LANGUAGE, EMOTION,
AND POLITICS IN SOUTH INDIA

Contemporary Indian Studies

Published in association with the American Institute of Indian Studies

Books in this series are recipients of the
Edward Cameron Dimock, Jr. Prize in the Indian Humanities
and the
Joseph W. Elder Prize in the Indian Social Sciences
awarded by the American Institute of Indian Studies and are published with the Institute's generous support.

A list of titles in this series appears at the back of the book.

Language, Emotion, and Politics in South India

The Making of a Mother Tongue

LISA MITCHELL

Indiana University Press
Bloomington and Indianapolis

This book is a publication of

Indiana University Press
601 North Morton Street
Bloomington, IN 47404-3797 USA

http://iupress.indiana.edu

Telephone orders 800-842-6796
Fax orders 812-855-7931
Orders by e-mail iuporder@indiana.edu

The paper used in this publication meets the minimum requirements of American National Standard for Information Sciences—Permanence of Paper for Printed Library Materials, ANSI Z39.48-1984.

Manufactured in the United States of America

Library of Congress Cataloging-in-Publication Data

Mitchell, Lisa, date
Language, emotion, and politics in south India : the making of a mother tongue / Lisa Mitchell.
p. cm. —(Contemporary Indian studies)
Includes bibliographical references and index.
ISBN 978-0-253-35301-6 (cloth : alk. paper) — ISBN 978-0-253-22069-1 (pbk. : alk. paper) 1. India, South—Languages—Political aspects. 2. Language policy—India, South. I. Title.
P119.32.I4M57 2009
306.44'909548—dc22
2008037984

1 2 3 4 5 14 13 12 11 10 09

For my parents,

Sara and Larry Mitchell,

who first taught me to pay attention to language

CONTENTS

ACKNOWLEDGMENTS

Far too many people have contributed either directly or indirectly to the researching and writing of this book to make it possible to mention them all; however, the following people do require special acknowledgment. Professor Velcheru Narayana Rao and Christopher Chekuri opened up a new world for me in the summer of 1995 with their spectacular Telugu language teaching. Narayana Rao-garu has continued to be a close reader and supportive mentor in subsequent years, and I have been grateful for Chris's continued intellectual exchange, both in Hyderabad and in the United States. I have also been fortunate to have been able to study Telugu with Dr. P. Venugopala Rao and Padmaja in Madras (before it was renamed Chennai), and with K. Vimala in Hyderabad.

In Hyderabad, Vimala not only provided me with the highest-quality language instruction, but her friendship and intellectual companionship gave me an ideal base for making an intellectual and social home in Hyderabad. Her parents, K. Purushottam and Bhagya Lakshmi, with whom I lived in 1995–96, welcomed me into their family and made me feel like their own daughter. I only wish that Purushottam-garu could have lived to read this book. His pride in my Telugu and his keen interest in my research made me feel that I was engaged in a worthwhile project. To both of them, and to Vimala, Shyam, Pratyush, and Pratheek, thank you. Professor Chekuri Rama Rao, retired from Osmania University's Linguistics Department, Professor K. K. Ranganathacharyalu and Dr. Pillalamarri Ramulu of the University of Hyderabad's Telugu Department, and Dr. Atluri Murali of the History Department at the University of Hyderabad have been generous with their time and intellectual suggestions. Over the years they have provided me with much-needed reading suggestions in Telugu literature and language and in the socio-political history of Andhra and have continued to be supportive mentors in subsequent years.

To R. Bhagya Lakshmi, my friend and flatmate in the Nallakunta neighborhood of Hyderabad, I owe the greatest debt. Her wide circle of friends—journalists, poets, writers, activists, and academics—filled our flat constantly with lively discussion, debate, song, poetry, and camaraderie, sustained by endless cups of tea; and her research assistance, both formal and informal, helped in a myriad of ways in making this project what it eventually became. R. V. Ramanamurthy, A. Suneetha, L. Chaitanya, and A. Sreenivasulu became great friends and have continued to act as intellectual interlocutors. The family of Sunil Kumar Bernard and Glory Premila; their sons Sunand and Praneeth; Glory's parents G. Seshaiah and Caroline; and her siblings and their families—James Vinay Kumar; Shoba, Vijay, and Komal; Paul Vinod and Annie; David Sukumar; Pramod; and Madhu—made me feel a part of their family, saw that I was always well provisioned on any railway journey, and humored my passion for their *majjiga chāru* and other Andhra delicacies. I am only sorry that Glory's mother did not live to see this work published. Vijay Kumar Johnson and his family, especially his sister Esther Subashini, also offered welcome diversions from my work. Others in Hyderabad whom I would like to thank for their conversations, assistance, and advice are Andreas D'Souza, Bharat Bhushan, Bindu, Diane D'Souza, Jagan Reddy, Jaya, Krishna Reddy, K. Lalita, Rammohan, Rekha, K. Sajaya, Sharmila, G. Shyamala, Vasudha, and all of the folks at Anveshi. The Anees family, Rizwana, Saleha, Fathima, and their parents, Mohammed Anees Ahmed Khan and Najma Begum, provided yet another home for me in Hyderabad. These relationships were established and strengthened during periods of fieldwork in Hyderabad in 1995–1997, 1999–2000, and again in 2002.

In Hyderabad, I benefited greatly from access to numerous institutions. I am especially indebted to C. Sambi Reddy and librarian I. S. N. Raju at Sundarayya Vignana Kendram for the use of their extensive collection of Telugu literature. I also want to thank the employees of the Andhra Pradesh State Archives, especially Narasimha Reddy, Koteshwar Rao, Krishna, A. John, and Divakar. Numerous people at Potti Sreeramulu Telugu University in Hyderabad guided me in various ways, both formally and informally. These included Professor N. Sivaramamurti, Professor J. Tirumala Rao, Dr. C. Mrinalini, Dr. K. Thomasaiah, Dr. M. Sankara Reddy, and all of the librarians in the Telugu University Library who were always willing to help me locate a book. Professor Bh. Krishnamurti, retired professor of linguistics from Osmania University; Dr. S. V. Rama Rao of Osmania University's Telugu Department; Dr. P. Krishna Moorthy, formerly assistant director of the A. P. State Archives; Dr. P. S. Gopala Krishnan and Sumanaspati Reddy at All-India Radio; B. Mallikarjuna Rao, Telugu Literary Research Society; R. Trivedi, additional secretary, Home Department, A. P. State Secretariat; the American Studies Research

Centre (now the Indo-American Centre for International Studies); and the Henry Martyn Institute of Islamic Studies all provided assistance that benefited my research.

In Nellore, I want to thank Dr. A. Subramanyam for his friendship, his open door, his introductions, his ongoing assistance and advice over the years, and his enthusiasm for my research. Through him I met innumerable people who helped me begin to answer the many questions I brought with me, especially V. Anantha Ramaiah and his wife, V. Kameswari. They not only welcomed me into their home, but Anantha Ramaiah-garu also shared with me his extensive archive and memories of the events of 1952, discussed in the introduction and chapter 6, and opened more doors through his extensive introductions in Nellore. Dr. C. V. Ramachandra Rao and Dr. C. Vasundhara shared their home, their extensive libraries, much rich conversation, and the best homemade *uppu mirapakāyulu.* Mala Kondaiah and his family gave me a warm welcome and introduced me to the joys of Nellore *chēpa pulusu.* I also want to thank those who helped me in the Nellore Town Hall Library, in the Collectorate Records Room, and in the Nellore Police Archives. The office of the Telugu weekly, the *Zamin Ryot,* graciously allowed me to use their meticulously maintained newspaper archive, and Chitti Babu provided assistance in copying news articles from 1952–53.

In Tirupati, A. Sreenivasulu, O. Uma, and Madana Sekar provided friendship and research assistance. Krishnam Raju at the Tirupati Regional Office of the State Archives, and Dr. P. S. Reddy and librarian P. Syama Rao in the Department of Telugu Studies, Sri Venkateswara University, provided generous research assistance. Dr. L. Rama Moorthy in the Physics Department at S. V. University graciously allowed me to use their microfilm reader.

In Chennai (formerly Madras), I want to thank Anand and Sivapriya for their wonderful hospitality always, Theodore Bhaskaran, Dr. M. S. S. Pandian, Professor G. V. S. R. Krishnamurthy at Madras University, Dr. A. R. Venkatachelapathy at the Madras Institute of Development Studies, and Anna Lockwood. Thota Bhavanarayana introduced me to a larger circle of Telugu journalists, poets, and creative minds residing in Madras. I also want to thank the Madras Literary Society; the Adyar Theosophical Society Library and Research Center, especially A. Swarnamukhi for her help; all of the employees at the Tamil Nadu State Archives, but particularly M. Sendurpandian, Dr. M. Sundara Raj, and M. Namasivayam; the

Connemara Library; the Roja Muthaiah Research Centre; and the Government Oriental Manuscripts Library and its curator, Dr. S. Soundorapandian. Vincent Joseph and Saroja Vincent at the Gurukal Theological Seminary Archives, formerly employees at the Madras State Archives, helped me to sort out which documents were moved from Madras to Hyderabad in the 1950s, and which were kept by the Tamil Nadu State Archives.

This project would not have been possible without the willingness of so many people throughout Andhra and southern India more generally to take time out of their busy schedules to share their memories, perspectives, and reflections. I particularly want to thank the families of the young men killed in police firings in Nellore in 1952 who graciously agreed to talk with me; others in Nellore, Kavali, Naidupet, Rapur, Gudur, and Sullurupetta who participated in the events of 1952; numerous people in Hyderabad, Warangal, Chennai, Thanjavur, Tirupati, Rajahmundry, Visakhapatnam, Vijayanagaram, Anakapalle, Kakinada, Narsupet, and Madanapalle; and others I met while traveling by train or bus throughout Andhra.

Other individuals and institutions who facilitated access to archival and library collections in India and London include K. Bujji Babu at the Visakhapatnam Regional Office of the State Archives and librarians at the Dr. V. S. Krishna Memorial Library, Andhra University in Visakhapatnam; P. Renuku, head librarian, Mansas Library, M. R. College, Vizianagaram and Dr. A. V. D. Sharma, head of the History Department at M. R. College; N. Viswanathan, Telugu Pandit at the Saraswati Mahal Library in Thanjavur; Y. S. Narasimha Rao, V. T. V. Subba Rao, and Markandeyulu at the Jubilee Public Library and Reading Room, Rajahmundry Town Hall, and Subramaniyam, Chandra Sekar, and Sanidhanam Narsimha Sarma at the Sri Gowthami Regional Library in Rajahmundry; the Nehru Memorial Museum and Library, the Secretariat Library, and the Sahitya Akademi Library in Delhi; and all of the staff of the Oriental and India Office Collection in the British Library in London. I especially want to thank Dr. Andrew Cook, who not only provided help in understanding the organization of the OIOC but also performed a miracle in locating Kavali Venkata Ramaswamy's *Map of Ancient Dekkan,* mentioned in chapter 1, which had become detached from its shelf mark during repairs and had been missing since the 1960s. Bill Siepmann in London also offered friendship, hospitality, and a diversion from the archives whenever needed.

Other scholars whom I encountered during the fieldwork process in various archives, libraries, towns, and cities in both India and England provided much-needed opportunities to reflect on my research at various stages, and I am grateful for their insights, good humor, and wisdom. A partial list includes Cassie Adcock, Syed Ali, Shahid Amin, Rick Asher, Gautam Bhadra, Ben Cohen, Lawrence Cohen, Kavita Datla, Richard Davis, Michael Fisher, Joyce Flueckiger, Omar Kutty, Genevieve Lakier, B. Uma Maheswari, Karuna Mantena, Rama Mantena, Abby McGowan, Rebecca Moore, Deepa Reddy, Sunita Reddy, Paula Richman, Yasmin Saikia, Regi Sammanasu, Peter Schmitthenner, Martha Selby, David Shulman, Cynthia Talbot, Katherine Ulrich, Arafaat Valiani, and Phillip Wagoner.

Premila and Prashant Paul and their extended "family" and friends in Madurai, and David Scott, Corinne Scott, Paul Gonsalves, Ruth Chandy, Kamaan, Rahul, and Chayant in Bangalore always provided a home for me and sustained me in multiple ways throughout my research visits to India. In Delhi, I want to thank Sudhir Chandra, Rohan D'Souza, Snehlata Gupta, Joseph Mathai, Revati Mathai, Jinka Nagaraju, Chandra Bhan Prasad, Meera Prasad, S. N. S. Rawat, Ved Rawat, Seema Rawat, Yogesh Rawat, Pooja Rawat, Sharmishta, and the many friends in Vidisha Apartments in Patparganj.

John Pemberton, Nicholas B. Dirks, Partha Chatterjee, E. Valentine Daniel, Indira Viswanathan Peterson, Thomas R. Trautmann, Velcheru Narayana Rao, Martha Selby, Phillip Wagoner, and Ramnarayan Rawat all offered close and insightful engagement with and suggestions on earlier drafts of this book. I feel extremely fortunate to have had the opportunity to learn from all of them, and their stamp on my intellectual development will be apparent in the pages that follow. Any remaining inaccuracies or unclarities are, however, my own. From John and my first cohort of classmates at the University of Washington I learned the practice of close reading. Other teachers and colleagues in the United States who have enriched my thinking on the topics addressed within this book include J. Bernard Bate, Aditya Behl, Susan Blum, S. Christopher Brown, Francis Cody, Deirdre delaCruz, Richard Eaton, Anne Feldhaus, Goutam Gajula, Pamila Gupta, Miyako Inoue, Marilyn Ivy, Sunila Kale, Sudipta Kaviraj, Naveeda Khan, Elizabeth Kolsky, Siddhartha Lokanandi, Ritty Lukose, Aruna Magier, Brinkley Messick, Rosalind Morris, Nauman Naqvi, Dard Neuman, Christian Novetzke, Deven Patel, Usharani Popuri, Bhavani Raman, Naoki Sakai, Cynthia Talbot, Arafaat Valiani, Roxanne Varzi,

Amanda Weidman, Anand Yang, and Vazira Zamindar. Portions of this book were presented to audiences at Potti Sreeramulu Telugu University, the Forum of Cultural Studies (FOCUS) Seminar at the University of Hyderabad, Anveshi Research Centre for Women's Studies, the Centre for Studies in Social Sciences' Cultural Studies Workshop, Colby College, Arizona State University, the University of Washington, the University of Chicago, Columbia University, the University of Michigan, Yale University, the University of California at Irvine, and the University of Pennsylvania. I am grateful for the many questions, comments, and suggestions that were shared by members of each of these audiences.

At Indiana University Press my editor Rebecca Tolen and her very able assistant Laura MacLeod shepherded me through my first foray into the book-publishing world and patiently bore with the multiple moves that delayed my completion of this manuscript. Scott Taylor of Indiana University's Graphic Services produced the maps included in this volume. Jamal J. Elias generously took time away from chairing both the South Asia Studies and Religious Studies Departments at the University of Pennsylvania to share his photographic expertise and give me a hand in cleaning up several old photographs and illustrations in preparation for their inclusion. I also want to thank Susan Wadley and the members of the American Institute of Indian Studies Publications Committee for including this book in their series on Contemporary Indian Studies.

Funding and support for this research came from Foreign Language and Area Studies grants; the American Institute of Indian Studies; the National Science Foundation; Columbia University; the Fulbright-Hays Doctoral Dissertation Research Abroad Program; and the Wenner-Gren Foundation. Dr. Pradeep Mehendiratta, Purnima Mehta, Rajendra Kumar, Mini Kumar, and Mr. Arora at the Delhi AIIS office deserve special mention for their assistance and support throughout much of the period of my research in India. The American Institute of Indian Studies and the Leonard Hastings Schoff Publication Fund of the University Seminars at Columbia University provided generous support toward this publication.

An earlier version of chapter 3 was previously published as "Making the Local Foreign: Shared Language and History in Southern India," in the *Journal of Linguistic Anthropology*, vol. 16, no. 2 (2006): 229–248. Earlier versions of several portions of chapters 4 and 5 were previously published as "Parallel Languages, Parallel Cultures: Language as a New Foundation for the Reorganisation of Knowledge and Practice in Southern India," in the

Indian Economic and Social History Review, vol. 42, no. 4 (2005): 443–465. I am grateful to the editors of these journals for permission to publish these sections in their present form.

My parents, Sara and Larry Mitchell, gave me the best foundation I could possibly have wanted and never stopped supporting me. Leela McElhinney Rawat arrived to brighten my life just as this manuscript went into its revision stages. Last, but not least, I wish to thank Ramnarayan Singh Rawat, who has shown me many times over just how rewarding the marriage of anthropology and history can be, and even more importantly, that you never know what you'll find in an archive until you spend time in one.

Philadelphia, Pennsylvania
July 2008

NOTE ON TRANSLITERATION AND SPELLING

Words from Indian languages that are commonly recognized in English, contemporary place-names, and personal names have been transliterated without diacritics. For all other terms transliterated from Indian languages, long vowels are marked (ā as in h*o*t; ī as in d*ee*p; ū as in f*oo*l; ē as in f*a*de; ō as in h*o*pe), and short vowels—half the length of their long counterparts—are left unmarked (a as in h*u*t; i as in d*i*p; u as in f*u*ll; e as in f*e*d; o as in the first o in *o*h-oh). An underdot beneath a consonant (ṭ, ṭh, ḍ, ḍh, ṇ, ṣ, ḷ) indicates a retroflex consonant, pronounced by curling the tip of the tongue back toward the palate and flipping it forward, except for ṛ, which indicates a vowel sound similar to the *ri* in mer*ri*ly. Ś is pronounced as the English *sh*. For consistency and to assist English readers I have departed from conventional Telugu transliteration practices in using ch (rather than c) to indicate the English *ch* sound and chh to indicate an aspirated *ch*. For Tamil words, ḻ indicates a retroflex *r*, and ṟ indicates a sound similar to an English *r* when single and a trilled *tr* when doubled. Within quotations I have kept an author's original transliteration scheme and markings. All translations from Telugu are my own unless otherwise indicated.

LANGUAGE, EMOTION, AND POLITICS IN SOUTH INDIA

Introduction: A New Emotional Commitment to Language

I find only one way out. It is to lay down life with no desire, with no hate and with determination. From yesterday I felt that if I delay I should be committing a sin. I am prepared to go through the ordeal of laying down my life.

—Potti Sriramulu, letter dated September 15, 1952, one month before beginning his final and fatal fast-unto-death

What conditions must exist in order for someone to be willing to die, not for a nation, but for a language? How must one think and feel about language for this to be possible? Southern India has become famous during the twentieth century as a place where many have appeared to experience such heightened passion for language that they have been willing to sacrifice their lives for its sake. On December 15, 1952, the fifty-eight-day fast of the linguistic state activist Potti Sriramulu culminated dramatically in his death in the south Indian city of Madras (today known as Chennai). Sriramulu had undertaken his well-publicized fast-unto-death in order to demand the formation of a separate Telugu-speaking administrative territory within the newly independent Indian nation, with Madras city as its capital.[1] His dissatisfaction with the arbitrary administrative regions established under British colonial rule and inherited by the new nation after the departure of the colonial government in 1947 (see Map 1), and his frustration with the marginalization of concerns raised by speakers of Telugu within the existing multilingual state, drew on the larger movement for a linguistically defined Telugu province launched forty years earlier.[2] The movement culminated in the days immediately following Sriramulu's death, as news of his fast's fatal conclusion caused people in towns and cities as far as 700 kilometers to the north to flock to those sites where news arrived first—the local railway stations. Soon reports of violence, processions, destruction of railway property, stoppage of trains, and looting began to circulate. In numerous towns, scores of others met their deaths or were injured by bullets as police struggled to maintain order amidst the unruly crowds. Just four days later, Prime Minister Jawaharlal Nehru responded to the widespread disorder, read by journalists, politicians, and historians alike as irrefutable evidence of the collective will of the people, by declaring the formation of a new Telugu linguistic state within the Indian nation. The new state was to be known as Andhra State and was to be created from the uncontested Telugu-speaking districts of the existing Madras State, though without the inclusion of the multilingual capital city of Madras (see Map 2).[3] Four years later additional Telugu-speaking districts from the neighboring state of Hyderabad were added, and the name of the state was changed to Andhra Pradesh.

Although pathbreaking in setting the stage for the later linguistic reorganization of the Indian nation, the historical transformations that invested new importance in the Telugu language did not affect this particular language alone. South Asia has witnessed the twentieth-century rise of widespread and unprecedented commitments to what are today claimed as "mother tongues," a concept not attested in any Indian language prior to the second half of the nineteenth century.[4] Numerous public protests, suicides, and other dramatic forms of evidence of emotional commitments to one's *māta bhāṣa, mātṛ bhāṣa,* or *tāymoḻi,* literally "mother tongue," began to appear throughout the subcontinent during the middle decades of the twentieth century. Sriramulu's fast itself followed two previous attempts at a fast-unto-death for a separate Telugu linguistic state undertaken by G. Sitaramaiah, known as Swami Sitaram. The first of Swami Sitaram's fasts, in August and September of 1951, was given up after thirty-five days, and the second, in May and June of 1952, was aborted after three weeks in response to appeals made by a number of political leaders. On February 21, 1952, the same year as Sriramulu's fast, in the northeastern part of the subcontinent in what is today Bangladesh, four young men sacrificed their lives to police bullets during language riots in the name of the Bengali language—martyrs whose deaths are today commemorated by an international annual "Mother Language Day."[5] In 1960–1961, Sant Fateh Singh and Master Tara Singh both undertook fasts-unto-death to demand that the Indian government

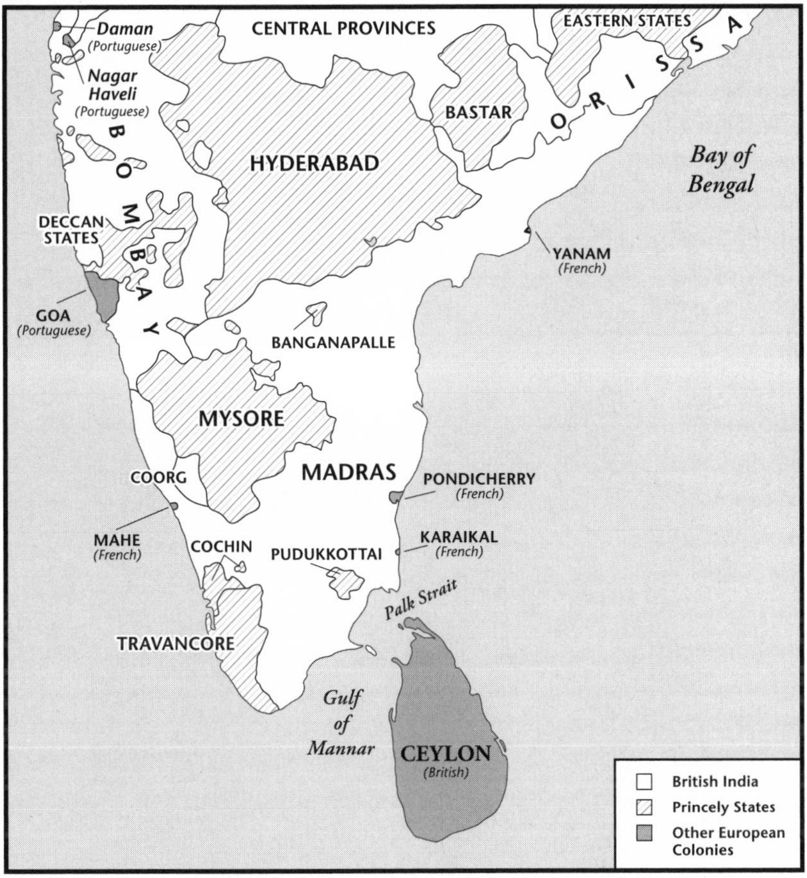

MAP 1. Map of major administrative regions of southern India prior to independence, 1947

establish a Punjabi-speaking state, though each effort was aborted before reaching its fatal conclusion, Tara Singh's after forty-eight days.[6] And in 1964–1965, a wave of language suicides again struck southern India. In January 1964, some three hundred kilometers to the south of Madras, a man named Chinnasami walked to the public space of the Tiruchirappalli railway station, doused himself liberally with kerosene, and set himself on fire, declaring tribute to the Tamil language as he died. The following year, eight others followed in Chinnasami's footsteps, five by publicly self-immolating themselves and three by consuming pesticide, all again proclaiming their loyalty to Tamil.[7]

Although Potti Sriramulu was the first to intentionally commit suicide

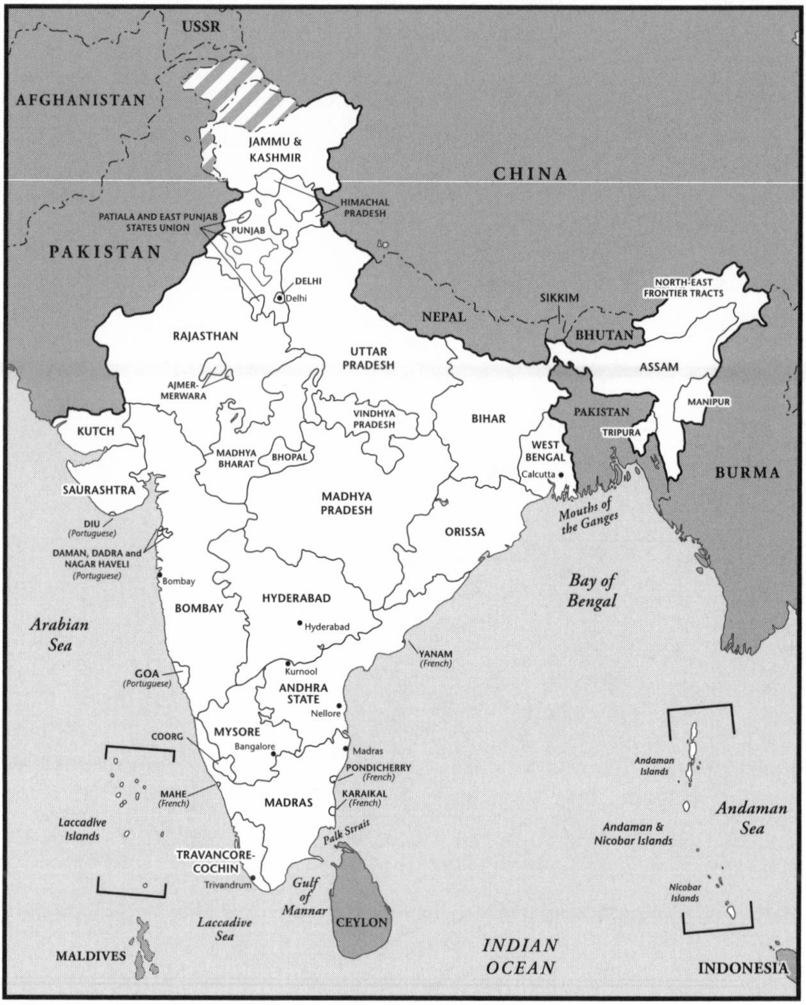

Map 2. Map of Indian administrative regions following the successful formation of Andhra State, October 1, 1953

in the name of his mother tongue, our story does not begin with his dramatic fast-unto-death in 1952. Not only can Sriramulu's passionate commitment to language not be explained by beginning our historical analysis in 1952, but it also cannot be adequately explained by examining his relationship to the Telugu language in isolation. The various sets of dramatic events in which death marks the recognition of language as a legitimate basis for collective identity were unthinkable just half a century earlier. Yet in each case historians and other scholars have paid little attention to why languages have quite suddenly become objects of such new and intense forms of affective attachment during the twentieth century. The past provides us no evidence of this type of committed devotion to language prior to the twentieth century. Even more importantly, it is clear that the rise of such emotional attachments has happened not just in relation to a single language, but rather in the context of many languages, all at approximately the same time.

Language in India

> *Government business in Southern India is chiefly transacted in the language of the Hindus, either Tamil, Telugu, Kannadi [Kannada], Malayalam or Marata [Marathi]; while the Mussalmans still speak Hindustani (as well as the local native tongue). . . . the modern Telugu contains a variety of Persian and Arabic expressions. In later years, some English words have crept into use.*
>
> —Charles Philip Brown, *Miśra Bhāṣā Nighaṇṭu: Dictionary of Mixed Telugu*, 1854

Six decades after gaining independence from Britain, 23 languages hold official status within India. In addition to the continued recognition of English as an official language, the Eighth Schedule to India's Constitution granted official status to Assamese, Bengali, Gujarati, Hindi, Kannada, Kashmiri, Malayalam, Marathi, Oriya, Punjabi, Sanskrit, Tamil, Telugu, and Urdu in 1950.[8] In 1967 Sindhi was added to the Eighth Schedule, followed by Konkani, Manipuri, and Nepali in 1992, and Bodo, Dogri, Maithili, and Santali in 2004, for a total of 22 "scheduled languages."[9] Today, most of these are used as official languages at the state level, with English and Hindi the primary languages used at the all-India Central Government level (see Map 3 for the present division of India into twenty-eight states and seven union territories). Yet these are still only a small fraction of the total number of languages that continue to be used in India today.[10] The 2001 census yielded raw data of 6,661 different responses to the question of "mother tongue." The census currently defines mother tongue as "the language spoken in childhood by the person's mother to

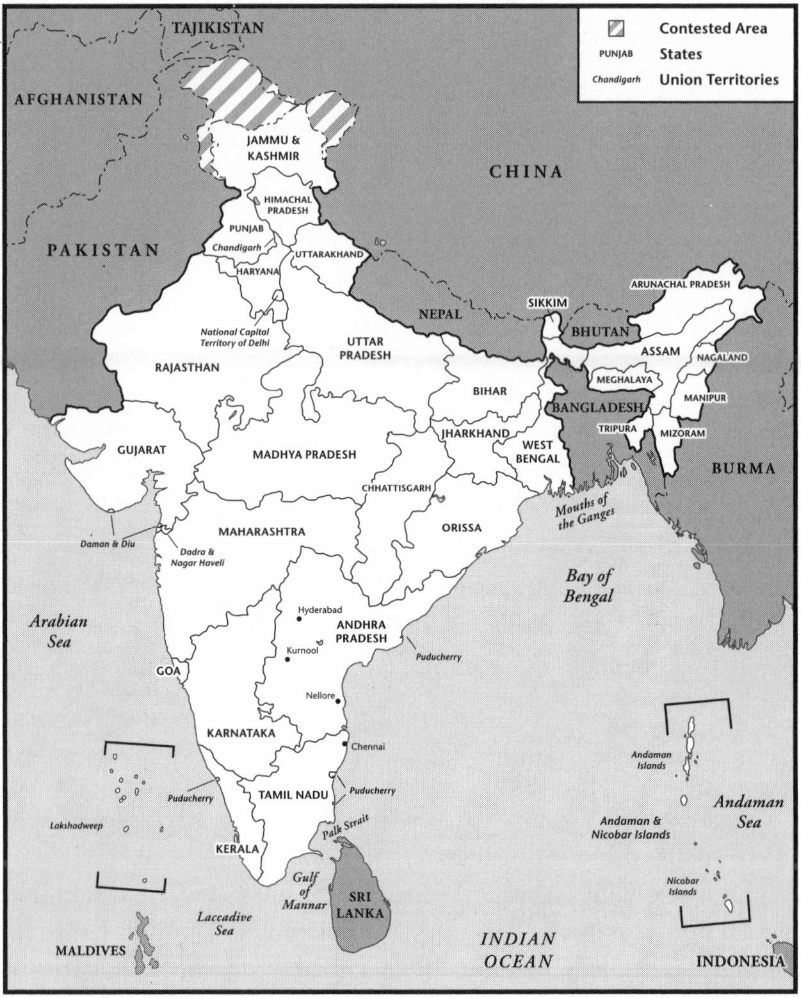

Map 3. Map of India, 2008

the person. If the mother died in infancy, the language mainly spoken in the person's home in childhood will be the mother tongue. In the case of infants and deaf mutes, the language usually spoken by the mother should be recorded. In case of doubt, the language mainly spoken in the household may be recorded."[11]

Linguists have grouped the 6,661 responses they received to the mother-tongue question into 1,635 "rationalized mother tongues," with an additional 1,957 languages designated as "unclassified." The 1,635 rationalized mother tongues have been further grouped into 122 different languages.[12] Hindi appears as the most widely spoken language in India today, or, more precisely, as the most widely identified mother tongue, claimed by 41.03 percent of the population, followed by Bengali (8.11 percent), Telugu (7.19 percent), Marathi (6.99 percent), and Tamil (5.91 percent) (see Table 1).[13] According to the most recent All-India Educational Survey, 43 different languages are used as media of instruction in Indian schools.[14] In addition, 47 languages are used at some level of public administration in India, 87 are used in the publication of newspapers, and 91 are used for radio broadcasts, making India one of the most multilingual nations in the world today.[15]

Nehru's decision to declare the formation of a new linguistically defined Andhra State in 1952 was significant as the very first successful culmination of a language movement in independent India, paving the way for similar demands in relation to other languages in subsequent years.[16] Within just a few short years of Andhra State's pathbreaking formation, mounting pressure nationwide resulted in the States Reorganisation Act of 1956, which redrew much of the map of India on linguistic lines. As a result, linguistic states became the new norm within the Indian nation rather than the exception, and Andhra State was expanded and renamed Andhra Pradesh (see Map 4). As the model for the geographic and political reorganization of the new Indian nation, the Telugu language movement is one of the most dramatic examples of the new twentieth-century emotional commitments to language. It is also of utmost importance for understanding the larger historical processes that led to the new positioning of languages within Indian society. An analysis of the historical dynamics and processes that led to these changes is therefore essential for understanding contemporary socio-political formations and activity in India more generally.

By way of contrast to the 1950s demand to reorganize the political territories of the Indian nation by defining them along linguistic lines, evidence from both British colonial and local Indian observers of the linguistic reality encountered by the British shortly after they assumed control of southern India toward the end of the eighteenth century suggests that they confronted a complex multilingualism. Vennelakanty Subba Rao, an interpreter for the Madras High Court in the 1820s, mentions in a journal of his life and times later published by his son that he used not only Telugu, Kannada, and English, but also Tamil, Marathi, Hindustani, Persian, and Sanskrit.[17] While it is clear that his professional employment as an interpreter accounts

Table I.

Most Widely Claimed Mother Tongues in India

RANK	LANGUAGE	NUMBER	PERCENTAGE OF POPULATION
1	Hindi	422,048,642	41.03
2	Bengali	83,369,769	8.11
3	Telugu	74,002,856	7.19
4	Marathi	71,936,894	6.99
5	Tamil	60,793,814	5.91
6	Urdu	51,536,111	5.01
7	Gujarati	46,091,617	4.48
8	Kannada	37,924,011	3.69
9	Malayalam	33,066,392	3.21
10	Oriya	33,017,446	3.21
11	Punjabi	29,102,477	2.83
12	Assamese	13,168,484	1.28
13	Maithili	12,179,122	1.18
14	Santali	6,469,600	0.63
15	Kashmiri	5,527,698	0.54
16	Nepali	2,871,749	0.28
17	Sindhi	2,535,485	0.25
18	Konkani	2,489,015	0.24
19	Dogri	2,282,589	0.22
20	Manipuri*	1,466,705	0.14
21	Bodo	1,350,478	0.13
22	Sanskrit	14,135	Negligible

Source: Scheduled languages in descending order of number of persons who returned the language as their mother tongue (Census of India, 2001).

Note: *Excludes figures of Paomata, Mao-Maram, and Purul subdivisions of Senapati district of Manipur for 2001.

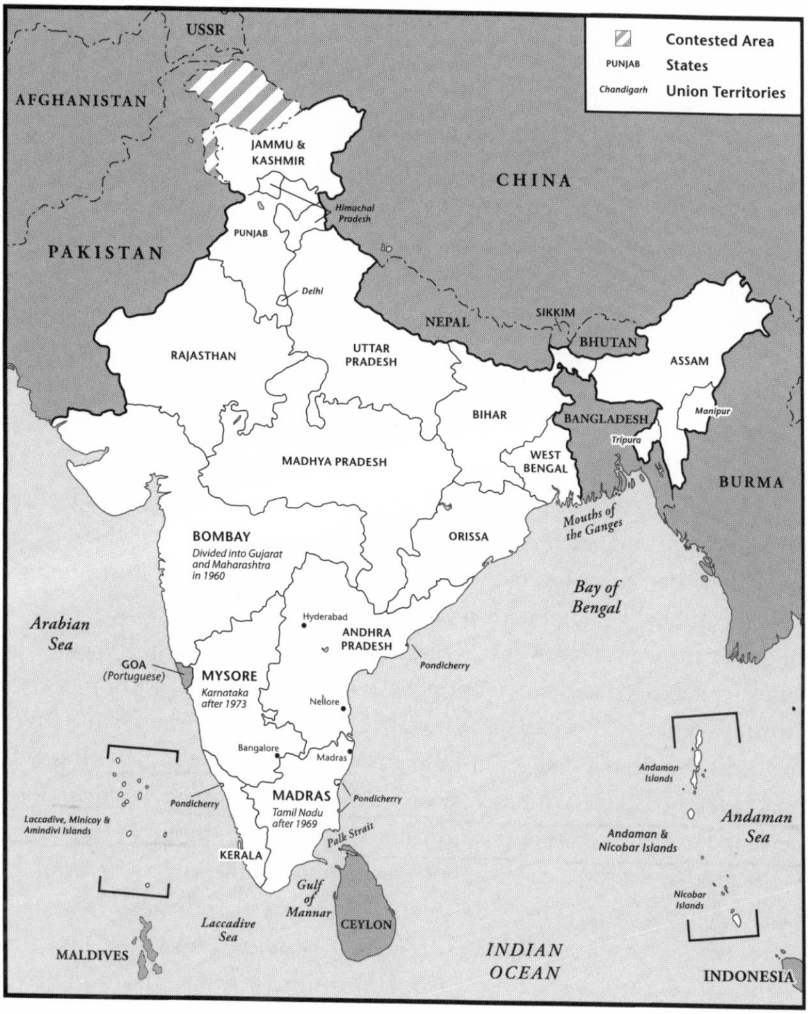

Map 4. Map of India following the States Reorganisation Act, November 1, 1956

for some of his extensive linguistic knowledge, the colonial administrator C. P. Brown, who was employed in various districts of the British colonial Madras Presidency between 1820 and 1854, similarly explains that Tamil, Telugu, Kannada, Malayalam, Marathi, Hindustani, Persian, Arabic, and English words were all used for the transaction of "government business in Southern India."[18] In addition, early printed textbooks such as *Pedda Bāla Śikṣa* [Expanded Child's Primer] included alphabets from multiple languages, suggesting that more than one script was typically learned by schoolchildren at the most basic level of education.[19] Literary gatherings and even individual poetic compositions and dramas of the medieval and early-modern periods were similarly multilingual. The poets associated with the court of the famous early-sixteenth-century Vijayanagara king Krishnadevaraya, who ruled from 1509 to 1529, composed in Kannada, Telugu, Sanskrit, and Tamil, among other languages.[20] The late-sixteenth-century Telugu text the *Rāyavācakamu,* a retrospective history of the Vijayanagara court, similarly portrays the multilingual nature of court life, quoting a lengthy description of the qualities required of a king taken from an earlier text. These include that he "be skilled in the eight languages, which are Sanskrit, Prakrit, Shauraseni, Magadhi, Paishachi, Chulika, Apabhramsa, and Tenugu [Telugu]."[21] The Nayaka courts of the late sixteenth through eighteenth centuries, which succeeded the Vijayanagara dynasty, produced a vast literature in Telugu, Tamil, and Sanskrit clearly aimed at a multilingual audience.[22] Courtly dramas of the period, such as Purushottama Dīkshituḍu's *Anna-dāna-mahā-nāṭakamu,* or "Great Drama of the Gift of Food," recorded in the Telugu script, combined Telugu with colloquial Tamil.[23] Indira Peterson's research on performance genres in the Maratha court of Thanjavur (1677–1855) has similarly demonstrated the multilingual nature of *yakṣagāna* and *kuṟavañchi* [fortune-teller] dance-dramas, which utilized Tamil, Marathi, Telugu, Sanskrit, and occasionally even English.[24] In much of the Indian subcontinent it was not unusual for literary production, pedagogy, government business, and everyday communication all to take place in multiple languages. Unlike today, however, one was not expected to be able to do everything in every language in order to claim competency. Instead, individual languages typically took on specialized roles. Telugu, for example, was, until the early twentieth century, learned by anyone in southern India who wanted to study Karnatic music—a specialized form of southern Indian music now regarded as classical—regardless of whether Telugu was used within other domains of a musician's life. In an era when languages are seen as attributes of persons rather than as tools to accomplish particular tasks, this is no longer true.[25]

One of the most common methods that has been used to approach the question of the emergence of mother tongues has been to examine separately what has occurred historically within each of several linguistically defined "worlds" (Bengali, Telugu, Punjabi, Tamil, etc.), treating each as a self-evident independent context. However, instead of simply limiting its analysis to a single domain, this book explores how it is that these "worlds" themselves came to be recognizable as distinct and separate domains around the beginning of the twentieth century. Of special interest, therefore, are the processes that have led speakers of particular languages to see themselves as having a separate history, literature, politics, and identity. In other words, this book asks how languages came to be viewed during the twentieth century as primary and natural foundations for the reorganization of a wide range of forms of knowledge and everyday practice. These include such practices as history writing, literary production, canon (re-)formation, pedagogy, political organization, and the representation of socio-cultural identities. Using Telugu as a specific case study without assuming that the Telugu language has always demarcated a separate domain will help to make more visible the historical processes that have made it seem so natural for languages to each possess their own individual histories, narratives, literatures, and peoples today. Because Telugu-speakers led the first successful movement for a separate linguistic state in independent India, their story of the making of a mother tongue is therefore a paradigmatic one, and readers interested in other parts of India or even other parts of the world will recognize pieces of this story that will prompt new understandings of related processes elsewhere.

Twentieth-Century Affective Attachments to Language

In the context of Telugu writing, one of the earliest explicit indications of the possibility of a new relationship to language appeared in 1893, some six decades before Potti Sriramulu's unprecedented fast-unto-death. In that year, the writer Gurujada Sriramamurti (1851–1899) solicited support for the publication of the second edition of his *Kavi Jīvitamulu,* or *Lives of [Telugu] Poets,* by opening his preface with an appeal [*vijñāpanamu*] addressed to *telugu dēśa bhāṣa abhimānulu,* or "those having affection for or pride in the language of the Telugu country."[26] In addressing his preface in this way, not only was Sriramamurti able to imagine an audience for his publication, but he also imagined one constituted and defined explicitly in relation to the language in which his text was composed. Although we can never be certain that his use of *abhimānulu* in relation to the language of the Telugu country was the very first use of the word in such a context, there is no evidence to suggest that it had ever been used in this way before.[27] Indeed, the explicit invocation of a new type of affective relationship to the Telugu language marks a subtle but fundamental change in the role of language within everyday life that was occurring in southern India during the last decades of the nineteenth century.

Sriramamurti's association of the emotion of *abhimānam*—"affection, pride, regard, care, love, favour," or "patronage and protection"—with a language as its object, extended its meaning in a novel way.[28] During the early twentieth century *abhimānam* began to assume important new connotations, leading to its most widespread use today in two new senses. The first is that of patriotism or political loyalty, not only in relation to language, but also in relation to one's nation or region (*dēśa*). The second contemporary use of *abhimānam* in the Telugu language is in relation to icons of popular culture, particularly movie actors. In such contexts it takes on the connotation of fan behavior or fan devotion. In some cases, these two meanings have coalesced around a single figure in the form of a film actor turned politician. The actor and former chief minister of the state of Andhra Pradesh, N. T. Rama Rao (NTR for short), who died in 1996, inspired just such an intensely affect-laden following, merging fan devotion with political loyalty among his followers. The term's use in the context of the Telugu language implies a similar intensity of affect and commitment to the personified figure of the language, *Telugu Talli* [Mother Telugu].

Sumathi Ramaswamy's groundbreaking work in the context of Tamil-speaking southern India has documented a similar phenomenon known in Tamil as *tamiḻpparṟu,* or "devotion to Tamil."[29] She uses a devotional framework to classify a wide range of forms of *tamiḻpparṟu* that she identifies as having been practiced and represented in southern India since the end of the nineteenth century. These new practices include the deification and worship of the Tamil language as a goddess; efforts to purify, cleanse, and protect Tamil against foreign encroachment and domination; the celebration of Tamil literary works and their authors; and the labor of publishing, circulating, and popularizing Tamil literature. The fact that her analysis—grounded in Tamil-language source materials beginning in 1891—dates from within two years of Gurujada Sriramamurti's novel appeal to those having affection for the language of the Telugu land, suggests that there was indeed a shift occurring in the representations and understandings of the relationship to language during the last decade of the nineteenth century. Her work furthermore suggests that the appearance of affective attachment to language at this precise historical moment was not restricted to either Telugu or Tamil alone, and prompts us to look beyond these individual languages and their immediate contexts to explain and historicize the phenomenon.

Ramaswamy's portrayal of *tamiḻppaṟṟu* is centrally concerned with rejecting the universalizing discourse of linguistic nationalism. Her objective is to demonstrate the distinctiveness of the devotion shown to Tamil when compared with European linguistic nationalism. She therefore rightfully refuses to allow Tamil linguistic devotion to be represented as "a (distorted) variant of something that has already happened elsewhere, but reenacted with local content."[30] Yet, in establishing the historical uniqueness of specific practices as purely "Tamil" (or purely "Telugu" for that matter), we must guard against projecting a historical unity of experience onto languages as natural foundations for independent and separate historical contexts or narratives. This is true even if we regard that apparent unity, as Ramaswamy insightfully portrays it, as "multiple, heterogeneous, and shot through with difference."[31] Isolating "Telugu," "Bengali," or "Tamil" processes from similar processes occurring in relation to other Indian languages ignores the complex multilingualism of pre-twentieth-century South Asia. It also treats pre-modern linguistic complexity as a variant of contemporary Indian multilingualism. All of this makes it difficult to recognize the possibility that a Tamil-speaking context, Bengali-speaking context, or Telugu-speaking context, each defined primarily in relation to a language, may itself be of recent origin. Drawing from the many Hindu-influenced practices associated with *tamiḻppaṟṟu,* Ramaswamy's work argues that to be a Tamil subject is to be a devotional subject. She documents the flexibility with which Tamil has—only since the 1890s—so easily and effectively been taken up as an object of devotion by a wide range of subjects. Scholars and poets, publicists and patrons, members of both privileged and underprivileged castes and classes, men and women, and even foreign missionaries have all helped to project a shared identity and shared context as Tamil-speakers in spite of whatever other differences may divide them. But given the dramatic reconfigurations of meanings and practices that occurred within nineteenth-century southern India, we must ask two important questions. First, how was the very concept of a subject changing during this period? And second, how were methods of representing subjects also undergoing transformations?

To answer these questions, we must also be careful not to project contemporary understandings of language onto the past. This will enable us to trace the emergence of monolingual worlds and subjectivities out of a complexly multilingual social field and identify the conditions that enabled their recognition as distinct and separate contexts. Chapter 1 does this by demonstrating how specific languages have gone from being understood and portrayed as natural features of particular local landscapes and environments to being experienced as inalienable attributes of human beings. As part of this transformation, languages ceased to be regarded primarily as tools or locally available resources and began to be refigured as the fundamental bases of individual identities. Chapter 2 extends the analysis of the transformations in the relationships to language in southern India by examining new twentieth-century methods of personifying languages. Newly portrayed as having biographical life narratives independent of their speakers, late-nineteenth-century languages began to be recognized as having had a birth at some point in the distant past. Nineteenth-century scholars identified clear stages of a language's progressive development and mapped out elaborate kinship relations with other languages.[32] Even the possibility of a language's death appeared as a new anxiety.[33] All of these new recognitions paved the way for a new full-fledged form of personification of language as a mother or goddess by the early twentieth century. The book then identifies and traces the contributions made to this process by transformations within three distinct though related domains: grammar, pedagogy, and translation. Chapter 3 examines shifts in the categories used to represent languages within the grammatical traditions of South Asia and their encounter with European language analysis practices. It uses both pre-colonial and colonial-era grammars, lexicons, and other meta-linguistic texts from southern India to demonstrate that a new concept of foreignness emerged during the nineteenth century that influenced domains far beyond those of concern to grammarians.

Chapter 4 pays careful attention to the role of printing within pedagogical practices of southern India. It argues that pandits were replaced by printed textbooks as the organizational foundation of curricular agendas, radically altering experiences of language and literacy. Educational practices that encouraged the acquisition of specific language domains—viewed as complementary to one another—within the particular contexts of their usage, gave way to printed textbooks that encouraged the study of a language as a discrete topic divorced from its context in preparation for doing things with it later on. Chapter 5 argues that by the late nineteenth century languages began to be perceived of as parallel to one another. This was accompanied by a new belief that it is possible to translate any language into any other language, and that anything that can be said or done in one language can be said or done equally well in any other language. Since languages ceased, as a result, to provide access to any unique content, they increasingly came to be valued as markers of identity rather than as unique mediums of knowledge or communication. Chapter 6, influenced by work in subaltern studies, uses ethnographic encounters in the coastal Andhra town of Nellore to demonstrate the effects of the processes elaborated in the preceding chapters. Oral narratives collected from individuals who participated in the events that led to the formation of a separate Telugu linguistic state in 1952 illustrate the ways in which the changes explored in earlier chapters have manifested themselves within southern India during the mid- to late twentieth century. These narratives also focus on the ways in which diverse personal experiences have been subsumed within dominant public narratives.

By closely examining the specific domains addressed by each of these six chapters, we can place the local idioms through which affective attachments to language are expressed within their larger contexts. Seen in this way, technological innovations, new structures of power and political mobilization, shifts in discursive networks and educational practices, and new sources of patronage and opportunities for consumption all become recognizable as important forces within our story. At the same time, this approach allows us to continue to insist, as Ramaswamy urges, that the story to be told in accounting for the language suicides of southern India is not simply a local version of a story already told elsewhere.

Advocates, Patrons, Devotees, and Fans

The shifts traced in this book do not, then, simply alter the definition of what it means to be a Telugu or a Tamil in the twentieth century; rather, they identify what has made it fundamentally possible to think of oneself as a member of a linguistically defined group—as a Telugu, a Bengali, a Punjabi, or a Tamilian, for example. By the early twentieth century, language had been mobilized to act not only as a new object of emotion, but also as the imagined foundation for the reorganization of knowledge, everyday practices, literary production, historical narratives, audiences, and ultimately populations. Although the idioms through which these new understandings of language have been expressed have been drawn from a range of already available local meanings, including the language of devotion, the fact that language was the site for this new constitution of subjects and new division of peoples was unique to no single language.

Just as the new form of emotional attachment identified as *abhimānam* was made apparent in Potti Sriramulu's dramatic fast-unto-death and in the tremendous following inspired by the Telugu film actor and politician N. T. Rama Rao, the devotional phenomenon identified in Tamil as *paṟṟu* appeared not only in the wave of language suicides documented in the 1960s, but also in the relationship to the renowned actor and former chief minister of Tamil Nadu, M. G. Ramachandran, popularly known as MGR. When MGR suffered a stroke in 1984, twenty-two people were reported to have expressed their *paṟṟu* by either self-immolating themselves or self-amputating a body part as an offering.[34] In the immediate wake of his death three years later, there were at least thirty-one confirmed self-immolations.[35] Thousands more showed their devotion by voluntarily having their heads tonsured in mourning.[36] Sara Dickey has documented the modern relationship between cinema fan clubs and the cultivation of voter bases in Tamil Nadu, suggesting again that the line between fan behavior and political loyalty, expressed in such terms as *abhimānam* and *paṟṟu,* has not always remained clear in southern India.[37]

In these examples of recent usage, *abhimānam* and *paṟṟu* both similarly indicate affective relationships between individuals and some sort of publicly available—and, most importantly, shared—object, be it a nation, language, or cinema star. Fans and patriots know that although their relationship with the object of their affection is an individual relationship, it is one that they share with many others, and thus they can imagine themselves as part of a much larger group of people with whom they may have little else in common other than the shared object of affection. They are regularly reminded of this shared attachment, often on a daily basis, through media coverage, participation in clubs, school activities, association memberships, institutional celebrations, memorials, and other events and activities that channel their attention in particular ways. It is easier to accept that the affective relationships described by the terms *abhimānam* and *paṟṟu* are new phenomena if we consider them in relation to a nation or to cinema stars. We recognize that both nations and cinema stars are themselves modern phenomena. However, affective attachment to language is not typically something we think of as a peculiarly modern phenomenon; indeed, many people would be quick to assume that an affective attachment to language of this nature has existed as long as language itself.

Although it is not uncommon to encounter praise and celebration of particular languages in pre-modern writings, experiences of affect associated with language in India prior to the late nineteenth century were quite different from the emotional attachments that have appeared more recently. There is much evidence that people prior to the nineteenth century took great pleasure in language, often portrayed as erotic pleasure. These pre-modern indications of an affective relationship to language—sometimes referred to as *rasa* (emotion, sentiment; aesthetic taste or pleasure; literary or artistic beauty)—typically emphasized the pleasures of using language and doing specific things with it. This type of representation of the experience of language should therefore not be confused with the more recent devotional types of emotional attachment to language represented by the terms *abhimānam* and *paṟṟu* and expressed through the passionate commitments, labors of love, and self-sacrifice witnessed in the twentieth century.

It will be easier to accept the novelty of this new affective attachment to language if we better understand its specific nature and twentieth-century manifestations. While Sumathi Ramaswamy's 1997 study has elaborated the new uses of the Tamil term *paṟṟu,* contemporaneous uses of the Telugu term *abhimānam* are less well documented. The 1903 edition of C. P. Brown's *Dictionary Telugu-English* gives the following definitions of *abhimānam:*

> ***abhimānamu*** [Skt.] n. Pride, self-esteem, haughtiness. Patronage, protection. Affection, regard, care, love, favour.
>
> ***dēśābhimānamu*** love of one's own country, patriotism.
>
> ***abhimāni*** n. He who loves . . . *Matābhimāni* a bigot. *Kulābhimāni* one who stands up for his caste. *Dēśābhimāni* the advocate for his country, he who loves his country, a patriot.[38]

Gwynn and Venkateswara Sastry's 1991 *Telugu-English Dictionary* gives a similar set of definitions, reversing, if anything, the relative emphasis on love in relation to pride:

> ***abhimānam*** n. 1. love, devotion, affection. 2. regard, liking, care. 3. favour, patronage; ***kulābhimānam*** showing favouritism towards o.'s community. 4. pride (in a good sense), self-respect, self-esteem. 5. pride (in a bad sense), arrogance.
>
> ***abhimāni*** [**pl. abhimānulu**] n. 1. one who loves or cares, one who has affection or regard. 2. admirer.[39]

The definition given by Apte's *Practical Sanskrit-English Dictionary* demonstrates the similarities between the Sanskrit *abhimāna* and its Telugu cognate:

> ***abhimāna*** 1. Pride (in a good sense), self-respect, honourable or worthy feeling; 2. Self-conceit, pride, arrogance, haughtiness, egotism, high opinion of oneself; 3. Referring all objects to self; 4. Conceit, conception; supposition, belief, opinion; 5. Knowledge, consciousness; 6. Affection, love; 7. Desire, wishing for; 8. Laying claim to; 9. Injury, killing, seeking to injure; 10. A sort of state occasioned by love.[40]

Calling to mind Freud's famous essay "The Antithetical Meaning of Primal Words," one is initially struck by the apparent embodiment of opposite meanings expressed within the same term: both "pride (in a good sense)" and "self-conceit," "pride (in a bad sense)," "arrogance"; both "affection, love" and "injury, killing, seeking to injure."[41] It is the third meaning in the Sanskrit definition above that suggests the key to the apparent tensions within both the Sanskrit and the Telugu definitions—that is, the quality of "referring all objects to oneself." Today one cannot be an *abhimāni* without also specifying the object of one's *abhimānam.* Indeed, what is central is the affective relationship between an *abhimāni* and an external object that can be referred back to oneself—an object that today helps to define oneself and one's identity. There can be no *abhimāni* without this defining and constitutive object of affection, admiration, or love.

The early-twentieth-century refiguring of languages as just such objects suggests that the extreme affective attachments to language represented by the deaths with which this book opened would have been unthinkable without the prior personification of a language in ways that made it available to become an object of love, pride, or devotional attachment. This involved not only the new attribution of a personified (and gendered) face to language in early-twentieth-century southern India, but also a process that for the first time granted to each individual language a biography, history, and kinship network of its own. This did not mean that Telugu had never before been personified, for there do exist pre-modern comparisons of the language to an eroticized young girl in which the poet takes delicious pleasure.[42] Instead, the personifications of mother tongues in twentieth-century southern India mark a transition to a new representation of one's mother tongue as a mother, a goddess, or a victim in need of protection, praise, patronage, service, or sacrifice.[43]

The Making of a "Mother Tongue" in a Global Context

The origins of the concept of a "mother tongue" are difficult to ascertain. In English, the use of the term "mother tongue" can be found at least as early as the fifteenth century to refer to one's native language or first language, often in the context of using a medium of communication that is more easily understandable or accessible than another medium, and therefore preferable for that reason.[44] References to the right to plead one's case before the law in one's mother tongue, for example, or to the greater ability to follow and understand religious proceedings and practices in one's mother tongue were not uncommon in pre-modern uses of the expression.[45] By the eighteenth century the idea of a mother tongue had begun to be associated with the language of nature, an idea that Richard Bauman and Charles Briggs have argued has been fundamental to the emergence of the concept of modernity.[46] In their book *Voices of Modernity,* they write that "Emerging out of eighteenth-century classical philology and coalescing in the philosophy of Johann Gottfried Herder [1744–1803] was a discursively founded framing of the advent of modernity that viewed language as a radically hybrid formation . . . inherently both natural and social, but in shifting proportions over the long course of human social evolution."[47] Such a hybrid emphasis on both the natural and the social dimensions of language allowed a romantic investment in the natural, unprocessed, and unrefined speech of the common people, what Herder referred to as the *Volk,* as the basis and foundation for claiming a national identity, while at the same time facilitating the acceptance of a hierarchy with which to justify existing social inequalities on the basis of language use.[48] For Herder, the language of the *Volk* was that which was most feeling-laden, and therefore most authentic, but also, in his view, the least over-burdened by excessive rationality. Herder's idea that the mother tongue—as a language of nature or as the natural language of "the people"—was the foundation of the nation had a widespread impact on nineteenth-century European ideas of nationalism. Both Herder and Jean-Jacques Rousseau (1712–1778) saw language as a "*sine qua non,* as the natural lifeblood of human culture and social demeanor in all its forms," positioning language in a new and important way within Europeans' understandings of themselves and the diversity they encountered in their increasingly expanding world.[49]

Although the European colonizers of India brought with them ideas about language that had a profound impact on the subcontinent, these ideas were received into an environment already rich with ideas and discourses about language. Bernard Cohn's pioneering work on colonial constructions of knowledge in South Asia has alerted us to the role of colonialism in creating the categories through which India has been experienced and written about within such colonial disciplines as anthropology, historical linguistics, and comparative religion.[50] A number of scholars who have followed him have argued that the emergence of linguistically grounded identities in the late nineteenth century was a result of the implementation of specific colonial administrative practices. These included the colonial census, the establishment of colonial districts on linguistic lines to aid in revenue collection, colonial educational policies, and the production of colonial language learning aids like grammars and lexicons.[51] However, much of this work has been more concerned with understanding the role of these new forms of knowledge within the logic of colonial rule than with tracing in great detail the effects of colonialism on local knowledge and practices. Cohn himself ends his pathbreaking article "The Command of Language and Language of Command" with a statement that stops just short of exploring the ways in which colonial re-framings of knowledge were experienced locally. Acknowledging that his primary interest is not in the impact of European scholarship and administrative policies on Indian thought and practices, he writes:

> The delineation of the cumulative effect of the results of the first half-century of the objectification and reordering through the application of European scholarly methods on Indian thought and culture is beyond the scope of this essay. The Indians who increasingly became drawn into the process of transformation of their own traditions and modes of thought were, however, far from passive.[52]

While acknowledging that local actors were not passive, the focus of much of the colonial constructions of knowledge scholarship has not been on illuminating specific shifts in local experience, practice, and perception, but rather on examining the practices of the colonial state.

In beginning my project where Cohn has left off, I am suggesting that much more attention has been placed on the causes of these changes than on the effects of the specific processes of local selection, transmission, and circulation and on understanding how consciousness, categories, meanings, and everyday practices have been refigured in new ways as a result.

Cohn's statement points out to us the insufficient attention that has been devoted to exploring the ways in which the British presence and practices in India were incorporated into, evaded, and otherwise confronted by local systems of signification. An emphasis on the latter allows us to identify and trace the anxieties, desires, and concerns of local knowledge experts—including poets, authors, publishers, interpreters, and schoolteachers—to illuminate the nuances of local systems of knowledge and their relationships to power. In this sense power is understood as a network of relations, meanings, and exchanges that are defined, produced, transmitted, and circulated in particular ways—a network that undergoes change whenever any one element within it is altered. How did local knowledge experts and others engage with and respond to the new forms of knowledge, new choices in the range of available practices, and new technologies and media introduced or mediated by the European colonial presence? Asking this question allows us to identify larger patterns of practice and understanding that both enabled and placed limits on the range of possibility within which actors—both local and colonial, though not necessarily in the same ways—could act, and the meanings attributed to these actions. Patronage, employment opportunities, outlets for creative expression, pedagogy, and even notions of what constitutes appropriate content of literature, history writing, education, and literacy underwent dramatic changes during the nineteenth century, bringing with them recognizable changes in the meanings and significance of virtually every activity linked to these domains.

Two features of the language movements of twentieth-century southern India make it clear that these emotional attachments to language are not simply local versions of a story already told in Europe or elsewhere. First, unlike the language-based political movements and nationalisms that swept through Europe from the late eighteenth century onward, language movements in India have not typically been separatist or nationalist movements. The leaders and followers of Indian language-based political movements have not sought to establish new and independent nations; instead they have desired recognition and rights within the existing Indian nation. In contrast, most language-based movements in Europe have either advocated, or actually resulted in, the creation of new nations. This suggests that the southern Indian story may have something to teach us about changing relationships to language elsewhere in the world. Not only can our story help to make visible features of change that have until now remained unnoticed, but it can also force us to question prevailing assumptions regarding the relationships between languages and nations that have gone unchallenged. Indeed, another of the questions this book answers is why the passionate attachments to language in India have not followed the European model of linguistic separatism that have so routinely culminated in the establishment of new nations.

Second, despite the disinterest in establishing separate nations, the intensity of the emotional commitments to language displayed in southern India appears to dramatically exceed similar attachments to language that have existed elsewhere in the world. The willingness of Sriramulu, Chinnasami, and others to die in very public ways demonstrates a conscious awareness of and ability to effectively use the power of new forms of mass media. Publicity did not simply magnify the implications of these martyrs' acts, but in a very real sense the twentieth-century communication networks of southern India actually created and circulated them as events in ways that would have previously been impossible. A well-publicized fast-unto-death and the selection of the most public location in the town of Tiruchirappalli to perform one's self-immolation suggest that this new form of attachment to language is not a private relationship, but rather one in which publicity plays an integral role. Potti Sriramulu, for example, began his fast with a clear sense of the role that the media would play in publicizing his concerns. He gave a great deal of thought to choosing a location that would maximize his impact, consulted widely with political leaders and fellow activists, issued regular press releases and weekly bulletins, and made public the most minute details concerning his health, bodily functions, and physical condition. One biographer tells us that "whenever Potti Sriramulu resort[ed] to a fast for a noble cause, he made rigorous correspondence with elders and gave press statements in order to mobilise the opinion of the elite and the general public in his favour."[53] Indeed, every aspect of his fast was meticulously documented and made public, from the color, size, and smell of each bowel movement to the number of ounces of saliva he produced.[54]

Chinnasami, too, had carefully calculated the impact of his actions. His suicide was not a spontaneous decision. Instead, he prepared carefully, choosing a location at the center of Tiruchirappalli's local communication network. As the site where the news literally arrived first in the town, the railway station's newsstands, bookshops, and coffee stalls were the most important local communication hubs in the 1960s. The station was therefore the most important site in the town for people to gather each day to read and discuss the newspapers delivered by early morning trains and converse with those getting down from trains arriving from distant locations. A decade earlier, in the wake of Potti Sriramulu's death, the railway stations throughout Coastal Andhra attracted crowds for precisely these same reasons. While conducting research into the events that followed Potti Sriramulu's death, I was already interested in the role of various forms of mass media. When I asked one former Andhra movement leader whether he had heard about Potti Sriramulu's death on the radio or read about it in the newspaper, he replied, "Hmm. Yes, radio was there. Newspaper was there. But, no, we heard about it in the street, and then we went immediately to the railway station to find out what *really* happened."[55] Sriramulu and Chinnasami both made calculated use of existing networks of communication to ensure that their actions would have maximum publicity coverage and attention.

In Europe, as in southern India, the defense of one's "mother tongue," whether in public or in private, is a learned behavior rather than a natural impulse. Yet, this does not mean that such learned behavior is insignificant or should be dismissed. Whenever a "mother tongue" is invoked, the first questions that should be asked are (1) what is at stake for the person claiming a mother tongue; and (2) what are the other languages against which the mother tongue is being defended and asserted? Any recognition of or claim to a mother tongue points to an awareness of multiple languages. Fiona Somerset and Nicholas Watson, in their book *The Vulgar Tongue,* have argued that a claim to a mother tongue is not simply a claim to a language, but also an acknowledgment of "a relation between one language situation and another." They write that the invocation of a mother tongue indicates an aspiration to transcend "the condition of *vernacularity*" by making a marginalized language "worthy to stand comparison with the classics" and therefore describes "not a language as such," but rather a situation in which the mother tongue is "at least notionally in the more embattled, or at least the less clear-cut, position" vis-à-vis another language.[56] In this sense, they point out that a claim to a mother tongue can be seen as a vehicle for access to increased power. It is "authority-seeking" as well as "authority-defying" in its attempt to redefine the existing reference points for status and decision making.[57] Peter Burke, in his book *Languages and Communities in Early Modern Europe,* similarly reminds us that sixteenth- and seventeenth-century defenses of regional vernacular languages not only stressed the "riches, abundance or copiousness of one language," but also drew attention to "the poverty of its rivals."[58] It is important to keep in mind this larger context of language competition and the ways that competition has encouraged the defense of language, but it is equally important that we understand why language has become a primary site for championing difference today.

This representation of embattlement against a rival language, or victimization and loss at the hands of its representatives, can also mobilize a mother tongue as an alibi for a powerful group to claim the right to represent those who are less powerful. Eric Hobsbawm writes that in an era before general primary education in Europe, "the actual or literal 'mother tongue,' i.e., the idiom children learned from illiterate mothers and spoke for everyday use, was certainly not in any sense a 'national language.'"[59] He goes on to say that even when claiming to be the "mother tongue" of the majority of the "people,"

> National languages are therefore almost always semi-artificial constructs, and occasionally, like modern Hebrew, virtually invented. They are the opposite of what nationalist mythology supposes them to be, namely the primordial foundations of national culture and the matrices of the national mind. They are usually attempts to devise a standardized idiom out of a multiplicity of actually spoken idioms, which are thereafter downgraded to dialects, the main problem in their construction being usually, which dialect to choose as the base of the standardized and homogenized language.

The concept of a "mother-tongue" invokes a romantic investment in the idea of language learned at the mother's breast. Yet in practice, the language championed as a "mother tongue" is almost always a regional variety associated with a socially and politically dominant group of people, albeit one that sees itself as victimized by yet another group of people perceived to be even more powerful or privileged. In Andhra Pradesh today, "standard" Telugu is a dialect associated with educated members of several dominant caste groups from the Krishna, East and West Godavari, and Guntur districts, representing the most agriculturally developed and prosperous region of coastal Andhra. While the knowledge of this linguistic inequity often inspires bitterness on the part of those whose varieties of Telugu have been marginalized, particularly among those from more economically disadvantaged districts, even this bitterness demonstrates the recognition that a standard language exists.

Whose Language? Whose Movement?

The Andhra movement was basically made up of a mass of middle-class peasants and students. . . . The actual toilers and laborers weren't involved.

—Former Andhra movement leader, August 12, 1998

As the quote above exemplifies, the common view of historians, journalists, and political leaders in Andhra is that the Telugu linguistic state movement was primarily a middle-class movement. Well documented are the widespread perceptions on the part of educated middle-class Telugu-speakers that they were excluded from or disadvantaged in consideration for government employment, educational opportunities, and other benefits when compared with other residents of the existing multilingual Madras State, particularly Tamil-speakers.[60] Early concerns emerged in response to a colonial policy established in 1895 to no longer recruit Telugu-speaking Hindus for military service.[61] By the early decades of the twentieth century, concerns centered on the under-representation of Telugu-speakers and residents of Telugu-dominated districts within government institutions and structures of employment.[62] Movement leaders drew up detailed tables that documented such statistics as the proportion of Telugu-speakers represented within various levels of government employment to demonstrate disproportionately low representation.[63] In 1904 the colonial government had established an explicit policy against recruiting government employees from among the Indian population via open competition, stating instead that a policy of general competition would create

> if not a monopoly, very nearly monopoly of posts conferred upon one section of the community [i.e., Brahmins]. This is a position which the government could not recognize with equanimity. It is the duty of the government to reconcile the conflicting claims of diverse races, rival religions and varying degrees of intellectual aptitude and adaptability. It is the duty of the government to see that all offices in their services are distributed as fairly and evenly as possible amongst all classes, castes, and communities.[64]

This statement suggests that the colonial government made explicit attempts in their recruitment of government employees to reflect the diversity of the general population with regard to race, religion, aptitude, caste, class, and community. However, as K. V. Narayana Rao remarks, "This solicitude of the Government to distribute jobs fairly to all categories of citizens did not extend to making similar adequate provision for the various linguistic groups" or for equitable geographic distribution of appointments.[65] Later there were also complaints regarding the distribution of hydroelectric power and investment in irrigation facilities, as well as concerns over the failure to appoint Telugu-speakers to the positions of executive councilors, limiting the influence of those from Telugu-dominated districts over major decisions regarding irrigation and electrical projects from 1921 to 1936.[66] The greater numbers of schools, colleges, and professional training institutions in the non-Telugu-dominated districts and the relative absence of rail connections in Telugu-dominated districts when compared with the Tamil-dominated districts of Madras State were also bones of contention for the advocates of a separate Andhra and caused much public discussion on the sources of what was referred to as the "backwardness" of the Andhras or Telugus.[67]

Similarly, the Tamil language movement is often explained as emerging out of the fear that if Hindi were to be established as the primary national language of India, Tamil-speakers would be disadvantaged in competitions for government jobs and university admissions at the national level. Chinnasami's self-immolation occurred when plans to implement Hindi as the national language were being revived after a temporary fifteen-year deferral of the question, during which time English was retained as a "transitional" language.[68] Both movements shared common fears of being economically and politically disadvantaged in relation to speakers of other languages. And indeed, many Telugu-speakers today continue to explain the movement for a separate state as primarily an issue of access to government employment and other economic, political, and educational opportunities, championed by those educated middle classes who most stood to benefit from the increased access to these benefits. Such statements are often made hand in hand with denials that language was ever something to feel emotional about. K. V. Narayana Rao's book *The Emergence of Andhra Pradesh,* for example, concludes that "it was the prospective political and economic advantages that might accrue to each region and, sometimes, to a predominant caste in that region, which really influenced the attitude of that region towards the formation of an Andhra province (or state) rather than an emotional or sentimental commitment to the Andhra identity."[69]

The huge gatherings at railway stations, the violence, the destruction of railway, police, and other government property, and the numerous deaths and injuries at the hands of police attempting to maintain order were all factors that influenced Prime Minister Jawaharlal Nehru to declare a separate Telugu linguistic state just four days after Sriramulu's death. One of a number of sites that figured significantly in reports of this violence and chaos was Nellore, a town of just over 350,000, and the headquarters of the district known by the same name. Nellore figured centrally both in the political development of the Andhra movement, dating from the first decades of the twentieth century, and in the final events leading to its culmination in December 1952. In the context of the massive crowds that formed around the Nellore Railway Station just days before the announcement of the formation of the new state, over two dozen people were shot by the police as they struggled to maintain some semblance of order. Out of these, four young men died from their bullet wounds. Since similar deaths and injuries occurred at the hands of police in other towns and cities of the coastal Telugu-speaking districts of Madras State—including Anakapalle, Visakhapatnam, Guntur, and Srikakulam—a close study of Nellore is useful in trying to understand these events. Although they were celebrated for their contribution to forcing Nehru's hand, little information is available regarding the actual individuals who were present at the railway station or who were injured and killed. Ethnographic and oral history research conducted in Nellore during the summer of 1998 and again during 2000 and 2002 gave me an opportunity to meet and talk with key individuals who had participated in the Andhra movement and in the events following Sriramulu's death, as well as with relatives of those who were killed in 1952. Efforts to track down these individuals and their surviving relatives nearly fifty years later led me to numerous neighboring smaller towns, including Kavali, Gudur, Sullarpet, Rapur, and Naidupet, and to several outlying villages.

In Nellore, I was fortunate to have access to the private archive of one of the former leaders of the Nellore Town Youth League in 1952, an organization that supported the agitation for a separate Andhra and raised funds for the victims of the police violence. In this archive I was able to examine the original money order receipts for the disbursements of these funds to those injured and to the relatives of those killed. The receipts, and the addresses they showed, became my starting points for locating these individuals fifty years later. Yet when I did actually track them down and speak with them, their stories introduced unsettling tensions into the seemingly seamless narratives that have come to dominate the historical and journalistic accounts of Andhra State and the movement for a separate Telugu linguistic province that I had already studied. The most surprising discovery was that the majority of those present at the "demonstrations" that occurred at the Nellore Railway Station were from lower-class and non-dominant-caste backgrounds, and many had little or no education. We know this because of the records kept by the Nellore Town Youth League documenting their fund-raising efforts and disbursements to the victims and their families. Their receipts show that almost half of those injured in the police firings in Nellore acknowledged receipt of relief funds with a thumbprint rather than a signature, indicating their lack of literacy.[70] If indeed the Andhra movement was truly a middle-class initiative, then why were so many people who stood to benefit so little from increased access for Telugu-speakers to government jobs and university admissions present at the railway station that day? The class and caste makeup of the crowds who gathered at the news of Potti Sriramulu's death, and its apparent contradiction of received assumptions regarding the Andhra movement, create an ideal paradox to use in analyzing the power of language to create the appearance of affective attachment during the twentieth century.

The Power of Language: Narratives of 1952

> *We heard that Potti Sriramulu had died. He died in Madras, they said. After that a big commotion [*pedda galāṭa*] happened here. Oh my, police stations, trains, gates were broken. At every place . . . police stations, everywhere, there was utter confusion [*ganddaragōḷam*]. . . . Such a spectacle [*tamāṣā*] that day.*
>
> —Retired railway mail service employee, age seventy-two, Nellore, April 15, 2002

"*Pedda galāṭa* [a big commotion] . . . *pedda galabha* [a huge fuss] . . . *gandaragōḷam* [utter confusion, complete disorder] . . . *tamāṣā* [a spectacle]." These are the words used by a retired railway mail service worker to describe events that occurred at the Nellore Railway Station on the eve of the declaration of a separate Telugu linguistic state in 1952.[71] The events included the police shootings on the crowd that took the life of his younger brother, then eighteen years old. His words form a striking contrast with the terms used by leaders of the political parties involved in the movement, journalists, historians, and other prominent citizens of the town of Nellore to describe the same events. For these latter individuals, the event was clearly remembered and recorded as a "demonstration," an "agitation," a crucial turning point within the *āndhra rāṣṭram udyamam* [the movement for a separate Andhra State], and most importantly, an expression of the popular will. The latter all used terms suggesting that the events were experienced within the larger narrative of the movement for a separate Andhra State. The stories of these events told by the relatives of those who were killed, however, also suggested larger narratives, though not necessarily ones anchored by a desire for Andhra State. At first, I thought the dramatic distinctions in word choices I was hearing must reflect differences between those who speak primarily in Telugu and those who are equally comfortable conducting their affairs in both English and Telugu. But as I began to talk with more people, gathering their memories of this same event and listening more carefully, I realized that this was not the case. Additional research revealed that even when speaking and writing in Telugu, political leaders, prominent citizens, and even journalists and historians used expressions like *vīrōchita pōrāṭa* [heroic struggle, heroic fight], *praja udyamam* [people's movement], and *janam lēchadam* [popular uprising],[72] even going so far as to suggest that the event was an expression of *āndhra prajānīkam yōkkakō-pōdrēkālu minnumuṭṭistunāyi* [the passions of the Telugu masses, once set in motion, touching the sky (rising sky high)].[73]

Given my interest in affective attachments to new objects and the appearance within new contexts of emotions previously undocumented, I found the reference to the rising passions of the Telugu masses in the last example above particularly intriguing. The key terms used—*udrēkam* "emotional tension, passion, excitement" (also "excess, increase"), and *prajānīkam* "the people, the masses, the general public"—brought together the two notions I was most curious about. I had already established the emergence of a decisively new affective attachment to language among literate upper-caste communities of the coastal districts of the colonial Madras Presidency from the last decades of the nineteenth century onward, represented in newly printed works like Gurujada Sriramamurti's *Lives of [Telugu] Poets.* A picture was forming of the interests and anxieties of those who had access to employment in government jobs and stood to gain from admission into government schools, colleges, and universities. Not surprisingly, these were the same communities and individuals who owned printing presses, established newspapers, journals, and literary forums, contributed to the social reform efforts of the day, and left written historical accounts. The complaints of these communities that they were institutionally under-represented when compared with their Tamil-speaking compatriots held a certain logic, and the statistics rallied in support of such complaints could clearly be seen as effective in drawing others from similar communities to support the cause.[74] Such claims also had the advantage of appearing to represent the interests of a huge population—all speakers of Telugu—an important factor in an era when representational claims and demands carried increasingly greater force than those made on behalf of a single individual.

Yet these literate individuals from the coastal districts of the predominately Telugu-speaking regions of the Madras Presidency still represented only a fraction of the total population of Telugu-speakers. The 1911 All-India Census, conducted at the same time as the first demands for a separate state were beginning to be formulated, showed a literate population of only 5.92 percent (10.56 percent of all men), and by 1951 this had increased to only 16.67 percent (24.95 of the male population).[75] Such statistics, and the explanations that the Telugu linguistic state movement was essentially a middle-class movement concerned with access to government jobs and university admissions, did little to explain the stakes, personal investments, and desires represented by the participation in these events of non-elites and non-literates, toilers and laborers, and members of non-dominant caste communities who stood to gain little from a new state.[76] At the same time, however, the contributions of the many already marginalized individuals who were present during agitations for a separate Telugu State are frequently further devalued and dismissed by the very same individuals who simultaneously claim that the Andhra movement represented the popular will. The desires and motives of the class of those who stood to gain from increased access to government employment and university education—the class from which most of the movement leaders came—made sense to me. But the motives of those who were not likely to gain increased access to education, government jobs, and similar opportunities with the creation of a new state are more difficult to explain and have not been adequately accounted for by existing literature on either the Andhra movement or linguistic nationalism. What could create such an investment in a separate Telugu linguistic state that so many non-elites and non-literates would be passionate enough about its achievement that they would be willing to sacrifice their lives? Arguments of false consciousness, offered by many I spoke with, or the conviction that many might have been paid by political parties to strengthen body counts at politically motivated and organized events (an explanation frequently offered for the presence of rural non-literates at political events and rallies in India) left little room for understanding the desires, anxieties, worldviews, and motives of those who actually participated. M. S. S. Pandian, for example, has cautioned us not to reduce language movements to sub-nationalist processes, but rather to recognize the various ways in which such movements may attract individuals to them for a wide variety of reasons, not all of which are consistent with the objectives of those who claim to act as spokespersons for these movements.[77] Why had those present during the agitations chosen to be there, and how could the discourse of attachment to language so easily come to be accepted as accounting for their presence? How has the idea of an emotional commitment to one's mother tongue displaced other possible explanations for the large-scale events that occurred in the wake of Potti Sriramulu's death in December 1952? These, then, are the questions that this book answers.

Explaining the New Commitments to a "Mother Tongue"

> *One can never understand this most ambiguous century [the nineteenth century] by describing the sequence of its periods. It must be demarcated simultaneously from both ends, i.e., from the last third of the eighteenth century and the first third of the twentieth.*
>
> —Martin Heidegger, *Nietzsche,* vol. 1

At one extreme, explanations for the Andhra movement see the crowds and widespread violence as irrefutable evidence of the passionate devotion to language and desire for a separate linguistically defined administrative territory. Those holding this view also frequently see such actions as the expression of the natural feelings possessed by any speaker toward his or her mother tongue. The repeated claims that the widespread commotion and violence signified that Telugu-speakers had "expressed themselves with one voice" to "demand the immediate formation of a separate state" and could be interpreted as clear expressions of a popular uprising (*janam lēchadam*) and heroic struggle (*vīrōchita pōrāṭa*) reflect this first extreme.[78] Even if we accept this explanation, which chapter 6 questions, we must still ask why such passionate feeling emerges only after the 1890s, and why it peaks in the middle of the twentieth century rather than earlier or later. At the opposite extreme, we find the repeated insistence by others that the Telugu linguistic state movement was "not something to be emotional about," but was a rational, matter-of-fact issue for members of the educated middle classes.[79] The participation of anyone other than a member of the middle class was explained to me either as false consciousness or elite manipulation, or with the assertion that some "people want their names to be published in papers. . . . That's all."[80] How were the lives of the four young men who were killed in Nellore in 1952, and the lives and actions of numerous others like them in Anakapalle, Visakhapatnam, Guntur, Srikakulam, and elsewhere absorbed so easily into narratives of language devotion and linguistic statehood despite the many contradictory claims about their actions that sought either to reduce them to blind devotion or to false consciousness? How, at the same time, were their actions able to be interpreted by Prime Minister Nehru and other political leaders as the deciding factor that led to the ultimate creation of a new linguistic state if they were not, in fact, manifesting devotion to a linguistic state?

Rather than reducing the explanations for the phenomenon of *telugu dēśa bhāṣa abhimānulu* to one of the two above extremes and reconciling this apparent contradiction through an explanation that would erase all meaning from the actions of those whose presence was most important, making them into nothing more than passive, unthinking pawns in a game in which the only real actors are educated elites, this book offers a third, and alternative, explanation. The following chapters use close attention to technological changes in transportation and communication, the restructuring of political power, and shifts in patronage, pedagogy, and the production of knowledge to trace the creation of a new role for language as a foundation for the reorganization of knowledge and practice in southern India. In focusing on the important and often overlooked ways in which technology and the reconfiguration of information networks appear in the story of the making of a mother tongue, I am drawing from the work of Frederich Kittler, who privileges "the network of technologies and institutions that allow a given culture to select, store, and process relevant data."[81] He argues that these "information networks can be described only when they are contrasted with one another." Rather than writing linear intellectual histories or focusing on chronologies of events, Kittler argues:

> Whether data, addresses, and commands circulate among pedagogy, Poetry, and philosophy, or among media technologies, psychophysics, and literature, *the difference changes the place value of every word.* In describing such feedback systems of senders, channels, and receivers, the instantaneous exposures or snapshots of a single moment can be of more help than intellectual histories.[82]

The following chapters help us understand the present by juxtaposing its discourse networks and the meanings they define with those of another moment. As such, I avoid relating the events of the nineteenth and twentieth centuries—particularly the events leading to the formation of linguistic states in southern India—in a simple chronological fashion. Instead, I selectively focus on particular moments that, in their contrast with the networks of other moments, reveal differences that can tell us something about contemporary experiences of language.

The book furthermore offers a set of reflections upon the practices that most effectively rallied and focused the attention, emotions, and actions of a wide spectrum of the population—if not the "masses," at least a spectrum much wider than the readers (and writers) of the new forms of print media circulating in late colonial and early independent India. Central to the discussion is the role of death and the discourse of loss, and the very public ways in which the marking of death has been employed to make silent bodies speak far more powerfully than the most persuasive of reasoned arguments disseminated via print media. The final chapter uses oral and written narratives of the events of December 1952 to produce a more nuanced understanding of the relationship between passion (impassioned action) and mass participation in an important twentieth-century sociocultural and political movement of southern India. It not only explores the nature of popular perception and participation within the process of democracy in India, but also the puzzling ambivalence over this participation expressed by political and social leaders and the ways in which public attention, emotion, and actions were shaped, sustained, and focused to make language appear to be a natural foundation for identity. In doing so, it illustrates how the earlier chapters answer important questions about the production of affective attachment to newly constituted objects and the motivation for action that stems from such attachments.

Archival, literary, and ethnographic materials collected from southern India suggest that the new meanings, passions, and subject positions linked to language that have appeared in the twentieth century have emerged in response to these very specific historical conditions of the nineteenth century. Residents of nineteenth-century southern India experienced dramatic reconfigurations of political power, to which they responded by experimenting with rapidly changing technologies and networks of communication and creating new patterns of patronage and consumption, each significantly mediated by British colonial policies and projects. In tracing the relationships between these various transformations, this book argues that it is only by understanding the very new role that language comes to play in modern India that we can fully explain the passions of those individuals who have given up their lives in the name of something newly identifiable as a "mother tongue."

CHAPTER I

From Language of the Land to Language of the People: Geography, Language, and Community in Southern India

Between the 1893 second edition of Gurujada Sriramamurti's *Lives of Poets,* in which his unprecedented appeal to those having an emotional attachment to the language of the Telugu country first appeared, and the 1913 third edition, which contained the same preface, a subtle but significant change was made to the opening line. Both prefaces bore Sriramamurti's name and the same date—February 1, 1893. Yet the 1913 preface was not an exact reprint of the one that had been published twenty years earlier. Instead of appealing to *telugu dēśa bhāṣa abhimānulu,* "those attached to the language of the Telugu country," as Sriramamurti's 1893 preface had, the 1913 preface opened with an appeal to *āndhra bhāṣa abhimānulu,* "those attached to the Andhra language."[1] The equation of the terms *telugu* and *āndhra* has a long, complicated, and not always uncontested history, and those who view these two terms as synonymous also usually assert that both can be used interchangeably to refer to a coterminous region, language, and people. The decision to alter the wording of the preface was not likely made by Sriramamurti, since he lived only until 1899, but was more likely initiated by his publisher, Vavilla Ramaswamy Sastri. His publisher may simply have felt that *āndhra* was aesthetically superior to the longer phrase *telugu dēśa,* and the matter may end there. However, there is another possibility, and that is that the term *dēśa,* the adjectival form of *dēśam,* "a country, land, territory; a district or subdivision of a country," could be eliminated because territory no longer formed the primary locus for identifying linguistic differences.[2] Instead, by 1913, evidence suggests that languages were no longer primarily associated with places but were increasingly imagined as inalienable attributes of people.

This does not mean that there was no longer any relationship between language and territory, or that there had never before been a relationship between the name of a dynastic family, king, or ruling group and the name of a language. Rather, I am arguing that the relationship between language and territory was for the first time explicitly represented as mediated by the people residing within the region.

The year of the publication of Sriramamurti's third edition, 1913, was, not coincidentally, the same year as the establishment of the Andhra Mahasabha, the association that spearheaded the movement for a separate Telugu linguistic state. It was also the year of the publication of Gidugu Venkata Ramamurthy's *Memorandum on Modern Telugu,* one of the most important documents in the movement to make written Telugu more closely resemble the spoken language of "the people."[3] These events suggest that by this second decade of the twentieth century, the Telugu language had indeed undergone a transformation that led to its recognition as the language of "the people." What Sriramamurti, in his tentative and uncertain appeal for an audience in 1893, needed to make explicit—the presence of a group of people defined and united by their shared relationship to a language—could, by 1913, be completely taken for granted.

Hidden within this seemingly innocent substitution of one term for another lies a shift from understanding language as a feature of a territory—*dēśa bhāṣa,* "language of the land"—to the acceptance of language as a personal attribute attached to particular people, viewed both as individuals and as members of a shared community defined in relation to that language. This latter understanding of language was expressed most obviously in the introduction of the new term *mātṛ bhāṣa,* literally "mother tongue," into the Telugu language around this same time. Without appearing to acknowledge any change at all, the subtle alteration in the representation of the role of language marked by the elision of the term *dēśa* draws our attention to the fact that by the time the third edition of Sriramamurti's *Lives of Poets* was published, a language was no longer considered something simply used by people as one of several possible media of communication. Instead, languages had also begun to be regarded as markers used to define and represent people, both individually and as members of a collectivity. The term *dēśa bhāṣa* had emphasized the language used in a particular place rather than the language used by a particular person or group of people. In Sriramamurti's 1893 preface, place was very clearly the determining factor for defining language, which in turn defined the *abhimānulu*—those attached to the language of the region—to whom Sriramamurti was appealing. In the 1913 edition, a reference to region can only be implied.

G. N. Reddy, in his introductory article in an edited volume on the history of the Telugu language, opens by asserting that "*Āndhram, Tenugu,* and *Telugu* are three names in use today for our language." He continues by identifying *Āndhram* as the term used to describe the language in Sanskrit texts and the others as used in Telugu literary compositions.[4] The adjectival form, *āndhra,* appears equally comfortably in designating a language (*āndhra bhāṣa*), region (*āndhra dēśam*), people (*āndhra prajalu*), or culture (*āndhra samskṛti*). The noun, *āndhram,* which appeared first in Sanskrit texts and later in Telugu-language texts, has been used alone to refer to either a language or a region. It is precisely the easy ambiguity between language and place that makes appear continuous that which is, in fact, highly discontinuous. Yet *telugu* and *āndhram* are not identical in their usage, nor are their English equivalents, Telugu and Andhra. In Telugu, *āndhram* as a noun can refer to either a region or a language but must take an altered ending to refer to a person (*āndhruḍu*) or people (*āndhrulu*). In contrast, *telugu,* when used in Telugu as a freestanding noun, with no additional endings, can only be used to refer to the language. It must be used as part of a compound or in adjectival form along with a noun to refer to a place (*telugu dēśam* or *telugunāḍu*), or single person (*teluguvāḍu*). This is further complicated by the fact that today Andhra is used in both English and Telugu as a short form for the proper name of the linguistic state, Andhra Pradesh. In English, Andhra as a noun can refer to a region, or, in the plural, to people (Andhras), but must be used in its adjectival form along with a noun to refer to a language (the Andhra language). The English proper noun Telugu, in contrast, is used today to refer to a language or a person in the singular but must be used in its adjectival form with a noun to refer to a place (the Telugu country or Telugu region).

"Andhra" and "Telugu": Region, Language, People

Although associations between the terms "Telugu" and "Andhra(m)" can be traced back at least to the fourteenth century, if not even earlier, the assertion that these two terms are synonymous has gained strength over the course of the past century. Since the beginning of the twentieth century historians and other authors have projected a continuous history, culture, and identity for both the Telugu country and its people. This has typically involved searching Telugu texts from the eleventh century onward (and Sanskrit texts before that), as well as even earlier inscriptions for evidence that might support the long existence of identification of a people with a shared collective sense of linguistic identity.[5] Although historically there has been no dearth of references to an Andhra region or to a Telugu region, there is little consistency in the landmarks used to demarcate such a region, suggesting that the terms may refer to different geographic territories in each context. In the absence of clear evidence, the present-day entity and boundaries of Andhra Pradesh are frequently anachronistically projected backward into time. In books published since the mid-1950s, an outline map of the contemporary state—created in its current form in 1956—is commonly used when representing much earlier periods of southern India, symbolizing a regional linguistic identity that is claimed to have already been well established centuries ago.

Beginning with the publication of the collections of lives of Telugu poets in the last decades of the nineteenth century, and the flood of subsequent publications that similarly sought to appeal to an audience marked by their relationship to Telugu, the twentieth century has seen a continuous process of consolidation of linguistic identification. Following the establishment of the Andhra Mahasabha and its demand for a separate linguistic state in the 1910s, activists from the districts of the colonial Madras Presidency where Telugu dominated were at the forefront of those demanding the restructuring of the Indian National Congress along linguistic lines that began to occur by 1917.[6] The Indian National Congress, formed in 1885 to advocate for greater Indian participation in the political and administrative structures of governance under British colonial rule, eventually accepted the principle of linguistic division as a fundamental organizational feature. The formation of the Andhra Provincial Congress Committee (APCC) was one of several provincial committees that helped pave the way for the subsequent complete reorganization of the Congress committees on linguistic lines. In the 1920s and 1930s the investment in a continuous Andhra history and past also took the form of attempts to comprehensively catalogue and document every Telugu literary work ever composed.[7] By the 1940s and 1950s it involved printing, reprinting, and editing critical and popular editions of the works of many of the now canonized poets identified with the Telugu land and people whose lives had already been well documented by this time. In both pre-colonial and post-colonial India, Telugu-speakers were pioneers in defining and asserting interests on a linguistic basis. After the establishment of a separate linguistic state in the 1950s, language and the assertion of shared linguistic identity appear to have diminished slightly as a focus of attention and concern in the context of Andhra Pradesh. However, in the 1980s, during the administration of the popular chief minister and former movie actor N. T. Rama Rao, statues of canonical Telugu literary and historical figures appeared along a main thoroughfare in the capital city of Hyderabad, and the Potti Sriramulu Telugu University was established. This institution—with departments of folklore, archaeology, history, comparative literature, music, dance, and astrology—has become a documentation and production site for Telugu culture. Although one cannot get a degree from this institution in computer science or information technology, despite Andhra's forceful presence in the global IT market, one can get a degree in virtually any subject relating to the history, representation, and performance of Telugu culture.

Although the fact that many people accept the terms "Andhra" and "Telugu" as synonymous facilitated the acceptance of the appellations Andhra State in 1953, following Nehru's December 1952 declaration, and Andhra Pradesh in 1956 for the expanded Telugu linguistic state, in practice, the assertion of the equivalence of these two terms has had a long history of contestation. While living in Andhra, I found that attitudes toward the interchangeability of these two terms correlated strongly with the region of Andhra Pradesh from which a person traced his or her origin. Contemporary Andhra Pradesh is today made up of three unofficial yet historically distinct and popularly recognized regions: Coastal Andhra, Rayalaseema, and Telangana (see Map 5). These three regional labels have largely replaced earlier territorial designations that covered some subsidiary area or that overlapped with what is today included in Andhra Pradesh.

The first label, Coastal Andhra, is used to refer to the predominantly Telugu-speaking districts along the eastern coast of India that were part of the British Madras Presidency until independence in 1947. This territory was also referred to as the Northern Circars at the time it was acquired by the British East India Company through a series of treaties first with the Mughal emperor in 1765 and later with the Nizam of Hyderabad in 1766, 1768, and 1788. Though the district names and their boundaries were different then, the Northern Circars included, from north to south, the territory today covered by the contemporary districts of Srikakulam,

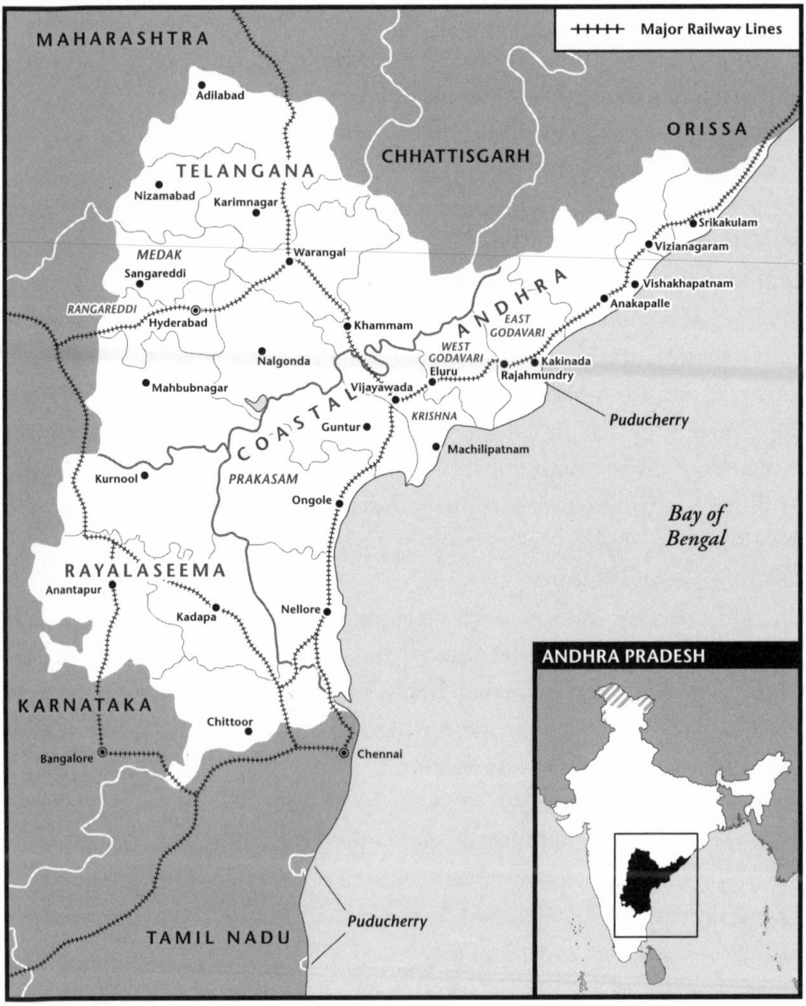

Map 5. Map of Andhra Pradesh
Note: Unless otherwise indicated, districts bear the same name as their major city (shown).

Vizianagaram, Visakhapatnam, East Godavari, West Godavari, Krishna, Guntur, and Prakasam, as well as two districts that are now part of the neighboring state of Orissa to the north, Ganjam and Gajapati. Along with a portion of what are today Prakasam and Chittoor districts, Nellore district was acquired by the British in 1801 from the Nawab of Arcot and is also now usually considered part of Coastal Andhra.

Rayalaseema, like Coastal Andhra, was also part of the British Madras

Presidency at the time of Indian independence. It was acquired by the Nizam of Hyderabad in 1800 following the fall of Tipu Sultan, and then ceded to the British East India Company. For this reason the region also came to be known as the Ceded Districts under British rule. Today Rayalaseema includes the contemporary districts of Kurnool, Anantapur, Kadapa, and Chittoor, and, for historical reasons, sometimes parts of Prakasam and Nellore districts, as well. Up until the time of the linguistic states reorganization of 1956, it also included Bellary district, today a part of the neighboring state of Karnataka to the west.

Telangana is the third popularly recognized division of Andhra Pradesh. The label is today used to refer to the districts of Andhra Pradesh that were once part of Hyderabad State, the largest of India's princely states during the period of British colonialism and a region never subject to direct British rule. These districts today include Adilabad, Nizamabad, Karimnagar, Medak, Warangal, Khammam, Ranga Reddy, Hyderabad, Nalgonda, and Mahbubnagar. At the time of independence in 1947, Hyderabad State chose to remain independent rather than join the new Indian union, an option that was offered to all of the princely states. This independence ended the following year in 1948 when the Indian government carried out a military operation that resulted in the annexation of Hyderabad State and its inclusion within the young Indian nation. The state was later divided along linguistic lines during the All-India Linguistic States Reorganisation of 1956, with predominantly Kannada-speaking districts joining the former princely state of Mysore State (which changed its name to Karnataka in 1973), predominantly Marathi-speaking districts joining Bombay State (which was divided linguistically into Maharashtra and Gujarat in 1960), and predominantly Telugu-speaking districts—some rather reluctantly—joining with Andhra State (Rayalaseema and Coastal Andhra) to form what was renamed Andhra Pradesh.[8]

This brief history of regional geographic labels is useful in revealing how much more important the role of language has become today in acting as the primary foundation for defining a geographic or political region. Many regions and dynasties today claimed by historians of Andhra as evidence of the continuous lineage of a Telugu linguistic people were, in fact, quite multilingual. We have already seen that Krishnadevaraya, the sixteenth-century ruler of the Vijayanagara dynasty, patronized poets who composed in Telugu, Kannada, Sanskrit, and Tamil, and ruled territory that now lies in Karnataka, Andhra Pradesh, Kerala, and Tamil Nadu. He is today celebrated as a Kannada hero by Kannada-speakers and a Telugu hero by Telugu-speakers and is included as a prominent hero in the histories of both contemporary groups.[9] The Northern Circars, with which Coastal Andhra roughly corresponded, included some regions that are today part of the neighboring Oriya linguistic state where Telugu inscriptions have also been found. Similarly, Rayalaseema once included regions that are dominated by Kannada-speakers and are now in the neighboring Kannada linguistic state of Karnataka. These facts attest to the complex multilingualism out of which present-day mother-tongue commitments and geopolitical reorganizations have grown. Few of the pre-modern regional labels that were once used but that have today all but disappeared from common usage—Kammarāṣṭramu, Pākanāḍu, Rēnāḍu, Vēngimaṇḍalamu, and Velanāḍu, to name just a few—corresponded exactly with a linguistically defined territory, perhaps explaining why these terms are no longer considered meaningful enough to be preserved in current usage.[10]

Prior to the formation of Andhra State in 1953, the term "Andhra" was used in ways that often gave little indication of its exact referent. The thirteenth-century poet Tikkana's use of the term *āndhrāvaḷi,* for example, has been translated as "the Andhra populace" and offered as evidence for the strengthening of "a consciousness of unity based on the use of Telugu" from about the late twelfth century onward.[11] In the passage in which this reference appears, however, Tikkana never specifically defines the extent of the term, nor does he indicate whether its foundational referent is a language, the name of the territory, or the name of the ruling dynasty. We should therefore be cautious about using a present-day understanding of the relationship between language and community to erase whatever we might be able to learn about the world that Tikkana himself experienced. As used by Tikkana, *āndhrāvaḷi* is a term open to interpretation. One possible translation of the term is "Andhra lineage," referring specifically to a particular family or dynasty and their descendants, or to the dynasty and its subjects and their descendants. The second part of the compound, *āvaḷi,* means literally "line, row" or "group, assembly" and is commonly found in terms such as *vaṃśāvaḷi,* meaning "genealogy" ("family/dynasty" plus "line/lineage"). It is also used to mean "string" or "garland" in a metaphorical sense. Velcheru Narayana Rao and David Shulman write of this reference that "The great poet Tikkana, in the thirteenth century, is apparently the first to refer to an imagined community named Andhra (*āndhrāvaḷi*), but the boundaries of this community are unknown."[12] They go on to suggest that in Tikkana's usage Andhra may have come to designate the region controlled by the Andhra dynasty, writing, "Originally, the term seems to be a purely dynastic family title," but that "by the medieval period, a conflation of the dynastic and regional terms was clearly well-established."[13] The distinction between *āndhrāvaḷi* understood as a dynastic/familial lineage and its region of domination, and a linguistically defined "population" is important, and we must be cautious about unduly conflating them by extending today's notions about language and identity into the past.

Coastal Andhra has historically been home to the richest and most well developed agricultural land and has therefore been wealthier than other predominantly Telugu-speaking regions. Residents of Coastal Andhra districts are therefore also the most likely to accept the terms "Andhra" and "Telugu" as synonymous, as are migrants from Coastal Andhra now residing in Telangana, including the many who have relocated to the capital city of Hyderabad. Those who identify as natives of Telangana have been the most ambivalent about being part of a state defined in relation to Telugu. Since the incorporation of Telangana into Andhra Pradesh in 1956, there has been an almost continuous movement to secede and form a separate state. Yet even this movement has found it difficult to avoid appealing to the logic of language as the foundation for political reorganization, emphasizing the distinctness of the Telugu spoken in Telangana from the language spoken in Coastal Andhra. Many native Telangana residents openly resent what they see as the colonization of Telangana by wealthy migrants from Coastal Andhra. This is expressed through sensitivity to the influx of migrants from the more prosperous Coastal Andhra districts who brought with them large amounts of capital and who now dominate many important areas of modern life, including media and publishing, politics, economic development, Internet technology, and even migration out of Andhra (to places like New Jersey, California, and Texas). Xiang Biao's ethnography of information technology workers from Andhra Pradesh, for example, suggests that "70 percent of Telugu IT professionals originated from coastal Andhra . . . and further, that 80 percent of these 70 percent hailed from just four districts located in the Godavari and Krishna river deltas—East Godavari, West Godavari, Krishna, and Guntur."[14] For many in the Telangana region, "Andhra" and its plural form are used contextually to refer specifically to the Coastal Andhra region of the state and to people from that region rather than to all speakers of Telugu or all residents of the state. For Coastal Andhra residents and migrants, the term is used much more broadly to refer to all areas where Telugu is spoken, to all areas within Andhra Pradesh, and to all people who speak Telugu as their mother tongue regardless of where they live today.

P. Chenchiah and Raja M. Bhujanga Rao, in their 1925 publication *A History of Telugu Literature,* define *āndhra dēśa* as "the land of the Āndhras," stating that "the classic and historic name for the people now known as Telugus is Āndhras."[15] For them, writing in 1925, it appears self-evident that the existence of a community of people preceded both the naming of the territory in which they lived and the language they spoke: "The early references on the whole make 'Āndhra' to be the appellation of a race, and we may take it that the name was first applied to a people, who in turn impressed it on the country they lived in, and on the language they spoke."[16] P. Raghunadha Rao's textbook of Andhra history, designed for use by B.A. and M.A. university students studying Andhra history and culture, similarly assumes the pre-existence of a community called the Andhras: "The language of the Andhras is variously known as Andhra Basha, Telugu and Tenugu. These appellations are used synonymously."[17] His title also projects the present-day geographic boundaries of the contemporary political state of Andhra Pradesh back into "the earliest times": *History and Culture of Andhra Pradesh from Earliest Times to the Present Day.* Chapter 1 begins with the Satavahana Dynasty (221 BCE to 218 CE), many centuries before the first inscriptional evidence of the Telugu language appeared.[18]

Cynthia Talbot's *Precolonial India in Practice: Society, Region, and Identity in Medieval Andhra* takes a more sophisticated approach to understanding pre-modern forms of identity.[19] Her attention to self-expressions of network affiliations and identities communicated through medieval religious endowments and other inscriptions provides a brilliant and unprecedented portrayal of southern India in the twelfth through fourteenth centuries. Given the power with which contemporary linguistic sensibilities have infused our views of the world and our perceptions of the past, it is not surprising that she conflates the use of language as a shared medium of communication with the use of language as marker of identity in her otherwise powerful account of pre-colonial practice and identity. She suggests, "In the sense that many other allegiances were circumscribed by the linguistic region, therefore, we can point to language as the most important cultural affiliation in the medieval South."[20] Yet it is not clear that the many other forms of allegiance she discusses actually were circumscribed by a linguistic region. Of the dozen or so maps she provides showing geographic distributions of inscriptions, major temples, and records left by the Kakatiya dynasty during the eleventh through fourteenth centuries, all use the borders of the contemporary state of Andhra Pradesh, an entity that has existed for only five decades. In using a contemporary outline map, she has chosen to leave out of her data set many significant features that would have been important in the lives of medieval residents of southern India and that would have helped to shape medieval self-perceptions of identity. Though clearly the vast inscriptional data available to Talbot made it necessary to define limits in order to complete a project of such magnitude, her decision to use contemporary political boundaries to do so has had the effect of making monolingual attachments like those experienced today appear more salient than they likely were. Many Telugu-language inscriptions that lie within contemporary Karnataka, Orissa, Tamil Nadu, and other contemporary neighboring linguistic states, significant temples that were parts of larger sectarian networks, and other records that lie outside the borders of the contemporary political state were excluded from analysis, suggesting that although the Kakatiya political network clearly used the Telugu language as a shared medium of communication, its domain never completely corresponded with the full extent of the region where Telugu was actually used. These omitted details suggest that although medieval rulers were occasionally known to have celebrated the use of Telugu, language was never the basis upon which a political territory or even an elite identity, much less a popular identity, was defined or delimited. The argument here is not that people did not recognize, value, or even praise distinct named languages like Telugu, for clearly they did; instead, we can see that these recognitions emphasized the utility of Telugu for accomplishing particular kinds of tasks or bestowing prestige on the user rather than celebrating the language as a marker of shared identity that excluded speakers of other languages.

The occasional associations between a king and a linguistically defined region have also frequently been taken by historians of Andhra as evidence of the longstanding existence of a shared linguistic identity held more popularly by the common people. A closer examination of these examples, however, further reinforces the argument that pre-modern references were to the "language of the land" rather than the "language of the people." The fourteenth-century poet Vidyanatha's description of the Kakatiya king Prataparudra (1295–1323) as "the lord of the Andhra realm" is offered as an example of the use of the term "Andhra" "to designate the entire territory inhabited by Telugu speakers."[21] Similarly, the god who is portrayed as appearing in a dream to the Vijayanagara king Krishnadevaraya in Krishnadevaraya's sixteenth-century composition the *Āmuktamālyada* describes himself in the dream as "a Telugu king" and Krishnadevaraya as "a Kannada king."[22] These references have been taken as pre-modern examples of a shared collective linguistic identity, yet what is most striking in each of these examples is the fact that it is only ever kings who are associated with languages or their regions in this way. In these rare examples there is no indication that this is a collective identity shared among a group of people.

Other evidence from these same time periods tells us that one of the qualities expected of an ideal king was that he be able to command multiple languages. In this sense, the fourteenth-century description of Prataparudra as a "lord of the Andhra realm" and the sixteenth-century references to a Telugu king and a Kannada king can be seen not as expressions of popularly shared collective identities but rather as royal claims to dominion over specific recognizable features of the locality or region—one of many ways of creating royal titles during the medieval period. This recognition further explains why it is only in reference to kings and not to the people or even to an elite class that we find expressions that can today be appropriated as evidence for a proto-linguistic identity. Although there is clearly evidence of shared use of the Telugu language in medieval inscriptions, a shared medium must be distinguished from self-identified markers of a shared identity. Religious practices, endowments, educational practices, sectarian affiliations, marriage networks, pilgrimage networks, trade relations, military recruitment, and political loyalties were neither defined by nor limited to only those using the same language. Neither oral communication nor written literacy was restricted to a single language, even by a king who claimed to be "the lord of the Andhra realm."

Talbot's representation of Kakatiya political dynamics as "a fluctuating political network composed in large part of a multitude of personal ties between lords and underlings" actually helps us to understand pre-modern forms of identity and power that, unlike twentieth-century politics, did not rely upon language as a marker of collective identification. In illustrating these various forms of personal ties, she makes an extremely important contribution to our understandings of pre-modern society in southern India and, as Sanjay Subrahmanyam has argued in a review of her book, challenges writings on medieval southern India that project "community" as the key to understanding early medieval state formation.[23] In light of this, her claim that "other levels of community were generally encompassed within the linguistic region" can perhaps best be read as an indication of the difficulty of recognizing that people using the same language in the past did not necessarily see themselves as members of the same community as is common today.[24]

A rare and notable exception to the easy equation of an Andhra region with the Telugu language can be found in the writing of G. V. Sitapati, who rightly points out that the term "Andhra" is not favored in all parts of the Telugu-speaking regions of southern India, and who refuses to accept the two terms as one and the same. In the introduction to his *History of Telugu Literature,* published in 1968, he writes: "as a student of the history of the language and of the people, I cannot accept the theory that the Telugu language is the same as, or has evolved from, 'Andhra' even supposing that there was ever a Prakrit [regional literary language] of that name, or that the Telugu people are the descendants of the Andhras. . . . It is no doubt true that the Andhra empire, in course of time, extended over a large part of the Telugu country but the Andhra empire and the Telugu country were never exactly co-extensive."[25] He offers a number of specific examples and then writes:

> Subsequent writers have taken a fancy to use Andhra to mean Telugu, for the language, the country or the people. Andhra sounds more dignified and enters into Sanskrit compounds more readily than Telugu, but whenever a reference was made to the mellifluous quality of the language, it was Telugu and not Andhra that was used. . . . It is only those that have been influenced by pedantry or politics who would use Andhra, but the ordinary people of this region always use Telugu to denote the language, and Telugus to denote the people that speak it as their mother-tongue. . . . It is only in recent times of political awakening and nationalism that Andhra became a favorite expression with the Telugus of the coastal districts. The people of Telangana use the word Telugu and are not in favour of using Andhra. This could be seen when recently there was a controversy about the name of the newly formed State, though finally it came to be known as Andhra Pradesh.[26]

Indeed, given that the dialect now accepted as "standard" Telugu comes from dominant caste communities in the Krishna, East and West Godavari, and Guntur districts of Coastal Andhra, and that most of the leaders of the movement for a separate Telugu linguistic state likewise had ties to Coastal Andhra, it is not surprising that other views have not received as much attention. When pressure was put on the Telugu-speaking districts of Telangana during the All-India Linguistic States Reorganisation in 1956 to join with Rayalaseema and Coastal Andhra (together Andhra State from 1953 to 1956), many from Telangana were opposed to union with their economically more powerful neighbors. The assertion of a correspondence between a region, language, and people—with its attempt to make synonymous the terms "Andhra" and "Telugu"—is the product of these very specific historical anxieties, political interests, and dominant agendas. In tracing these historical dynamics, we can identify a transition from a vague and never clearly defined relationship between territory and language to the emergence of language as a foundation for the imagination of a new form of community and political identity during the twentieth century.

From Medium to Marker

The remainder of this chapter distinguishes the late-nineteenth-century shifts in the experience of language from those caused by the rise of vernacular languages as literary languages in the early part of the second millennium.[27] It also differentiates the changes of the past century and a half from the new relationship to language apparent during the sixteenth to eighteenth centuries.[28] Key to these distinctions, I argue, is the shift from shared usage of a specific, named linguistic medium in these earlier periods to the explicit invocation of a language as a marker of one's identity. While it is clear that the use of Telugu has expanded to new domains over the course of the past millennium, both in inscriptions as demonstrated by Talbot and in literary production as discussed by Sheldon Pollock and by Narayana Rao and Shulman, it is also clear that shared usage of a language does not necessarily carry with it a recognition of shared membership within a common community. The distinction between language as medium and language as marker is of central importance in understanding how languages have been experienced historically. A common source of misunderstanding that often emerges within discussions of the rise of linguistic identities centers on the very different ways in which the term "identity" has been used. Pollock, for example, views the choice of languages in which literary texts are composed at the beginning of the second millennium as constituting "an intricate social phenomenon that necessarily comprises an element—however hard to capture—of cultural identity formation."[29] Yet he is also careful to distinguish these choices from the type of modern identifications which emerge in the late nineteenth and early twentieth centuries. Writes Pollock,

> Nowhere in the manifold data on language, identity, and polity for precolonial South Asia does anything like ethnicity—which for the purposes of this discussion we may define as the politicization of group sentiment—seem to find clear expression. . . . There never was in South Asia a linkage of "blood" and "tongue" as already in medieval Europe—even the concept "mother tongue" is unknown—and cultures were not closed systems.[30]

Even though he recognizes that the meaning of identity at the beginning of the second millennium must have differed from its meaning toward the end of that millennium, for Pollock, the fact that writers chose to compose their works in specific languages at particular historical moments is taken as evidence of a process of cultural identity formation. Yet even here, we must be careful not to assume that choice of language automatically implies a choice of community. Instead, recognizing the multilingualism of those who engaged in such "choices" helps us to recognize the rise of literary production in regional vernacular languages around the turn of the second millennium not as an assertion of a new cultural identity in opposition to a pre-existing elite identity, but rather as the adoption of a new linguistic medium for extending an already powerful identity. Viewed in this way, the literary vernacularization away from Sanskrit and into regional Indian languages that occurred in the second millennium can be read as a new strategy for preserving and extending existing identities rather than as the exercise of a choice between distinct linguistically defined communities.

Evidence from many of the writings popularly celebrated as the earliest Telugu literature suggests that choosing to write in Telugu rather than Sanskrit had little to do with asserting a new identity in opposition to the existing dominant and orthodox elite identity represented by Sanskritic brahmanical culture, and a great deal to do with expanding that elite culture and identity into new realms. The decision of the eleventh-century poet Nannaya to compose a version of the classic Sanskrit epic the *Mahabharata* in Telugu, which has been canonized by many as the first Telugu literary composition, is frequently offered as evidence of the emergence of a new linguistically defined Telugu "culture."[31] However, it can, in fact, be read as just the opposite—as an attempt to prevent the spread and expansion of an already existing anti-brahmanical heterodox identity by expanding orthodox meanings and practices via yet another available linguistic medium. S. Nagaraju has written of the already well-established Jain literary writings present in Telugu prior to Nannaya that have largely been ignored by literary historians of Telugu.[32] His observations suggest that by composing the *Mahabharata* in Telugu, Nannaya was actively countering an already established heterodox Jain identity that used Telugu as a medium for spreading itself rather than as a marker of membership in its community. For both Nannaya and for the authors of the Jain literature that preceded his compositions, Telugu was the medium in which contestations over cultural supremacy occurred rather than an assertion by elite brahmanical or Jain-influenced writers that they shared a common culture and saw themselves as members of the same community. Indeed, these two groups clearly did not identify with one another. Much of the self-identification of each of these groups came from defining themselves in opposition to one another's practices. Orthodox Brahmins and, from the brahmanical perspective, the heterodox Jains disagreed over the recognition of *varna-jati* [caste-groups], the role of textually based prescriptions for religious practice, and the necessity of priest-mediated worship. There is little evidence during most of the past millennium that language choice was ever considered one of these distinguishing practices of collective imagination. Instead, contestations over the necessity and validity of the above-mentioned practices were carried out in a variety of linguistic mediums, Telugu being only one of these mediums. It was not until the early twentieth century that language choice began to be deployed and claimed as a marker of identity rather than simply a medium for contestation over other sorts of non-linguistic identities.

In discussing the rise of the use of Telugu in inscriptions during the sixth through ninth centuries, Nagaraju writes that "[a] recognizable regional/ethnic consciousness began to surface; the tool used (Telugu) became the symbol of their unity and identity."[33] Although he provides much evidence that Telugu was indeed used as a tool, examples of Telugu being invoked as a "symbol of . . . unity and identity" are conspicuously absent. In fact, the evidence he provides makes a strong case for the opposite. Telugu inscriptions from the sixth through ninth centuries suggest that great conflicts were occurring during this period and were being reflected in the written records of the era. Of the Telugu inscriptions found in the Rayalaseema region of what is today Andhra Pradesh, Nagaraju writes:

> The rise of the Cāḷukyas of Bādāmi in neighboring north Karnataka and the consolidation of power by the Pallavas at Kāncīpūram, both engaged in bitter warfare with each other in an everlasting power struggle, made this mid-lying territory a region of strategic importance. A number of inscriptions of this period reveal that armies of both rival powers traversed this region off and on, and an equally appreciable number of vīragals (hero stones) show that this was also the scene of conflict often, and that the local population had an active participation in these.[34]

He goes on to state that both during this period and slightly later, many of the earliest to use Telugu in inscriptions "were of non-brahmanical extraction."[35] Although he calls these same individuals "protagonists of Telugu culture," he then goes on to observe that "inscriptions of the tenth and eleventh centuries reveal that there is a sudden rise in the number of Brahman military generals in the service of the Eastern Cāḷukya rulers, perhaps as a counter move."[36] It is precisely the fact that both those "of non-brahmanical extraction" and Brahmins themselves were using Telugu during the tenth and eleventh centuries that suggests that language was being used as a medium for contesting community—community defined not by language but by political/dynastic affiliation or religious practice.

Nagaraju acknowledges the fact that the Telugu language had become a site for contestations in his discussion of the eleventh-century poet Nannaya:

> Amidst the galaxy of Telugu poets of the age spreading the revolutionary message, Nannaya stands alone as the defender of traditional brahmanical systems. Nannaya, though born in an orthodox Brahman family of that age, and well versed in traditional learning in Sanskrit, *vedas* and *śāstras,* deviated from the norm of brahmanical scholarship of the day and used the vernacular in writing the Mahābhārata—perhaps to counteract the new movement with the same weapon it had begun to wield in the course of propagation of its message.[37]

Nagaraju's statement makes it clear that far from asserting a Telugu linguistic identity in opposition to a Sanskrit linguistic identity, Nannaya is much more concerned with extending an identity already consolidated—one, as Nagaraju nicely points out, based in the *vedas* and *śāstras.* If Sanskrit is insufficient for the task of extending this Vedic brahmanical identification, Nannaya is happy to use Telugu. As Nagaraju makes clear, language—the Telugu language—was a weapon, a medium, and a tool for accomplishing a specific purpose, not itself an assertion of an identity. Clearly the medium had not yet become the message in eleventh-century southern India. Language was indeed a choice, as both Pollock and Nagaraju have argued, but it was a choice influenced by the battles one chose to fight and the contexts in which one wanted to fight them, not evidence of a choice of new identity.

Shared religious practice—e.g., Jainism, Śaivism, or Brahminism—formed one important foundation for the assertion of common identity, and each of the groups thus defined took advantage of the available languages of the land to advance their agendas and expand their communities. The strength of works like S. Nagaraju's and Cynthia Talbot's is their exploration of these other types of pre-modern identities—religious affiliations, military statuses, royally bestowed titles, and trading networks among them—many of which have disappeared today. Nagaraju cites Mallikarjuna Panditaradhya's mid-twelfth-century *Śivatattvasāramu,* which asserts that "one should not borrow or lend, sell or buy, or look at or speak pleasantly with those degraded with their souls turned away from Śiva" and that "one should not sleep in the same bed, sit on an equal seat, move along or live together with those who are degraded with their souls turned away from Śiva."[38] Indeed, so strong is the assertion of collective identity among devotees of Śiva (*Śivabhaktas*) that although "surely no living beings should be injured intentionally; yet, without any thinking, one may kill those sinners who revile Śiva."[39] Among all of the explicit prohibitions and rules of conduct for shared *Śivabhakta* identity, language does not figure at all, either by name or as a distinguishing marker. Likewise, Cynthia Talbot's careful readings of early Telugu and Sanskrit inscriptions offer copious evidence of the new kinds of networks and solidarities that were forming in medieval southern India—religious, military, personal, and commercial—many of which relied upon the Telugu language as one of several mediums for their representation and expression.

From *Dēśa Bhāṣa* to *Mātṛ Bhāṣa*

Once described as distinctive features of landscapes (*dēśa bhāṣalu*), by the twentieth century languages had begun to be characterized as personal attributes of individuals (*mātr̥ bhāṣalu,* or "mother tongues"). In tracing this transformation, we can identify the ways in which languages have come to be represented as natural and inalienable features of individual subjects and of collectivities of subjects, displacing almost completely earlier understandings of the role of language. One important genre of writing that appears in southern India during the nineteenth century is that of pilgrimage narratives or travelogues, and one of the earliest of these is Enugula Veeraswamy's 1830–1831 *Kāśiyātra Charitramu,* or the story of his fifteen-month pilgrimage to Kashi (Varanasi or Benares).[40] Veeraswamy's text reads like an early ethnography, with detailed descriptions of the various features of the local cultures and terrains he encountered and particular information that might be of interest to future pilgrims. He describes a variety of aspects of the landscape and physical geography and gives examples of the local flora and fauna, agricultural products, customs, and everyday practices he encountered as he traveled by palanquin from Madras to Varanasi and back. Somewhere between the Godavari River and Hyderabad city, he makes the following series of observations:

> After leaving Cuddapah there are rarely people who know and speak in Tamil. Telugu words are most commonly—and musically—spoken. . . . Hindustani and Persian words are very common in this region—people speak mixing those words in with Telugu. The flies are very troublesome in this area.[41]

There are several striking features of this passage. First, not only in this passage but throughout Veeraswamy's entire narrative people are consistently represented as knowing, speaking with, or using language, as though it is a tool or something externally available to them. They are never identified descriptively as people defined by their language or "mother tongue"—as Tamilians (*tamil̠l̠u, tamil̠vāḷḷu,* or *aravabhāṣavāḷḷu*), Telugus or Andhras, Marathas, Kannadigas, or Malayalis. "*Aravabhāṣa telisi māṭlāḍa taginavāru,*" writes Veeraswamy, "one who knows and speaks Tamil," not "*aravabhāṣavāru*" or "*tamil̠vāru*" (a Tamilian or Tamil-language person) or some variation thereof, as might be more common today.

Second, without missing a beat Veeraswamy goes directly from discussing the mixture of Hindustani and Persian with Telugu to commenting on the nuisance caused by the flies in this region, as though both are somehow equally pertinent as descriptions of the local region. His comments about languages used in the region come in the middle of a general discussion of other features of the area. He mentions that the bathing ghats in this place are inconvenient, that there is a severe lack of shade, that currently the river is high and very wide with several islands in the middle, that it is the custom on both banks of the Krishna River to present four annas to each Brahmin family, along with a blouse piece for each married woman whose husband is alive. He also mentions a few local phrases he finds idiosyncratic and unfamiliar and then goes on to discuss the insect population, explaining that the local people attribute the pestilence to the heavy rains. Although local idiosyncratic language usage is of interest to Veeraswamy in identifying local habits, there is no sense in this text of 1830–1831 that the Telugu language or any other named language plays any special role in defining the identities of the people and places he encounters. If language does play a role, it is no more significant in constituting identities than the food habits, soil quality, and insect population of the place.

Third, Veeraswamy's account suggests that the presence of multiple languages within a single village, region, court, or territory was very much an accepted and commonplace state of affairs. Rather than commenting on the presence of multiple languages in a single place as we might today (as an exception to a mother-tongue mono-linguistic identity viewed as the norm), Veeraswamy begins his comments on language by pointing out the absence of a particular language in any given village, town, or geographic territory as he passed through the landscape. This suggests that the absence of a particular language is more noteworthy than its presence. A few pages later, again in the middle of a longer passage describing local features along the route between Hyderabad and Nagpur, Veeraswamy writes: "Telugu is rarely present beginning from Kayaru onwards. Brahmins and other *jātis* (communities or caste groups) speak with the Mahārāṣṭra language here. Hindustani and Turakabhāṣa [Persian] are common to all the people."[42] Again, we see that Veeraswamy refers to languages much in the manner of tools that are used by people, in some cases by members of particular castes or communities, in other cases by the whole population. The grammatical post-position "*tō*" (meaning "with"), added as it is to *mahārāṣṭra bhāṣa,* suggests a translation closer to "speak with the *mahārāṣṭra* language," rather than "speak the *mahārāṣṭra* language," with *mahārāṣṭra* the name of the region rather than the language itself. But whereas the notions of being a Brahmin or a member of another *jāti* are present as identities, language is never linked to people as something that identifies them explicitly as belonging to a particular group. Rather, members of particular defined groups (Brahmins or other *jātis*) use certain languages (often more than one), and the languages are portrayed as distinct from their users. Indeed, two languages—Hindustani and Turakabhāṣa—not one, are described by Veeraswamy as commonly used among "all the people" [*sarvajana*], again suggesting that "the people" are not imagined collectively as a linguistic group in relation to a single shared language.

As in the earlier passage, the use of particular languages and words is treated in this second description like any other local practice, no more or less linked to identity than any other practice or custom. His comments on local language use follow a series of observations concerning the availability of provisions and water, and the proximity of Brahmin establishments, and are immediately followed by details concerning local food habits. In fact, in the very next sentence, without a break, Veeraswamy writes, "People from Godavari onwards, particularly the superior sort, take one meal only a day. Those who cannot stand this, eat *aṭukulu* [pounded rice flakes] at night as tiffin. Taking a second meal is as objectionable as a third meal eaten in our parts by children, invalids and people who are not accustomed to following strict regulations."[43] Language appears in Veeraswamy's description to be no more constitutive of identity than the number of meals taken per day by residents of the region, the types of food eaten, and other local customs. Since all of these practices can in some sense be equally taken as constitutive of identity, it is clear that language's rise to greater significance than the number of meals taken or other local practices, and the corresponding shift from language of the land to language of the people, must have occurred sometime after 1830–1831.

Many of the literary excerpts that have been used to support the argument that Telugu linguistic identity is as old as the language itself can also help us see that language was regarded as a feature of the local environment rather than a feature of the common people living in a locale. A common saying in Telugu, which appears in the Vijayanagara king Krishnadevaraya's early-sixteenth-century poem *Āmukta-mālyada* and a century earlier in Vinukonda Vallabharaya's *Krīḍābhirāmamu,* is *dēśabhāṣālandu telugu lessa,* "among all the languages of the land, Telugu is the best." Its explicit inclusion of Telugu among the languages of the land [*dēśa bhāṣālu*] makes clear the identification of Telugu as a local or regional language in contrast to Sanskrit, the *dēva bhāṣa* [language of the gods], representing the received way, path, or model [*mārga*] in opposition to the local or regionally specific [*dēśa*]. Velcheru Narayana Rao has written that this phrase "has acquired new meaning in the context of post-nineteenth-century linguistic nationalism, as a slogan of superiority for Telugu people."[44] He goes on, however, to distinguish between the patriotism behind its meaning today and the linguistic context in which this statement was first made. He writes: "there is no evidence of language serving as a symbol of 'national' identity before the nineteenth century. There were Telugu-speaking people, Telugu land . . . but no Telugu people whose identity was formed by the 'mother-tongue.'"[45] How then, do we get from the language of the land to the language of the people and the birth of "mother tongues" in southern India?

The Census and Its Categories: Race, Nation, Mother Tongue

Between the first (incomplete) attempt at an All-India Census in 1871 and the All-India Decennial Census of 1881, the category "mother tongue" was added as a new "head of information" to the census enumerator's schedule in the Madras Presidency.[46] Although there was no heading designed to gather information about languages and their usage in the 1871 census schedule for the Madras Presidency (or in the Bombay and Bengal Presidencies, the other two major territorial divisions under British colonial rule), that year's census report nevertheless carried statistics concerning "six well-defined linguistic boundaries" within the presidency. The report listed the numbers of persons speaking each of six languages (Telugu, Tamil, Canarese [Kannada], Malayalam, Tulu, and Ooriya).[47] How was it possible for census officials to calculate the number of people speaking each language without including a single question to this effect within the census schedule? The answer is that these figures were arrived at not by counting actual numbers of people claiming to speak each language, but by calculating the population living within certain pre-determined "linguistic boundaries." In some cases, these linguistic boundaries were coterminous with district boundaries. The census report tells us that in cases of "districts in which more than one language is current," the population at the *taluk* (a sub-district grouping of villages) or village level was used to calculate the total number of speakers of each language.[48]

In using such a method to calculate the total number of speakers of each language, it is clear that the census administrators of 1871 assumed that language use was distributed geographically, and that therefore, territory determined language. If a respondent to the census resided in Godavari

District, then he or she was assumed to be a speaker of Telugu and counted as such; those who lived in Trichinopoly District were counted as speakers of Tamil. In fact, the census office had virtually no role in determining these linguistic boundaries. In his report, W. R. Cornish, sanitary commissioner for Madras, "In-Charge" of the Census Office, and author of the *Report on the Census of the Madras Presidency, 1871,* thanks the Revenue Survey Department for "the preparation of maps showing the density of population and linguistic boundaries," and "the Collectors of districts in which more than one language is current, for information regarding the linguistic boundaries."[49] Such an acknowledgment suggests that once linguistic boundaries had been determined, the Census Office needed only to total the populations of the districts, taluks, or villages included within each boundary in order to arrive at their totals. How the Revenue Survey Department and the district collectors would have determined these boundaries in 1871 is not clear, except that they, too, seem to have assumed that place determined language, possibly drawing their views from local attitudes toward language. Such an assumption is yet another example of treating languages as features of territory or region rather than as inalienable aspects of individuals as is considered natural today. The approach of the 1871 census administrators also suggests, in turn, a reliance on those individuals and sources of knowledge with whom the revenue officials and the collector's office dealt most closely—village accountants and headmen, large landowners, and other village residents empowered to collect revenue or keep records. In more than just a few cases, these individuals favored language use that differed significantly from that used by artisans, smaller landowners, or landless laborers who together typically made up the greater percentage of the population. This likely influenced their representation of local language use to both the survey department and the collector. In many instances the language use of those who were landless (including tribal and nomadic groups) was completely disregarded when determining linguistic boundaries, since those with no hereditary rights to land were considered mobile and therefore more likely to move out of the territorial unit in question, an attitude that continued to prevail even during the 1950s' linguistic state reorganizations.[50]

Although there was no category for language on the 1871 census schedule, column six was headed "Race or Nationality or Country of Birth," sandwiched between column seven, "Occupation," and columns four and five, headed "Religion" and "Caste or Class," respectively.[51] Given today's linguistically defined ethnic categorizations, one might expect that this would be a category that could accommodate such a language-based ethnic identification; however, a closer look at the census instructions and the sample entries provided to enumerators proves that this is not the case. Instructions for column six clarify: "The race or nationality or country of birth should be given in the general terms thus: English, French, Madrassee, Bengallee, &c.; when this information cannot be given, the general terms Hindoo, Mussalman, &c., will suffice."[52] By today's criteria, these instructions are truly remarkable. The first set of "general terms" suggests not so much an ethnic or racial identification as an association with a geographically bounded political territory—England, France, the Madras Presidency, the Bengal Presidency, and so on, with race equated with the geographic location of residence. Yet the instructions go on to specify that if the former cannot be determined, then one term from among a *second* apparently unrelated set of "general terms" should be entered. From this second set, the enumerator can choose such terms as Hindu, Muslim, and so on. Lest one think these to be repetitive of column four, "Religion," for that earlier category the enumerator is instructed: "Amongst Hindoos the entry will generally be Shiva, Vishnava, or Lingayet; amongst Mussalmans, Sunnee or Shea; amongst Christians, Protestant or Roman Catholic."[53]

A "Specimen Form of Schedule Filled Up" is provided along with the instructions to enumerators. On this, three sample residential compounds are enumerated. For the first compound, consisting of two houses, the "Race or Nationality or Country of Birth" of all eleven men and seven women residing in the compound is indicated as "Hindoo." Column six for the members of the second compound, occupied by nine men and eight women, is designated "Mussulman." The third compound—occupied by a man named John D'Cruz, his wife, their six children, an additional thirty-year-old woman named Anne Gomiz, and eight others, apparently domestic servants—is the most remarkable by today's understandings. Under the heading "Race or Nationality or Country of Birth," all of the D'Cruzes and Anne Gomiz are designated "Madrassee." Their religion is listed as Protestant, and their "Caste or Class," Eurasian. Of the eight additional people listed for this compound, all of the four males (two adults and two children) and two of the four females (one adult and one child) are listed as Roman Catholic under religion, with the remaining two women (one adult and one child) listed as "Siva" (Saivite). "Caste or Class" is listed as Pariah for all eight. The designation listed in column six for

"Race or Nationality or Country of Birth," however, forces one to reconsider all existing assumptions about what many of these categories and designations meant in 1871 southern India. All of the latter eight identified as Pariahs—both the six Roman Catholics and the two Saivites—are listed as Hindoos.[54] The Eurasian D'Cruzes are the only ones characterized as Madrasees; all of the rest are identified as either Hindus or Muslims—even if they're Christian!

By 1881, some of these puzzling categories had been sorted out. Nationality had been reduced to five possible responses: Hindus, Muhammadans, Eurasians, Europeans, and Others (including "Not Stated").[55] The category of religion had likewise been simplified, also limited to five possible responses: Hindus, Muhammadans, Christians, Jains, and Others, though with "Buddhists, Jains, and Native Christians" still identified as "Hindu" by nationality.[56] But instead of the 6 languages mentioned in the 1871 census, the 1881 returns showed 73 different languages, "of which 48 are Asiatic and 25 non-Asiatic."[57]

Despite attempts to clarify matters of nationality and religion, it is clear that in the results of the 1881 census, language is already being asked to stand in for "nationality." In the report's analysis of language use and distribution, authored by Lewis McIver of the Madras Civil Service, language is repeatedly invoked as evidence of historical origins. For example, McIver claims that the mother tongue indicated on the census returns by Muslims can be used to determine whether a Muslim is native to the region or an immigrant: "*Hindustani,* or the Dekhani form of Hindustani, is the language of the Mussulmans exclusive of the Mappillas, whose language is Malayalam, and of the Labbais, whose language is Tamil. This recognized fact is perhaps the best guide to the numbers of the immigrant Mussulmans and their descendants."[58] The preoccupation with nativity and origin and the belief that it can be ascertained with reference to a single mother tongue are asserted even in the face of other possibilities. The report continues by stating:

> There are in some districts immigrant Mussulmans who have forgotten Hindustani, and there are a few immigrants other than Mussulmans who speak Hindustani as their native language. But these are unimportant in number. That Hindustani fairly marks the immigrant Mussulman and his descendants is confirmed by the proportions in the districts where it is known that the immigrant population is largest and the Labbais comparatively few.[59]

The possibility of "forgetting" a language or adopting a new mother tongue is viewed by the British census administration as unlikely or numerically insignificant at best, as error or fiction at worst.

This tendency to doubt the census returns rather than to question their own ideas about language classification is particularly true in reference to the statistics on European languages. Toward the very end of the chapter on language, the report states that

> 35,628 claim English as their mother tongue. According to the imperfect nationality returns the total number of Europeans and Eurasians in the Presidency is only 32,734, so that it would appear that some 3,000 natives have claimed English as their mother tongue. But the matter is worse than this, for 40,142 claim European mother tongues, which is an excess of between 7,000 and 8,000. It is probable, however, that nearly all those claiming Portuguese are Eurasians: 2,665 of such cases occur in Malabar and, as has been noted above, the Eurasians have been understated for Malabar. Of the apparent surplus of 7,408 no doubt a considerable section is not real, but represents the omitted Eurasians.[60]

According to the report, it is inconceivable that a respondent who was neither European nor Eurasian could think of his or her mother tongue as English or Portuguese. The only way the census office can accept the large number of non-Europeans who have claimed a European language as their mother tongue is to assume that errors have occurred in calculating the actual number of Eurasians. In such a reading of the census statistics on nationality and language, we already see language beginning to be used to define nationality. What appears in 1881 to be a contradiction between the categories of language and nationality is resolved by McIver by making the latter more closely resemble the former. And in doing so, by 1881 language had been institutionally recognized as an attribute of individuals rather than of territories, as had been the case in the previous decade.

Printing and Patronage in Nineteenth-Century South India

The discussion of the census's shift from using geographic territory to determine language in 1871 to identifying the mother tongues of individual census respondents in 1881 suggests that the establishment of language as a distinguishing feature of individuals did not occur until the last decades of the nineteenth century. But this does not mean that other potential bases for new assertions of identity (and invitations to identify with these bases) were not already being experimented with during the turbulent reconfigurations of power that were occurring in southern India in the first half of the nineteenth century. Colonial political and economic reorganization, the introduction of printing, changes in educational practices, and the disappearance of old sources of patronage all played a role in the struggle to formulate new attachments, affiliations, and sources of stability (both economic and otherwise). In 1829—almost half a century before Gurujada Sriramamurti first began to think about publishing a volume detailing the lives of specifically Telugu poets—Kavali Venkata Ramaswami published a work entitled *Biographical Sketches of Dekkan Poets,* containing descriptions of poets who composed in Sanskrit, Telugu, Tamil, and Marathi.[61] Two years earlier, in 1827, Ramaswami had published a work entitled *A New Map of the Ancient Division of the Deckan,* and the following year, in 1828, a companion to this work, entitled *Descriptive and Historical Sketches of Cities and Places in the Dekkan.*[62] Taken together, these three works suggest the emergence of a new relationship between geography, history, literary production, and collective identification, though not yet one defined by language. Indeed, Ramaswami's attempt to appeal to new audiences by using the Deccan region as the foundation for a shared identification suggests that there were efforts to create new kinds of collective identities that preceded, and may even have competed with, the construction of the linguistic socio-political identities upon which southern India was ultimately reorganized in the 1950s. From his vantage point, at least, embedded as he was within an extremely multilingual world, the linguistic identifications of the twentieth century were not yet a foregone conclusion.[63] Things could have turned out differently.

Although ultimately unsuccessful in creating an audience that recognized the Deccan region as a basis for shared collective identity, Ramaswami demonstrated one of the most creative responses to what I have elsewhere characterized as the "crisis of patronage" that occurred in relationship to literary production under the conditions of British colonial rule in nineteenth-century India.[64] Yet despite this, possibly because he was ultimately not successful, he has largely been dismissed by historians who view him as insignificant in comparison with his more obliging and conventional brothers, Boraiah and Lakshmaiah, who were praised by the first surveyor general of India, Colonel Colin Mackenzie, for their reliable and faithful service as his most valued assistants.[65] Although Ramaswami was also employed by Mackenzie for a time, Mackenzie appears to have regarded him much more negatively.[66] The perpetuation of these attitudes has made it difficult for us to recognize the challenges faced by the heirs to the literary traditions of southern India, among whom Ramaswami would have included himself, and the very creative ways in which they responded to the new conditions in which they found themselves.[67] By the beginning of the nineteenth century, pre-colonial dynastic rulers had largely been replaced by the colonial state. Although willing to finance and support certain limited kinds of writings, including grammars and textbooks for the use of their own administrators, the colonial state was clearly a much less reliable and generous patron, with an attitude toward local languages and those who manipulate them very different from their pre-colonial predecessors.

Narayana Rao and Shulman have characterized pre-colonial attitudes toward language as investing language with great creative ability to constitute power.[68] Poets of this period, they argue, were literally (not just figuratively) capable of creating kings and other high-status beings through their use of words alone. In return, poets received ongoing patronage from those whose status and power they flattered and helped to create and perpetuate. However, the conditions of colonial rule had altered land ownership patterns, economic exchange networks, and educational structures to such an extent that outside of the colonial state there were few individuals remaining who were wealthy or powerful enough to act as substantial patrons of major literary endeavors. The colonial administrator A. D. Campbell, for example, recognized the extent to which colonial policies had impoverished their local subjects. In an 1823 report he observed not only that fewer local residents were able to send their children to school since the British had assumed governance, but that

> this is ascribable to the gradual but general impoverishment of the country. The means of the manufacturing classes have been of late years greatly diminished by the introduction of our own European manufactures in lieu of the Indian cotton fabrics. The removal of many of our troops from our own territories to the distant frontiers of our newly subsidized allies has also, of late years, affected the demand for grain; the transfer of the capital of the country from the native governments and their officers, who liberally expended it in India,

> to Europeans, restricted by law from employing it even temporarily in India, and daily drawing it from the land, has likewise tended to this effect, which has not been alleviated by a less rigid enforcement of the revenue due to the state.[69]

Clearly, colonial attitudes toward local languages and opportunities for acquiring both literary skills and literary patronage in early-nineteenth-century India were dramatically more limited than they once had been, leading to what we can only view as a "crisis of patronage."

Accordingly, even the limited patronage offered by the colonial state was of a very different nature when compared with the forms of support to which poets had grown accustomed. Rather than a land grant that would provide a permanent livelihood to a writer, the colonial administration preferred to purchase the copyright to a composition outright with a one-time cash settlement, much to the dismay of many nineteenth-century authors. Thomas Trautmann has discovered archival records of the extended correspondence between Mamadi Venkaya, author of the first alphabetized Telugu dictionary (discussed in chapter 3), and the Madras government over the College of Fort St. George Board's offer to purchase the copyright to his dictionary.[70] Mediated by the collector of Masulipatnam over a period of several years from 1811 though 1813, it is clear that two very different ideas of patronage were at work. The Madras government offered to purchase the copyright to the dictionary (without a commitment to publish it) for a one-time cash payment of 1,000 star pagodas, while Mamadi Venkaya anticipated that his chosen patron, clearly capable in his mind of bestowing great gifts, might offer him a reward for his efforts in the form of a permanent tax-free grant of land or a perpetual pension. Rejecting the College Board's one-time cash offer, Venkaya wrote that his Telugu dictionary, along with a second, Sanskrit, dictionary, were intended "as a present to the Honourable the Governor in Council, and hoping by that means to merit his favour to such a degree as to get some durable allowance settled for the support of my family."[71] He persisted against the government's reluctance in a subsequent letter, writing,

> I left the matter entirely to the will and pleasure of the Government, but as the Board wishes to ascertain the same from myself, I can only intimate, that I have a family whose expenses amount to one Pagoda pr. Day, but that I shall be satisfied with such quantity of land in the neighborhood of Masulipatnam, as the Government may deem an

> adequate compensation for the transfer already mentioned. I expect it will be granted to continue to all my posterity.[72]

Trautmann comments, "It is clear that Mamadi Venkayya expected the Governor of Madras to play the role of a discerning and liberal patron, a raja of sorts." When the collector responded by informing him that the fulfillment of such a request was impossible in the wake of the permanent settlement of the land around Masulipatnam, Trautmann further observes that Venkaya was "not entirely convinced that the era of tax-free grants of land in perpetuity was over," as his continued correspondence in pursuit of just such a settlement made clear.[73]

In the face of such dismaying changes, there are several features of Ramaswami's efforts to cultivate and produce some of the first collective patrons in India that make him unique for his era. He was the first Indian, and likely the first private individual in India, to utilize the new technology of lithography to produce an original map, and he was one of the very earliest in India to experiment with the use of subscriptions to finance his book publishing.[74] Both of these experiments with the newly available technologies of lithography and printing were likely taken up as a response to the dramatic decline in the availability of single wealthy patrons, be they the state or other powerful individual patrons. And though the Deccan was ultimately not a basis for shared identity that resonated with audiences and made them recognize themselves, the methods of attempting to cultivate and interact with such an imagined audience were adopted by others in subsequent decades to more effective ends. By the end of the nineteenth century, someone like Gurujada Sriramamurti was able to use these methods to successfully flatter the sensibilities of an audience that imagined itself in relation to language in order to bring into being his own new collective patron.

Second, Ramaswami was one of the first individuals to adapt existing genealogical techniques to a collective audience. Literary production up until the nineteenth century was generally organized around a king, court, dynasty, wealthy patron, sect, or lineage (genealogical or intellectual). Poets and playwrights portrayed genealogies in ways that brought glory to their patron and, if successful, expected to receive support for their livelihood in return. Ramaswami's *Map of the Ancient Division of the Deckan* and its companion, *Descriptive and Historical Sketches of Cities and Places in the Dekkan,* depart from this in attempting to build a framework that will appeal to multiple patrons simultaneously. Instead of composing a genealogy praising the lineage of a single patron, Ramaswami's *Biographical Sketches of Dekkan Poets* sought to produce a collective genealogy by writing about individual poets who spanned a geographic territory that transcended any single historical or contemporary dynasty. The region he identifies as the Deccan on the map and within his *Descriptive and Historical Sketches* includes portions of many different political territories of the nineteenth and earlier centuries, not any single one, and his *Biographical Sketches* includes discussions of literary figures who composed in at least four different languages. Indeed, there is little that unites them all except for the simple fact that they all lived (and died) within the Dekkan.[75]

And third, Ramaswami was the first person to synthesize and publish material collected by Colin Mackenzie, who amassed one of the largest archives of local histories and inscriptions ever to be collected in southern India.[76] As someone who had previously served in the employ of Mackenzie, Ramaswami was uniquely positioned to utilize the documents that he and others had collected for Mackenzie. Several years after Mackenzie's death we begin to see evidence of Ramaswami publishing his own works organizing and synthesizing materials collected while in Mackenzie's employ, in the late 1820s from Calcutta, 1830s from Madras, and 1840s from Bombay. Since Mackenzie himself never had the time, or perhaps the inclination, to publish any of the materials he collected, Ramaswami's efforts represent the first significant effort to publish anything from this vast archive. From the range of people listed as subscribers on the last pages of many of his works, we can assume he moved with—or at the very least had the ear of—a rather cosmopolitan crowd, though little else is known of Ramaswami except for the record left by his publications. His subscribers included such well-known individuals as Raja Rammohan Roy in Calcutta, prominent commercial families in Bombay, and large numbers of English and other European patrons who subscribed to one or more of his publications.[77]

As I have argued extensively elsewhere, it is precisely Ramaswami's earlier engagement with the colonial enterprise that makes his later work an ideal site for examining the ways in which local residents of India were making use of newly available media, technologies, and, most importantly, techniques of representation in order to negotiate the new terrains of employment opportunities and categories of knowledge that were being constructed under colonial conditions. All of his published works appear to have been produced under his own motivation and toward his own ends. There is no evidence that any of his many publications were commissioned by the East India Company, or by other Europeans, though some are dedicated to colonial officials.[78] While he may have been interested in appealing to an English-reading audience, given that most of his publications are in English, Ramaswami appears to have been acting entirely on his own initiative both in choosing what to write and publish, as well as in generating support for his publications.

Ultimately, Ramaswami's attempt to articulate a Deccan regional identity (or proto-regional identity), with its legitimizing map, history, and literature represented by his three texts, did not endure. Within decades it had come to be displaced by more effective and efficient constituencies—indeed potential audiences and subscribers/patrons—who were defined in relation to language. The historical record has been particularly unkind to Ramaswami. Compared with his elder brothers Borraiah and Laksmaiah, whose loyalty and commitment to Colonel Colin Mackenzie and his project ensured that they found some mention in the colonial archive, Ramaswami and his many original works have been neglected. The publication of C. V. Ramachandra Rao's account of the Kavali brothers is an important counter to this trend.[79] Of the three brothers, Ramaswami—more rebellious than his elder brothers by all accounts—was the only one to both envision and take steps to try to bring into existence new possibilities enabled by the dramatic changes with which he was confronted. That he was ultimately less than successful does not mean that we should ignore his attempts. Indeed, his experiments with very new technologies of representation—lithography and printing in particular—almost immediately after they became popularly available in India, and his uncanny ability to create and cultivate new sources of patronage suggest that he was able to anticipate what was to come far better than either of his brothers.

A final word is necessary to connect these three texts of Ramaswami's with the writing more than half a century later of Gurujada Sriramamurti and those who followed. Although Ramaswami does not yet use language as a foundational category in his reorganization and representation of geographic territory, history, and literary production, it is clear that he is experimenting with new possibilities that could serve as an organizational foundation in appealing to multiple potential patrons and readers. In the absence of a king, substantial landowner, or other wealthy patron, demands for new forms of patronage and new forms of political representation were inevitable. Ramaswami's writings, though perhaps never widely disseminated or read, are nevertheless a significant attempt to grapple with the rapidly changing dynamics of power, authority, and knowledge that were occurring in nineteenth-century colonial India. His texts responded to a demand that had not yet been explicitly identified or articulated. In doing so, they anticipated a need for new foundational categories capable of bearing the weight of the new audiences, forms of identities, and political reorganization that eventually enabled both regional and national demands for political power.

By recognizing how the linguistic identifications that appear so natural today may have come to make sense only within a very particular restructuring of knowledge, technology, patronage, authority, and relations of power during the nineteenth century, we can see that such identifications were neither necessary nor imaginable prior to the nineteenth century. In his explicit appeal to his audience, Gurujada Sriramamurti, like Kavali Venkata Ramaswami before him, was using the publication of his *Lives of Poets* to respond to the implicit demands around him. Rather than viewing language as playing a constant and stable role throughout the past centuries, such an approach helps us begin to see the ways in which language has been experienced in dramatically different ways in the not-so-distant past. From *dēśa bhāṣa*—language as one of many features of a territory or landscape—at the beginning of the nineteenth century to *mātṛ bhāṣa*—language as an inalienable aspect of each and every individual—the places and functions of languages within a larger frame of reference had changed dramatically by the end of the century.

CHAPTER 2

Making a Subject of Language

To our mother Telugu, a garland of jasmine flowers
Camphor flames to the mother who gave birth to us
Our mother, who showers us freely with gold in her heart,
Compassion in her gaze, riches and good fortune in her smile

When the rippling Godavari River flows
When the rapid Krishna River runs
Golden crops ripen
And milky white pearls appear

The rare arts of Amaravati city
The notes which spring from the throat of Tyagayya
The sweet beautiful sounds from the pen of Tikkayya
She is present and endures in all of these.

With the strength of Rudramma, the faithfulness of Mallamma,
The intellect and cleverness of Timmarusu, the power of Krishnarayalu
We'll keep singing your songs and dancing your dances
Until our ears resound with your echoes.
Hail Mother Telugu, hail Mother Telugu!

—Shankarambadi Sundarachari, Mā Telugu Tallikī Mallepū Daṇḍa
[A Garland of Jasmine Flowers for Our Mother Telugu]

By the twentieth century, in addition to the shift from language as a feature of the landscape to language as a defining characteristic of individuals, a second transformation was under way in the representation of language in southern India. The Telugu language, like many other languages used in India, increasingly came to be personified more elaborately than had ever previously been the case. It also, for the first time, began to be imagined and described as having a life of its own independent of the speakers and writers who used it. Although sometimes metaphorically portrayed as an eroticized maiden in which a poet might take pleasure, the Telugu language was experienced up to the nineteenth century primarily as a medium for written and oral communication; for linguistic play, artistic and musical pleasure, and the demonstration of technical virtuosity; for religious and literary education; and for inscriptions, record keeping, and accounting. By the end of the nineteenth century, however, the Telugu language also began to be experienced as a new personified object of adoration, pride, and devotion, as a specific subject of study, pedagogy, and attention in its own right, and as a marker of identity. During the nineteenth century, the Telugu language acquired a number of new attributes, including a birth and, as Rama Mantena has argued in her work on language and historical time, stages of development and a progressive life narrative.[1] It also gained a family tree, kinship relations with other languages, and the possibility of its own death. All of these acquisitions led eventually to a new full-fledged personification of the Telugu language by the early decades of the twentieth century. From this point onward, the Telugu language began to appear in a new personified and gendered form as *Telugu Talli,* "Mother Telugu," represented in human-like form—often as a goddess—in descriptive narratives, poems, songs, and artistic renderings (see Figures 2.1 and 2.2).[2]

When Gurujada Sriramamurti published his *Lives of Poets,* not only was his use of the term *abhimānulu* to define a community of readers in relation to Telugu a new innovation, but the context in which it appeared—a text consisting entirely of biographical narratives of the lives of Telugu poets—was itself a new phenomenon when he published his first edition in 1878. The bringing together within a single printed collection of biographies of poets from a wide range of historical time periods, geographic locations, and sectarian backgrounds solely on the basis of their shared use of Telugu was unprecedented. As we have already seen in the case of Kavali Venkata Ramaswami's publications, there were by the nineteenth cen-

FIGURE 2.1. Andhra Pradesh tourism minister J. Geeta Reddy, dressed as Telugu Talli, performing the state anthem *Mā Telugu Tallikī, Mallepū Daṇḍa* [A Garland of Jasmine Flowers for Our Mother Telugu], Legislators Cultural Meet, Hyderabad, March 30, 2005. PHOTO: K. Gajendran/*The Hindu Photo Archives* (used by permission).

tury already contexts in which multiple poets and their work would have been brought together in a single manuscript, composition, or occasion. Before the nineteenth century, poets were sometimes anthologized and grouped together in association with a particular intellectual lineage, literary school, genre, or sectarian affiliation (e.g., Viraśaivite, Vaiṣnavite, Jain), or by virtue of their common association with a particular dynasty, king, or other patron. Popular legend, for example, has retroactively associated eight great poets, the *aṣṭa-dig-gajas,* with the sixteenth-century court of Krishnadevaraya.[3] However, it was not until the end of the nineteenth century that these eight poets—and indeed, Krishnadevaraya himself—came to be celebrated as specifically Telugu poets rather than as representatives of the rich multilingual literary culture that existed at his court. The Nayaka period that followed the decline of Vijayanagara in the late sixteenth to eighteenth centuries was similarly multilingual. Velcheru Narayana Rao, David Shulman, and Sanjay Subrahmanyam have written that "[t]he Nayaka courts produced a large literature in Telugu, Sanskrit, and Tamil, aimed at an educated multi-lingual audience of courtiers, courtesans,

FIGURE 2.2. New statue of Telugu Talli garlanded during an event in honor of the Telugu language, Visakhapatnam, August 29, 2005. PHOTO: C. V. Subrahmanyam/*The Hindu Photo Archives* (used by permission).

pandits and officials."[4] The practice of creating, citing, circulating, and exchanging the short freestanding literary verses known as *cāṭu* (a popular oral poetic genre that thrived during this period in southern India) often brought poets of different time periods, literary traditions, and genres into one another's presence in the space of a single verse. In these cases the intertextuality of different literary styles, metrical patterns, and traditions was precisely the point of these oral exchanges that pit the skill and wit of one celebrated poet against another.[5] However, even in these encounters poets were brought together not as "Telugu," "Sanskrit," or "Kannada" poets, but simply as poets (*kavulu*), doing what they do best—playing with language. Indeed, as Narayana Rao and Shulman have shown, not only were individual members of this community typically multilingual, but it was not uncommon for poetic compositions to be multilingual. "Language boundaries were porous," they write, "and *cāṭu* verses moved easily from one language to another."[6] Even in cases where a linguistic encounter, a composition, or an anthologized collection appeared only in a single language, such as Telugu, it was the poets' shared usage of literary conventions and the values being enacted through their participation that united them.[7] The language itself was not what marked or denoted their membership. In other words, during this early-modern era language neither marked poets nor made claims upon them as exclusively "Telugu," "Tamil," "Sanskrit," or other linguistically defined poets.

This distinction—between language as medium and language as explicit marker of shared identity—is also apparent in Gurujada Sriramamurti's emphasis not on the works of the poets he has collected together but on their lives, as suggested by the title of his book, *Kavi Jīvitamulu* [Lives of Poets]. Rather than demonstrating a concern with their literary compositions and their usage of language—something that preoccupied the literary commentators who preceded him—Sriramamurti is primarily interested in the identities of the poets he has selected. He wants to portray them as ideal representatives of the Telugu language and as real people who actually lived. Although the first to appeal to the sensibilities of a collective audience defined in relation to the Telugu language, Sriramamurti was not the only person to conceive of the idea of publishing a collection of biographies of Telugu poets during the last decades of the nineteenth century. We can see Sriramamurti's *Lives of Poets* as one step in the larger cultural transformation that ultimately enabled the recognition of a biographical life narrative and personification of the Telugu language by the early twentieth century. At least five distinct stages within this cultural transformation can be identified. Though in many cases these stages overlap with one another, in rough order, they include: (1) shifts in patronage and technologies of production that produced new attempts to represent poets in ways that would define and appeal to larger audiences; (2) the adoption of new styles and literary techniques for representing human subjects through narrative; (3) the introduction of chronological ordering within the representation of collections of poets; (4) the conversion of these histories of multiple poets into a single history of a language rather than a collection of histories of individual poets of the same language; and (5) the production of a full-fledged biography of a language, representing a language as possessing a life of its own, independent of its speakers. This representation of language as a new type of independent and personified subject is, in turn, an integral feature of the rise of the new types of affective attachment to language that appeared in the twentieth century.

Shifts in Patronage and Technologies of Circulation

In the first stage, under similar circumstances as those that led to the unprecedented experimental attempts of Kavali Venkata Ramaswami to appeal to a collective Deccan identity in the 1820s, authors sought to compose new types of literary works that would appeal to a shared collective sensibility they either believed already existed or thought could be created within their potential audiences. Like Ramaswami, later poets and litterateurs were even more motivated by the disappearance of the wealthy individual patrons who had earlier constituted the primary form of support for poets and their literary labors, and by the new forms of technology that were becoming increasingly accessible at a more popular level during the last decades of the nineteenth century. Although Ramaswami's innovative experiments with the new technologies of lithography and print to appeal to an audience that defined itself in relation to the Deccan region ultimately failed, he did pave the way for later authors like Gurujada Sriramamurti, who sought to appeal to an audience defined in relation to the language of publication. In publishing his first edition of *Kavi Jīvitamulu* in 1878, Sriramamurti had completed only a small part of the larger project he envisioned.[8] His later 1893 preface describes this earlier first edition as an experiment when he tells us that he began publishing his lives of poets "in order to see what the reception would be like among my fellow countrymen [*dēśasthulu*]."[9] His uncertainty is significant, for it suggests that the existence of a ready-made audience for such a work was by no means a given in his mind. The response must have been positive, for when the second part of his first edition was published in 1882, it was immediately prescribed by the Education Department of Madras University as a textbook for that year's B.A. examination. Encouraged, Sriramamurti continued to publish the remaining sections in the Telugu journal *Prabandha Kalpavalli.* It was only with the publication of what Sriramamurti refers to as the second edition in 1893, that all of these parts appeared together for the first time.

Though the first to publish, Sriramamurti was not alone in his ability to imagine an audience defined in relation to their shared use of the Telugu language. In 1887, Kandukuri Viresalingam (1848–1919) published the first volume of his three-volume *Āndhra Kavula Charitramu* [Biographical History of Andhra Poets], a work that similarly sought to bring together a collection of the lives of poets on the sole basis of their shared use of Telugu. Viresalingam's volume was extremely well received and was eventually selected for inclusion in the syllabus for the First Examination in Arts at Madras University in 1890. The second and third volumes appeared in 1894 and 1897, respectively, and were received with similar acclaim. Prior to these last decades of the nineteenth century, such a catalogue of literary production organized around the Telugu language had never before existed and had likely never before even been imagined. Yet together, Sriramamurti's and Viresalingam's texts anticipated a flood of subsequent works—histories, biographies, anthologies, encyclopedias, and compendia—that were explicitly organized and written in relation to the Telugu language.

The Lives of Poets: New Forms of Representation through Narrative

Sriramamurti's and Viresalingam's departures from earlier literary compositions are dramatic for two reasons. First, as we have seen in the case of Sriramamurti's *Lives of Poets,* their organizational strategy to include poets solely on the basis of the fact that each composed in Telugu (even if many also composed in other languages as well, including Sanskrit, Kannada, Tamil, and Marathi) displaced earlier organizational frameworks. Although from today's vantage point shared language may seem to be enough of a natural commonality for them all to be included within the pages of a single work, there is nothing to suggest that the sharing of a single language would have then been enough to override the potentially much more divisive differences of time, place, religious sect, dynasty, and genre. The East India Company administrator C. P. Brown, for example, wrote in 1840 of finding two ostensibly "Telugu" lexicons, "the *Śiva Āndhram* and its rival, the *Viṣṇu Āndhram,*" identical except for the final line of each verse which praises the deity named in the title. Writes Brown, "Thus we find even a dictionary dedicated to Siva and using his name as the chorus of every memorial stanza: an artifice met by a Vaishnavite [worshipper of the god Vishnu] philologist, who stole the verses and appended the name of his patron idol."[10] Indeed, the fact that names of deities in the titles of early lexicons were common, as in the *Sāmba Nighanṭuvu,* which invokes an epithet of the god Śiva, suggests that sectarian commitments were important foundations for identification. Never before had poets from such diverse backgrounds and locations been written about together within a single literary project using language as the sole foundation for the mutual recognition of commonality.[11]

Second, Sriramamurti's primary concern is not with reproducing, anthologizing, analyzing, or even introducing the actual literary works that had brought each poet to the attention of the world. He chose instead to focus on the poets themselves, relating incidents of their lives, biographical information, anecdotes, and stories about them, many of which had previously circulated only orally. Similarly, Viresalingam, like Sriramamurti and Ramaswami before him, emphasized the lives of Telugu poets in his *Āndhra Kavula Charitramu,* although he did, for the first time, provide short excerpts of some of their most important works.

The 1870s and 1880s saw not only the emergence of the first works on the lives of Telugu poets but also the first novels and the first modern biographies published in Telugu. Viresalingam claimed that his own novel *Rājaśēkhara Charitramu,* an adaptation of Oliver Goldsmith's *The Vicar of Wakefield,* serialized in 1878 and published in book form in 1880, was the very first Telugu novel.[12] Telugu literary historians have also argued that the biographical form in Telugu began first with translations into Telugu of biographies originally written in English, such as the translation of a biography of John Bunyan published in Telugu in 1856.[13] Viresalingam wrote Telugu biographies of Jesus, the poet Shelley, and Queen Victoria. What both of these genres—the novel and biography—shared was a new form of representing human subjects. Lives were being conveyed through narrative in a new way, and in this sense, the new Telugu novels and biographies mark the formation and representation of a very new type of subject.

The Telugu term *charitra[mu]* commonly appeared in titles of both novels and biographies during the last decades of the nineteenth century. Viresalingam used *charitramu* in the title of his first novel on the life of the fictitious protagonist Rajasekhara (*Rājaśēkhara Charitramu*) and also within the title of his biographical history of Andhra poets (*Āndhra Kavula Charitramu*). Indeed, many of the earliest novels use *charitramu* in their titles, in combination with the name of their main protagonist. Narahari Gopalakrishna Chetty's *Sri Ranga Raja Charitramu* [The Story of Sri Ranga Raja], published in 1872, is another example of this phenomenon, and there are numerous others. Glossed in English both as "history" and as "tale, story, account, narrative," the term *charitramu* reveals a relationship between the genres of biography and novel that—although perhaps also present in English—is not readily apparent.[14] This is in part because of the specific history of the relationships, emergence, and definition of genres in European literature, and in part because of the specific role of the novel within the history of Telugu literature. The 1903 edition of C. P. Brown's *Dictionary Telugu-English* includes the following entry: "*charita, charitra, charitamu, charitramu* [Skt.] n. History, tale, narrative. Behaviour, conduct."[15] This 1903 definition distinguishes two meanings, but collapses "history" and "tale" as comparable forms of narratives and gives a second meaning of "behaviour, conduct." Almost a century later, in 1991, J. P. L. Gwynn's *Telugu-English Dictionary* groups these meanings rather differently. Here we are given the following distinct entries:

> **charita**[**m**] n. 1. nature, character; **wāḍi** ~ **manchidi kādu** his character is not good. 2. history, tale, narrative; see **wīra** ~.
>
> **charitra** n. 1. history. 2. tale, story, account, narrative.
>
> **wīracharitam** n. tale of heroes, epic; **palanāṭi** ~ the epic of Palnad.

Although "nature, character" is still grouped separately from "history, tale, narrative" in the definition of *charita[m]*, "history" has been separated from "tale, story, account, narrative" for the definition of *charitra*. This suggests a regrouping that reflects the growing adoption of a European distinction between "fact" and "fiction" and between "history" and "story." In creating such categories, European divisions of literary production recognize these distinctions as more important than other differences that might be noted. What appear to an English reader to be two distinct forms of narrative—history and fiction—are both able to be accommodated with little tension within a single Telugu term. One must, however, be careful not to assume (as colonial and other scholars have been prone to do) that readers (and authors) were not conscious of any distinction between fact and fiction. Rather, as Narayana Rao, Shulman, and Subrahmanyam have argued, in the context of south Indian literary production it was not considered necessary to denote this distinction explicitly in the titles and classifications of each individual work. They offer numerous examples that suggest that readers of texts in medieval and early-modern southern India were able to make distinctions between fact and fiction through textual clues, making the explicit marking of a single text as either fact or fiction unnecessary.[16] Both could be contained within a single work, with readers able to negotiate the distinction through other indicators.

The use of *charitra* in the titles of Telugu biographies and novels emphasizes features that these genres share—features that maintain continuity with earlier literary forms in Telugu also using *charitra* in the title but that also show important departures in their extension to new objects. The portrayal of the qualities of a model individual and the demonstration of how these qualities were acquired or developed emerge in both early Telugu novels and biographies as decidedly more important than the differences between fact and fiction, history and novel. In Telugu, *charitam/charitra* is also used both within the term for "epic" (*vīracharitam,* "hero story") and within titles of novels, a striking contrast to the separation of epics from novels as two distinct genres often defined in opposition to one another within the history of European literature.[17] We must not, however, immediately assume that this distinction is relevant and applicable within Telugu literature. Instead, it pays us to consider the similar ways in which novels, biographies, and even epics may have functioned (and may still function) within larger structures of social relations, knowledge, and political organization within southern India.

There are three aspects of the use of the term *charitra* in late-nineteenth-century southern India that suggest similarities in the ways in which both novels and biographies operated within society. First, the protagonists within the new form of the novel introduced into Telugu in the 1870s shared with the subjects of the biographical form a location within self-contained narratives of individual and autonomous subjectivity. In other words, the protagonists of the titles are the subjects of each text. The primary focus is no longer on narrating the genealogy of the significant forebears (intellectual or biological) that preceded an individual. Instead, the protagonist's own lifespan and progression from birth to death forms the new object of narration and forces the narrative forward. Second, the fact that *charitra* was also used to mean "behaviour, conduct" (in 1903) and "nature, character" (in 1991) signals the fact that the term was frequently used to describe texts and narratives that modeled exemplary behavior, carrying over a meaning that was clearly present in the verse *charitras* of earlier centuries. Although what defined exemplary behavior was also changing rapidly during the nineteenth century, it is clear that *charitra*—at least as it was initially used in the titles of novels and biographies—continued to be used to describe those texts that best exemplified the model behavior of the era. Viresalingam's *Rajasekhara Charitramu,* for example, and many other Telugu novels of the late nineteenth century and early twentieth century did exactly this. In his 1878 novel Viresalingam clearly imagined a new type of model individual (though he did not yet have a term for it) and wrote in order to popularize a new mode of conduct exemplified by this individual. In writing about *Rajasekhara Charitramu,* D. Anjaneyulu, one of Viresalingam's biographers, marks Viresalingam's break with earlier literary protagonists as something completely new in Telugu literature, stating:

> From the traditional preoccupation with mythology, legend and romance among the writers of the day, we have come down here to social life in all its realism. The prince of noble birth, who used to be the traditional hero of the *Prabandhas* and the *Kavyas* [has] given place here to the average householder, so familiar in life to the contemporary reader.[18]

Indeed, Anjeneyulu points out that Viresalingam's protagonist Rajasekhara is a good, generous, and kind man who "suffers, not from the wrath of God or a holy saint, but due to his own weakness—mainly in the shape of vulnerability to flattery and propensity to live beyond his means for love of ostentation." He goes on to tell us that in Viresalingam's portrayal of his new model subject, "[t]he good man comes out the ordeal in good shape, because it was the author's belief that if providence was just, virtue was bound to win in the end."[19]

Passages throughout the novel suggest Viresalingam had an educated, rational, thrifty, unostentatious, and virtuous model subject in mind, in the shape of the reformed and now wise Rajasekhara we see by the end of the novel. *Rajasekhara Charitramu* is filled with satire of actions Viresalingam considers uneducated, foolish, or superstitious. But the passages that most directly indicate to the reader the kind of model character Viresalingam has in mind occur in the last few pages of the novel, after Rajasekhara has become impoverished and imprisoned through his own ignorance and pride, has been redeemed to his previous standard of living through benevolent intervention, and has clearly learned his lesson:

> From that time onward Rajasekhara, having gained dear experience from the conduct of the astrologer and others of that ilk, took good care never to allow himself to be puffed up by empty adulations, not to squander his money, and steadily refused to believe anyone his friend who approached him with oily words. [. . .] He became, too, a firm disbeliever in *mantras* and alchemy, with all kindred arts. [. . . B]oth Rajasekhara and his descendants became disbelievers in astrology as well. On account of the trials he had undergone through debts contracted for gratuities at Rukmini's wedding, Rajasekhara determined never again to go into debt. From that time onward he wasted no money on useless show, but continued most moderate in all his expenditures; and, content with what God had granted him, bestowed upon the poor alms of what he possessed. Preserving truth and kindheartedness inviolate even in his dreams—treasuring ever in his heart the golden maxim that "Virtue is victory"—and departing not the length of a fly's foot from the path of righteousness, he conducted himself honestly in the sight of all men, gained the reputation in the land of being a good man, and spent the rest of his days in affluence and happiness, surrounded by numerous grandsons and granddaughters. [. . . M]any of his numerous host of relatives, too, who by dishonest practices had enjoyed the pleasures of sin for a season, learned by Rajasekhara's upright walk that honesty is the only source of enduring good, and finally entered the path he trod so unerringly.[20]

Although Viresalingam's model individual may only represent a reformed ideal within a brahmanical Hindu worldview, it is clear that his novel (and other novels published in the decades after this) did seek to represent an ideal for conduct and behavior, and the use of *charita/charitramu* further reflects and reinforces this goal. It also points to the significance of the individual subject as the foundation of these new narratives. The story is about Rajasekhara, his trials and tribulations, and his path through experience to great knowledge and virtue. The chronological unfolding of events within the protagonist's life grounds the novel's narrative and gives it an overall coherence. His virtue is portrayed as emerging from the lessons he learns within his own life's experiences rather than being inherited from virtuous forebears.

Third, the new protagonists of late-nineteenth- and early-twentieth-century *charitras*—both novels and biographies—differed from the protagonists of the verse *charitras* composed in earlier centuries. Subjects of earlier *charitras* had been limited—almost without exception—to saints and founders of religious sects, deities, military heroes, kings, and other royal figures, suggesting that only certain types of individuals displaying exemplary characteristics (as defined by each era) were worthy of becoming the subject of a *charitra.* A very early Sanskrit *charitra* was written about the Buddha, and one of the earliest Telugu *charitras* is Ekamranatha's sixteenth-century *Prataparudra Charitramu,* written about the Kakatiya king Prataparudra. But the subjects of the new prose *charitras* of the late nineteenth and early twentieth centuries included not only ordinary individuals but also inanimate (though often personified) entities such as collectivities of subjects (beginning first with poets), language itself, territories, and eventually linguistically defined communities. It is not long after the publication of Sriramamurti's and Viresalingam's volumes of the biographical lives of Telugu poets that we begin to see biographical historical narratives of first the Telugu land, then the Telugu language, and finally the Telugu people. The first *charitra* of the Telugu region was published in 1890.[21] Six years later, a *charitra* of the Telugu language, P. Gopala Rao Naidu's *Āndhra Bhāṣā Charitra Sangrahamu* [Summary of the History of the Andhra Language], was published—almost twenty years after the first novels and the first collection of the lives of Telugu poets.[22] But although it appears to be an easy move from the writing of *charitras* of individual subjects—both historic figures in the form of biographies and fictional figures in the form of novels—to the writing of a *charitra* of the Telugu territory and language, it was not until 1910 that the first *charitra* of the Telugu *people* appeared with Chilukuri Veerabhadra Rao's multivolume *Āndhrula Charitramu* [History of the Andhras].[23]

"The Simple Order of Time" and "The Natural Divisions of a Life": Chronology and New Narrative Structures

The second line of Sriramamurti's preface to *Kavi Jīvitamulu* reveals the source of his inspiration for such a collection of biographies of poets. "Beginning from 1876, having conceived how useful within the Andhra language a book like Macaulay's Critical and Biographical Essays of Poets (in the English language) which I had read earlier during my education, would be, and having published some works and developed relationships with many important people concerned with such matters, I began publishing [biographies of poets] in order to see what the reception would be like among my fellow countrymen [*dēśasthulu*]."[24] This statement not only indicates Sriramamurti's uncertainty of the existence of an audience for his publication but also reveals the source of his inspiration—the essays of Thomas Babington Macaulay. Although Sriramamurti had obviously been influenced by the essays about English poets and other historical figures that he had read in school, this was not already a tried and tested genre within the literary production of Indian languages.

Biographical essays by Thomas Babington Macaulay, Samuel Johnson, and others were standard fixtures on the syllabus at Madras University and other colleges and high schools in the latter part of the nineteenth century. A study guide to Macaulay's *Essay on Johnson* illustrates one of the narrative strategies for creating the unity of this newly represented subject that would have been repeatedly modeled in one form or another for school and college students in south India during the late nineteenth century:

> The Essay on Johnson follows its theme, the life and works of Samuel Johnson, with the directness of a straight-forward narrative which never once loses sight of its main character, and follows only one single thread of interest. [. . . T]he essay was written as a biographical sketch for the Encyclopedia Britannica. [. . .] It is the simple order of actual events that determines Macaulay's arrangement of the Essay on Johnson; and his knowledge of the eighteenth century and his honest conviction that Johnson was its great central figure keeps its subject dominant over all related subjects with a supremacy that makes for the simplest and clearest form of unity. In general the essay may be said to be based upon the following fundamental topics:—
>
> I. Johnson's Early Life,
> II. Johnson's Early Struggles in London,
> III. Johnson's Early Literary Work,
> IV. The Period of Success,
> V. The Period of Decline,
> VI. Last Years and Death,
> VII. Assured Position of Johnson.
>
> A glance shows, then, . . . that its discussion proceeds upon the simple order of time, that its divisions are natural divisions of

> Johnson's life, that its unity is firm, that it presents a brief, plain conclusion.[25]

"The simple order of time" and the "natural divisions" of a life—these features make up the unity of Macaulay's essay. Such essays were taught in Indian schools as models for the composition of essays of others' lives. They have also made it possible for readers to imagine and frame a similar structure for their own lives, a structure dominated by "one single thread of interest" and organized by "the simple order of actual events."

This emphasis upon chronology and the linear unfolding of time became the object of increasing attention and comment by the end of the nineteenth century, and we can identify it as the third stage in the larger socio-cultural transformation that occurred toward the end of the nineteenth century. In 1896, the prominent literary scholar and historian Jayanti Ramayya published *An Essay on Telugu Language and Literature.*[26] In this essay Ramayya makes a striking comparison among the first three attempts at cataloguing Telugu literary production. He hastily dismisses Ramaswami's 1829 *Biographical Sketches of the Deccan Poets* as well as Sriramamurti's 1878 *Lives of Poets* as lacking in historicity. He writes, "neither of these works is exhaustive and no attempt has been made in either to fix the chronology of the poets. They merely record some of the local traditions and anecdotes regarding the poets with brief notices of their principal works."[27] In contrast to these two works, Viresalingam's 1887 *Āndhra Kavula Charitramu* is the recipient of Ramayya's great praise. Ramayya writes: "The next attempt has been made by Rao Bahadur Kandukuri Veeresalingam Garu whose work I consider to be the best of its kind. His book is arranged chronologically and he has attempted, with [a] great deal of success, to fix the time at which each poet lived. He has also, where possible, given brief sketches of the lives of the poets."[28] In emphasizing the importance of a linear chronology linking, or "fixing," as Ramayya puts it, the lives of each poet within a larger narrative of the progression of Telugu language and literature—something he feels Viresalingam does, but Ramaswami and Sriramamurti do not—Ramayya betrays the entry of a new value into the discourse of Telugu intellectual circles. One can furthermore speculate that it is not simply coincidental that Viresalingam's title includes the term *charitra,* while Ramaswami's and Sriramamurti's titles do not. Clearly the linear progression of time and the chronological events and occurrences within a single life had by this time gained new importance within the structuring of narratives and the composition of a subject, and the use of *charitra* in the titles of these new works reflected these new values.

Viresalingam's biographical history eclipsed Sriramamurti's to such an extent that many later literary historians cite it as the first history of Telugu literature as well as the first history of Telugu poets, completely ignoring Sriramamurti's earlier publication. G. V. Sitapati, for example, in his 1968 *History of Telugu Literature,* writes:

> Viresalingam Pantulu is again the first in the writing of History of Telugu Literature but what he actually wrote was *Andhra Kavula Charitra* (The Lives of Telugu Poets) arranged in chronological order. . . . About the same time Guruzada Sri Ramamurti wrote his Lives of Telugu Poets under the title of *Kavi Jivitamulu.* But he did not arrange them according to the chronological order. He classified them under headings such as *Purana Kavulu, Prabandha Kavulu,* etc. and he selected only the leading poets.[29]

Although the literary historian Arudra disagrees with this dismissive view of Sriramamurti's accomplishment, his thirteen-volume *Samagra Āndhra Sāhityam* [Complete Andhra Literature] offers us further evidence that Viresalingam's work displaced Sriramamurti's in most people's minds. He writes:

> Sri Ramamurti's *Kavi Jivitamulu* prompted the writing of other works of that sort. In 1887 Kandukuri Viresalingam published the first part of his *Andhra Kavula Charitramu.* Sri Ramamurti acknowledged that Viresalingam's work contained many poets' names that his own work did not. Therefore, in the literary world Viresalingam's book gradually became established as the authoritative work. Sri Ramamurti's composition gained a name as a bundle of myths and legends. But in reality, Sri Ramamurti also did not fail to discuss historical matters.[30]

By the last decade of the nineteenth century, a linear narrative was expected not only when reporting on the lives of each individual poet, but also when reporting on the life of the language itself. No longer was an author admired simply for collecting a group of poets or works into a single volume, relating anecdotes and stories of their lives. Instead, an author was also expected to locate each poet accurately within a larger narrative, using each poet and literary work to represent an aspect of the development of the Telugu language.

Once poets had been regrouped explicitly in relation to the language in which they composed, it became difficult not to view them within the larger context of the linear progress of the Telugu language. Each poet included in these works began to be seen not simply as a poet but as a Telugu poet. Instead of representing themselves, their patrons, particular literary genres, or particular sectarian concerns, each poet began to be expected to signify a stage in the development of the language. Indeed, at the turn of the twentieth century the significance of each poet to the larger history of Telugu became dramatically more important than the actual literature each had produced. Determining the exact dates that each poet lived and died, as Viresalingam attempted, provided markers within the larger narrative of the history of the language. Nannaya Bhatt, who produced the first Telugu retelling of the Sanskrit epic the *Mahabharata* in the eleventh century, is still celebrated as an author of the *Mahabharata,* but he has become even more important as the received canonical "first" poet of Telugu.[31] The meaning of each work and, more importantly, of each poet was altered in light of their reframing within this new history of Telugu. Such histories of literary production provided the earliest biographical narratives of the development of the language, but it wasn't long before other independent histories of the Telugu language, region, and people followed. All of these narratives reframed the Telugu language as an entity capable of moving through history independently of its speakers, making it appear to have a life of its own.

But this still does not account for why poets rather than other significant historical figures should form the initial significant site for the emergence of the Telugu language as a foundational organizational category. Why, for example, do we not see published during these last decades of the nineteenth century collections of the lives of Telugu saints, religious leaders, kings, or statesmen? During the medieval period, individual religious figures, such as saints, mystics, and founders of new devotional movements, as well as kings, princes, and military heroes, often formed the objects of *prabandha* (a style of literature combing verse and ornate prose developed in the fifteenth and sixteenth centuries) and *kāvya* (poetic literary compositions), very often including the term *charitra* in their titles. But these accounts (frequently more hagiographic than biographical, though even this distinction needs to be examined more closely) were never collected together and organized on the basis of a shared language background, and they therefore never exclusively stressed the importance of language to their identities. They were typically only devoted to a single historical figure and his or her lineage.[32]

Sriramamurti's acknowledgment of Macaulay's essays as the inspiration for his *Kavi Jīvitamulu* presents us with a puzzle and suggests that Sriramamurti was not simply adopting an existing European literary form, but rather was adjusting it to suit local needs and conditions. Although Macaulay's essays have been collected and published in numerous combinations, including one edition entitled *Critical and Historical Essays* and another entitled *Biographical and Historical Sketches,* an edition of his work entitled *Critical and Biographical Essays of Poets,* the title cited by Sriramamurti, does not appear to have been published. Although it is possible that this could have been a special edition of Macaulay's essays prepared specifically for college use in India, it is more likely that Sriramamurti may be misremembering the title or may have read an edition of Samuel Johnson's *Lives of Poets,* which also included Macaulay's essay on Johnson. This point is important only because Macaulay's collections of essays all combine essays on poets with essays on statesmen, earls, dukes, kings, queens, bishops, and other significant historical figures. If the work that Sriramamurti read as part of his education had included statesmen, kings, and other historical figures along with poets, we are left with the problem of explaining why his essays concern only poets and leave aside the other important historical figures he could also have included. His emphasis forces us to consider what is significant about poets and their lives that they should exclusively be used to mark the initial site of the emergence of Telugu as a foundational organizational category. There are two main points to consider in answering this question.

First, poets are recognized primarily for their skillful manipulation of language. Constructing narratives of poets as autonomous subjects defines them as subjects explicitly in relation to language. In composing a *charitra* of Telugu poets—poets marked as authors specifically in relation to Telugu, regardless of the many other languages in which they may also have composed—the shared relationship to one particular language is the only thing that unites the individuals selected for inclusion within the work. Yet the poets selected are also distanced from the language in which each composed literature. It is not the works of the authors that are primarily featured, but rather their lives. The poets are abstracted from the specific literary and historical contexts in which their poetry was originally composed and reconstructed as self-contained and autonomous agents and subjects of the narratives about them. In such a *charitra,* the emphasis is on the significant events of a poet's life related chronologically: birth, education, significant formative events, publications and contributions to society, and death, giving primary continuity to the single thread of each individual life rather than to the court, genre, religious institution, or sectarian movement of which the poet may have been a part. Each poet's life merits a separate narrative, which is set off from the narratives of the lives of other poets by headings. Rather than relating the history of Telugu poets within a single continuous narrative, Sriramamurti's work, like Viresalingam's, was published as a collection of individual narratives. Even when the influences on a particular poet's life and works were included in the narrative, these influences were portrayed as external to the life of the poet, acting on it from outside. Whereas statesmen, saints, and military heroes may have had important relationships to a particular language or languages, this relationship does not constitute their identity or their occupation in the same way that it does with poets or literary figures. Thus, although it is equally possible to construct a self-contained narrative of the life of a statesman, saint, or military hero as an autonomous subject, only narratives of literary figures emphasize this new subject's relationship to language.

Second, the poet's relationship to language in a volume of the lives of Telugu poets parallels that of the reader's, particularly if potential readers are also defined by the language in which the work is composed. Language becomes the only common point that all are imagined to share. Just as poets from many different geographic and dynastic regions, historical time periods, literary traditions, genres, sects, and communities are all united within the pages of a single text on the basis of their shared language, so too are readers from many different caste backgrounds, sectarian affiliations, educational experiences, socio-economic contexts, occupations, and regions united in reading the same text. Indeed, the only thing shared by all of the poets and all of the potential readers respectively would have been the Telugu language. As Benedict Anderson has argued, printing enabled people to imagine themselves as sharing a community and an identity with people they had never met and might never meet, people not related to them by blood, marriage, or personal face-to-face connection.[33]

Texts like Sriramamurti's *Kavi Jīvitamulu* and Viresalingam's *Āndhra Kavula Charitramu* shift the emphasis from poets as authors to poets as central characters in novelized renditions of their own lives. Although still subjects in relation to the object of language, and central subjects within the events of their biographies, they also became objects—objects of study in classrooms and textbooks, and objects of knowledge. One of the most significant features of these two biographical texts of Telugu poets is that they made available stories about Telugu poets—as characters acting as the subjects of their own life narratives, as objects of academic study, and as heroes of stories in which people took pleasure—long before printed editions of the works composed by many of these same poets were widely and easily accessible. Although palm leaf copies of the works of many of the featured poets may have been in existence, such copies were rare and not freely available in the way that printed editions later became, especially after the popularization of public reading rooms and libraries in many towns throughout south India.[34] Furthermore, it was several decades before many of the texts that first made these poets famous began to be issued in printed form. Probably the earliest and best example of this process can be seen in the circulation of the stories [*kathalu*] told about the popular sixteenth-century court poet Tenali Ramakrishna.

The first known printed collection of the popular oral tales about the much-loved poet-jester Tenali Ramakrishna, famous for his practical jokes and quick wit, appeared in 1860. Also popularly known as Tenali Ramalingadu, a number of later literary historians have heatedly debated the question of whether the celebrated joker and hero of these popular tales is, in fact, the same person as the historically verifiable sixteenth-century poet of the same name. Regardless of the historical accuracy of this association, it is clear that Sriramamurti believed them to be the same person and wrote about Tenali Ramakrishna as both a great poet and a quick-witted jester.[35] Several Telugu literary historians have attributed the first printed collection of Tenali Ramakrishna stories to Sriramamurti, though it was more likely produced by Nelaturu Venkatasubba Sastri, since Sriramamurti would only have been nine in 1860 when this first collection was published.[36] Subsequently, there were at least eight (likely many more) additional printed collections of stories about Tenali Ramakrishna published by different authors between 1860 and 1917, and each was reprinted numerous times. In contrast to these works *about* Tenali Ramakrishna, the first printed edition of a work composed *by* Tenali Ramakrishna, the *kāvya* composition *Pānduranga Mahātmya,* was published only much later, in 1923, sixty-three years after the first collection of stories about the poet.[37] As the literary historian Arudra writes, "It was common among all of the well-known publishers—Vavilla Ramaswami Sastrulu & Sons, Westward & Co., N. V.

Gopal & Co.—that anytime any one of them published a book of Tenali Ramakrishna stories written under any name and by any writer, that book would keep on being reprinted over and over again."[38] Clearly there was little doubt that printed stories *about* popular poets would sell—much better perhaps than the literature composed *by* the same poets.[39]

What then does it mean to begin circulating printed versions of popular oral tales long before printed versions of written palm-leaf works, and stories about poets prior to the compositions by those same poets? Tapping into stories with which audiences were already familiar may well have done more to create an audience (and a market) for printed books than did other less widely known works, including those works for which the poets had initially gained their reputations, though perhaps only within a limited circle. Printed versions of well-known oral stories also appear to have been more popular than original ("novel") stories with which potential audiences were unfamiliar. This is demonstrated by the remarkable demand that existed for the repeated reprinting of any collection of Tenali Ramakrishna stories, a demand that far surpassed the demand for the new novels that were appearing around the same time. Yet this oral genre also paved the way for the later novelization of poets' lives. Just as Sriramamurti admitted that his attempt to publish the first part of his *Kavi Jīvitamulu* was intended as an experiment to test the waters, it is likely that what were initially picked up by early publishers of print literature were stories that were less experimental, ones that already held social currency at the popular level and were therefore likely to succeed. By first publishing stories with which a larger public could already identify, writers and publishers were able to gradually move from genres already popular toward the introduction of more novel genres.

Biography of a Language

Writing self-contained biographical narratives of poets in relation to a single language paved the way for language to become its own subject. And, indeed, it was not long after the publication of Sriramamurti's and Viresalingam's volumes of the biographical lives of Telugu poets that histories of the Telugu language began to appear. The chronological narrative structure found in the biographical essays and even in the novels mentioned above soon adapted itself to relating the life of the language, including its "birth" and distinct stages of its "development" up through its maturity to the present day. In 1896, the same year that Jayanti Ramayya published his *Essay on Telugu Language and Literature,* two other important works were published that illustrate the fourth significant stage in the larger cultural transformation toward the personification of language. The first biographical narrative [*charitra*] of the Telugu language—P. Gopala Rao Naidu's *Āndhra Bhāṣā Charitra Sangrahamu* [Summary of the History of the Andhra Language], mentioned earlier—was published in that year, as was K. V. R. Krishna Rao's essay *Āndhra Bhāṣa Abhivṛddhi* [The Development of the Telugu Language].[40] K. V. R. Krishna Rao was a *zamindar* (landlord) of Polavaram, near Rajahmundry in East Godavari District of contemporary Coastal Andhra. The association of language with the idea of *abhivṛddhi,* "increase, growth, expansion; progress, improvement, development," within Telugu literary discussions, as exemplified by Krishna Rao, marks yet another subtle change in the way language was conceptualized within intellectual circles of late-nineteenth-century southern India.[41] It includes the appearance of a new discourse attributing a birth to languages, the possibility that a language might one day die, and the establishment of family trees and kinship networks for languages.

We can see the possibility of the death of language first imagined in the middle of the nineteenth century. Perhaps the very first reference to the death of a language in South Asia occurred in relationship to Sanskrit. In an article on the death of Sanskrit, Sheldon Pollock has documented this historic first. He writes, "In the memorable year of 1857, a Gujurati poet, Dalpatrām Dahyabhai, was the first to speak of the death of Sanskrit:

> All the feasts and great donations
> King Bhoja gave the Brahmans
> were obsequies he made on finding
> the language of the gods had died.
> Seated in state Bajirao performed
> its after-death rite with great pomp.
> And today, the best of kings across the land
> observe its yearly memorial.[42]

It wasn't long after this that the life and death of a people came to be associated, not with their geographic location or even with their shared cultural practices, but with the life and death of their "language." By the end of the century, the argument that the death of a language also meant the disappearance of its speakers and therefore the disappearance of "a people" had become increasingly common. In 1900, V. S. Srinivasa Sastri, writing in Madras, could claim in all reasonableness that "in a people's speech is bound up its entire life . . . and that to talk complacently of the disappearance of that speech is to talk of the disappearance of the people itself."[43]

Such statements draw our attention to the ease with which death and other assertions of loss—real or imagined—circulate more easily than many other sorts of discourse. Potti Sriramulu's fast-unto-death, the numerous deaths of others in his wake, or the fear of the death of one's language were all able to mobilize a crowd as no previous meeting, demonstration, or rally had been able to for the cause of a separate Telugu linguistic state. I was repeatedly struck during conversations with people throughout southern India at the ease with which stories of loss in relationship to the formation of Andhra State circulated far beyond what I thought its reach would have been. One young woman in Hyderabad, not yet thirty years old and clearly not yet born at the time of the declaration of a separate Andhra State in 1952, told me how unfair it was that "we lost Madras. They took it from us."[44] The intensity of the passion of this young woman at what she perceived of as an unjust theft initially shocked me. In her case, not only had the discourse of loss been conveyed from one generation to another, but it had also traveled from the coastal region of southern India, where her family was originally from, inland more than five hundred miles to Hyderabad, the present capital of the state in Telangana. Another told me, "we were cheated out of Madras by that Rajagopalacharya [chief minister of Madras State in the period preceding the formation of Andhra State]. He was a tricky one, that one."[45] An older man living in Madras also blamed Rajagopalacharya, popularly known as "Rajaji," for the loss of Madras, saying, "Don't quote me on this, but Madras *is* a Telugu city. This was Rajaji's slight of hand. In 1937 or 1938 he carried out a referendum in which the key question was 'Do you speak Tamil?' not 'What language do you speak?'"[46] And yet another retired lecturer from Nellore who had participated in the movement as a young man expressed the unfairness slightly differently, while also pointing out the contradictions of the entire notion of linguistic identities, when he said of this leader of Tamil Nadu, "Even Rajagopalacharya himself has Telugu origins."[47] As an injustice made tangible, death and its associated discourse of loss are injustices easily conveyed from one generation to another even under conditions of migration.

The Personification of the Telugu Language

In August 2002, fifty years after Potti Sriramulu's death, a new statue of the goddess Telugu Talli [Mother Telugu], the personification of the Telugu language and emblem of the contemporary Telugu linguistic state of Andhra Pradesh, appeared in front of the Andhra Pradesh Secretariat in the state capital, Hyderabad. Today it can be seen standing just next to a similar statue of linguistic state martyr Potti Sriramulu, whose story opened this book (see Figure 2.3). Inaugurated by Andhra Pradesh chief minister Nara Chandrababu Naidu the following month, this 11.6-foot statue replaced another statue of Telugu Talli commissioned by an earlier chief minister, N. T. Rama Rao, in the 1980s, that stood for almost two decades in another location nearby. In 1999 a contractor's crew broke the original Telugu Talli statue in two while attempting to relocate it in order to make way for the construction of a new highway overpass, christened "Telugu Talli flyover" at its opening in 2005. The city's longest flyover, or overpass, it was initiated as part of the chief minister's *Swarna Andhra Pradesh* [Golden Andhra Pradesh] program of development and modernization.

As the personified representation of the Telugu language, Telugu Talli has come to stand not only for the Telugu language but also for its speakers and for the linguistically defined territory that has formed the basis for the modern state of Andhra Pradesh. Frequently pictured superimposed upon or rising up out of an outline map of Andhra Pradesh, Telugu Talli appears in government publications, advertisements, schoolbooks, poetry, and songs. The context in which the earlier statue of Telugu Talli met her irreparable end suggests that when faced with the realization of a "golden Andhra Pradesh," even Telugu Talli herself (not to mention the language she represents) must give way to "progress." At the same time, the speed with which she was reincarnated, not far from her original location, also suggests her continued necessity, especially in the eyes of political leaders. What was particularly striking, however, was that when she rematerialized this time, she appeared framed in a subtly different—but fundamentally significant—way. The words inscribed upon the stone slab that forms her pedestal today appeared not in Telugu, the language she represents, but rather in English. The irony of this linguistic displacement was not lost upon cultural commentators, particularly those critical of the Telugu Desam Party, the party of Chandrababu Naidu, the chief minister

FIGURE 2.3. Statue of Potti Sriramulu with statue of Telugu Talli in the background, Secretariat Road, Hyderabad, 2006. PHOTO: P. V. Sivakumar/*The Hindu Photo Archives* (used by permission).

of the state at the time. As their way of marking the anniversary of Andhra Pradesh Formation Day on November 1, 2002, the front page of that day's edition of the Telugu daily newspaper *Vaartha* carried a photo of the new statue, showing both Telugu Talli herself and the English inscription on her pedestal below. The English inscription identified her by name, identified her sponsor, the Municipal Corporation of Hyderabad, and listed the names of the officials responsible for her dedication and inauguration, with Chandrababu Naidu's name featured most prominently. Alongside the photograph of the statue floats a large caption in Telugu script, asking "Mother Telugu, where's Telugu?"[48] Below, a longer caption elaborates:

> This is the fate which has befallen the mother tongue [*mātṛbhāṣa*] Telugu under the Telugu Desam government. Government leaders who have no knowledge of Telugu and who are telling us to learn English, have themselves composed even what's on the stone slab of the Telugu Talli statue without Telugu. Seeing the miserable condition which has befallen her language, Telugu Talli is silently weeping.[49]

Such representations of Telugu Talli indicate one of the most recent stages in the historical shift surrounding the relationship to language in southern India.

The emergence of language as a foundation for the assertion of a new cultural community and collective identity has made possible the changes in the relationship to language that have enabled such a collective identity to appear completely natural. The Telugu language and script today appear nowhere on the statue of Telugu Talli. Instead, the entire inscription appears in the English language in Roman script. As the new statue suggests, the actual use of Telugu is no longer essential to representations of the Telugu language, people, and territory. What matters is the idea of Telugu. By the twentieth century the relationship to language in southern India had undergone a shift from its earlier usage as a medium of communication to its representation today as a marker of cultural identity. Indeed, it is not uncommon today for individuals with no knowledge of Telugu at all—children of Telugu-speaking migrants to the United States, for example—to consider themselves "Telugu." Actual knowledge of a language is not essential for language to be seen as an attribute of someone's identity today.

Telugu Talli's proximity to political power—her location just in front of the state secretariat, her sponsorship by the Municipal Corporation of Hyderabad, rather than by a civic or cultural organization, the list of political figures involved in her dedication and inauguration, and the annual

FIGURE 2.4. Telugu Desam president N. Chandrababu Naidu after garlanding the statue of Telugu Talli in Hyderabad, November 1, 2004, the 48th anniversary of the Andhra Pradesh State Formation Day. PHOTO: Mohammed Yousuf/*The Hindu Photo Archives* (used by permission).

garlanding of her statue by prominent politicians—is just the most recent manifestation of her long association with political contexts and bodies (see Figure 2.4). This association helps draw our attention to the fact that language has become a basis not simply for new cultural identities but also for the articulation of uniquely political identities and forces us to consider changes in what it means to be "political." The first personified appearance of Telugu in pictorial form coincided precisely with the emergence of a political movement for a separate Telugu linguistic state in the second decade of the twentieth century. In 1913, for example, the year of the first Andhra Conference and the year in which the Andhra Province Standing Committee was formed, an image of Mother Andhra in personified form appeared in the fourth annual number of the periodical *Andhra Patrika.* The illustration shows a sari-clad woman labeled Andhra rising up out of a map of what is today the southeastern part of India, showing the neighboring territories of Madras Presidency, Mysore, Haidrabad [Hyderabad], the Central Provinces, and the Bay of Bengal (see Figure 2.5). Titled "The Blessings of the Mother—Āndhra Mātā Śīrvachanamu," it is significant that the predominantly Telugu-speaking portions of Hyderabad—the former princely state—were not yet imagined as part of the region represented by Mother Andhra.

A second image in the same issue shows Bhāratamāta [Mother India] blessing the Āndhra Bāla [Andhra Child]. This second image places Andhra in relationship to the larger imagined nation of India, as one among her many children. Such a representation also reflects the acceptance of India's languages as parallel and equivalent to one another, representing identical functions for separate and distinct constituencies within independent monolingual worlds rather than overlapping and complementary functions within a multilingual setting. Unlike the eroticized representations of the rare pre-colonial personifications of Telugu, these twentieth-century portrayals of a personified Telugu have removed all traces of the erotic pleasure that once provided a metaphor for the enjoyment of language. Instead, language can be seen as taking on the characteristics of a female deity, a process that occurs in relation to both Telugu and Tamil, ultimately culminating in the creation of the new deities, Telugu Talli [Mother Telugu] and Tamiḻttāy [Mother Tamil]. This personification of language is also gendered, establishing the ideal *abhimāni* as a specifically male subject.[50] In addition, the proximity of Telugu Talli to political power and political movements suggests that it is her political role that is most significant and raises questions about the relationship between "politics" and "culture."

FIGURE 2.5. The Blessings of the Mother—Āndhra Mātā Śīrvachanamu, *Andhra Patrika,* 1913.

Indeed, it suggests that cultural identities—whether defined by language or any other foundation—are central to the functioning of politics in India today.

Questions concerning the relationship between language and socio-political formations in twentieth-century southern India are also closely linked to changes in the relationship between Telugu and other languages.

The assertion of the naturalness of a single linguistic identity requires the distancing of potential group members from other competing identities—in this case, other languages. In light of the many multilingual residents of southern India, this presents a unique challenge to the process of making linguistic identity appear natural. We can see a glimpse of this in an excerpt taken from a series of ethnographic interviews conducted in several locations near the present-day border between the states of Andhra Pradesh and Tamil Nadu. Interviews with three brothers and their mother—part of an extended family currently spread out over parts of Tamil Nadu, Andhra Pradesh, and the adjacent state of Karnataka—reveal that some members of the younger generation of this family currently self-identify as Tamilians, and others as Telugus, and that some members of the older generation refuse to choose a single linguistic identity. I first interviewed the eldest of the three brothers, born in 1967, who currently lives in a town in Andhra Pradesh not far from the Tamil Nadu border.[51] After asking him a wide range of other questions, I finally asked him to identify his mother tongue (*mātṛbhāṣa*). Without hesitation, he replied that his mother tongue was Tamil, but he went on to say that because he has lived in Andhra for so long, these days he thinks of himself as a Telugu. Later, the second brother, born the following year in 1968 and now living in another district in Andhra Pradesh not far from the Karnataka border, also agreed to be interviewed. When asked the very same question concerning his *mātṛbhāṣa* or mother tongue, this brother, only one year younger, replied without hesitation that his mother tongue was Telugu.[52] Two brothers, only one year apart and raised in the very same household, today claim two different "mother tongues."

After interviewing the eldest brother, the third and youngest brother joined the two of us over lunch. It was clear that my questions had intrigued the eldest brother, particularly those questions dealing with linguistic identity, causing him to think about himself in ways he had never previously. He began asking many of my questions to the youngest brother, and the two discussed the matter for some time while I listened. Finally, they concluded that although both spoke Tamil and Telugu at home while growing up, they were indeed Telugu, and they went on to decide that the crucial moment that determined this occurred when they started primary school—in a Telugu medium school, since they were residing in Andhra. Today, both have married Telugu-speaking wives who speak no Tamil, and both live in predominantly Telugu-speaking regions of Andhra Pradesh. The eldest brother's young son has grown up speaking mainly Telugu, although he plans to teach him Tamil. As they talked, they explained that their mother, whom they described as speaking Tamil, Telugu, and Kannada equally fluently, was one of nine children—seven daughters and two sons. At some point their mother's father, originally born in a small village in what is now Andhra Pradesh, not far from the Tamil Nadu border, took a job in Madras, and the family moved there. Today, their mother's two brothers and four of her sisters live in Madras. "Their children are studying in Tamil and growing up as Tamilians," explained the youngest brother. Of their own mother, and two other aunts who now live in Andhra Pradesh, he concluded that "their children are turning into Telugus."[53] The fact that some members of a single family have today come to feel themselves "Telugu," while others from the same family now feel "Tamil" makes a strong case for arguing that the acquisition of a linguistic identity is indeed a historical process, rather than any sort of primordial natural identification.

The use of a discourse of loss and victimization at the hands of others, sometimes portrayed as competing linguistic groups, other times portrayed as group members whose interests are opposed to those of the majority, has been particularly effective in shoring up a Telugu definition of identity. The image of mother Telugu "silently weeping" at the "miserable condition which has befallen her language" effectively utilizes this discourse of loss and victimization in a way that has reoccurred throughout the past century. At times Telugu identity is asserted in opposition to languages that have come to serve as the foundations for neighboring territorial and political claims, such as Tamil, Kannada, Marathi, and Oriya. At other moments such an identity is asserted in opposition to more powerful languages, such as English, which have come to assume new roles within everyday life. In both cases these assertions are strikingly different from the pre-modern assertions of Telugu language that occurred in opposition to Sanskrit and the cultural meanings represented by Sanskrit. As Velcheru Narayana Rao has observed, medieval and early-modern representations of language in southern India distinguished between *dēśa bhāṣa,* the language of the land, and *dēva bhāṣa,* the language of the gods, or Sanskrit.[54] Although a particular *dēśa bhāṣa* might be celebrated as more beautiful than others, as in the statement circulated by Vallabharaya in the fifteenth century and Krishnadevaraya in the sixteenth century that "among all the languages of the land, Telugu is the best [*dēśabhāṣālandu Telugu lessa*]," one does not perceive a sense of victimization of one *dēśa bhāṣa* at the hands of another within pre-nineteenth-century writings, nor does one see the representation of the victimization of one *dēśa bhāṣa*'s speakers at the hands of another's. Rather, as the larger context of both Vallabharaya and Krishnadevaraya's statements makes clear, languages served complementary functions within a much larger multilingual context, albeit one in which the primary contrast was between Sanskrit and regional languages. The championing of Telugu in this case indicates not a defense of one language against the oppression of another, but rather an acknowledgment that poets and other literate individuals of that era had the capacity to choose from among a range of languages. In the preface to his sixteenth-century *Āmukta-mālyada,* Krishnadevaraya has a dream in which he is exhorted by the god who appears in his dream to compose a work in Telugu. The god goes on by saying,

> Why Telugu? You might ask.
> This is the Telugu land.
> I am the lord of Telugu.
> There is nothing sweeter.
> Because you speak Telugu,
> many kings come to serve you.
> Among all the languages of the land,
> Telugu is best.[55]

The implication is that the poet king Krishnadevaraya has the ability to compose in any of a number of languages. That Telugu is more worthy because it is someone's mother tongue or only tongue is not the claim being made.

The personification of languages represents them first and foremost as consolidated subjects, completely independent of other languages save for their kinship relationships, and independent even of their speakers. They exist as entities with lives parallel to those of other languages. Such externalized representations of language create alienation from linguistic acts and require the enactment of an affective attachment to language in order to reattach language to self, this time not to all language acts in general but to a specific "mother tongue." Scarcely apparent even to those who have experienced this shift, such a distinction can only be perceived by holding up the system of one moment against the system of another and looking for the tensions and contradictions that come to light as a result. Indeed, so natural do people regard their mother tongues today that most find it unthinkable to imagine that a relationship to language ever existed without a mother tongue.

CHAPTER 3

Making the Local Foreign: Shared Language and History in Southern India

[L]ocal dialects of Telugu vary; and we may be able to speak that of Kadapa, while unable to understand that of Rāja-mahēndra-varam, or Condapilli, or Visākha-patnam.

—C. P. Brown, *A Grammar of the Telugu Language,* 1857

While conducting fieldwork in 1998, I met a longtime friend who had married the previous year. Born and brought up in the city of Hyderabad, the capital of Andhra Pradesh, my friend—a schoolteacher educated in English medium schools who had grown up speaking primarily Telugu at home and English, Telugu, and Hindi in Hyderabad's public spaces—had married a man from a small village in the Coastal Andhra district of West Godavari, some five hundred kilometers east of Hyderabad. As we talked about her first year of married life, she happened to remark that for the first six months of their marriage she was able to understand very little of what her husband was saying. It was not just that their accents were different, but that the words each used for different objects and actions and the ways in which they formed verbs were unfamiliar. Yet despite their difficulties in understanding one another, both found it completely natural to claim that they spoke the same language—Telugu. What, then, does it mean to say that one shares a common language with another, if not that one finds the other's speech mutually intelligible? And conversely, what does it mean for language to be foreign, if not that it is unintelligible?

In the past two centuries in southern India, mutual intelligibility has increasingly been displaced as the criterion for defining what constitutes shared language—in theory, if not also in practice. Instead, as Naoki Sakai has observed, in most places in the world today appeals to history and common origin have come to be decisive factors in determining what defines the language shared by a group of people.[1] Historical consciousness—an awareness of the origins of language and the etymologies of words—has come to define and constitute not only what it means to share language in southern India, but also what it means for linguistic practices to be considered "local" or "native" as opposed to "foreign." India has had a long formal tradition of language analysis, dating to at least the fourth century BCE, and played a central role within the discovery of the Indo-European language family and the birth of historical and comparative linguistics. Yet under colonial rule, the ideologies of language present within Indian grammatical traditions were transformed while simultaneously made to appear unchanging.

By invoking the concept of language ideologies, I am drawing attention to what Kathryn Woolard and Bambi Schieffelin have characterized as the "cultural conceptions of language—its nature, structure, and use" and "conceptions of communicative behavior as an enactment of a collective order."[2] Put another way, language ideologies function as culturally specific mediating links between language use and social structures. These ways of imagining languages and relationships between languages frequently underpin social institutions, including, in Woolard and Schieffelin's conceptualization, such social institutions as "the nation-state, schooling, gender, dispute-settlement, and law."[3] It is perhaps not surprising that colonial contexts of various sorts have provided one of the most visible sites for conflict between different language ideologies, bringing competing language ideologies into relief, and India during the British colonial period provides us with a useful example of this. For these reasons, a close examination of the mechanisms through which historical linguistic ideology came to dominate is of importance for anyone who accepts claims that rely on an awareness of the origins of words and languages.

Widely unquestioned as a scientific method of classifying and analyzing language use worldwide and making languages tell the deep history of the world's peoples and their movements, the historical linguistic methodologies that grew out of colonial comparative philology have enabled, in the words of Joseph Errington, "language difference [to] become a resource—like gender, race, and class—for figuring and naturalizing inequality."[4]

They have made possible the definition, management, and policing of difference in both colonial and postcolonial contexts in very new ways. At the same time, comparative historical linguistic analysis is still widely regarded as a universal method of knowledge production, existing outside of any particular linguistic ideology. More carefully historicizing the practices of comparative philology enables us to see them as only one method of approaching and classifying language use. Despite historical linguistics' dramatic implications for the present-day construction and politicization of language identities, its methods can be contrasted with other language ideologies that have been effaced under its impact.

While not suggesting that all aspects of the consideration of language remained constant in the medieval and early-modern periods, this chapter argues that rather than being understood in relation to foreignness or identity (one's own or another's), prior to the nineteenth century language use was formally differentiated in terms that could be measured along a spectrum of intelligibility. At one end of this spectrum, pre-colonial linguistic analyses of language (Sanskrit as well as regional literary languages like Telugu) described those features of language that were capable of traveling farthest over both time and space (though, significantly, not class) while still maintaining intelligibility. Because of their ability to be intelligible over large expenses of space and time, these features were therefore also identified with the greatest levels of prestige, education, and refinement. At the other end of the spectrum, increasingly local language use was intelligible within progressively more geographically narrow domains. Moving toward this end of the spectrum meant that language was comprehensible only within a restricted territory, region, set of villages, or social group. Such an understanding returns us to an earlier meaning of the term "Sanskrit"—one denoting not a discrete language but rather a codified register of highly refined and manipulated language governed by a set of rules. These rules enabled its use and comprehensibility by learned classes throughout South and much of Southeast Asia who also commanded other forms of more local language use. Although such a spectrum of language usage in relationship to intelligibility still exists in practice in southern India, these distinctions are no longer of primary importance, and, indeed, as the following discussion demonstrates, the formal vocabulary for describing such differences has largely been lost. It has been replaced by terms—in some cases the same terms—that take their meanings from a system defined almost exclusively in relation to historical origins. These earlier formal ideas about language made possible the recognition of particular categories of language as appropriate for particular uses rather than for particular users, especially among literate elites who routinely commanded multiple scripts and language styles. The new categories of grammatical analysis formulated in the nineteenth century had wide-ranging implications for the ways in which both literate and non-literate individuals and groups began to think about everyday linguistic practices, features of group difference, and the categories through which these are experienced.

Categories of Language Analysis

The categories through which the Telugu language has been understood within southern Indian grammatical discourses may initially seem rather esoteric and removed from everyday popular linguistic practices, especially given the dominance of literate brahmanical elites within these discourses. However, it is here, within the realm of meta-linguistic discourses, that many of the distinctions between the local and the foreign were first worked out, laying the groundwork for the adoption of new understandings of these distinctions at a popular level. Although dominated by elites, the discussions and writings on language that emerged in the nineteenth century took place most prominently within educational institutions established by the British colonial government, and the ramifications of these conversations for students from all castes and communities were profound. By the mid-twentieth century the implications of these ideas had spread even to non-literate sections of the population. Almost all of the important political movements of twentieth-century southern India have appealed to the commonality of shared language defined in relation to origins as a partial or complete foundation for their claims. These include the Andhra linguistic state movement; other twentieth-century linguistic state movements leading to the 1956 All-India Linguistic States Reorganisation; the Telangana separatist movement; and the Dravidian and Non-Brahmin movements, which appealed to shared linguistic kinship among speakers of the south Indian Dravidian languages—Tamil, Telugu, Kannada, and Malayalam—and labeled those who used Sanskrit (namely Brahmins) or other Indo-European languages (associated with northern India) as foreigners and oppressors.[5] Most of the specific details that made such foundations available and imaginable as platforms for defining who

Table 3.1.

Framing and Definitions of "anyadēśyam" and "accha telugu"

AUTHOR	FRAMING OF *anyadēśyam*	DEFINITION OF *dēśyam*	DEFINITION OF *anyadēśyam*	FRAMING OF *accha telugu*	DEFINITION OF *accha telugu*
Mulaghatika Ketana (13th C.)				one of five types of words, listed after *tatsama* and *tadbhava* and before *dēśyam* and *grāmyam*	*accha tenugu*—"those words that are known to everyone"
Kakunuri Appakavi (17th C.)	one of two subcategories of (*andhra*) *dēśyam*	*shuddhāndhrams*—"all those words and expressions spoken plainly and clearly by the various peoples of all the cities and places of the Andhra region, not including the obscure territory"	*anyadēśajāndhrams*—"the Telugu words that Andhras, having stayed in many regions, have spoken together with the speech acquired in various places"	describes literary works that do not include *tatsama* words	"those splendid literary works that do not allow tatsamas and that mix tadbhavas and those three varieties of dēśyams that are called *kēvalāndhrams* [*shuddhāndhrams*, *anyadēśajāndhrams*, and *grāmyams*]"
Mamadi Venkaya (1806)	a subcategory of *dēśyam*		*anyadēśyam*—"the people of Andhra, otherwise called Trilingam, have frequented other countries and mixed their language with that of these several countries"		

Table 3.1. (continued)

AUTHOR	FRAMING OF *anyadēśyam*	DEFINITION OF *dēśyam*	DEFINITION OF *anyadēśyam*	FRAMING OF *accha telugu*	DEFINITION OF *accha telugu*
Vedam Pattabirama Sastri (d. 1820, published posthumously in 1825)	one of two subcategories of *dēśyam*	*andhradēśyam*—"words understood clearly"	*anyadēśyam*—"words with meanings that are not so clear, which sometimes have non-Telugu-sounding letters, or sometimes also sound like Telugu"		
A. D. Campbell (1816)	separate fifth category, in addition to *dēśyam, tatsama, tadbhava,* and *grāmyam*	*dēśyam*—"language of the land" (includes *acchadēśyam*—"pure language of the land")	*anyadēśyam*—"foreign"	*acchadēśyam*—a more emphatic term for *dēśyam*	"the pure language of the land"
Francis Ellis (1816)	one of four main categories, in addition to *dēśyam, tatsama,* and *tadhbhava* (replaces *grāmyam*)	*dēśyam* (or *accha telugu*)—"pure native terms" (includes *grāmyam*—"rustic dialect; not authorized by the rules of Grammar")	*anyadēśyam*—"terms borrowed from other countries"	synonymous with *dēśyam*	"pure native terms"

Table 3.1. (continued)

AUTHOR	FRAMING OF ***anyadēśyam***	DEFINITION OF ***dēśyam***	DEFINITION OF ***anyadēśyam***	FRAMING OF ***accha telugu***	DEFINITION OF ***accha telugu***
Ravipati Gurumurti Sastri (1836)	one of two subcategories of *dēśyam*	*acchadēśyam*—"words of the Telugu region"	*anyadēśyam*—"words of the Dravida, etc. regions used with Telugu cases"	*acchadēśyam*—one of two subcategories of *dēśyam*	"words of the Telugu region"
C. P. Brown (1840)	subcategory of *dēśyam*	*dēśyam*—"primeval; cannot be traced to any root"	*anyadēśyam*—"local"		
C. P. Brown (1852)		"n.s. A dialect, obsolete or local expression. Idiom, provincialism. Adj. Idiomatic, provincial. . . . Desya words are those the root of which is unknown: many are used by the oldest and best poets. . . . Some are Sanskrit"			"Telugu without Sanskrit words"

Table 3.1. (continued)

AUTHOR	FRAMING OF *anyadēśyam*	DEFINITION OF *dēśyam*	DEFINITION OF *anyadēśyam*	FRAMING OF *accha telugu*	DEFINITION OF *accha telugu*
C. P. Brown (1857)	subcategory of *dēśyam*	*dēśyam*—"country dialect; language of the land"; includes "aboriginal" words	*anyadēśyam*—"local expressions peculiar to the foreign countries"	Included within *dēśyam;* used to describe a dialect rather than a category of words	"'Pure Telugu' the name given to a dialect used more or less in all poems, wherein the author shuns Sanscrit words: or, if obliged to use them, softens the sound, changing Vishnu into Vennudu, &c."
Brown's Telugu-English Dictionary (2nd ed., 1903)	original four categories abandoned in favor of "four strata": pure Telugu, Sanskrit, Hindustani, and English	"adj. Belonging to the country. *Native.* n. The language of a country, a vernacular; a vernacular term. Desya words are opposed to foreign words"			"Telugu without foreign words"

was included and who excluded from these movements were worked out in the colonial context before they were taken up more popularly.[6] I do not mean to imply that nineteenth-century scholars anticipated the political formations and social movements of the twentieth century at the time they were working out the categories discussed within this chapter. My point is simply that many of the categories of identity and difference that provided foundations for later political and social movements were established as categories during the nineteenth century. Before an identity was able to be taken up and used for socio-political mobilization, it had to first be made available within popular discourse.

Telugu meta-linguistic texts composed up to the end of the nineteenth century analyzed words through a system of categories originally borrowed from the Sanskrit *vyākaraṇa* (linguistic analysis) tradition. The *vyākaraṇa* tradition, evidence of which goes back at least as early as work of the poet-scholar Panini, who likely lived around the fourth century BCE, sought to account for the entire lexicon of known words though a system that combined a comprehensive list of verbal roots with a set of concise rules for transforming these roots into every other linguistic element. This system was further refined to describe the more regionally specific Indian literary languages ("Prakrits"), as they were used in current speech and writing. The earliest grammarians of Telugu, writing in Sanskrit, picked up the main features of this system, and added to it. The *vyākaraṇa* system included the categories of *tatsama* ("the same as it"; equivalent to Sanskrit), *tadbhava* ("of the nature of it"; derived from Sanskrit; altered), and *dēśya* (not derived from grammar; of the country or region; of a particular place). Telugu grammarians added a fourth category, *grāmya* (of the village; rustic; vulgar), which typically denoted words considered inappropriate for use in literary compositions. *Āndhra Śabda Chintāmaṇi,* a grammatical treatise on Telugu popularly (though controversially) attributed to the eleventh-century poet Nannaya Bhatt but likely composed in the sixteenth century, uses these four categories.[7] So, too, do the many authors who have offered commentaries upon this text who together have come to make up what Boddupalli Purushottam labels "The Traditional School" of Telugu grammar.[8] The thirteenth-century Mulaghatika Ketana, who explicitly claims to be the first Telugu grammarian, but whose work has not prompted the same production of commentaries, also uses the same four categories, along with a somewhat ambiguous fifth category, *accha tenugu,* today glossed as "pure Telugu" (see Table 3.1 for other definitions of *accha tenugu/telugu*).[9]

In his seventeenth-century commentary on *Āndhra Śabda Chintāmaṇi,* Kakunuri Appakavi likewise writes that there are "four kinds of Telugu—tatsama, tadbhava, dēśya, and grāmya bhāṣa."[10] He further refines his analysis by defining two sub-types of *dēśya* and by introducing his own version of *accha tenugu.*[11] More recent grammarians of the nineteenth century like Vedam Pattabhirama Sastri (1760–1820), Ravipati Gurumurti Sastri (1770–1836), and Paravastu Chinnaya Suri (1802–1860) likewise begin with these four categories, adding further refinements later in their texts.[12] Given their adoption of similar categories of analysis, a superficial examination of Telugu grammars might suggest a uniformity of meanings unquestioningly shared by all who have used these four categories over the past eight centuries. However, closer readings reveal not only that analysis is not restricted to these categories alone, but also that there is not always consensus over what each of these terms actually means in practice. A reading of the usages of these terms in a number of prominent grammarians of Telugu will demonstrate how notions of the local and the foreign in relation to historical origins—notions that have made possible the kind of parallel and exclusive regional socio-political linguistic identifications one encounters in south India today—have come to be constructed in their present forms.

The Absence of "The Foreign" in Pre-colonial Telugu Grammars

No category commensurable with what we would today characterize as "the foreign" is apparent within the pre-colonial *vyākaraṇa* language analysis system. Although the term *mlēccha* ("barbarous" or "foreign") did exist, both in Sanskrit and in Telugu, it is rarely found within linguistic analyses of language. It was not until a new ideology dominated by historical origins and derivations was introduced that an explicit idea of foreignness began to appear in the context of grammatical analysis. Eivind Kahrs has argued that early Indian grammarians were concerned with describing not *one* language in opposition to others but *all* language, and that "nothing like language development or linguistic change through time is accounted for."[13] Although later grammarians classified words according to their relationship to Sanskrit (*tatsama* and *tadbhava*), they show little explicit concern with identifying specific relationships with languages other than Sanskrit or with describing historical changes in language over time that may have produced what later became distinct languages.[14] According to

Kahrs, the language described by Panini "is timeless" and "comprises all linguistic facts known to him."[15] Kahrs further suggests that the Western understanding of *tadbhava* as "'derived from Sanskrit' . . . implies the concepts of 'time' and 'linguistic change' from a Western framework," causing "serious misinterpretations of Indian grammar." He goes on to argue:

> The Western usage of the Indian term flavours the meaning of that term with Western presuppositions, concealing completely what the term originally signified in its Indian context. The risk, then, is that a purely Western conceptual framework with presuppositions and aims of its own is introduced into ancient Indian grammar in a disguised way, that is, under the cover of an Indian term.[16]

Kahrs concludes that despite its virtual acceptance today, "the adoption of the term *tadbhava* in the sense of 'derived from Sanskrit' was a feat of Western authors."[17] He instead advocates either "leaving the term untranslated" or recognizing a meaning closer to "located in it, i.e., in Sanskrit."[18]

The primary category used for words with no relationship to Sanskrit—*dēśya,* today glossed as "of the region"—has been used by Telugu grammarians to classify words that have not been derived from grammar but that are still acceptable in literary usage. According to Boddupalli Purushottam, this follows the Prakrit grammarian Hemachandra, in his *Dēśināmamālā,* who defines *dēśi* as "such words that are not derived by grammar and even when derived, are not current in Sanskrit dictionaries. . . . Such words are further defined . . . as not including provincial dialects, but only such Prakrit words as are current through ages, without beginning."[19] Yet so powerful was the European emphasis on historical origins that this meaning of unknown origins and timelessness was rejected even when recognized as the clearly stated intention of earlier authors. The colonial administrator Alexander Duncan Campbell, for example, writing in 1816 in response to the universal agreement he identified within Telugu grammars that the origins of *dēśya* words are unknown, states, "Why the origin of this class of terms is supposed to be unascertained has not been stated; nor can I conceive how so erroneous a conclusion could have been adopted."[20] His obvious bewilderment at the definitions offered by earlier Telugu grammarians should be taken not as an indication that pre-colonial south Indian grammarians were wrong, but as evidence that Indian and European colonial approaches to linguistic categories were not completely commensurable. Today, although the term *dēśya* is not incompatible with the earlier emphasis on the lack of grammatical derivation, its identification of words not simply as being used within a particular region, but also as originating in that region, is more exclusively emphasized.

The argument that the *vyākaraṇa* tradition was unconcerned with something understandable as "the foreign" at the beginning of the nineteenth century can best be supported by tracing the many difficulties encountered by early British grammarians of Telugu in interpreting Telugu linguistic categories. Frustrated by the lack of easy translatability between Telugu and English labels, British scholars of Telugu struggled for nearly half a century to make local classifications correspond with their own notions of language. In attempting to force commensurability, British scholars of southern Indian languages frequently adjusted categories to suit their own understandings. But by citing local authorities and using local terms and categories in their writings, they managed to make it appear that their own understandings of language had always already been present in the very local texts they used to support their arguments. Ultimately they inserted a new notion of the "foreign" into a system which, although itself not static over the preceding centuries, had never before contained such a category. Three examples will make this clear.

Rewriting Telugu Grammar

In the first example, the colonial administrators Alexander Duncan Campbell, author of *A Grammar of the Teloogoo Language,* first published in 1816, and Francis Whyte Ellis, who established the first south Indian college for English civil servants, and whose "Note to the Introduction" is included within Campbell's book, both subtly redefine a system of language analysis while attributing it to "Native Grammarians" and "Native Authors."[21] Now known primarily for its proof of the Dravidian family of languages—the first text to suggest the familial kinship between Tamil, Telugu, Kannada, and Malayalam, and, more significantly, their dissimilarity from Sanskrit and the languages of northern India—their work holds a significant place in the history of comparative and historical linguistics, as recent work by Thomas Trautmann has made clear.[22] Yet Ellis and Campbell's citations of local grammarians have never been questioned. Indeed, as Trautmann observes, their "discovery" of the Dravidian family of languages was made possible by the system of etymological analyses of roots used within the *vyākaraṇa* tradition.[23] In his grammar, Campbell summarizes what he views as the Telugu etymological system of language analysis:

> [I]t is certain that every Teloogoo Grammarian, from the days of Nunnia Bhutt [Nannaya Bhatt] to the present period, considers the two languages [Sanskrit and Telugu] as derived from sources entirely distinct; for each commences his work by classing the words of the language under four separate heads, which they distinguish by the respective names of *dēśyamu,* language of the land, *tatsamamu,* Sanscrit derivatives, *tadbhavamu,* Sanscrit corruptions, and *gramyamu,* provincial terms.[24]

Although Campbell lists the same four categories used by Indian authors, he has rearranged the order in which they have customarily been presented, beginning first with *dēśyam,* rather than with *tatsama* and *tadbhava.* He also glosses *dēśyamu* as "language of the land" rather than emphasizing its non-derivation from grammar, as Telugu scholars have done. His next words, however, are even more striking, for he states, "To these, later authors have added *anyadēśyamu,* foreign words or those from other lands."[25] The way that Campbell defines and frames *anyadēśyam* is significant, for never before had it been listed as a separate category of analysis. Instead, whenever it was introduced, it was always listed as a subdivision of the *dēśyam* category (see Table 3.1 for examples of the various framings and definitions of *dēśyam* and *anyadēśyam* offered by Indian and British authors).[26] Campbell later acknowledges this fact, but in a way that dramatically masks the significance of the intervention he's making. At the beginning of his third chapter, he expands his definition of *anyadēśyamu,* writing that it includes "words from other countries, sometimes given as a subdivision of the first Class [*dēśyam*], and comprising, according to the definition of ancient writers, words adopted from the dialects current in the Canarese, Mahratta, Guzerat, and Dravida provinces only, but now also including several of Persian, Hindoostanee, and English origin."[27]

Campbell's understanding of *anyadēśyamu,* based as it is on an assumption of an origin located outside the local, makes it difficult for him to accept it as a sub-category within the *dēśyam* category, especially given his definition of *dēśyam* as "language of the land." He clearly recognizes that Indian grammarians have understood the *dēśyam* category differently from his own interpretation when he writes that he cannot "conceive how so erroneous a conclusion could have been adopted" that "the origin of this class of terms is supposed to be unascertained." But he is unwilling to accept this, writing instead that

> the name given to them by all Sanscrit Grammarians, by the whole body of the people . . . at once points out their derivation. This name is dēśyam, a noun used either as a substantive or an adjective, in the former sense denoting *a country or land,* in the latter, in which it is here used, implying *that which belongs to the country or land;* it marks the words in question, not as merely "current in the country," but as the growth and produce of the land; it would be difficult to define more precisely the origin of any words, and to this class must we look for the pure Teloogoo—for the true *language of the land.*[28]

Not only does he reject *dēśyam* as categorizing terms of unascertained origin, but he also rejects any possibility that this category may refer simply to usage that is, as he puts it, "current in the country." Instead, he insists on understanding *dēśyam* exclusively in terms of the category's classification of the *origins* of words. Ultimately, with this definition he can only accommodate *anyadēśyam* by removing it completely from within the category of *dēśyam,* promoting it to a separate category of its own and defining it, like *dēśyam,* in terms of origins. In effect, he has redefined *anyadēśyam* in opposition to *dēśyam* rather than including it, as Indian grammarians had done, as a subset of the *dēśyam* category.

Ellis takes Campbell's framing of the classification used by "Native Grammarians" one step further removed from the cited texts. Rather than considering *anyadēśyam* an additional fifth category as Campbell has, he replaces one of the four original primary categories with it, reordering the four according to what he calls their "natural order." He writes:

> [T]he language may be divided into four branches, of which the following is the natural order. Dēśyam or Atsu-Telugu *pure native terms,* constituting the basis of this language and, generally, also, of the other dialects of southern India; Anya-dēśyam *terms borrowed from other Countries,* chiefly of the same derivation as the preceding; Tatsamam, *pure Sanscrit terms,* the Telugu affixes being substituted for those of the original language; Tadbhavam, *Sanscrit derivatives,* received into the Telugu, direct, or through one of the six Prācrits, and in all instances more or less corrupted.[29]

With this act, he not only reframes but also redefines both *dēśyam* and *anyadēśyam.* The category he displaces in this act, *grāmyam,* is relegated to a new position outside of this system of four categories, while also simultaneously incorporated into the first category with the comment, "[t]he Grāmyam (literally the *rustic* dialect from *Grāmam* Sans. *a village*) is not a constituent portion of the language, but is formed from the Atsu-Telugu by contraction, or by some permutation of the letters not authorized by the rules of Grammar."[30] For Ellis, *grāmyam* has become the new *dēśyam*, used to classify whatever is seen as not derived from grammar, with no reference to origins.

There is even more substantial evidence that Ellis's definitions of *dēśyam* and *anyadēśyam* do not correspond with previously existing meanings of these terms. Ellis, in his introduction, relies heavily on his own translation of the preface of Mamadi Venkaya's *Āndhra Dīpika,* the first alphabetized Telugu dictionary, composed around 1806.[31] Venkaya uses the four categories in their customary order: *tatsama, tadbhava, dēśyam,* and *grāmyam.* Ellis intersperses his own comments in between lengthy quotations from Venkaya (rearranged, translated, and interpreted by Ellis). He translates Venkaya's definition by writing, "Dēśyam, in other words Andhra, or Telugu, is of two kinds; the language which originated in the country of Telingana, and Anya-dēśyam, or the language of foreign countries intermixed with it."[32] After equating *dēśyam* with the Telugu language, he then elaborates on *anyadēśyam* words by discussing the examples used by Appakavi and Venkaya to illustrate the subcategory. It is here that the tensions within Ellis's translations of *dēśyam* and *anyadēśyam* become most problematic, for he writes:

> The examples are of Anya-dēśyam terms in which aspirates, not belonging to the thirty letters proper to the Telugu, occur . . . ; of those which have a final long vowel . . . ; and lastly, of difficult words, *inappropriately ranked among Anya-dēśyam terms.* . . . Of the list given by the author as examples of the several kinds of Anya-dēśyam terms, the whole of the words in the first are of uncertain derivation; those in the second are either Hindustani or they are terms the last syllable of which has been casually lengthened. . . . Most of those in the last list are common to the southern dialects.[33]

Upon encountering terms that he believes are "inappropriately ranked" among what he considers to be terms of "foreign" origin, Ellis might have been given pause to reconsider his definition. But instead of modifying his translation to accommodate the examples given, Ellis awkwardly insists upon the inappropriateness of their inclusion within the category of *anyadēśyam* words and implies the ignorance of the Telugu scholars he cites. By equating *dēśyam* with "native" and opposing it to *anyadēśyam,* Ellis is for the first time making these categories available for the kinds of regional ethnic identifications with language that many today accept as natural. The implications of this move—a sleight of hand almost invisible to today's sensibilities—for the ethnic politicization of language is tremendous. His reading further suggests that we must look carefully in order to understand the different ways in which language, identity, and alterity were experienced and perceived prior to the arrival of the British.

From Local to Foreign

In the second example, we see the colonial administrator Charles Philip Brown struggle for almost two decades to define this same term, *anyadēśyam,* first glossing it simply as "local" in an 1840 publication and only later, in an 1857 publication, defining it as "foreign."[34] But these glosses of Telugu categories are meaningless without understanding the roles each plays within its larger system of meaning, both Brown's and the system he is encountering. It is the attempt to understand these terms within their own contexts while at the same time making them correspond to English categories that causes so much difficulty for Brown. Most today would accept his later use (and Ellis's) of "foreign" to gloss *anyadeśya,* as the term consistently gets translated as such in many Indian languages today. "Local," Brown's earlier definition, may be more difficult for contemporary readers to accept, and we may initially want to suggest that he simply got it wrong. Yet his "mistake" (though I hesitate to call it that) points to an incommensurability between categories of thought, and it is therefore important to explain why he initially defined it the way he did, as well as why he later abandoned this definition. An examination of the systems of meaning within which the term *anyadeśya* appears will tease out nuances of this term that have more recently—in an era when subcontinental regional linguistic identifications and differentiations have become paramount—been completely effaced. It also makes more obvious how two terms we now read as absolute opposites—"local" and "foreign"—could once have been accommodated as compatible understandings of the same category.

In his 1840 "Essay on the Language and Literature of the Telugus," Brown closely follows the seventeenth-century grammarian Appakavi, cited earlier, dividing Telugu words into four classes: "I. Tatsama, II. Tadbhava, III. Desya, IV. Gramya."[35] Like Appakavi, he also defines *anyadēśya* as a subdivision of *dēśya:*

> Desya, or primitive Telugu words . . . like the corresponding English words are primeval and cannot be traced to any root. *A subdivision of this class is Anyadesya, or local.* . . . some of which are supposed to be Tamil and others are Canada [Kannada]: just as we consider some of our words English, others Scotch, and others Irish.[36]

Brown goes on to assign words from Hindustani to the fourth category, *grāmya,* defining the latter as "barbarisms including all Hindustani and other corruptions."[37]

However, by the 1850s, Brown's glossing of *anyadēśya* has shifted subtly but significantly to encompass a notion much closer to today's meaning of "foreign." In the second edition of Brown's *Grammar of the Telugu Language,* he includes an appendix entitled "On Etymology. Tatsamamu, Tadbhavamu, Desyamu, and Gramyamu."[38] His comments reveal his disdain for the competence of Indian grammarians:

> Telugu Grammarians have discussed at great length some points of Etymology which more properly appertain to a Dictionary or separate philological treatise. . . . These topics are allowed to retain a place in the grammar, because learned natives are so much addicted to talking on etymology: *of which in general, they have no clear notions:* I will merely state enough to solve the riddle: while on the native mode, this one theme would occupy a whole volume.[39]

He then goes on to devote a few paragraphs to each of the four categories in their customary order. His definition of *dēśyam,* however, has changed, for he writes, "such words . . . being aboriginal, like the corresponding words in English are called the Desya, country dialect, or language of the land. One class of these is denominated anya-desyamu or Dialect being local expressions peculiar to the *foreign* countries."[40] Here he manages to accommodate the tensions he encounters in trying to make commensurable two systems of linguistic analysis by defining *anyadēśyam* as both local and foreign. Whereas, for Brown, *dēśya* words originate within the local territory, *anyadēśyam* terms are used locally but originate in foreign places. By grouping all four categories under the heading "On Etymology," Brown reveals his interest in the etymologies or origins of words—an interest that exceeds all other methods of classifying the Telugu vocabulary he has encountered, and blinds him to other possibilities present within the "addiction" he attributes to "learned natives." Arguably, the reason Telugu grammarians appeared to Brown to "have no clear notions" of etymology was that they were not exclusively discussing etymologies at all, but rather were using these categories to sanction the appropriateness of words for use in literary compositions by assessing the extent of their intelligibility according to grammatical rules.

The seventeenth-century Appakavi, cited by Venkaya, Ellis, and Brown (above), was the first Telugu scholar to use a category like *anyadēśya.* Appakavi writes, "There are two varieties of āndhradēśyams—*shuddhāndhrams* and *anyadēśajāndhrams.*"[41] He defines *shuddhāndhrams* as "all those words and expressions spoken plainly and clearly by the various peoples of all the cities and places of the Andhra region, not including the obscure territory."[42] He then goes on to write that "the Telugu that Andhras, having stayed in many regions, have spoken together with the speech acquired in various places, those words are anyadēśajāndhrams."[43] Although Ellis interprets this as "terms introduced into Telugu from foreign countries," others have understood it differently.[44]

Boddupalli Purushottam has glossed Appakavi's term *anyadēśajāndhrams* as words "that belong to various dialects," quite a different understanding from Ellis's, and one that suggests an interest in the diversity of usage rather than a preoccupation with origins.[45] We can read just a hint of this tension through Ellis's translation of Mamadi Venkaya's comment on Appakavi's definition of *anyadēśajāndhrams:* "The people of Andhra, otherwise called Trilingam, have, as Appacavi [Appakavi] states above, frequented other countries and mixed their language with that of these several countries."[46] Rather than words of other countries being introduced into Telugu as we might expect of foreign loan words, Venkaya, and Appakavi before him, suggest that changes have occurred to Telugu words introduced into other regions. In other words, Telugu terms have undergone changes as they have traveled, been used elsewhere, and returned. Such an understanding of *anyadēśajāndhrams* also helps to account for the examples given by Appakavi (and Venkaya after him), which include sounds not found in the Telugu alphabet, as well as vowel lengthenings and complex words not generally familiar throughout all places where Telugu is spoken. What Appakavi's definitions of the two sub-categories of *dēśyam* suggest, then, is an emphasis upon clarity and ease of understanding throughout the territory where Telugu is used. However, what Ellis, Campbell, and Brown have emphasized is a concern not with clarity, but with the origins and etymologies of words.

Most Telugu grammars written by Indian authors in the early decades of the nineteenth century also adopted the term *anyadēśya* as a subdivision of the *dēśya* category. Many were written by pandits employed by colonial institutions established, not for native education, but for the education of British civil servants. The production of grammars suitable for the use of colonial administrators ensured their publication by the colonial government. One of the earliest was Vedam Pattabhirama Sastri's *Āndhra Vyākaraṇamu,* first published posthumously in 1825. Pattabhirama Sastri was head Sanskrit and Telugu master at the College of Fort St. George in Madras until his death in 1820. Pattabhirama Sastri seems to have worked quite closely with both Ellis and Campbell, as he mentions Ellis in his grammar, and Ellis and Campbell both acknowledge Pattabhirama Sastri.[47] For this reason, the marked differences between Pattabhirama Sastri's 1825 analysis and those of Ellis and Campbell are particularly striking. Like earlier *vyākaraṇa* texts, Pattabhirama Sastri's text lists four main categories and then promises to explain the characteristics of each "with clarity" in Telugu verse. After describing *tadbhava* and *tatsama* words, he turns to *dēśya* words:

> In accordance with the general flow of Telugu words used by the people, there are among dēsya words, two types: āndhradēsyams and anyadēsyams. Those words which are understood clearly are āndhradēsyams. . . . Those with meanings which are not so clear, which sometimes have non-Telugu sounding letters, or sometimes also sound like Telugu, are called anyadēsyams.[48]

Pattabhirama Sastri's definitions, like Appakavi's before him, are concerned with describing the level of clarity and ease of understanding of different types of words, rather than the origins of the words grouped in each category. All three British scholars—Campbell, Ellis, and Brown—along with many later historians of languages, view these earlier *vyākaraṇa* analyses of words as exclusively etymological analyses, as Brown's heading "On Etymology" and framing of the categories suggest. None entertain the possibility that these categories might also (or even primarily) be concerned with evaluating the comprehensibility of words and their appropriateness for use within literary compositions that seek to be intelligible beyond one's immediate locality.

Inventing "Pure" Telugu

The third example concerns the significant reframing and redefining by Ellis, Campbell, and Brown of the term that the two former scholars both equate with *dēśyam,* and the latter struggles to account for: "*atsu-*" or *accha-Telugu.* Ellis, as we have seen above, treats *dēśyam* and "*atsu-Telugu*" as completely synonymous, defining them as labels for "pure native terms."[49] Campbell, likewise, equates the two terms, calling the latter simply more emphatic than the former: "*Déshyumoo,* or, as it is more emphatically termed, *Utsu Déshyumoo* [accha dēśyamu], the *pure* language of the land."[50] This effacement of any differences between *dēśya* and *accha Telugu* is a crucial step for both Campbell and Ellis in enabling them to construct a new notion of foreignness within their system of language analysis. And their equation of both terms with "pure" Telugu sets up an inverse relationship between the purity of language on the one hand and its foreignness on the other. The notion of purity in relationship to language may, to the modern reader, appear unsurprising. Yet, it is important to clarify what the idea of a "pure" language assumes. For Ellis, Campbell, and certainly Brown, the more "foreign" words present in a language, the less "pure" and more "corrupted" it is.

But was this notion of purity also the concern of pre-colonial southern Indian grammarians? Thomas Trautmann has suggested that the emerging practices of historical and comparative linguistics of the late eighteenth and early nineteenth centuries drew heavily from the Sanskrit *vyākaraṇa* tradition in working out many of the principles used to account for the origins and development of contemporary differences in languages and cultures.[51] While this may be true, this is not the same as suggesting that a concern with origins was the primary focus of *vyākaraṇa* linguistic analyses. However, the comparative and historical linguistic theoretical frameworks influenced by Leibniz (1646–1716), Jones (1746–1794), Grimm (1785–1863), Rask (1787–1832), Bopp (1791–1867), and others were so compelling that once accepted it was difficult to view the models of analysis that predated them outside of this newly developing model. Thus, scholars like Campbell, Ellis, and Brown, influenced as they were by these emerging structures of knowledge, found it difficult to view the *vyākaraṇa* tradition outside of a historical linguistic framework.

As scholars of Sanskrit have recognized, the earliest understandings of Sanskrit (*samskṛt*) viewed it not as an isolated language, but as a register of refined language use that was highly manipulated and elaborated—the opposite pole on a continuum from natural, unmodified speech (*prākṛt*).[52] Daud Ali, for example, reminds us that the earliest "fully enunciated theory of 'Sanskrit' is to be found in an aesthetic rather than grammatical text," the *Nāṭyaśāstra*.[53] The *Nāṭyaśāstra* characterizes Sanskrit and Prakrit as different registers of refinement in speech—registers that could have been and often were used within a single context. Ali writes:

> According to the *Nāṭyaśāstra,* stage-recitation could be divided into two varieties of speech—"refined" (*samskṛta*) and "natural" (*prākṛta*). The central feature of refined speech was its adherence to phonetic and grammatical rules as set down in treatises on grammar. It was described with derivatives of the root *sam* + √*kṛ*, denoting something manipulated, refined, or even adorned to achieve a specific result. . . . [In contrast,] natural speech was *diverse and particular.* The *Nāṭyaśāstra* lists a variety of such ways of speaking (*prākṛtas*), each known by its region of origin—Māgadhī, Āvantī, Śauraseni, etc. . . . [T]hese forms of speech were associated with different social ranks, and like the postures and gaits in the drama, they reflected the essential qualities of the characters who spoke them. . . . [R]efined recitation was only to be used in the case of upper-caste males and heroes of different varieties, while natural recitation was to be assigned to women, people in disguise, Jains, ascetics, mendicants, jugglers, children, people possessed of low houses, transvestites, and women of low birth. . . . Śauraseni, for example, was spoken by heroines and courtly women while Magadhi was suitable for guards of the royal harem. Though each form of natural speech could function as a mode of communication in its own right, as a whole they were considered *less intelligible* (*gamakatva*) *and expressive* (*abhihitatva*) than refined speech.[54]

Recalling that Sanskrit and the Prakrits were once thought of as different registers of speech within a single linguistic context, and that they reflected different functions, degrees of refinement, and levels of intelligibility rather than different ethnic identities, helps us to see how the categories of southern Indian language analysis could once have been more concerned with describing levels of clarity and expressiveness than with establishing origins.

This view enables us to see *tatsama* and *tadbhava* as categories indicating not the pure origins of words and their level of corruption, but rather their general familiarity over the widest possible territory. Sheldon

Pollock reminds us of Sanskrit's use in inscriptions not only within the Indian subcontinent but as far afield as Burma, Thailand, Cambodia, Laos, Vietnam, Malaysia, and Indonesia, all "with a simultaneity that is again striking."[55] *Tatsama* words would have been recognizable over the largest possible area, and *tadbhava* terms, also responsive to the rules of grammar, would have been recognizable with some effort. *Dēśya* terms would have been recognizable over a much narrower range of territory, unfamiliar to elites living in distant places precisely because they cannot be derived via grammatical rules. The last category, *grāmya* terms, would have been the least recognizable of all, known only within a very localized region, and thus most inappropriate in literary compositions. Such an understanding also makes it difficult for us to find a central place for the notions of purity and corruption—so favored by Ellis, Campbell, and Brown—within precolonial *vyākaraṇa* understandings.

The term *accha tenugu* (also *accha Telugu*) has an equally dramatic history of changes in meaning. Current dictionaries define *accha tenugu* as "pure" or "unmixed" Telugu.[56] Yet what this has meant in practice has not always been constant. The earliest use appears in Ketana's thirteenth-century Sanskrit grammar of Telugu, *Āndhra Bhāṣā Bhūṣaṇamu.* Unlike most other grammarians examined, Ketana begins his discussion with five, rather than four, categories, introduced in the following order: "I will make known, each by itself, the five types called tatsama, tadbhava, accha tenugu, then dēśya and grāmya language."[57] However, there is little consensus over what Ketana actually meant by his use of the term *accha tenugu.* Writes Boddupalli Purushottam:

> Keetana [Kētana] confuses us in using this term. He uses the term *ačča tenugu* in between *tatsama* and *tadbhava* (verse 19) and spontaneously quotes examples. . . . He concludes by stating that words of this type, well-known to the people come under this category. But these are dēśyas. He does not seem to discriminate the two groups. All *dēśyas* are no doubt *ačča tenugu* but not vice-versa. Again he states in another verse (27) that except *tatsamas,* the four other categories, i.e., *tadbhavas, ačča tenugu, dēśyas* and *grāmyas* may be called *ačča tenugu* and creates further confusion.[58]

It is clear, however, that regardless of this confusion, for Ketana, "those words which are known to everyone are called accha tenugu."[59] The confusion over Ketana's thirteenth-century understanding of the term *accha tenugu* likely stems from the perspective from which we in the present have been inclined to read these categories—as descriptions of the origins of words, rather than as indexes of their comprehensibility and therefore literary appropriateness.

The sixteenth-century poet Ponnikanti Telaganna is generally considered the first poet to have composed in "pure" (*accha*) Telugu.[60] However, a fact frequently overlooked—particularly in an era when past evidence of continuous and pure Telugu identity is so strongly desired—is that what *accha tenugu* meant in the sixteenth century and what it means today are very different. In the sixteenth-century court of Malik Ibrahim Kutub Shah, the sultan of Golconda, where Ponnikanti Telaganna made his living, to compose in *accha tenugu* meant to avoid using any Sanskrit or Prakrit words.[61] Ponnikanti Telaganna freely used many Persian and other words today identifiable as "non-Telugu" in his *accha tenugu* poetry, calling into question more recent notions of *accha tenugu* as a pure language devoid of "foreign" terms. Appakavi, too, in the seventeenth century used the term *accha tenugu,* though not as a descriptive category for words. Instead, much as it is used in the sixteenth century, he used it to characterize literary works. Having defined and discussed *shuddhāndhrams* and *anyadēśajāndhrams,* his two sub-categories of *āndhradēśyams,* he goes on to state that "Those splended literary works that do not allow tatsamas and that mix tadbhavas and those three varieties of dēśyams which are called *kēvalāndhrams* [*shuddhāndhrams, anyadēśajāndhrams,* and *grāmyams*] are called *accha tenugu* in Telugu."[62] However, later authors, particularly British scholars, finding the term available to describe Telugu language use in some sort of "pure" state, use it not only to characterize literary texts, but also to categorize the words used within these texts.

By the nineteenth century, the notion of *accha tenugu* had begun to be positioned in a completely new way, as a sub-category of *dēśyam* in opposition to *anyadēśyam.* Although Pattabhirama Sastri does not use the term, he does use the term *āndhradēśyam* in roughly the same manner that Appakavi has used *shuddhāndhram,* which, along with *anyadēśyam,* make up the two subcategories of *dēśyam.* It is within this structural position that the term *accha* reappears. Ravipati Gurumurti Sastri, author of *Tenugu Vyākaraṇamu,* published in 1836, succeeded Pattabhirama Sastri as the head Telugu master at the College of Fort St. George following the latter's death in 1820. Gurumurti Sastri also begins his discussion of the categories used to analyze Telugu words by writing that "there are four kinds: dēsyamu, tatsamamu, tadbhavamu, and grāmyamu." He then elaborates on these categories in a way that reflects the influence of his British employers, writing that "There are two kinds of dēsyamu: acchadēsyam and anyadēśyam. Words of the Telugu region are acchadēśyams. Words of the Dravida, etc. regions which are used with Telugu cases are anyadēśyams."[63] Like his predecessor, Gurumurti Sastri also worked closely with British scholars and administrators. He is identified in the first edition of his grammar as a "servant of A. D. Campbell," and C. P. Brown credits Gurumurti Sastri in his 1840 essay.[64]

Two innovations in Gurumurti Sastri's grammar suggest he was impacted by conversations taking place at the College of Fort St. George (much more than Pattabhirama Sastri). First, he places *dēśyam* as the very first category in his list of four, as both Ellis and Campbell have done, and second, he characterizes *anyadēśya* terms as "words of the Dravida, etc. regions." Whereas Pattabhirama Sastri, writing in 1825, characterized the difference between *andhradēśya* and *anyadēśya* words in terms of their clarity and common familiarity throughout the Telugu-speaking regions, Gurumurti Sastri, in line with Campbell and Ellis, emphasizes their regional origins. With Gurumurti Sastri we see the present-day understandings of *acchadēśyam* (categorizing words of "pure" local Telugu origin) and *anyadēśyam* (indicating words with origins in "other regions") beginning to crystallize.

Brown is also troubled by the term *accha tenugu,* and here, too, European influences on local understandings of language are noticeable. In the 1857 edition of his grammar, Brown extends his definition of *dēśyamu* by including within it *accha tenugu,* which he describes as "'Pure Telugu' the name given to a dialect used more or less in all poems, wherein the author shuns Sanscrit words: or, if obliged to use them, softens the sound, changing Vishnu into Vennudu, &c."[65] Brown, in line with Appakavi, uses the term to describe a type of usage of Telugu rather than particular words. Five years earlier, in the first edition of his Telugu-English dictionary, Brown had defined *accha tenugu* as "Telugu without Sanskrit words."[66] However, by the 1903 second edition of his dictionary, edited after his death, *accha tenugu* had come to be defined as "Telugu without *foreign* words" (whether due to Brown or his later editors we do not know).[67]

Similarly, definitions for *dēśyam* likewise underwent a subtle shift in meaning between these two editions. In the 1852 first edition, Brown defined *dēśyam* as, "n.s. A dialect, obsolete or local expression. Idiom, provincialism. Adj. Idiomatic, provincial. . . . Desya words are those the root of which is unknown: many are used by the oldest and best poets. . . . Some are Sanskrit."[68] But by 1903, an era in which nationalist feelings had become well established, *dēśyam*—defined, as it now is, in opposition to the firmly established notion of the "foreign"—comes to be clearly and simply construed as "native." In the 1903 edition of Brown's dictionary, the definition of *dēśyam* given is "adj. Belonging to the country. *Native.* n. The language of a country, a vernacular; a vernacular term. *Desya words are opposed to foreign words.*"[69] The most curious feature of Brown's earlier 1852 definition of *dēśyam* is the very last line, indicating that some *dēśya* words are Sanskrit. Such an inclusion of Sanskrit words within the category of *dēśyam,* abandoned by 1903, makes sense only if we accept that the pre-colonial categories of *vyākaraṇa* analysis did not correspond to the discrete languages (e.g., Sanskrit, Telugu, Tamil, Persian) recognized today, but rather referred to some specific characteristic of language as used in practice, such as intelligibility or relationship to grammar. By the beginning of the twentieth century, a distinction between the universal and the particular or the codified and the uncodified had given way to a distinction between the foreign and the native. A new idea of the "foreign"—based not upon intelligibility, but solely upon origins—had become firmly established as the reference point for both *accha tenugu* and *dēśyam.*

New Categories of Language Classification

The descriptive categories discussed thus far do not easily map onto discrete "languages" as British scholars wanted to assume. This is significant in part because it suggests that what we identify today as discrete "languages"—Sanskrit, Telugu, Marathi, Tamil, English, Persian—though already present within discourse as recognizable terms and entities, were not necessarily the most significant categories in the analysis, organization, and even experience of linguistic knowledge. The categories used by pre-colonial Telugu *vyākaraṇa* texts do not refer to a discrete and bounded Telugu language, but rather are descriptive catalogues of the linguistic practices within a particular territory, used to evaluate the level of codification, appropriateness, and intelligibility of particular types of words within literary compositions. Colonial administrators sought to re-define languages in relation to the etymological origins of words and their historical changes over time, rather than in relation to the linguistic practices present in a particular place. For pre-colonial Indian grammarians of regional linguistic practices, some usages were recognized as more effective than others for particular purposes. All categories of language use—*tatsama, tadbhava, dēśya,* and *grāmya*—were seen as part of the language of the region. Where they differed was in the extent of their comprehensibility beyond the local. Although pre-colonial grammarians used these descriptive categories in a prescriptive manner to accept some usages as appropriate for use in literary compositions, it was only colonial grammarians who began to define some local usage as Telugu and other usage as "not Telugu."

In between the publication of his *Essay on the Language and Literature of the Telugus* in 1840 and the second edition of his *Grammar of the Telugu Language* in 1857, C. P. Brown published his 1854 *Miśra Bhāṣā Nighaṇṭu: Brown's Dictionary of Mixed Telugu.* An obsession with the purity of the Telugu language and his concern with expelling foreign words are obvious throughout his preface, despite his acknowledgment that this mixed language was what was most commonly used "in business, letters, and conversation."[70] Writes Brown, "To each word in the vocabulary I have appended a Telugu synonyme. This will aid those who wish to get rid of these foreign words. Perhaps one word in twenty may merit preservation. But in talking and writing Telugu we ought to avoid this mixed dialect."[71] Exactly why we ought to avoid the foreign words present in this "mixed" dialect, given that all of them are "current" and comprehensible among the populace, is, however, not explained. Perhaps it is to make it easier for scholars such as Brown to analyze the language into its constituent "source" languages, or for other Europeans to learn the language. Indeed, Brown comments that "due to the introduction of many foreign words into . . . the modern Telugu, . . . [t]he present vocabulary of the Mixed dialects therefore forms a requisite supplement to a Dictionary of the Telugu language: and it contains only those phrases which are current among the natives."[72] Ultimately rejecting mutual intelligibility and currency among the populace as the criteria for defining what should and should not be considered part of the language, Brown—like other British scholars of Telugu—opts for parameters based firmly in the origins of words. If its origin is foreign, it isn't really Telugu, suggests Brown, regardless of its currency within everyday speech and writing.

So it should not then be surprising that by 1903 a new classification of the elements of Telugu has been established along strictly historical linguistic lines, abandoning completely the pre-colonial categories we have been discussing thus far and settling instead for categories mapping directly onto what are today identifiable as discrete languages. The editors of the 1903 edition of Brown's Telugu-English dictionary collectively write:

> In the formation of modern Telugu, four strata are distinctly visible. The lowest of these consists of the pure Telugu element. . . . The second element . . . is that which has come from Sanskrit. . . . The third element . . . is that which has come from, or at least through, Hindustani. Under the term Hindustani we have included all Persian and Arabic words which have come into use in Telugu. . . . The fourth element is the English one.[73]

From a system of classification that grouped words according to their clarity, comprehensibility, and relationship to grammar, we have arrived at an analysis that breaks the language down into its source languages. Though obviously not exclusively responsible for the adoption of discrete languages as foundations for the reorganization of various forms of knowledge and the emergence of new linguistic identities within southern India during the twentieth century, the meta-linguistic movements discussed within this chapter have made available the categories through which not only language use in southern India but also literatures, histories, and even peoples are perceived and experienced today.

CHAPTER 4

From Pandit to Primer: Pedagogy and Its Mediums

The historical adventures of speaking do not form a continuum and so do not constitute a history of ideas. They are marked by breaks that in a single stroke can consign entire discourse networks to oblivion, and they have plateaus that make one forget the advance of armies and hours even during the winters of world wars.

—Friedrich Kittler, *Discourse Networks 1800/1900*

[E]very image of the past that is not recognized by the present as one of its own concerns threatens to disappear irretrievably.

—Walter Benjamin, "Theses on the Philosophy of History"

On November 22, 1820, Vennelakanty Subba Rao (Vennelacunty Soob Row), translator and interpreter in the Madras *Sudr* [High] Court, addressed a long letter to the newly formed Madras School Book Society, to which he had just been nominated as a member. In his letter he describes in detail existing educational practices within "the several subordinate provinces subject to the Presidency of Fort St. George" and offers suggestions for changes that "will tend to the general improvement of the knowledge of literature."[1] Yet when at the end of his ten-page letter he finally turns to his specific recommendations, his solution to what he sees as the existing educational problems is to recommend the publication of a list of books "for the better improvement, therefore, *of the knowledge of the several languages.*"[2] In moving from a proposal for the "general improvement of the knowledge of literature" in his first paragraph, to a solution prescribing "the better improvement . . . of the knowledge of the several languages" in the last paragraph, we have arrived at one of the most important sites of nineteenth-century educational intervention.

In proposing the improvement of language as the most valuable object of education, Subba Rao is signaling the fact that by the early decades of the nineteenth century the acquisition of linguistic competency simply through usage alone was no longer considered sufficient. Both colonial and local reformers were beginning to argue that systematic comprehensive knowledge of language—both grammar and meaning—was necessary as a basis for further education and training, and most importantly, as a foundation for doing things with language later on. In tracing this change it is tempting to suggest that nineteenth-century southern India witnessed a shift from language experienced primarily as a medium to an increased experience of language as an object. This may at first glance appear to be true, since we can certainly identify further evidence of a shift from experiencing language in use to thinking about it as a freestanding object of knowledge, abstractly divorced from actual usage. Yet such an assessment would not be wholly accurate, since a focus on language as a medium or, more precisely, on languages as separate and distinct mediums—each with advantages and disadvantages to be debated—was itself something new that emerged not long after the emphasis on language learning became an educational objective in its own right. It was not until the 1830s and the debates between the European Orientalists (who promoted the study of Indian classics through Indian languages as the primary media of instruction) and the Anglicists and utilitarians (who advocated the study of English literature through English as the medium of instruction) that the question of linguistic medium was extensively debated.[3] The focus of this chapter, then, is the emergence of language as a new object of attention and intervention. It explores the shift from learning language in use to learning languages as discrete and separate objects—a shift epitomized by the transition from pandits and schoolteachers to printed primers and textbooks as the central everyday organizing forces within educational practice in southern India.

In arguing that language became a new object in the early decades of the nineteenth century, I am not suggesting that languages within southern India had never before been recognizable prior to that time, or that people did not previously think of languages as discrete and distinguishable entities. Clearly they did. People learned to read, write, and speak specific languages, acquired skills to greater or lesser degrees in one or more, were proud or ashamed of those skills, even boasted about them and berated the skills of others. Languages could be—and were—listed, counted, inventoried, and analyzed. In referring to languages as new objects of pedagogical attention, then, I am not suggesting that languages had never before been thought of as objects. Instead, what I am arguing is that in learning and acquiring varied linguistic skills, the explicit goal of "learning language" was rarely the aim of formal or informal education. Linguistic competency came along the way—as a by-product of learning to do specific things with languages—reading, memorizing, reciting, writing accounts, composing letters, copying documents, keeping records, making proclamations, inscribing grants, or any of the other many things that people do with language. Sometimes this happened in a formal educational setting; more often it happened elsewhere. As Subba Rao astutely observed in 1820, "It may be admitted that a man acquires more knowledge of the language subsequently to his leaving school than prior thereto."[4] Much of what one needed to learn to do, one learned as and when—and most of all in the context where—it was required. And most importantly, in being acquired in use rather than as separate objects of knowledge, such skills were frequently specific to particular linguistic mediums. There was neither the need nor the desire to be able to do everything one could do in one language in every other language as well. In this sense, we can think of linguistic domains prior to the nineteenth century as complementary to one another. By the end of the nineteenth century, however, languages were increasingly viewed as parallel to one another, with the assumption that any function that could be performed in one language could also be performed in any other language equally well.

Such a subtle, but dramatic, transition from linguistic competencies acquired in use to languages acquired as objects may initially appear unlikely, especially given the overwhelming reality of the contemporary experiences of language within which most readers today live, and the careful reader will immediately seek out some historical example to try and disprove this suggestion. To support this argument, then, the remainder of this chapter explores the movement from pandit to primer as the central source of educational organization, agenda, and content. In examining this shift, I trace the displacement of the cultivation of memory as an effect of the emergence of printed storage media, particularly school textbooks and other printed books, demonstrating in the process exactly how language became a new object of pedagogical attention. I also explore the new role of "culture" within education that emerged in the twentieth century, and conclude by arguing that language not only provided a medium for the acquisition of that which was accepted in the twentieth century as "knowledge," but also began to act as a marker for cultural identification.

We have already seen in chapter 1 evidence of the new literate milieu characterized by Velcheru Narayana Rao, David Shulman, and Sanjay Subrahmanyam as *karaṇam* culture, which crystallized in southern India between the sixteenth and the eighteenth centuries. They argue that this culture marked a break with earlier forms of literate culture, consisting as it did of a "newly emerging middle-range group of graphically literate communities, who used writing as a medium not merely for preservation or recording but also for communication—perhaps for the first time in the history of southern India."[5] One of the central features of this culture was its polyglossia, with such individuals typically navigating multiple linguistic codes and scripts.[6] They quote the fifteenth-century poet Srinatha's praise of his patron as one of the earliest representations of the prototypical values possessed by this culture:

> Arabic, Turkish, Oriya, Kannaḍa, Telugu, Gandhari, Gujarati,
> Malayalam, the barbarous languages of the Śakas, Sind and Sauvira,
> the Karahāṭa language, and many other exotic tongues—
> Annaya of the Areti family had amazing control over them all in the assemblies.
> When Annaya sends letters on behalf of Ana Vema Reddi
> to the Sultan Ahmad Shah in Persian,
> his letters traced on paper are a festival for the eyes.[7]

Like the mid-sixteenth-century text cited in the introduction that declared the qualities of a good king to include being skilled "in the eight languages, which are Sanskrit, Prakrit, Shauraseni, Magadhi, Paishachi, Chulika, Apabhramsha, and Telugu," such representations demonstrate the value that was placed on an ability to control multiple linguistic domains, scripts, and functions.[8] To be skilled in the use of multiple linguistic domains was clearly an important value during this era of decentralized political organization, an era remembered for its absence of any single overarching political structure. In our current era, when literacy means the ability to read and write one's mother tongue, it is easy to forget that different relationships to language once existed.

It is not coincidental that the shift from the acquisition of multiple languages in the contexts and spaces of their use to an emphasis on learning the grammar of one "mother tongue" as a foundation for doing things with the language coincided with the advent of printing within southern India. Although often remarked upon, most accounts of the development of printing treat it primarily as an additive feature. Such portrayals fail to take seriously the ways in which printing transformed everyday experience, practices, relationships, and interactions. Attitudes toward language, definitions of accuracy and error, the functions of orality and memory, the meaning of truth and fiction, and the very role of "meaning" itself all underwent revolutionary changes in nineteenth-century southern India in conjunction with the introduction of printing. One of the sites most dramatically affected by printing was that of pedagogy. This chapter, then, examines the role of printing in reorienting pedagogy in southern India around the explicit acquisition of language. In doing so, I argue that printed textbooks did not simply replace the manuscripts which preceded them, but that they occasioned an entire restructuring of the meanings, practices, participants, goals, and agendas related to the process of becoming educated. Indeed, even what it meant to be "educated" had changed by the beginning of the twentieth century.

Pedagogy in Nineteenth-Century Southern India

A 1950 report on educational methods draws attention to twentieth-century attitudes toward the learned scholars or pandits associated with pre-modern forms of knowledge as the central source, repository, and organizer of the educational agenda. The report observes:

> The pandit's aim in mass education was a mixed one of moral and religious instruction, incidential [*sic*] imparting of information, and a considerable extent of entertainment and recreation. . . . In the case of his students, most of whom either lived with him or at least spent a large part of the day with him, the pandit's aim was one of communicating to them as much of his scholarship as he could, or chose according to his estimate of each individual student's capacity: the method of exposition the students learnt from their *guru* chiefly by observation and imitation. The teacher's aim is far different; it is

> one of developing in the children language "skills," such as control of sound by muscular effort, which concerns pronunciation, the intellectual work of "understanding" the content of a sentence, which concerns meaning, and above all the "purpose" or "intention" of writing, that is to say, the ability to achieve some end, such as persuasion which is a matter of motive and will. . . . Similarly, the teacher does not directly entertain his children; his aim is to enable children through their own reading to obtain entertainment and recreation.[9]

From the perspective of the twentieth century, the nineteenth-century pandit's goal was to communicate "as much of his scholarship as he could" to his students. His task was not to impart some externally defined educational agenda to his students. He himself was the agenda. Whatever he knew, he passed on to his students. In the next paragraph of the report, this difference is made even clearer: "From his students he expected ultimately *a stamp of his own scholarship.*"[10] To twentieth-century eyes, the goal of the pandit appeared to be the replication of himself in his students. The pandit was the repository of the knowledge his students would learn. His memory was the location of storage, his own knowledge the definition of what was to be taught, and his oratory the medium. Whatever language competencies the pandit possessed, in whichever languages and scripts he knew, he in turn passed on to his students. Books, or manuscripts if they were available, were incidental and certainly defined neither the goal nor the method of evaluating a student's education.

Second, "the students learnt from their *guru* chiefly by observation and imitation." To twentieth-century sensibilities it appeared that the pandit gave little attention to how his students learned. Building "skills" to use in life, laying a foundation for later self-education or employment, and even the level of comprehension of the meaning of what students were taught were not the focus of the pandit's agenda. According to the report,

> The pandit was only in a general way concerned with the ultimate results of his teaching. In the case of the masses to whom he expounded a theme his immediate concern was a good reception—the creation of an effective impression. This needed a technique of judicious display of his skill and knowledge without altogether boring his audiences while entertaining them. The skillful pandit built with words a picture as vivid as one on the modern cinema screen. His reputation as well as his material reward depended on the impression he made.[11]

The pandit, himself gifted with language, used his own words to educate his students.

In contrast, the report views the teacher's agenda as one of cultivating "skills," and most significantly, skills in the effective use of language. It explicitly states, "The teacher's aim is far different [from the pandit's]; it is one of developing in the children language 'skills.'" Although the pandit may have been gifted in his own use of language—be it in some combination of Sanskrit, Telugu, Tamil, Marathi, or any other language—he was not explicitly concerned with encouraging the linguistic skills of his students, at least not separately from his other aims. To the extent that he himself was skilled with language, he wanted to make over his students in his own image, but imitation and observation were the methods employed, placing the responsibility on the students. Language was never singled out as an explicit object of knowledge. But the teacher in twentieth-century schools, the report continues, "has to test his pupils at every stage of their attainments and progress towards the different aims he has set to achieve. For his emoluments he is not dependent on the 'impression' he creates nor on the amount of learning he displays; he receives a fixed salary and his work and the group amidst which he works are also well-defined."[12] As objects of knowledge themselves, specific language skills, in a specific language, had become targets of testing and evaluation. The agenda of the twentieth-century schoolteacher was not simply to replicate himself, but rather to achieve a certain externally defined agenda, one often laid out in textbooks, even if the availability of textbooks was limited and a school possessed only a single copy.

Vennelakanty Subba Rao, the translator and interpreter with whom this chapter opened, made strikingly similar critiques of educational practices more than a century earlier. Judging from the above 1950 report's use of the past tense when referring to the pandit, and Subba Rao's own future-oriented proposals for change in 1820, we can think of the two as situated on opposite ends of what lies between them. Born in a village near Ongole (in what is today Prakasam District of Andhra Pradesh) in 1784, Subba Rao occupied a wide range of official positions in the service of the East India Company and its English administrators from the age of fifteen onward, holding titles as various as writer, head writer, *munshee* (scribe), accountant, translator, and interpreter. He died in 1839, just short of his fifty-fifth birthday. In addition to his writings for the Madras School Book Society, Subba Rao also left behind a very unusual journal, detailing the life, family history, education, travels, and employment of an early-nineteenth-century

Brahmin civil servant, which his son, Vennelacunty Venkata Gopal Row, a district munsiff at Trivellore, arranged to have published in 1873.[13]

A prominent theme throughout his journal is Subba Rao's concern with the improvement of, as he puts it, "education among the natives, my countrymen."[14] And central to this project of improvement is the introduction of grammar into the school curriculum. Number one on the list of recommended texts Subba Rao suggests need to be produced and encouraged by the Madras School Book Society are "abridgments of the existing Telugu, Tamil, Canada [Kannada] and Mahratta [Marathi] Grammars written in prose and explained in the modern languages."[15] He complains at length in both his journal and in his letter to the School Book Society about the lack of attention given in schools to the knowledge of grammar:

> It is very much to be lamented that neither the Grammar nor any books of morals are taught to students in this country in the earlier part of their study in schools. The study of these books would, beyond all doubt, render the education accomplished, and it is entirely owing to this omission that we often find grammatical errors in the native writings and correspondence. The study of the Grammar *in every language* would appear absolutely necessary for perfectness and while such very foundation is neglected, how is it possible that any correct knowledge of a language can be expected? . . . [G]enerally his whole acquirements are by no means perfect, for, in the very beginning of his education, he is not educated as he ought. The imperfectness now stated is entirely attributable to the negligence of studying the Grammar and the chief Books of morality.[16]

Although he goes on to make a list of other books he feels would be of benefit in schools—including books of moral tales and mathematics written "in prose in the modern tongues"—it is clear that it is the introduction of the study of grammar into schools that he feels would most improve education in the region.[17]

Subba Rao's critiques of existing practices and his proposals for introducing new textbooks, shaped as they were by his own experience in service to the colonial administration, anticipate the observations made by the colonial administrator A. D. Campbell several years later. Campbell—remembered most for his grammar of the Telugu language, first published in 1816 for the use of English civil servants learning Indian languages—also took a keen interest in local education. He was critical of the ways in which the East India Company's economic policies had diminished native education during the second half of the eighteenth and early part of the nineteenth centuries and was a strong advocate of greater company involvement in opening and supporting local schools. In 1823, while serving as the collector for Bellary District, Campbell submitted a report entitled "On the State of Education of the Natives in Southern India" in which he was particularly emphatic in his demonstration of the ways in which policies of the colonial East India Company had seriously eroded the quality and prevalence of education within the Madras Presidency. "Imperfect, however, as the present education of the natives is," writes Campbell, "there are few who possess the means to command it for their children."[18] It has not always been this way, he continues, writing that today "of nearly a million souls in this district, not 7,000 are now at schools. . . . In many villages where formerly there were schools, there are now *none;* and in many others where there were large schools, now only a few children of the most opulent are taught, others being unable, from poverty, to attend, or to pay what is demanded." The state of education in the Madras Presidency of the 1820s was then newly impoverished—a clear result of the economic policies of the colonial administration. Campbell reports that the low percentage of children receiving formal education and the limited number of years they remained in school were a direct result of the introduction of the cheap cottons from the newly industrialized mills of Manchester, the changing impact of the company's military forces on the demand for grain, the extraction of capital, and rigid policies of revenue collection. In short, concludes Campbell, it is because of the British that "[t]he greater part of the middling and lower classes of the people are now unable to defray the expenses incident upon the education of their offspring, while their necessities require the assistance of their children as soon as their tender limbs are capable of the smallest labour."[19]

Like Subba Rao, Campbell was also concerned about the lack of appropriate books specifically addressing "the principles of the vernacular languages themselves." After listing the Ramayana, the Mahabharata, and the Bhagavad Gita, the three texts he found in manuscript form in almost every school, and a number of less common texts read in a few schools for "religious purposes or amusement," he writes:

> The books on the principles of the vernacular languages themselves, are the several dictionaries and grammars, such as the *Nighantoo* [dictionary or lexicon], *Umara* [Amara Kosha], *Subdamumburee,*

> *Shubdeemunee Durpana, Vyacurna* [Vyākaraṇa], *Andradeepecva, Andranamasungraha, &c. &c.,* but these last and similar books *which are most essential,* and without which no accurate or extensive knowledge of the vernacular languages can be attained, are, from the high price of manuscripts and the general poverty of the masters, of all books the most uncommon in the native schools, and such of them as are found are, in consequence of the ignorance, carelessness and indolence of copyists in general, full of blunders, and in every way most incorrect and imperfect. . . . It is not to be wondered at, with such imperfect education, that in writing a common letter to their friends, orthographical errors and other violations of grammar, may be met with in almost every line written by a native.[20]

Campbell agreed with Subba Rao that of all the (manuscript) books, those concerned with language were the least commonly found in local schools. And the result of this failure to study the language properly at the most basic level, claim both of these men, is imperfect education.

Both Subba Rao and Campbell also bemoan the lack of qualifications among existing teachers in local schools and their general failure and inability to convey necessary skills to their students. "It is true," writes Subba Rao, referring to the very short list of manuscripts commonly found in schools, "that the boys read the aforesaid books in the school, but they do not understand any part of their meaning, for the teacher himself hardly knows it. The reading of the books, therefore, is obviously to no other purpose than to obtain a steadiness and general practice of reading any paper, letter, accounts, &c."[21] Campbell echoes this, writing, "The chief defects in the native schools are the nature of the books and learning taught, and the want of competent masters."[22] Most teachers, argues Campbell, are capable only of instructing students in the pronunciation and memorization of syllables but do not understand the meaning of what they teach:

> Indeed few teachers can explain, and still fewer scholars understand the purport of the numerous books which they thus learn to repeat from memory. Every schoolboy can repeat *verbatim* a vast number of verses, of the meaning of which he knows no more than the parrot that has been taught to utter certain words. Accordingly, from studies in which he has spent many a day of laborious but fruitless toil, the native scholar gains no improvement, except the exercise of memory and the power to read and write on the common business of life; he makes no addition to his stock of useful knowledge, and acquires no moral impressions.[23]

Both Subba Rao and Campbell, then, advocate first and foremost the development and publication of simplified books that will assist in the improvement of not just language but "the several languages" explicitly. "For the better improvement, therefore, of the knowledge of the several languages, I most submissively beg leave to recommend the publication of the undermentioned books to be printed and disposed of for a moderate price to be fixed by the Society," concludes Subba Rao in his 1820 letter to the Madras School Book Society.[24] "The Government," agrees Campbell, "could not promote the improved education of their native subjects in these districts more than by patronizing versions, in the common prose and spoken dialect, of the most moral parts of their popular poets and elementary works, now committed to memory in unintelligible verse. He who could read would then understand what he reads, which is far from the case at present."[25] According to early-nineteenth-century educational reformers, if the pandit could not make his students achieve an understanding of what they read, then the introduction of appropriate textbooks was needed to produce this result.

Printing in the Madras Presidency

The shift from pandit to primer as the organizing principle of educational content cannot be viewed outside of the larger historical conditions of the nineteenth century. Christian missionary activity, administrative decisions made by both the British Parliament and the East India Company's Board of Control, the new demands of colonial employment, the advent of printing in southern India, and the establishment of educational and literary societies all had effects on educational practice in the Madras Presidency and on experiences of language. It is not surprising that this new focus on the language and learning of "the natives" occurred shortly after the passage of the British Parliament's Charter Act of 1813, which not only extended the East India Company's charter for an additional twenty years, but also for the first time made England responsible for the education of its native subjects. In obligating the company to adopt measures "as may tend to the introduction among them of useful knowledge, and of religious and moral improvement," the Charter Act ushered in a new colonial agenda.[26]

That local reformers should take up an emphasis upon language as the most effective means for improving local education at this particular historical moment is cause to reflect, especially given the slowness with which the East India Company administration manifested its interest in "native education" in actual practice. Although language was already heavily emphasized by colonial administrators as a primary object of education by the second decade of the nineteenth century, this was an agenda almost exclusively directed toward the benefit of civil servants newly arrived from England and had little direct impact on native education. The College of Fort St. George was established in Madras by the East India Company in 1812, with two main objectives: "to apply the zealous and undivided attention of the junior civil servants to the study of the native languages, and to correct the preference formerly given to the study of such of those languages as are least useful to the public service," particularly Sanskrit and Arabic.[27] Despite the 1813 Charter Act's new emphasis on native education as a concern of the East India Company, native education did not become a serious target of British attention until more than a decade later. And the question of language as it pertained to native education (most centrally the question of whether English or vernacular mediums were most appropriate) was not heavily debated until the 1830s, leading up to Governor-General William Bentinck's English Education Act of 1835. The act finally established English as the medium of instruction in government-supported Indian educational institutions. Yet Subba Rao's letter is evidence that local reformers felt that language was the key to improving education not just for newly arriving young civil servants from England but also for local students, long before language within Indian education became a colonial preoccupation.

There were other forces afoot, as well. The early decades of the nineteenth century also saw the use of printing presses spread beyond the printing of single-sheet forms, proclamations, and pamphlets (to which printing had been restricted during the second half of the eighteenth century), to the printing of periodicals and books. The first printing press in Madras was acquired during the British siege of French-controlled Pondicherry in 1761 and carried to Madras.[28] Because the East India Company administrators were not interested in maintaining the press, they gave it to missionaries of the Society for the Promotion of Christian Knowledge (SPCK) in Vepery, on the outskirts of Madras town, where it could be used by the missionaries whenever it was not needed for official jobs.[29] Initially, the press seems to have been little used for the printing of books. As B. S. Kesavan has written, the press was used primarily for "proclamations and such for the Company, alphabets and calendars for the missionaries."[30] Some of the printed items that have been preserved from this period are "a single-sheet powers of attorney in English and a page of herbal remedies in Portuguese, both from 1764," and a calendar for 1767.[31] Graham Shaw has found evidence that Francis W. Ellis, who was at the time employed by the Madras Mint, may have been the first to prepare a set of Telugu type in 1800. But similarly to the way in which the earliest English typesetting was used only for government forms, bills of credit, and flyers, Ellis apparently used his Telugu type in November of 1800 to prepare two thousand copies of a "Government advertisement respecting inoculation."[32] No copies have survived. Katharine Smith Diehl has also suggested that unlike the College of Fort William in Calcutta, which had a variety of independent printers it could rely upon, the government at Fort St. George in Madras was more limited in its options. She argues that much of the government's early printing was done by the Orphan Asylum Press (also referred to as the Madras Male Asylum Press, or simply the Asylum Press) in Egmore, Madras.[33] It is not clear exactly when the Government of Madras first acquired and began using a press of its own under its own name.[34] However, in 1812, the same year that the College of Fort St. George was established by the Madras government, money was also made available for the establishment of a college press.[35] A. D. Campbell's *A Grammar of the Teloogoo Language,* one of the first books printed by the College Press, was published in 1816. Yet these earliest printing efforts were intended not for the education of the native population of Madras Presidency but to assist in the education of the East India Company's civil servants who had just arrived from England.

It was not until 1820 and the formation of the Madras School Book Society that efforts first began to be directed toward the production of schoolbooks for use by local students. These efforts were initially supported primarily through donations and subscriptions from private Europeans, many of whom were also civil servants; the government was not yet officially involved in the publication of textbooks for native education, their priority being textbooks for use by European civil servants acquiring vernacular languages. In 1826, Thomas Munro, then governor of the Madras Presidency and a supporter of native education, allocated Rs. 700 a month to the School Book Society specifically for the printing of textbooks to be used for native education and for the salaries of teachers willing to prepare them.[36] In bemoaning the existing lack of adequate teachers and schools,

Munro writes: "Teachers, in general, do not earn more than six or seven rupees monthly, which is not enough to induce men properly qualified to follow the profession. It may also be said, that the general ignorance of the teachers themselves is one cause why none of them draw together a large body of scholars."[37] Despite the shift that Munro's financial commitment may mark, Gauri Viswanathan has pointed out that "political philosophy and cultural policy converged to work toward clearly discernible common ends" during the first two and a half decades of the nineteenth century, making this period of British rule appear "as a period of relative inactivity in education."[38] The actions taken in the first half of the 1820s to reform the teaching of language in native schools were a combination of local and private European initiative and were not yet under official patronage of the East India Company administration.

The proposal that primers be introduced to compensate for the inadequacies of pandits, then, dates almost from the earliest days of book publishing in Madras. Yet the appearance in southern India of printing was also responsible for introducing new options that made pandits—and their pedagogy—subject to a comparison that had never before occurred—indeed, it could never before have occurred. Without printing and the possibility of primers that printing enabled, the scrutiny to which southern Indian educational practices, and language in particular, became subject could not have been imagined—either under conditions of colonialism or otherwise. Substituting or supplementing pandits with textbooks created the appearance of inadequacy where none had earlier been perceived. Textbooks then, became the "other" of pandits, the other that made them appear to be different from what they were not. "The study of these books would, beyond all doubt, render the education accomplished," wrote Subba Rao in 1820, "and it is entirely owing to this omission that we often find grammatical errors in the native writings and correspondence."[39] Textbooks would improve the quality of students' language usage where pandits had failed—a failure never before recognized before the advent of printing.

Early Telugu Primers

One of the earliest primers—and certainly the most popular for many subsequent decades—was *Bāla Śikṣa* [A Child's Primer]. First compiled around 1832, hardly a decade after the establishment of the Madras School Book Society, *Bāla Śikṣa* was followed by an enlarged edition in 1865, entitled *Pedda Bāla Śikṣa* [Expanded Child's Primer].[40] It is this expanded version, more comprehensive than *Bāla Śikṣa,* which is remembered with nostalgia by many speakers of Telugu in Andhra today. For generations of schoolchildren, having "read *Pedda Bāla Śikṣa*" was equivalent to having gained an education. This single volume contained the most important knowledge that was thought necessary for schoolchildren to learn at the most basic level. While I was doing fieldwork in Hyderabad, a thirty-five-year-old friend there once remarked that when he was growing up, elders would often ask (in Telugu), "Have you learned *Pedda Bāla Śikṣa?*" Inevitably he and the other children would nod and say yes, they had, even though by their time *Pedda Bāla Śikṣa* was no longer used in the schools my friend and his contemporaries attended.

Even as children my friend and his contemporaries knew enough to equate having studied *Pedda Bāla Śikṣa* with having acquired an education, and they were embarrassed to admit that they hadn't read it, an admission synonymous with acknowledging their ignorance and lack of education. My friend's sixty-year-old mother, however, vividly remembered studying *Pedda Bāla Śikṣa,* and could still recite most of its contents from memory.[41] Clearly the printed textbook had been made synonymous with education, but at the same time, it also completely refigured the structure of selection, storage and transmission of what was considered knowledge. In effect, it changed what people viewed as knowledge itself. In 1820, Subba Rao could write that "when a young man is to be married, the parents of the bride examine him in some instances whether he is a good reader of books, or not; and when they find him in the affirmative, they feel a complete satisfaction and are proud that their son-in-law is a clever reader." He wrote this in 1820 with the clear assumption that the young man's future in-laws would be proud at the correct pronunciation and fluency with which the young man read aloud, regardless of his comprehension or lack thereof of what he was reading. But within the next few decades, such pride-inducing talents were no longer sufficient to even be recognized as skills.

With printing one could suddenly do things with language never before imagined, and skills that had formerly been impressive ceased to impress. Even more significantly, disciplines previously crucial to the preservation of knowledge—not only pronunciation, but also such abilities as the cultivation of memory—could be abandoned or reframed as mere entertainment with impunity. Although introduced to compensate for the inadequacies of existing pandits, the effect of textbooks was much greater than a simple substitution (for manuscripts or for pandits) or addition within an otherwise static system. It didn't simply produce more of something that had previously already been available in manuscript form. Instead, it caused a reorganization of the very nature of education. Printing produced, structured, stored, and transmitted data in new ways, affecting not only notions of what constituted knowledge but also specific practices at each stage of acquisition, circulation, and retrieval. Printing created access to a new corpus of materials never before standardized at the primary level of education and changed educational objectives by placing emphasis on new skills and competencies. It also revolutionized methods of transmission of these materials and skills to students and dramatically altered notions of correctness and error.

At the time that they were proposed, the educational reforms of the nineteenth century and the values (if not the motives) expressed by their advocates appeared to many as self-evident and worth championing. The acquisition of "meaningful knowledge" quite suddenly became an urgent agenda, making existing educational practices appear in comparison as nothing more than "fruitless toil." A scholar once lauded for a prodigious memory was now inadequate in only being able to "repeat *verbatim* a vast number of verses, of the meaning of which he knows no more than the parrot that has been taught to utter certain words."[42] This was the dominant view held by both members of the local intelligentsia like Subba Rao and by colonial officials like Campbell. For these early-nineteenth-century critics and for us today it is difficult to imagine what a pre-print perspective on the world would have felt like. No one has ever seriously advocated a return to that "fruitless toil," and the reason for this is simply that such toil cannot and does not appear "fruitless" until the introduction of printing. Only then does it become possible to imagine the practice of memorization as a waste of time.

Śikṣa: From Sound to Meaning

There is no better example of this than the changes that occurred in the meaning of the term *śikṣa* itself. Used in the title of *Pedda Bāla Śikṣa, śikṣa* means not only instruction or education, but also discipline, correction, or punishment. However, one of its earliest known usages refers to a treatise that teaches correct pronunciation of the language of the Vedas. The emphasis on correct pronunciation, with no particular attention to meaning or comprehension, embedded as it is as one of the earliest meanings of *śikṣa,* is a value that came to be reviled by nineteenth-century educational reformers. To these nineteenth-century enthusiasts, the value placed on correct pronunciation for its own sake, independent of an understanding of meaning, was incomprehensible and appeared a misplaced emphasis. Yet to a member of a pre-print discursive network, where even handwritten manuscripts were somewhat rare, expensive, inconsistent, and impermanent, subject as they were to the vagaries of weather, insects, and age, such a value was crucial to the preservation and transmission of knowledge (regardless of whatever we may today think of that knowledge and the societal inequities it may have produced or reinforced). A memorized text, however, once gained, could not be taken away, destroyed, lost, or stolen and could be passed on to a young scholar in the same way it was acquired.

The significance of this pre-print emphasis on memory was brought home to me in August 2000, while I was doing fieldwork in Hyderabad. Heavy rains had flooded the library of the Sundarayya Vignana Kendram (SVK), a non-profit institution established in 1988 in memory of P. Sundarayya, freedom fighter, Communist leader, and popular hero of the Telangana peasant uprising of the 1940s. This library holds an outstanding collection of Telugu and Urdu books, a collection I had already used extensively, and the news of the complete submersion of the library in the worst rains Hyderabad had seen in forty-six years was devastating. Given that the building that housed the library was built only in the late 1980s, in a neighborhood that had not yet been settled forty-six years ago, no one had anticipated the possibility of flooding. Even worse, the space designated for the library was actually a partial basement, much of it below the street level. Over the years, SVK had become a popular destination for the private libraries of Telugu scholars upon their deaths, and the library's accumulation of entire lives' worth of scholarship had made it one of the richest Telugu collections in modern Andhra. A comment made following the flood by a fellow scholar of southern Indian literature that "there's no substitute in the end for memorizing all the classical literature and carrying it in your head," brings into relief the fact that an analysis of cultural practices must not ignore the ways in which access to and incorporation of particular technologies have made specific practices possible.[43]

How is it, then, that certain practices central to the storage and preservation of knowledge, like the cultivation of memory or an emphasis on correct pronunciation, can suddenly be thought of as a waste of time? To answer this question, let us turn to the ways in which printed media—books, journals, reference works, and periodicals—replaced the need for the cultivation of memory. If the memory of the pandit provided the method of selection and storage for what was conveyed to the next generation of scholars, then the printed book almost completely superseded the pandit. Given the cost and rarity of manuscript books in southern India at the beginning of the nineteenth century, their use in classrooms was irregular at best, frequently restricted to what Campbell regarded as a few "incorrect and imperfect" error-ridden texts. Ram Raz, another member of the Madras School Book Society, reflected upon his own experiences with memorized manuscript knowledge in an 1824 report entitled "A Short Sketch of the State of Education among the Natives at Bangalore":

> The first book which the boys are taught is the *Bālarāmāyanam,* the abstract history of Rāma, taken from the Sanscrit Rāmāyana by Vālmici, and written in Telugu characters. . . . It is distressing to hear the erroneous sentences, the vitiated orthography, and the wrong pauses, with which the children are taught to read this book in a Telugu school; nor can it be expected otherwise, while the manuscript copies from which they read are full of errors, and the masters and the scholars are equally ignorant of the meaning. . . . When the scholars have committed Bālarāmāyanam to memory, which, though it contains no more than a hundred stanzas, yet takes to many of them six months [*sic*]. They then proceed to learn the whole or a part of the *Amara-Cōsā,* a lexicon of the Sanscrit language in blank verse, consisting of three cāndās or parts. . . . This also, they commit to memory from an incorrect copy, and for my own part, it cost me a great deal of trouble, when I first entered on the study of Sanscrit, to correct the errors with which I had learnt this work in my early age at school.[44]

J. Mangamma tells the story of the preparation of the first printed version of this last text mentioned by Ram Raz, the *Amara Kosha,* printed in Serampore in 1808. "On the establishment of the College of Fort William [in Calcutta]," she writes, "efforts were made to secure a good dictionary of Sanskrit and the *Amara cosha* was selected. Colebrooke, being a Sanskrit scholar, was asked to make the work useful for the students learning the language. He used not less than half a dozen copies in original." She goes on to describe the manuscripts he consulted in preparing the first printed edition of the *Amara Kosha:*

> One was a transcript collated with a copy in Devanagari which had been carefully examined by Sir William Jones. Jones had inserted an English interpretation in it. The second was a transcript in Devanagari character with a commentary and notes in the Canara dialect. It contained numerous passages unnoticed in the most approved commentaries. A third copy used by him was one in Devanagari character with a brief and imperfect interpretation in Hindi. The fourth was a copy in Bengali characters, while the fifth was with a Sanskrit commentary by one Rama Sarma. When necessary, Colebrooke also referred to copies from local people.[45]

Each of the copies he consulted was different, not only in the "errors" it contained, but also in script and language of commentaries, as well as its inclusion or exclusion of many specific passages, reminding us that within a manuscript tradition, texts could be and were easily adapted, condensed, or expanded for specific uses within particular contexts.

Each time a manuscript was copied it was copied for a particular person and was usually created with a very specific audience in mind (often the copyist himself or herself). As a researcher, my own field notebooks come to mind as an example of this process, as I think about how many times I copy extracts from books that I have read, interspersing them with my own comments. I copy only those portions that I anticipate might be useful to me, or which move or inspire me, and I frequently frame and position them in new ways, using them toward my own ends. In an era of not only printing but also photocopying, scanning, and computers, this analogy with the production of manuscripts can only be of limited use. However, we can be sure that what appeared to Ram Raz as "errors" in 1824 would have been nearly impossible to perceive had he not later been able to consult a printed version of the same text in which pains had been taken to compare several versions, rather than simply recopying the most conveniently available single manuscript. C. P. Brown, famous for having prepared manuscripts for printing by assembling "upwards of a dozen manuscript versions" of a single text along with a group of local language scholars to adjudicate the multiple versions, epitomizes this post-print equation of "variation" with "error." Encountering an overwhelming array of differences between the many manuscript versions of what were thought of as the same text, Brown could only declare that they "swarmed with errors."[46] Printing, and in particular the process of comparing multiple manuscript copies of a text in order to prepare an authoritative printed version, introduced possibilities never previously made available, bringing certain comparisons into relief that could not previously have been perceived. Knowledge once learned, skills previously acquired, and variations that once were difficult even to recognize, all appeared differently to critics with the advent of printing.

Memory: From Practice to Performance

In his 1910 autobiography, Kandukuri Viresalingam, the author of the Biographical History of Andhra Poets [*Āndhra Kavula Charitramu*] we met in chapter 2, describes in great detail his virtuosity in *aṣṭāvadhānam,* or the art of attending to eight [*aṣṭa*] different matters simultaneously.[47] The passage appears rather unexpectedly in the middle of a chapter relating the early stages of his work as a teacher and journalist from 1870 to 1880, and more specifically it is framed within an account of his establishment of the monthly Telugu journal *Vivēka Vardhini,* first published in 1874. Central to his concerns within the journal is an agenda of social reform. It is therefore puzzling why such a description of his skill in the performance of memory should appear here, immediately preceded as it is by a description of his efforts at advocating women's education and establishing schools for girls and followed immediately by his recollection of a campaign "to curb immorality in the higher classes." He writes:

> In those days I could compose verse extempore, with the same facility with which I delivered talks in prose. So some friends in Dhowleswaram desired that I should hold a session in *Ashtāvadhānam,* and I held one shortly afterwards, in a private house, before a few friends. Though it was my first effort, it seemed to fill them all with wonder and admiration.
>
> The same day, news of the performance spread in the town, and the officials of the place, who could not attend it for lack of notice, most earnestly requested that I should repeat the performance and in a public place [*bahiranga-sthalamu*], where they might all attend. So I promised to do so the following week in our school.[48]

Telugu scholars particularly adept at *avadhānam,* "the skill of remembering many different matters," often had the suffix "*-avadhānulu*" appended to their names.[49] As a demonstration of technical virtuosity, the evocation of wonder and admiration Viresalingam suggests it provoked further elevated a value essential to the preservation and transmission of knowledge within pre-print society in southern India. Viresalingam continues his account with a detailed description of the specific activities in which he simultaneously engaged when performing this display:

> The items in it were:
>
> 1. *Versification:* In this, I responded to ten people and gave them ten verses on the themes they suggested and in the meter they prescribed, letter by letter.
> 2. *Vyastakshari:* This item dealt with two passages, one in Telugu and the other in Sanskrit, each consisting of thirty-two letters. The letters were numbered, then cut into separate pieces, mixed up and given to me without any order, from time to time, while I was engaged with other items in the *Avadhānam.* In the end I put all the letters together mentally, in their proper sequence and delivered the two passages correctly.
> 3. *Nishēdākshari:* In this, I had to abstain from using the forbidden letters in each line, and compose a verse, letter by letter.
> 4. *Samasyā Pooranam:* In this, keeping in mind a given line, I composed line by line, in the midst of the *Avadhānam,* a verse into which the *samasya* line fit perfectly.
>
> 5, 6, and 7. *Chess, Cards, and Conversation:* While attending to items 1 to 4, I had to engage also in a game of chess, in a game of cards, and in holding conversation in a cogent and consistent way, all simultaneously.
>
> 8. *Counting Flowers:* While attending to all of the items mentioned above, I kept count also of the flowers that were thrown at my back from behind, one at a time, and at varying intervals of time.[50]

Viresalingam comments on his *avadhānam* performance: "It was a mighty feat of concentration, but lay people and ignorant people attributed it to black magic and thought, in spite of my friends' assurances to the contrary, that I was a devotee of some dark spirits." Following his performance, Viresalingam tells us that he gave one more at the insistence of friends but then decided thereafter to refuse further demands. He concludes the episode by asserting, "I realized then that it was only entertainment to fill idle moments and brought no real benefit either to the world or to me. So however much people begged of me afterwards, I refused to repeat a performance which entailed so much strain on my intellect and at the same time benefitted no one."[51]

Why should Viresalingam suddenly choose to disavow what had been viewed until then as one of the most accomplished demonstrations of a skill highly valued by society, promising never again to engage in what he now saw as a useless activity? And why at this particular moment? Positioned as it is in the midst of an account of his earliest publishing activities, we might initially be confused by his inclusion of the episode in this particular location within his larger narrative, as well as by his sudden change of view. By way of comparison, let us juxtapose Viresalingam's discussion of *avadhānam* with the roughly contemporaneous discussion of U. V. Swaminatha Iyer, who writes in his autobiography:

> On several occasions, the experts in *avatāṇam* arrived in the monastery to exhibit their skills. Their range would extend from eight to sixteen to thirty-two or even one hundred simultaneous tasks. Watching such feats with amazement we felt a desire to cultivate the art of *avatāṇam* ourselves. We practiced. Then one day I performed the feat in the gathering of my fellow-students and my pupils. Some of those present indicated a line of poetry for incorporation in a stanza. Some asked for the clarification of their doubts. Some quoted old poems for me to repeat. Some set problems in arithmetic. I gave to all these the proper answers. The one gift necessary for *avatāṇam* is an unfailing memory. . . . Thus involved in the composition of poems often, my ability to compose poems improved. This made others happy, and I got more and more encouragement.[52]

Although not precisely dated, both Swaminatha Iyer and Viresalingam describe events in the mid- to late 1870s, yet their contexts and attitudes are strikingly different. Although Viresalingam gives us no history of the practice or the context in which he learned to perform *avadhānam,* his description suggests that the practice has been moved from one context to a new one—from a private home to a public venue [*bahiranga-sthalamu*]. And furthermore, his claim that the audience included "lay people and ignorant people" who "attributed it to black magic and thought . . . that I was a devotee of some dark spirits" suggests that the practice had been extended to a new audience, beyond its original context of practice, and was being newly experienced by groups of people who had never before seen or heard of the practice.

In Swaminatha Iyer's description, *avatāṇam* was restricted to the context of the monastery in which he was both a teacher and a student. Although experts came from outside the monastery to perform, their performances spurred younger scholars like Swaminatha Iyer to practice in emulation of their elders. The value each writer placed on the practice could also not be more different. Whereas Viresalingam concludes by remarking that "it was only entertainment to fill idle moments and brought no real benefit either to the world or to me," Swaminatha Iyer concludes with the remark that "[t]hus involved in the composition of poems often, my ability to compose poems improved."

The key to understanding this puzzling passage in Viresalingam's autobiography lies, I believe, in the fact that Viresalingam was not only an educational reformer but also one of the earliest owners of a printing press in Coastal Andhra. Both of these factors positioned Viresalingam uniquely to recognize the ways in which printing was altering the value of cultivating memory. Viresalingam's journal, *Vivēka Vardhini,* was initially published in Madras, since in 1874 when he started the journal there was no printing press in the Coastal Andhra town of Rajahmundry where he lived (see Map 5, p. 40). In 1875 he was able to purchase a press with the help of five other partners, three of whom were powerful local merchants.[53] In 1875–76, this press was one of only four printing presses in the entire district of Godavari and the only one in the town of Rajahmundry.[54] Since the press was kept in Viresalingam's home, he had an exceptional vantage point from which to perceive the impact of printing. With printing suddenly easily available as a medium of storage and transmission of essential knowledge, memory no longer played the crucial role it once had. The fact that Viresalingam included this unusual passage in the midst of his account of the establishment of his own printing press and first periodical suggests that at some level—even if only subconsciously—he had been influenced by the role of printing in his own disavowal of the celebration of memory.

A final comment on this incident concerns the fate of that which gets left behind by a new discourse network. In some cases, something no longer recognized as valuable gets consigned to oblivion and is simply forgotten. We can see Viresalingam's comment that "lay people and ignorant people attributed it to black magic" and the accusations that he might be "a devotee of some dark spirits" as one possible fate of practices for which a new discourse network can no longer find a place or meaning. But these marks of recognition of the new place of memory in a post-print world—both those made by Viresalingam and those made by his critics—do not mean that the practice of *avadhānam* disappeared by the end of the nineteenth century. In fact, Velcheru Narayana Rao and David Shulman have argued that it underwent a popular resurgence during the early decades of the twentieth century. This suggests that, in fact, the type of public performance of *avadhānam* in which Viresalingam was engaged may actually have been something new, despite its use of a name associated with a previously existing practice.[55] What appeared as a "popular resurgence" may, in fact, simply have been the extension of *avadhānam* to new contexts and the recognition of a shift from limited in-group participation to public stage performances. The crucial difference is that audience members no longer are active fellow practitioners waiting to take their own turn, but rather are passive consumers seeking to be awed or entertained. In their discussion of the community that participated in the creation and circulation of oral *cāṭu* verses, Narayana Rao and Shulman observe some of the changes that printing introduced into the world of oral versification—a world that today gives a prominent place to the practice of *avadhānam.* They list, for example, shifts in the concept of factuality that printing produced, a decline in imaginative possibilities and collective creative collaboration, and new understandings of the nature of authorship, all occasioned by printing.[56] Their conclusion is that eventually, "with the repeated interference of a printed text, improvisations and textual variations practically disappear," and "in the new environment, there is little room for communal creation of *cāṭu* verses; instead the community is reduced to the role of their consumer."[57] Indeed, the recent surge in the popularity of *cāṭu* verses exchanged via the Internet within Telugu-speaking communities outside of India and the wild popularity of *avadhānam* performances at local and national gatherings of Telugu non-resident Indians (NRIs) living outside of India suggest that these practices have been reframed as entertainment and, even more, as markers of culture. From active participant in a milieu where *cāṭu* verses were used as a medium for competition, verbal play, the honing of memory, and the development of the ability to manipulate language, to passive consumer of *cāṭu* verses as objects, entertainment, or markers of "culture," it is difficult to consider these entities quite entirely the same. Despite the fact that both practices bear the same name, little else about the practices appears similar today. Their contexts and purposes have both changed.

Yet, despite their ultimate assertion that printing has dramatically altered practices of oral versification, Narayana Rao and Shulman also maintain that the initial effect of printing is to stimulate oral culture in a manner completely consistent with medieval practices. They argue that poets who performed *avadhānam* in the early decades of the twentieth century "still belonged entirely to the organic *cāṭu* world, continuous with the medieval past."[58] Furthermore, they assert that "patterns of patronage, composition, and circulation were essentially no different from those in Śrīnātha's time [late fourteenth and early fifteenth centuries], even though the poets now traveled by train, and their verses came to be printed."[59] Although printing may initially have offered an impetus for pre-print practices to expand their circulation, it is clear from their description that ultimately the social world of oral versification changed irreversibly by the twentieth century. Narayana Rao and Shulman write that

> the *cāṭu* community itself was fast changing its form. It was no longer the village elite gathered under the banyan tree. Rather, we are dealing with a graphically literate middle class, distributed over cities and towns and given to reading newspapers or, later, to watching TV. People of this class do not sing verses; such recitation has gone out of fashion. They merely listen to verses. Furthermore, the printing press eventually rendered both verse and meter obsolete. The primary mode of poetry for most readers—who read silently in the privacy of their homes—has become the nonmetrical prose poem (*vacana-kavitvam*). A silent world of individual readers, rather than communal listeners, is not hospitable to the *cāṭu*.[60]

There is little question that the production, circulation, and consumption of *cāṭu* verses changed with the advent of printing, yet the precise nature of these changes requires further consideration.

First, let us look more closely at what we know about the context of *avadhānam* performances at the turn of the century. As Narayana Rao and Shulman have argued, "The early decades of the twentieth century witnessed a profound renewal of oral versification, led by Divākarla Tirupati Śāstri (1872–1920) and Cellapilla Venkaṭa Śāstri (1870–1950)."[61] Born in the same decade in which Telugu periodicals first began to circulate popularly, these two poets are located by Narayana Rao and Shulman within a continuous *cāṭu* culture which stretches from the sixteenth century or even earlier into the twentieth century. Yet it is interesting that the specialty of these poets, their claim to fame, is not simply their *cāṭu* verses but more specifically their performance of *avadhānam*. *Avadhānam,* however, is a very particular context for the creation of new *cāṭu* verses and one not mentioned at all in Narayana Rao and Shulman's book until the last half dozen or so pages, in the final section devoted to *cāṭu* in the twentieth century. No mention is made of *avadhānam* as a primary context for the production, stimulation, and circulation of *cāṭu* verses in earlier centuries. Already this makes one suspicious that this apparent "renewal" of oral versification, might, in fact, be something decidedly new.

For one thing, the practice of *avadhānam*—as illustrated by the case of Viresalingam in the 1870s—is consistently characterized as a "performance." Here is Narayana Rao and Shulman's description of the context:

> These two poets, popularly known together as Tirupati-Venkaṭa-Kavulu, "the Tirupati-Venkaṭa poets," or *jaṇṭa-kavulu,* "Twin Poets," performed phenomenal feats of oral improvisation and memory all over Andhra. Their specialty was *śatāvadhāna:* dozens of "questioners," *pṛcchakas,* up to a hundred, would announce their names and give the poets problem questions, puzzles, or a riddle-line meant to become part of a verse; the poets would have to improvise correct answers, in verse, in the order in which they were asked, one line at a time, thus producing a *muktaka* [separate stanza] verse for each questioner. At the end of the performance, the poets had to recite again, in the proper order, all the (hundred or so) verses they had composed. Their performances, rich with fun, scholarly skill, and wit, energized the literary community and produced a veritable beehive of oral verses. On street corners, in restaurants, clubs, and at gatherings of friends, people would recite the latest verses of Tirupati-Venkaṭa-Kavulu.[62]

Although they use the performances' stimulation of the circulation of new verses within the larger literary community to argue that such a gathering marked continuity with earlier patterns of "patronage, composition, and circulation," several questions remain. If we consider the events staged by these two poets along with Viresalingam's *avadhānam* a few decades earlier, it becomes clear that the audiences in question are already consumers, merely by virtue of the framing of the event as a "performance," and an apparently "public" one at that. Viresalingam's *avadhānam* is held in a school, not under a banyan tree amid a gathering of the village elite, and the event is advertised, open to anyone who cared to attend. Indeed, the context suggests that *avadhānam* is something that has the power to bring a new "public" into being. It is also clear that not everyone in the audience was already familiar with the nature of *avadhānam* prior to Viresalingam's performances. A community already familiar with and accustomed to participating in such verbal demonstrations would hardly suspect a fellow *avadhānam* practitioner of black magic, no matter how much virtuosity he demonstrated. Then, too, we have the celebrity of the practitioners—the very small number of known authors of the new *cāṭu* verses that people were reciting on street corners and in restaurants in much the manner of cinema songs and dialogues today. Now you can make donations to support a certain number of days or hours of *avadhānam* by famous performers and purchase video CDs of celebrated *avadhānam* practitioners.[63] Pay-per-view Telugu entertainment websites also offer video footage of *avadhānam* performances for those who cannot be present in the audience in person.[64] The rivalry and verbal wit of *avadhānam* practitioners might resemble that of an earlier era, but it is clear that the printing press, and later other forms of mass media, have radically changed the circulation of the practice of *avadhānam* from something actively participated in to performances passively consumed.

Most of all, printing gives a new place and meaning to *avadhānam* within a larger set of relations, reframing it as entertainment. Indeed, far from representing "a reaction to the encroachment of modern printing upon the domain of popular communication," as Narayana Rao and Shulman speculate, the "amazing popularity and success" of Tirupati-Venkaṭa-Kavulu actually marks the novelty of the activity in which they were engaging.[65] No longer reflecting a set of skills to aspire to, or inviting participation, performers of *avadhānam* in a post-print world are exactly that—performers, entertainers who delight and fascinate their audiences. In fact, the practice of *avadhānam* today is unthinkable in a small group made up only of participants, not because it has "gone out of fashion," but because today *avadhānam* cannot exist without a stage and an audience. That participation by the audience members is as unnecessary as their presence is necessary is made evident by the fact, which Narayana Rao and Shulman note, that "*Śatāvadhānis,* or even *sahasrāvadhānis,* who compose verses extempore in answer to the demands of a hundred or a thousand *pṛcchakas,* have become popular on television and in public performance in the cities."[66]

Memory has been reframed not only in the classroom but also within the larger changes in the social world occasioned by printing. No longer celebrated as a central value necessary to the preservation and transmission of "knowledge," practices altered and reframed by the introduction of printing do not necessarily simply disappear. Rather they can take on new meanings and assume new roles within larger structures, relations, and everyday practices. In this case, printing has transformed practices associated with memory into public performances. As such, these new performances serve a new function—that of constituting, marking, and bearing witness to the existence of shared community among those who no longer share one another's lives in any day-to-day fashion. Evidence that this is the case can be found in the fact that the most popular contexts for *avadhānam* today are large urban centers in the Telugu-speaking regions of India, and the occasional (often annual) meetings of expatriate Telugu organizations outside of India. Regional associations like the Telugu Literary and Cultural Association (TLCA) in New York or the Telugu Association of Metro Atlanta (TAMA) and annual meetings of national organizations like the Telugu Association of North America (TANA) or the American Telugu Association (ATA) have all hosted successful *avadhānam* events, with plans for more. As one U.S.-based conference organizer remarked, "*aṣṭāvadhānam* has become one of the most watched literary events at these conferences. Therefore, in our efforts to please our paying patrons, we will continue with this tradition too."[67] And another audience member commented, "I have been noticing that ever since Medasani Mohan [one of the most celebrated performers of *avadhānam*] in Houston '89, this event has been playing to packed halls."[68] Indeed, given the popularity of such events, one can think of their most important function today as that of uniting people into some sort of new community—a community whose very existence depends upon the basis of a shared linguistic identity.

From Literacy to "Cultural Literacy": A "New" *Pedda Bāla Śikṣa*

A last example of the displacement of the cultural centrality of memory in southern Indian pedagogy relates to the teaching and learning of prosody—the rules for metrical versification. In 1999, during the annual Hyderabad Book Fair held on the grounds of Nizam College, a friend found among the other treasures avid book buyers appreciate a recent publication of the early Telugu primer discussed earlier, *Pedda Bāla Śikṣa.* He bought a copy and showed it to me that evening while I was having dinner with his family. It was clear that my friend, a college lecturer in Hyderabad, had bought the book out of nostalgia, and indeed, the edition—published in 1998—explicitly marketed itself in precisely that way. The fact that it had already gone into a second printing suggests that the first printing had sold well. Given my friend's interest in the book, it is likely that most of the copies made their way into middle-class households where English was as comfortably used as Telugu, households much like that of my friend's. An advertisement on the back of the book—and the only English used in the entire book—proclaimed, "This book is designed basing on the concept of Cultural Literacy. *What Every Person in the Telugu Country Needs to Know!*"[69] Although my friend had never studied *Pedda Bāla Śikṣa,* he valued its place as an icon of Telugu education and bought it as a curiosity as much as anything. Later I had a chance to compare this new 400-page 1998 edition with a copy of the original 90-page 1865 edition, the first to be titled *Pedda Bāla Śikṣa,* as opposed to simply *Bāla Śikṣa.* The changes and additions were numerous, but even more striking than the topics and material that had been added were the contents that had been eliminated in the new edition.

One of the very few subjects that was eliminated completely between the 1865 edition and the 1998 publication of *Pedda Bāla Śikṣa* was the study of *chhandassu* or poetic meter. Nearly six of the ninety pages of the 1865 edition of *Pedda Bāla Śikṣa* were devoted to "*Chandōlakṣaṇa Viṣayamulu*" [Matters of Metrical Rules]. This section laid out the rules of *chhandassu* and instructed students in the patterns of metrical versification that were used by Telugu poets. Being skilled at *chhandassu* was useful not only in composing poetry but also in memorizing and recalling lengthy verse compositions [*kāvya*]. Knowing which meter a given composition used made it easier to recall and recite. No mention was made of *chhandassu* at all in the 1998 edition, suggesting that, as a subject, it no longer found a place within that range of knowledge that "every person in the Telugu country needs to know."

So what did "every person in the Telugu country" need to know at the end of the twentieth century? *Sāmskṛtika sākṣarāskata*—the principle upon which the new edition of *Pedda Bāla Śikṣa* was compiled—is a category that clearly did not exist in the nineteenth century. Indeed, so uncertain is Buddiga Subbarayan, the author of the 1998 edition of *Pedda Bāla Śikṣa,* that his audience will understand the term, that he chooses to explicitly gloss the phrase with an English translation (written in Telugu script) as "cultural literacy—core knowledge." Along with chapters devoted to the Telugu language, children's literature, literature, general knowledge, and knowledge of the world, chapter 2 of the 1998 edition is entitled "Foundation of Cultural Tradition" [*Samskṛtī Sampradāya Pīṭham*]. It includes topics such as religious knowledge—selections from the Vedas, Vedanta, Hindu prayers [*hinduvula prārthanalu*], the Bhagavad Gita, pictures and names of various deities, and a very few pages devoted to Christian and Muslim "tradition" [*sampradāyam*], as well as festivals, names of the Telugu years and months, astrological signs, and patterns of *muggulu* (rice flour designs laid freshly each morning in front of one's doorstep).

From Subba Rao's desire for textbooks to assist in the improvement of language in 1820, we have arrived at the end of the twentieth century at a desire for "the necessary foundation stones for language-cultures" [*bhāsāsamskṛtuluku kāvalsina punādirāḷḷu*] in Buddiga Subbarayan's *Pedda Bāla Śikṣa.* Yet in his 1998 preface Buddiga Subbarayan suggests that this has been the purpose of *Pedda Bāla Śikṣa* all along, from its very inception a century and a half earlier. He writes that

> probably around 1832, Puduru Chandalawada Sitaramasastri, one great pandit, created the gift of *Pedda Bāla Śiksha* in Telugu . . . and handed it over to the Telugu community [*telugu jātiki*]. *It included the subjects of knowledge—those topics of language—which form the necessary foundation stones of language-cultures* [*bhāsāsamskṛtuluku kāvalsina punādirāḷḷu*]: the letters, their combinations, secondary forms of consonants, simple words, words made of two, three and four letters, easy sentences, proverbs, prosody rules, things associated with traditional culture, subjects relating to historical, geographic, and scientific matters known today, established forms and ways of speaking.[70]

"Topics of language" have now become the most important "subjects of knowledge," just as Subba Rao proposed nearly two centuries earlier. But the purpose is no longer the general improvement of the knowledge of literature or the making perfect of one's accomplishments. Instead, "those topics of language" now provide the foundation stones of language-cultures, and impart "cultural literacy" in place of literacy. Such a partitioning of cultural knowledge from other types of knowledge, and even more its easy marketability, can be read as an indication of the level of desire for precisely those practices and meanings that people are most afraid of losing—those things that no longer find a place within the rest of what is considered knowledge of today.

From a primer designed to replace pandits and convey the essential knowledge required by primary students in southern India in the nineteenth century, to a repository of a specifically cultural literacy at the end of the twentieth century, the various incarnations of *Pedda Bāla Śikṣa* mirror the positions and roles of language within larger patterns of change in southern India. From a medium used along with other languages in a complementary way to an object of acquisition, we finally find the Telugu language at the end of the twentieth century marking out the boundaries of culture as a separate domain. Like the shift from learning language in use at the beginning of the nineteenth century to learning language as an object and foundation for further learning a century later, such an explicit partitioning of "cultural" knowledge from other types of knowledge, and its packaging within the covers of a book as an object to be acquired, suggest something important about the idea of "culture" today. No longer something experienced in practice, or known through usage, "culture" appears today in precisely those locations where people most fear it has disappeared. In urban areas and abroad, not only language but culture, too, is packaged as an object for easy consumption. Whether one buys it in a book or appreciates it from a seat in an auditorium, in either case the consumer is no longer an active participant in the production of culture. Subba Rao's desire to make language the most important object of education has transformed this object—language—into Subbarayan's "foundation stone for language-cultures" (*bhāsā-samskṛtulu*) today.

CHAPTER 5

From the Art of Memory to the Practice of Translation: Making Languages Parallel

When Vennelakanty Subba Rao made his recommendations to the Madras School Book Society in 1820, he was not just interested in the improvement of students' use of unbounded, undifferentiated language in general. Nor was he exclusively interested in the improvement of one particular language over all others. Instead, his proposal specifically addressed "the better improvement, therefore, *of the knowledge of the several languages.*" Indeed, "the several languages" appeared in the early decades of the nineteenth century as the most important target for improving education within the districts subject to the administration of the Madras Presidency.[1] Central to the attention and educational intervention addressed toward this newfound focus was the plural nature of the objects of knowledge in question. Reformers increasingly began to see the accumulation of linguistic skills, registers, and mediums acquired in context or through everyday usage as inadequate, believing it essential to mark them as explicit objects of instruction. But rather than grouping these objectives together by specific task—the deciphering of handwriting, the reading of scripts, the writing of official correspondence, the singing of the Ramayana, or the recitation of lexical knowledge—the objectives of education began to be defined along linguistic lines. Increasingly, students were expected not simply to add each of these accomplishments to their repertoire in whatever language or languages each could be done, but rather to acquire a more general basic knowledge of Telugu, Tamil, English, Sanskrit, Kannada, or Persian.

As chapter 4 has argued, this reorientation of educational objectives increasingly meant studying the grammar of any one of these languages as a prerequisite for doing other things with the language. Although the *vyākaraṇa* tradition had made grammatical knowledge of languages available for centuries in southern India, existing evidence suggests that grammatical texts were never studied at the primary level as a prerequisite for later use of linguistic mediums. Instead, they tended to be taken up for advanced study by already established scholars and poets. Texts such as Mulaghatika Ketana's thirteenth-century *Āndhra Bhāṣā Bhūṣaṇamu,* the classic *Āndhra Śabda Chintāmaṇi,* popularly attributed to Nannaya Bhatt, and Kakunuri Appakavi's seventeenth-century commentary upon it (see chapter 3), were not considered relevant to the basic education of schoolchildren. Educational reformers of the early decades of the nineteenth century correctly observed that these texts were seldom to be found in schools.[2] What has been less remarked upon, however, is the fact that this new attention to educational objectives caused languages to begin to be thought of as separate, distinct, and, most of all, parallel mediums. With the advent of such a perspective, languages increasingly came to be viewed not as registers—their uses specific to particular tasks and contexts—but as complete in and of themselves, sufficient for any and all tasks and contexts within a newly geographically and linguistically defined community.

Indeed by the end of the nineteenth century the idea of the existence of linguistic communities increasing replaced task or context as the primary factor in determining and defining language use. This had dramatic effects in numerous realms, but particularly upon notions of what it meant to be literate. At the very beginning of the nineteenth century someone in southern India might find it perfectly natural to compose an official letter in Persian, record a land transaction in Marathi, send a personal note to a relative in Telugu, perform religious ablutions in Sanskrit, and barter with the vegetable vendor in Tamil, all in the course of a single day. If one wasn't comfortable with the language required for the specific task, then one engaged a specialist to perform the function—be it religious, administrative, or even the writing of a personal letter. However, by the beginning of the twentieth century, such contextual and task-specific language use was increasingly converted into different registers of the same language. More and more, people came to expect that—if not all of these functions—then at least most of them could be performed within a single language. And what's more, people increasingly began to feel that all of these things could be performed in any language equally well, though not necessarily by the same person. The shift to a recognition of "the several languages" that Subba Rao's report marks paved the way for languages to be experienced as separate but equally acceptable mediums, eventually creating the expectation that languages exist in parallel to one another. By the beginning of the twentieth century, a new belief in universal translatability made it seem that anything that could be said in one language could be said equally effectively (if not as elegantly) in any other language. From that moment hence, as Naoki Sakai has compelling argued in another context, "to be able to read and write" ceased to mean "to operate in more than one linguistic medium."[3] Instead, literacy began for the first time to be regulated "by the demand that the primary function of writing should be to transcribe what is suggested by 'mother tongue.'"[4] Indeed, in addition to the domains of geography, literary production, history writing, grammar, and pedagogy discussed in earlier chapters, the concept of literacy was similarly being reorganized in relation to the new idea of a "mother tongue."

An exploration of three specific aspects of this shift can help make clearer the implications of the new experience of languages as parallel entities and objects of knowledge. This chapter first traces the shift from "doing things with language" to "doing things with languages." It demonstrates how this is intimately linked to the transition from learning languages in use to acquiring them as discrete and independent objects of knowledge, largely divorced from context. Second, the chapter explores the role of lexicons in establishing languages as parallel to one another. Pre-colonial lexicons organized words topically and were little concerned with the origins of words as long as their usage was attested by earlier literary works. These lexicons were displaced during the nineteenth century by alphabetized word lists or dictionaries that were newly preoccupied with origins and purity. These new dictionaries and word lists represented languages as separate from but nevertheless equivalent to one another. Such a shift marks a significant, but seldom recognized, reorganization of knowledge production, transmission, and circulation. In the third section, I argue that new practices of translation played a central role not only in the nineteenth-century transition from verse to prose, and from literary language to a form of writing that more closely approximated spoken language, but also in making languages appear to be parallel and equivalent to one another. Together, these three examples demonstrate a transformation that I argue is fundamental to the emergence of languages as new markers and foundations of "culture" and "identity" in the twentieth century.

From Language to Languages

Benedict Anderson's classic study of the origin and spread of nationalism has based its argument upon the effects of a print capitalism simultaneously consumed by multitudes. Though each act of reading is a private individual act, Anderson writes that "each communicant is well aware that the ceremony he performs is being replicated simultaneously by thousands (or millions) of others of whose existence he is confident, yet of whose identity he has not the slightest notion."[5] Using Europe as a model, he argues that the logic of capitalism motivated the spread of literature into vernacular languages in order to expand markets into the much larger non-elite masses who did not know Latin, which in turn created fertile ground for the birth of imagined communities. Yet Anderson makes a crucial assumption that does not hold in the context of nineteenth-century southern India. Even more importantly, this assumption is represented by him as a universal, when in fact his observation refers to a phenomenon locatable very specifically not only in place but also in time. He asserts that "then and now the bulk of mankind is monoglot."[6] His assumption of monoglossia—suggesting that everything most people do is done within a single discrete and consolidated "language"—was not only not applicable to many places in South Asia in the eighteenth and nineteenth centuries, but it arguably was not applicable in much of the world at one time or another, and may still not be. Indeed, the very idea of monoglossia itself requires historicization and can be seen as only one of many possible ways of organizing and categorizing the multitude of speech acts the average person engages in each day. It is clear that everyone in the world commands more than one linguistic domain and can function linguistically in more than one specific context, regardless of how one chooses to define domain and context. Whether the language acts performed in these different domains and contexts are popularly considered to belong to the same language is largely a matter for historical inquiry. At various times and places individuals and communities have organized, grouped, and labeled linguistic acts in very different ways. As chapter 3 has demonstrated, a system in which languages were defined by their intelligibility over distance and time was displaced during the nineteenth century by a system that defined languages on the basis of their origins. Sanskrit, today irrefutably recognized as a distinct language, originated not as a "language" but as one very specific register of linguistic use.

Even today—in an era when linguistic identities have gained importance—the idea of monoglossia still does not reflect the everyday practices of many. It is exceedingly common for people in India today to routinely use two, three, or even more languages in the course of a typical day. Such practices are not restricted to the well-educated, many of whom were educated under a "three-language formula" advocated by the government as a way of coping with India's national linguistic diversity. It is equally common for unlettered domestic workers, auto rickshaw drivers, or manual laborers to speak two or more languages, particularly in urban areas, where almost 30 percent of India's population lives. The domestic worker in the home of a friend of mine in Bangalore—a young woman with only a few years of formal education, employed by a woman with family ties to Kerala who grew up in Bangalore and by her Kolkata-born husband—is a typical example. This employee speaks English and Hindi with her employers, Kannada in the market, Tamil with her siblings, and Telugu with me whenever I visit. Even when someone does not command all of the linguistic registers they personally require, they frequently have recourse to a relative or specialist who does, as in the case of villagers wishing to send a letter to a relative in another part of the country, file a petition, or fill up a legal form. Even if these tasks are conducted in what we would today think of as the same language, the register is often so unfamiliar to the one requesting the service as to be, for all intents and purposes, a different language.

Nevertheless, most people in situations like these today have learned to label their language use in accordance with the well-accepted names of languages widely known today, recognizing that they speak "different" languages. H. M. J. Maier, in another, though similar, context, has argued that this was not always the case.[7] He demonstrates that people in the Dutch East Indies were taught under colonial rule—at roughly the same time that similar processes were under way in India—to think of their own linguistic practices in new ways, increasingly aligning their customary linguistic practices with a sense of group identity. Maier characterizes this transition as one in which the existence of heteroglossia has been replaced by polyglossia. Following Bakhtin, who reminds us that language "is unitary only as an abstract grammatical system . . . taken in isolation," Maier characterizes a heteroglossic attitude toward language as

> a complex interaction of utterances, discourses, speech-genres, "languages" which—far from being unitary, far from circling around generally accepted centers of authority—formed a continuum of mostly spoken forms, in a number of not very clearly defined domains and a great amount of variation. A slippery continuum, that is, a continuous switching between codes and styles. In the Indies, linguistic differences were great no doubt but they were not felt to be unsur-

> mountable; nobody was able to give an exact definition of how the system worked, and yet most people managed to maintain themselves in it. Somehow differences did not really matter. Somehow things worked to the satisfaction of all of those involved. Call it linguistic co-existence, acceptance, appreciation. Call it heteroglossia.[8]

In India, there were certainly centers of authority in relation to language, but such heteroglossia clearly applied both within speech and within the writing practices of graphically literate communities in southern India. We can see this, for example, in the lack of uniformity even in the very names of languages that were used in pre-colonial southern India. Tamil, for example, has been known as *arava bhāṣa, drāvida bhāṣa,* and *malabar,* and Telugu as *tenugu, tilinga, kaling, trilinga bhāṣa, gentoo,* and *āndhra bhāṣa.* Furthermore, the borders between one language and another were not always clear, especially in the context of spoken language and the absence of written scripts. Even the presence of distinct scripts was not necessarily a reliable indicator of separate languages, as it was not uncommon for the same language to be represented by multiple scripts. Maier's Bhaktinian representation of language is therefore equally applicable to the way people experienced language in pre-modern southern India. Although many people in India today still do not experience the monoglossia imagined by Anderson to be the norm in the world, most, particularly those exposed to formal education, have undergone a transition from heteroglossic language use (which can be described but never counted) to a recognition of polyglossic languages (which can be counted, listed, compared, and contrasted).

The new polyglossic understanding of languages asserted that anything that could be said or done in any one language should be able to be said or done in any other language, audience notwithstanding. This new experience of language also altered what it meant to be literate. Rather than doing some things in one language and others in another language according to the specific task at hand, as a literate person in southern India at the beginning of the nineteenth century would have done, by the early twentieth century it was increasing believed that someone literate should be capable of doing everything that needed to be done within a single language. Some examples will make this clearer.

One of the first differences that strikes the reader of the 1865 and 1998 editions of the classic Telugu primer *Pedda Bāla Śikṣa,* introduced in chapter 4, is the fact that the 1865 edition opens, just after its Telugu preface, not with the Telugu alphabet but with the English and Tamil alphabets. These alphabets are labeled in Telugu script, "*inglīṣu akṣaramulu*" [English letters] and "*arava akṣaramulu*" [Tamil letters].[9] The next page of the primer shows a chart of Tamil letter combinations, demonstrating how letters are formed when each consonant is used with different vowels. Only then do students receive an introduction to the Telugu letters, first vowels and then the consonants, followed by their combinations. Although numbered as prefatory pages in the 1865 edition, separate from the main text, the fact that the English alphabet and the Tamil alphabet were both considered important enough to be included in this popular primer in 1865 suggests that the average schoolchild in southern India in 1865 would have needed to learn these alphabets along with the Telugu alphabet. Whether this reflects the location of publication in the multilingual colonial administrative city of Madras, or whether it reflects the reality of employment opportunities, basic skills needed, and social understandings of literacy throughout the larger Madras Presidency of the era is not self-evident from this text alone. However, other evidence concerning nineteenth-century educational practices is available for examination that can help to put this inclusion of the Tamil and English alphabets into historical perspective.

Education in Subba Rao's lifetime (1784–1839) was not restricted to a single linguistic medium. Particular languages and scripts—Telugu, Sanskrit, and Tamil most often, but also Kannada, Marathi, English, and Persian—were employed in the course of a day as necessitated by the knowledge of the pandit, the nature of the lesson, and the common usage of the region. Languages were recognized as distinct, but the use of each was governed by task and context rather than by a linguistic identity claimed either by the speaker or his or her interlocutor. In describing education in the various districts subject to the administration of Fort St. George, Subba Rao writes:

> The mode of teaching all the vernacular languages is almost the same, though the Tamil has a less number of letters in the Alphabet. In this, the books in which lessons are given to boys in the first instance are in the Tamil language. The Devanagari characters are those in which the Sanskrit is generally written, but as Telugu, Canada [Kannada], Grandham and Balabonda have the same number of letters as Devanagari, the Sanskrit books in the south of India are written in all these languages with equal correctness.[10]

How surprising to contemporary language sensibilities is Subba Rao's description of learning the Tamil script first—not because it is the primary medium of instruction or the mother tongue of the young scholars in question, but because it has fewer letters and is therefore easier for students to begin with. Indeed, often a variety of linguistic scripts were considered equally relevant, or at least interchangeable, at the primary educational level, with no single script accorded special privilege.[11] The Telugu alphabet, with (in the nineteenth century) fifty-seven letters, was considered somewhat more difficult than Tamil to learn—a more advanced lesson to be mastered only after one had already learned the shorter Tamil alphabet.

In describing the progression from an alphabet with fewer letters to alphabets with more letters, Subba Rao is describing a context in which competency in reading a range of scripts (and forms of handwriting) was considered necessary.[12] Although in 1820 there is clearly some flexibility in the choice of script used when writing any particular text, the ability to read those same texts in whichever script they were encountered was an accepted part of an adequate basic (not advanced) education.[13] Campbell, after outlining the basic primary skills taught in the schools of Bellary District, writes: "The other parts of a native education consist in deciphering various kinds of hand-writing in public, and other letters which the schoolmaster collects from different sources, writing common letters, drawing up forms of agreement, reading fables and legendary tales and committing various kinds of poetry to memory, chiefly with a view to attain distinctness and clearness in pronunciation, together with readiness and correctness in reading any kind of composition."[14] This is not to say that every child in every school in the Madras Presidency learned every language used within the Madras Presidency, but rather that a student commonly acquired the ability to read multiple scripts as needed and as samples were available. Subba Rao mentions, for example, that his younger brother, whose education Subba Rao supervised following his father's death, had "acquired tolerable knowledge in five different languages" by the age of fourteen.[15] Although he never lists them explicitly in one place, his various accounts of his own employment suggest that he could conduct necessary tasks in at least some registers in not only Telugu, Kannada, and English, but also Tamil, Marathi, Hindustani, Persian, and Sanskrit.[16] The scripts students would have learned to read would have been determined not by any sense of "mother tongue" or "foreignness" as we would think of them today, but rather in relation to the specific contexts in which a student learned particular functions and according to the availability of written texts and the knowledge of the teacher. If not learned in school, scripts would have been acquired in the specific contexts in which they were used.

In light of all of this, the inclusion in an 1865 Telugu primer of the Tamil alphabet seems much less remarkable. What does become necessary to account for, however, is the absence of the Tamil alphabet in later editions of *Pedda Bāla Śikṣa.* The 1998 edition, for example, like the 1865 edition, opens with an introduction to the letters of the alphabet. But unlike the 1865 edition, the 1998 version begins with the Telugu letters alone, accompanied by charts showing their combinations and followed in progression by simple Telugu two-letter words, then three- and four-letter words, and other useful words. It is only much later, in the sixth and final chapter, "Foundation of World Knowledge" [*Lōka Vijñāna Pīṭham*], that the English, Hindi, and Greek alphabets, with the names of each letter in Telugu, appear in a miscellaneous section headed "Useful Knowledge" [*Paniki Vacchē Parijñānam*]. Appearing as the very last item in the final section of this last chapter, these two pages (one containing both the English and Hindi alphabets, the second showing the Greek letters) accompany such other useful items as mathematical terms and tables (four pages); principles of health (one page); a separate page on rabies and its prevention; a chart showing ideal height-weight proportions for men and women; a list of birthstones and their corresponding (English) months; measurement conversions; Baufort's scale of wind speed measurement; a chart of comparative electrical expenditures; and three pages of model letters for use in correspondence.

Not only has the Tamil alphabet disappeared, but the alphabets other than Telugu that are included—English, Hindi, and Greek alphabets—are reframed as objects of "useful world knowledge." No longer are they presented as essential basic tools for mediating the immediate written and spoken world; rather, they are presented as items in an assortment of miscellaneous reference topics. Each alphabet has ceased to be one *dēśa bhāṣa* among many available mediums—one of many features of a local landscape available to be used as needed, becoming instead freestanding objects of useful knowledge. This shift from acquiring language in use to acquiring languages as discrete objects can also be seen in actual descriptions of educational practices. Subba Rao's journal, for example, paints a portrait of education gained as much through everyday practice as in the classroom, providing us with a rare window on the educational practices of the early nineteenth century. Apprenticeships, paid or unpaid, provided most of a young person's education, and what little school education did occur generally did not include a great number of books. In his accounts of his own educational experience, Subba Rao describes how Manchella Paupiah, the son of one his paternal aunts, taught him "how to write accounts and letters."[17] Later, through another family connection, he obtained an apprenticeship in the Pay-Office at Guntoor, where "the Pay-master, Mr. Henry Wilson, allowed me a Madras Pagoda or 4 Rs. per mensem for my subsistence and I improved myself in writing the English accounts in his office."[18]

Despite his own largely informal education, it is clear that as an advocate of "the several languages," Subba Rao has already begun to think in terms of the organization of education around languages. He makes references to several schools that he identifies as a "Telugu school" or an "English school." Yet, apprenticeships were by far the most common form of education during this period, and a young man with some rudimentary knowledge of reading and writing would be dispatched to work for little or no money in an office where a relative or other known person was already placed. In assisting the senior relative, either formally or informally, the young man would acquire whatever specific skills were necessary for the job in question—keeping accounts, perfecting penmanship, copying correspondence, and learning to write letters, reports, and memoranda according to well-established formulas. Subba Rao describes his cousins and brothers gaining their educations in just such a manner, usually apprenticed for little or no wages by the age of fourteen. In this way, a young person acquired a range of linguistic skills that did not necessarily seek to exhaust all of the functions and tasks possible within any particular language.

Although the death of his father appears to have disrupted his studies, Subba Rao's account of his own education (and that of his brother and cousin whom he also undertook to have educated under his care) differs little from his later generalization of educational practices, found in the proposal he wrote to the Madras School Book Society in 1820:

> A boy in this country leaves school at about ten or eleven years of age, and without the least regard for the completion of his education follows generally the profession of his family. If his father be employed as a servant in any public *Cutcherry* [court or office], the son goes there and learns to write the accounts, and when he is found to be able to write a tolerable hand, his relatives exert themselves to obtain for him a situation, and little care is thence taken whether or not he turns out a good master of this language.[19]

Clearly, in Subba Rao's mind at least, the knowledge of language specifically had until then never been made a priority within the school education of the day, a problem—as discussed in the first section of this chapter—he felt needed to be rectified. According to Subba Rao, current custom in the early part of the nineteenth century dictated that languages were to be acquired through practice, added as needed in particular situations, and if they were not well acquired, no one much seemed to care. It was this attitude that reformers of the era most wished to see changed.

What little time students did spend in school appears to have followed a common routine. Subba Rao provides a detailed description of the educational practices in a typical school, telling us that a student

> is first taught to learn the alphabet by causing him to write the same with the thumb of his right hand on sand, and when he has got them by heart, he is required to write them with a piece of slate on a Board prepared for the particular purpose and blackened by coals and the juice of certain leaves. The pupil now arriving at the stage of understanding the characters, he is taught the syllables and the spelling part of the Orthography; after which short names of the divine and human beings are taught to be written, and when he is found to be able to write down any name he is told, the further progress is, that he is taught to write on cadjan leaves with an iron pen, beginning at first to form large ciphers, and when sufficiently able to do them well, he reads an abridgement of the holy Book (Ramayanum) in Sanscrit by receiving lessons of a single verse every evening to be got by heart before he goes to the school the next morning.[20]

Campbell's description is almost identical. Having learned to read and write letters and syllables in one or more of the vernacular languages, students then proceeded to read the Ramayana—in Sanskrit, though written in a vernacular script. Subba Rao and Campbell both expressed frustration that pronunciation, or "steadiness and general practice of reading any paper, letter, accounts, &c" was more important than "understand[ing] any part of their meaning.[21] Knowledge of any specific language—beyond its correct pronunciation and the student's ability to read and write its script fluently—or a canon of literature defined exclusively by that language was not the goal. This was true even though schools were, by the 1820s, already characterized as specifically Telugu, Tamil, Kannada, or English schools.

The school day typically began at six in the morning and continued until at least six in the evening, with two breaks for the students to return home for breakfast and the midday meal. After the midday meal, Subba Rao reports, "they all attend the school regularly and receiving from their master or his deputy fresh lessons, they read them until half after five, after which they all stand up with great submission before their master, and repeat aloud the names of the years (sixty in number), the months, days of the week, the planets, the stars, the different festivals, the remarkable days &c."[22] He goes on to explain that the typical education included only a few books in manuscript form written on either palm leaves or paper, with occasional printed books by the 1830s:

> Independently of the holy book above referred to several other books are also read by the students in the school, of which the most in use are here-under stated. A part of the Ameracosa [written in Sanskrit but generally read in one of the vernacular scripts] comprising the names of the deities, of the quarters, the divisions of time, the different musical instruments, the divisions of the earth, the towns, plants, animals, &c., some books of morals; a part of the Arithmetic and Mathematics and several easy extracts from the holy books are also read.[23]

Campbell's description similarly emphasized the limited number of manuscript books available: "The three books which are most common in all the schools, and which are used indiscriminately by the several castes, are the *Ramayanum, Maha-Bharata* and *Bhagrata [Bhagavad Gita]*."[24] Multiple copies of the same text were unlikely within any given school. Students were expected to learn to read whatever was available. Writing at this basic level consisted in being able to compose each character in a pleasing and legible manner, while the goal of reading was decipherment—"to obtain a steadiness and general practice of reading any paper, letter, accounts, &c."

Lexicons New and Old

Lexicography is a second domain in which the shift from learning to command different complementary registers of language through usage in specific contexts gave way to learning languages as discrete and separable objects. We see changes in the production of lexicons, dictionaries, and other texts that catalogued words in one way or another. During the nineteenth century a shift occurred away from topically arranged verse lexicons in favor of alphabetized word lists and "dictionaries," no longer composed in verse, and, unlike pre-colonial lexicons, clearly impossible to memorize. What's more, these new word lists were frequently arranged as parallel word lists, showing three, six, or sometimes as many as a dozen different languages lined up parallel to one another. In these new lexicons each language was allotted its own column, and each column was expected to contain a unique term for each idea that could be expressed in any of the other languages. The following discussion explores this dramatic change in lexicons, focusing on the nature and purpose of each type of lexicon, their assumptions about language and languages, and their effects upon their users.

We have already seen a reflection of the linguistic practices of the first half of the nineteenth century in C. P. Brown's *Miśra Bhāṣā Nighaṇṭu: Brown's Dictionary of Mixed Telugu,* published in 1854, first introduced in chapter 3. Though by no means the first Telugu dictionary composed by a European, its premise represented a prevailing mid-nineteenth-century view of language held by European administrators and others. In compiling such a dictionary, Brown was explicitly attempting to account for language as it was used in everyday life. The English subtitle found inside the book on the first page describes it as "A Dictionary of the Mixed Dialects Used in Telugu: Explaining Foreign Words, Arabic, Hindustani, &c. that occur in business, letters, and conversation."[25] The fact that Brown views "those phrases which are current among the natives" as a supplement—something additional to but also attempting to bring to completion by filling in a gap rather than a central work in its own right—suggests his attitude toward "mixed" usage.[26] In terms of actual everyday usage, however, such a dictionary was far from a supplement. Few long-time local residents would have required such a lexicon given its reflection of their existing everyday knowledge. Its usefulness was primarily for the newly arrived colonial administrators who found local linguistic practices bewildering.

Thomas Trautmann has traced the rise and fall of the notion of "mixed" languages in England and continental Europe, arguing that it was the colonial encounter with Indian philological and grammatical traditions that made possible many of the most revolutionary changes in European thinking about language in the late eighteenth and nineteenth centuries. He argues that during the first half of the nineteenth century, "the belief that certain languages of today are 'stock' or 'original' languages and other are 'mixed,' or indeed that all languages consist of an ancient core vocabulary plus later mixtures from other languages" held sway as the dominant etymological theory.[27] He also argues that the biblical origins of this and other etymological theorizing—including the dominant contemporary methodologies of historical and comparative linguistics—have largely been forgotten today. By the second of half of the nineteenth century, however, "the notion of a mixed language had not only lost its value but was regarded as an obstacle by the New Grammarians: 'Es gibt kein Mischgesprach'—there is no such thing as a mixed language—was their slogan."[28] Indeed, following Brown's *Dictionary of Mixed Telugu* in 1854, there were no additional attempts to portray Telugu as a "mixed" language.

C. P. Brown's attempts to produce a dictionary of Telugu were not the first. The same British administrators and students of Telugu who encountered pre-existing local linguistic analysis (*vyākaraṇa*) practices (introduced in chapter 3) were also confronted with well-developed lexical cataloguing practices that similarly predated their own arrival on the subcontinent. Precolonial lexicons of southern India demonstrated a high degree of comfort with precisely the type of "mixed" language British administrators like C. P. Brown found so frustrating. However, unlike Brown, they were not primarily concerned with everyday speech. Instead, pre-colonial lexicons were generated by compiling lists of words that had been previously attested in highly regarded literary works [*kāvya*]. The words were organized topically and arranged in verse form, making them easy to memorize. What was key to determining the inclusion or exclusion of particular words within such lexicons was not their "purity" as Telugu words, but their appropriateness for use in Telugu kāvya, defined according to whether they had ever been used in a literary work before, and their intelligibility beyond the immediate geographic context of composition. If a particular word could not be attested in any earlier well-regarded work of poetic literature, it was much less likely to be included. As a result, such lexicons reflected the literary language used in educated verse compositions rather than the language of everyday speech. There is also some evidence that verse lexicons may have existed in oral form long before they were ever written down.[29] Regardless, it is clear that even written lexicons were frequently memorized and passed on orally, even though they may also have existed in manuscript form. Indeed, the distinction between written and oral texts is not always easy to identify, since a text passed on orally may have been committed to a manuscript only later on. We know from Subba Rao and Campbell that the Sanskrit verse lexicon *Amara Kōśa* was still being partially and sometimes entirely committed to memory by schoolchildren in the 1820s. A Telugu adaptation of the *Amara Kōśa* known as the *Śiva Āndhra,* also composed in verse, was also widely memorized. C. P. Brown, for example, mentions that among several other vocabularies and lexicons widely found, "The Siva Andhra is, like its Sanscrit model the Amara Cosha, very widely taught—about one quarter of the Cosha is taught to nearly every school-boy."[30]

One of the earliest recorded Telugu lexicons was the *Āndhra Nāma Sangrahamu* [Compilation of Telugu Words], attributed to the poet Paidipati Lakshmana (c. 1600). Following this, the poet Adidam Surakavi composed a supplement to Lakshmana's lexicon, known as *Āndhra Nāma Śēṣamu* [The Remaining Telugu Words], also in verse form. This supplement contained only additional words that were attested in *kāvya* compositions but that did not already appear in Paidipati Lakshmana's composition. These two vocabularies, along with an additional supplement, *Sāmba Nighaṇṭuvu* [Sāmba Lexicon, after one of the many epithets of Śiva], composed by Kasturi Ranga Kavi in the mid-eighteenth century, are popularly known today as the *Nighaṇṭu Trayam* [Trio of Lexicons] and are often found collected together in one manuscript or book. Another early Telugu verse lexicon is Ganapavarapu Venkata Rao's *Vēnkaṭēśāndhram,* compiled in 1684.[31] It consists of 108 verses, each of which ends with "*pankajāpta vikasa venkaṭesa*" ["blossoming beloved lotus Lord Vēnkaṭēśa"].

Almost all pre-colonial lexicons, whether composed in Sanskrit or in Telugu, were organized topically rather than alphabetically, providing poets with lists of synonyms and related words that enabled them to complete a given verse by selecting a word conforming to the appropriate metrical pattern. Pre-colonial lexicons were most often organized according to five divisions: *Dēva Vargu* [category of words relating to deities], *Mānava Vargu* [category of words relating to humans], *Sthāvara Vargu* [category of words relating to places or immovable things], *Tiryag Vargu* [category of words relating to animals], and *Nānārtha Vargu* [category of words with multiple meanings]. Each division contained words likely to be used when writing of the topic in question. For example, the category pertaining to deities typically included not only various titles, euphemisms, epithets, and names of deities, but also words used for describing their attributes, vehicles, identifying weapons, tools, and common actions. The classification system used by *Āndhra Nāma Sangrahamu, Āndhra Nāma Śēṣamu,* and *Sāmba Nighaṇṭuvu* exemplifies this organizational framework.

That colonial lexicographical practices initially tried to build upon these existing lexicons is made evident by C. P. Brown's early attempt to compile an alphabetized dictionary of the Telugu language, entitled *Karkambāḍi Nighaṇṭuvu.*[32] Although he never published it, Brown enlisted the help of several pandits to reorganize into alphabetical order all of the words found in a number of existing verse lexicons—including *Āndhra Nāma Sangrahamu, Āndhra Nāma Śēṣamu, Vēnkaṭēśāndhram,* and *Sāmba Nighaṇṭuvu.* The ultimate lack of interest in publishing this compilation points to the fact that pre-colonial *nighaṇṭus* and colonial dictionaries were not only organized differently but also served wholly different purposes. Indeed, despite the tendency to translate *nighaṇṭu* as "dictionary," one can hardly consider them within the same category of texts. Pre-colonial lexicons were intended to be used for composing, reading, understanding, or remembering *kāvya* literature. But colonial-era lexicons were designed to be used for language learning and translation. Colonial-era lexicons, then, were not a continuation of existing southern Indian linguistic practices. They represented an entirely new way of thinking about, cataloguing, and ultimately using language.

By the early decades of the twentieth century, this new understanding of language had spread to new domains, prompting among other things a raging controversy over the nature of written Telugu to be used in schools. One of the frustrations that the self-proclaimed "modernists"—those who advocated a form of written Telugu more closely resembling educated speech—had with the language found in pre-colonial lexicons was its redundancy. Gidugu Venkata Ramamurthy, author of the 1913 *Memorandum on Modern Telugu* and advocate of the use of a new form of written Telugu that more closely resembled spoken language, expressed his frustration with the great variety of terms available in literary Telugu, criticizing the fact that no subtle shades of meaning were indicated by the many variant terms. Such synonyms played a useful role if one needed them to fulfill a particular metrical pattern. However, Ramamurthy's view of these endless variants was that "[t]he Pandit swallows all this stuff and prescribes it to his pupil for his literary salvation. Variety is a merit in his own language; it is a demerit in the modern dialect. The variants in a living language will develop into synonyms expressing delicate differences in meaning, whereas the Pandit's variants remain a useless load on the memory."[33] By now it should not be a surprise that by the second decade of the twentieth century memory would appear in such a devalued manner in Ramamurthy's impassioned plea for the modernization of Telugu. Rejecting what he could only see as a useless load created by linguistic variants that expressed no subtle differences in shades of meaning, Ramamurthy instead explicitly advocated a form of language that was easily translatable. This again suggests that the purpose not only of lexicons but even of languages had dramatically shifted from tools to assist in the practice of memory and recall to tools assisting in the practice of translation.

C. P. Brown, half a century before Ramamurthy, was equally frustrated by what he felt to be the redundancy of literary Telugu. Criticizing the taste of many *kāvya* poets, he writes:

> rhetorical flourishes are far more prominent in those poems which are written in stanzas; doubtless each of these admired works contains a *kernal* of really pleasing poetry, but this is preceded by many a page of ill judged rhetoric, wherein the poet is evidently a mere grammarian. . . . He rejoices in synonymes, and the dictionary is never out of his thoughts. In many stanzas (particularly in the meter called sisa) the same thought is thrice reiterated with a mere change of phrase. Thus "*the fair maid decked out with these jewels entered the presence of the king. The bright damsel arrayed with these gems passed into the court of the prince. Such were the adornments of the beauteous nymph when approaching the royal threshold.*" Such passages possess an undeniable value as regards the foreigner, who will find these stanzas a most convenient substitute for the Amara Cosha and similar vocabularies of synonymes. But the taste they display is paltry enough.[34]

Print technology changed southern Indian lexicons almost irrevocably. Printing made appear irrelevant and redundant much of the apparatus that had previously supported the art of memory. Exactly those same techniques that ensured that literary works could survive and travel in space and time and still be understood were now dismissed as "redundant" and "a useless load on the memory."

Finally, most pre-colonial verse lexicons mixed Sanskrit words with Telugu words. Even more remarkably, lexicons also included words today identified as Persian or Arabic, as well as words from Kannada and other regional vernacular languages. Since their purpose was to catalogue words attested in literary usage, this often included words later considered not strictly of Telugu origin. Grouped together as these words were by topic and context of usage, no special designation was provided within pre-colonial lexicons to indicate the etymology or origin of each word. As we have seen in chapter 3, even compositions in sixteenth-century *accha Telugu,* or what is today defined as "pure" Telugu, frequently included Persian, Marathi, Tamil, and Kannada words, though they avoided Sanskrit terms.[35] What a contrast with the lexicons that were to come.

By the end of the eighteenth century, missionaries and subsequently colonial administrators (with C. P. Brown among them) began to develop lexicons less frustrating and more suitable for their purposes than the *nighaṇṭus* that already existed. The most striking feature of these new lexicons was their multilingual nature, though in a very different sense from pre-colonial lexicons. Most early European lexicons of Indian languages consisted of two or more languages, not intermixed, but rather lined up parallel to one another. One of the earliest European lexicons to include languages of the Indian subcontinent was a small vocabulary printed in Halle in 1782. It consisted of 53 words, each listed in eleven different sub-continental languages written in Roman script. Arranged topically, much like the Amara Kosha, this lexicon, entitled *Symphona sive undecim Lingvarum Orientalism-Discors Exhibita Concordia Tamulicae, Videlicet Granthanicae, Telugicae, Samscrutamicae, Marathicae, Balabandicae, Canaricae, Hindostanicae, Cuncanicae, Gutzaraticae and Peguanicae, non Caracteristicae, Qvibus, ut explicative Harmonica adjecta est Latina-Editore,* listed body parts, words pertaining to the cosmos (such as sun, moon, sky, and stars), animals, everyday life (such as house, water, and tree), and pronouns.[36] It wasn't long, however, before the needs of the era began to demand the reorganization of lexicographical knowledge in a manner more easily applicable to the tasks of colonial governance. The needs of the era were, of course, primarily needs for translation. In 1808, H. T. Colebrooke's 393-page version of the *Amara Kōśa* was printed in Serampore, using Devanagari script along with English.[37] This included English translations of all of the Sanskrit terms, Colebrooke's commentary, and, most significantly, an alphabetized English index of 219 pages. With an index longer than the original text, Colebrooke's *Amara Kōśa* was able to be used either for its original purposes or by Englishmen engaged in language learning or translation. As such, this text marks a kind of hybrid transition from one form of lexicon to another. Ultimately, later European attempts to create usable lexicons would abandon the topical arrangement entirely, keeping only the alphabetized lists.

The nineteenth century saw a flood of multi-lingual lexicons, written in most of the vernacular scripts common to southern India and containing various combinations of languages. These texts were also increasingly organized alphabetically. *A Polyglot Vocabulary in the English, Teloogoo and Tamil Languages* was published in 1851, with a second edition in 1862, suggesting that it found a ready market.[38] *The English, Tamil, Telugu and Hindustani Sonmalai, or An easy way of learning to speak four languages* was published in 1880, and a *Telugu, Canarees, Tamil, English and Hindustani Pañchabhāṣīya* [Five Language] *Vocabulary,* was printed in Kannada script in 1887.[39] Not all titles used English as the standard reference point. Some did not even include English at all. *Trībhāṣa-manjari (Se-zubani): A Vocabulary in Telugu, Hindi, and Persian,* for example, was printed in Telugu script in Masulipatam in 1890.[40] By the end of the nineteenth century many of these lexicons contained as many as six different languages. V. Madhura-Muttu Mudaliyar's *Ṣaṭ-bhāṣā-Śabdārtha Chandrika: A Vocabulary Containing Six Languages, viz. Telugu, Kannada, Tamil, English, Hindustani, and Marathi* was printed in Telugu in 1896, and P. S. Rangasvami Rau's *The Linguist's Self-instructor (in Telugu, Kannada, Malayalam, Marathi, Tamil, and English)* appeared in 1900.[41] These represent only a few of the dozens of multilingual lexicons published throughout southern India between 1850 and 1910.[42] While some were intended to teach spoken language, the majority were oriented toward translation, some explicitly so, such as Sivashankara Pandyaji's *Āndhra Hūna Bhāṣantarikarna Chintāmaṇi* [Telugu-English Translation Guide], published in 1886.[43] Without exception all of these lexicons were organized as parallel word lists, the assumption being that a word in any language must have a ready equivalent in each and every other language. Each column demanded a unique word that corresponded to the same meaning in every other column, and lexicographers worked hard to find one.

Such lexicons reflected the increasingly common attitude toward language use in southern India that had emerged by the end of the nineteenth century. Rather than thinking of the linguistic domains in which specific tasks and functions were carried out as relating to one another in a complementary way, residents of southern India had increasingly begun to expect that most functions could be carried out in a single "language." That people sometimes needed to resort to another "language" increasingly had less to do with the nature of any given task—an important consideration of an earlier era—but rather was more and more defined by the person or people with whom one wanted to interact. No longer did the task, context, nature, or characteristics of any particular language determine linguistic choice; by the beginning of the twentieth century one chose one's words according to the linguistic identity of the person with whom one was speaking. Chapter 1 has demonstrated that by the end of the nineteenth century language had ceased to be considered a feature of the landscape or a characteristic of a particular context (independent of the people who populated that context) and was increasingly thought of as a characteristic of people. To the extent that language had earlier been regarded as a reflection of identity it was linked to an individual's role within society rather than to something that would be recognizable as a linguistic identity. Chapter 3 has suggested that what was a contextually defined register in one context later became regarded as a "language." As we have seen, Sanskrit is the example of this *par excellence*, but many other "languages" of an earlier era were associated in dramatic traditions with particular types of characters and therefore functioned in a manner more closely resembling contextually defined linguistic registers of today, rather than what we today think of as languages. Actors who played villains or demons, for example, frequently spoke Apabrahmsa while only the royal hero was permitted to declaim in Sanskrit, making language itself an indicator of a character's role within the story (or within society). In modern dramatic traditions beginning in the late nineteenth century, characters within a performance were increasingly expected to speak in the "same" language, even if they used it in slightly different ways.[44] Clearly, by the beginning of the twentieth century, the experience of language in southern India, and the manner of grouping linguistic acts and selecting appropriate mediums, had changed irrevocably.

Translation and the Production of Languages

The final location in which we can see this transition to languages as separate, discrete, and parallel objects is in the domain of translation. As languages began to be considered parallel to one another rather than complementary, they also began to be thought of as universally translatable. People began to believe that anything that could be said or written in one language must, by definition, be able to be said or written in any other language. As their attitudes toward language changed, so did the ways they thought about acquiring languages. Indeed, even ideas about what constituted "knowing" a language began to change. As languages increasingly began to be seen as completely translatable, whatever content could previously be expressed in only one particular language ceased to be experienced as unique to that particular language. The effects of such a change cannot be underestimated. Immersed as any modern reader is within a contemporary linguistic sensibility, this distinction may be difficult to appreciate. As late as the early twentieth century, it was accepted that the only language through which one could learn the style of music today known as Karnatic music was through the Telugu language. In the early decades of the twentieth century, the Tamil music movement, which advocated the need to learn music in one's own "mother tongue," changed this assumption.[45] Similarly, the Tamil worship movement challenged the existing use of Sanskrit for temple and other ritual use, again advocating the right to use one's "mother tongue" for such specialized practices.[46] When we talk of learning multiple languages in pre-print southern India, what many today forget is that we are not talking of learning to do everything in every language. To "learn a language" today means to attempt (with varying degrees of success) to acquire the ability to do in that language what you can already do in another language. But this was not the case in pre-print southern India, and for many, it is not be the case even now. One learned to do different things with different languages, but not—and this is key—the same things with every language. Indeed, if you could do a particular task in one language, it was often quite unnecessary to learn how to do it in another language.

Translation is generally understood today as the practice of saying or doing something in one language that has already been said or done in another. Such an understanding of translation sets up a relationship between languages that assumes them already to be equivalent—or at least able to be made so. Naoki Sakai has questioned this accepted notion of translation as a practice that bridges two already pre-existing, but separate, linguistic mediums. Instead, he suggests that it is translation itself that is responsible for bringing these "languages" into being, making particular sets of linguistic practices appear to belong to two separate bodies of language. According to Sakai,

> Strictly speaking, it is not because two different language entities are given that we have to translate (or interpret) one text into another; it is because translation *articulates* languages so that we may postulate the two unities of the translating and the translated languages as if they were autonomous and closed entities through *a certain representation of translation.*[47]

He goes on to argue that not only languages but also ethnicities are "irreparably associated with the problematic of translation."[48]

When the British colonial administrators who took an interest in local south Indian languages first began to engage with local understandings of language, evidence suggests that they encountered a much different attitude toward the relationship between languages. However, they did not always recognize that this is what they were encountering. We can see this especially well in their attitudes toward what they took to be translation. Colonial administrators assumed that the relationship that existed between the linguistic domains they encountered in southern India reflected the same practices of translation from one language to another with which they were most familiar. In his widely read "Essay on the Language and Literature of the Telugus," published in the *Madras Journal of Literature and Science* in 1839 and again as a short book in 1840, C. P. Brown epitomizes this misunderstanding:

> We may here remark that the Telugu translators take liberties more than poetical with their originals, for they consider a general outline quite sufficient to form a copy: thus they omit, transpose and insert, whatever they please. In the life of Krishna, not only has the translator (Bammera Potu Raz) amplified the passages regarding love and beauty, but has omitted and transposed, what he pleased. He has even gone further and changed the story in some places, giving statements which are not found in the Sanscrit original. Besides (possibly wishing to conceal these deviations), the Telugu translators in *all* books set aside the numerical order of the Sanscrit, melting down ten or twelve (adhyaya) chapters into one (asvasa) book or canto. Thus it is not easy to trace in the original any passage regarding which comparison may be required.[49]

Brown's accusations of liberty, omission, transposition, insertion, and deceit point to a dramatic difference both in the "requirements" expected of language and in understandings of the relationships between languages. For Brown, the goal of translation was to say exactly the same thing in the language of translation that had been said in the original—with no additions, subtractions, or transpositions. Brown granted little value to anything that might make the new composition more suited to its new context if it entailed altering the text viewed as the "original" in any way. He also required that he be able to compare what he took to be a "translation" with its "original." However, Brown's goals and requirements of the practice of "translation" were not necessarily shared by the poets he was reading.

The literary works Brown encountered demonstrated a much different sense of purpose from Brown's own. The compositions of many of the authors he encountered told stories that their audiences already knew and loved—the *Ramayana, Mahabharata, Bhagavad Gita,* and *Panchatantra,* for example. In retelling a story already known to audiences, the point was precisely to say something already known, but to say it in a new way. Often this was intended to bring pleasure to an audience; other times it was an intellectual challenge to the poet. The many versions of the Ramayana told without using any labial consonants (*m, b, bh, p, ph*) or versions conforming strictly to a particular meter are examples of the latter type of projects. The entire genre of *dvyarthi kāvya,* "double-meaning compositions," in which two or sometimes even three stories are told simultaneously, depending on where one breaks a series of syllables into words, likewise suggests that the pleasure experienced by a poet in accomplishing a particularly challenging linguistic feat was as important a value as bringing pleasure to an audience.[50] Clearly, the agendas of pre-colonial poets differed greatly from what colonial administrators expected to encounter in Telugu literature.

Most accounts of the history of Telugu literature suggest that unlike other literatures of southern India, Telugu literature began as translation. The work celebrated as the earliest Telugu literary text, Nannaya Bhatt's *Mahabharata,* was composed in the early-eleventh-century court of Raja Raja Narendra of the Chalukyan dynasty.[51] It is typically characterized in English as a Telugu "translation" of the Sanskrit *Mahabharata.* P. Chenchiah and M. Bhujanga Rao, writing in 1925, have suggested four historical periods of Telugu literature based on the dominant literary modes of each period—periods of translation, expansion, abridgement, and imitation. They identify the first period, the period of translation, as spanning the eleventh to fifteenth centuries.[52] G. V. Sitapati, writing in 1968, likewise suggests that for the first five centuries, "a predominant part of Telugu literature consisted of translations of the Epics and Puranas."[53] Even after the fifteenth century, "translations" from Sanskrit continued to play an important role in Telugu literature, and frequently the same epics and stories—especially the Mahabharata, the Ramayana, and the Panchatantra—were repeatedly "translated" by different poets and scholars. The *Kavitraya,* or "Great Poet Trio" of Nannaya (eleventh century), Tikkana (thirteenth century), and Errapragada (fourteenth century) are consistently celebrated as the great fathers of Telugu literature, and all three are described as working on a "translation" of the lengthy Mahabharata from Sanskrit into Telugu, a task too big for any of them alone. Even in the nineteenth century many of the most significant literary figures established themselves by composing "translations" of the very same stories "translated" by their predecessors. For example, Telugu pandits of the Presidency College in Madras, Kokkonda Venkataratnam and Kandukuri Viresalingam, following their predecessor Chinnaya Suri, all composed prose translations of the Sanskrit *Panchatantra,* and all entitled their works *Nītichandrika.*[54] This suggests that those occupying (or desirous of occupying) particular positions in a literary hierarchy may have felt compelled to attempt similar literary challenges.[55]

What was at stake for the authors of such "translations"? What exactly was entailed by the "translations" composed by the *Kavitraya* and their contemporaries, the "translations" composed during the Nayaka period that overlapped with the arrival of British colonialism, and those composed by Telugu pandits at the Presidency College under colonial rule? And in what ways did each of these types of "translation" resemble notions of "translation" brought to India by the British and the enormous labor of "translation," to which entire departments of the colonial administration were devoted? That the texts produced by the individuals in these different time periods, writing under dramatically different conditions, have all come to be characterized as "translations" is rather remarkable. Not only were the agendas and conditions of production, transmission, and reception different in each case, but notions concerning the relationships between languages were also incommensurable. The story of colonial encounters with language in southern India includes the story of efforts to bring very different sensibilities regarding language into a single frame of discourse.

That this was the case can be supported by examining the shifts in definitions of a series of terms relating to "translation" that occurred during the nineteenth and twentieth centuries. The word most commonly used in Telugu today for the English term "translation" is *anuvādamu.* Yet it appears that *anuvādamu* has not always been equivalent to the English notion of "translation." A related Sanskrit cognate has been defined as "a supplementary repetition," "repetition by way of explanation, illustration or corroboration," or an "explanatory repetition or reference to what is already mentioned such as paraphrase or free translation."[56] Another related Sanskrit term, *anuvādya,* is used in grammar to denote a "subject which is supposed to be already known," suggesting that the term may be most appropriate for describing a type of translation in which the subject of the translation is already known. It is not surprising then, that it should be used for describing the many retellings of stories already well known to their readers or listeners, such as the Mahabharata, the Ramayana, or the Panchatantra.

William Brown's Telugu-English Dictionary of 1818 does not list any of the words that later come to be equated with the English term "translation." P. Sankaranarayana's *English-Telugu Dictionary,* first published in 1897, also does not include *anuvādamu* in its definition of "translation" but does mention two other terms, *bhāṣāntarīkaraṇamu* and *tarjumā,* and further glosses these two terms in English as both "translation" and "rendering into another language, interpretation." By the time of the publication of the second edition of C. P. Brown's *Telugu-English Dictionary* in 1903 (not to be confused with William Brown's 1818 dictionary), *anuvādamu* is finally given a listing as a Telugu word, but it is defined similarly to the Sanskrit, as "tautology, repetition," in contrast with the listings for *bhāṣantaramu* and *tarjumā,* both defined simply as "a translation." This definition of *anuvādamu* as "repetition" at the very beginning of the twentieth century can be contrasted with the definition given by the most recently published Telugu-English dictionary, published in 1991, in which *anuvādam* is translated simply as "translation," with no additional explanation or interpretation.

That colonial understandings of "translation" differed greatly from local understandings should not surprise us, since what the colonial bureaucracy sought to do was to "translate" new ideas and information from one language into another in which these same ideas and topics did not already exist. Often this meant "translating" English into local languages in order to reach an audience unfamiliar with specific information. Inoculation announcements, health and sanitation advisories, legal codes, and literature considered moral and uplifting, as well as revenue and other administrative policies, were subject to colonial translation practices. Far from translations being experienced as new retellings of stories or topics already known to an audience, English colonial officials saw translation as a way to convey information not yet known to a new audience. In arriving by the end of the twentieth century at a definition of *anuvādamu* as "translation," we can conclude that a shift had occurred in the meaning of the Telugu word *anuvādamu,* from "repetition" and "retelling" (of that which is already known) to "translation" (of that which is not yet known).

Another clue to shifts in linguistic signification relating to "translation" can be seen at a particular moment during the late nineteenth century that coincides with the publication of what was at the time viewed as the first Telugu novel, Kandukuri Viresalingam's *Rājaśēkhara Charitramu.*[57] With the publication of this "first novel," it appears that it quite suddenly became important to assert a difference between a "translation" and an "adaptation," a distinction that had not previously been important to emphasize, and that perhaps had not previously even existed. We can see this new distinction as an effect of attempts to make British and local understandings of translation commensurable. Kandukuri Viresalingam, the author of *Rājaśēkhara Charitramu,* described his novel as a *swēchānusaraṇamu* of Oliver Goldsmith's *The Vicar of Wakefield.* Today *swēchānusaraṇamu* would be translated into English as a "free adaptation," though earlier definitions of the second word in the term, *anusaraṇamu,* suggest a different relationship with the terms discussed above that have come to be equated with the English "translation." The second edition of C. P. Brown's *Telugu-English Dictionary* (1903) defines *anusaraṇamu* as "following, going after, serving or attending on another," but by 1991, Gwynn gives the definition simply as "adaptation."[58] Although it appears that *anusaraṇamu* and *anuvādamu* were originally much closer in meaning to one another than they are today, it is clear that by the last decades of the nineteenth century the two had begun to be explicitly distinguished in opposition to one another. Viresalingam was not writing an *anuvādamu* of *The Vicar of Wakefield.* He was explicit in asserting that he was making a *swēcha anusaraṇamu.* The terms used today have come to take their definitions in contrast to one another in a way not suggested by their earlier definitions.

Several decades later (and not long after the publication of Viresalingam's autobiography), in June of 1912, Gidugu Venkata Ramamurthy (1862–1940), professor of history at the Raja's College, Parlakimidi, in the British-administered Madras Presidency of South India, wrote his *Memorandum on Modern Telugu.* This text explicitly laid out for the first time an agenda and justification for the reform of written Telugu to make it more closely resemble educated spoken Telugu, an agenda first prefigured in 1897 by Gurujada Appa Rao in his play *Kanyāśulkam,* which used a more spoken form of Telugu than had previously been used in dramas.[59] Published the following year in 1913, Ramamurthy's *Memorandum on Modern Telugu* reflected a displacement in understandings and expectations of language and its role in society and the newly emerging nation. This was not the only document important to a debate that emerged at the end of the nineteenth century, raged most intensely between 1911 and 1914, and continued in some form even through the 1970s.[60] However, Ramamurthy's *Memorandum* was significant as the first document that clearly and systematically enumerated the positions of a self-proclaimed modernist school, which he called the "Modern Telugu Movement."[61] By 1910 when the Secondary School Leaving Certificate Board made Telugu composition and translation compulsory subjects for the school final and intermediate classes, the terms of the debate were already emerging.[62] It was in the *Memorandum* that Ramamurthy explicitly delineated the two camps and defined them in opposition to each other. For Ramamurthy, these two camps were represented by the "Members of the Telugu Academy," who later came to be known as "the classicists," and the members of the Modern Telugu Movement, later known as "the modernists."[63] The former advocated the use of "literary Telugu" (language attested by earlier literary works) for school and college examinations, instruction, and textbooks; the latter advocated the use of the "spoken Telugu" of the educated classes as the written form to be used in schools and colleges—a style of writing that was at that moment not yet clearly defined in either theory or practice. Descriptions of the actual language used in the writings of members of each of these groups indicate that the Telugu in which their arguments were written and disseminated did not easily fall into the very categories they were asserting. Bh. Krishnamurti writes, "While G. V. Ramamurti succeeded in shaking up the confidence of the classicists to write in the so-called pure literary dialect, he failed to offer clear illustrations or models for the modern spoken language he was advocating. His own writing represented an arbitrary admixture of classical and modern nominal and verbal forms although he would not have used such a style in speech."[64]

An overlooked but crucial detail within this debate is the fact that all of the earliest documents over the form of written Telugu, including Ramamurthy's *Memorandum,* were written in English for a predominantly British administrative audience. Only much later, when both "sides" began appealing to a wider public for support of their positions, were their arguments disseminated in Telugu as well. Indeed, the often invisible role played by English in these debates is important, not only as the language in which the discussion is initially carried out, but also in its critical positioning in relation to both of the newly emerging "classical" and "modern" Telugus. Although Ramamurthy claims to be comparing and contrasting "modern spoken" Telugu with "classical literary" Telugu, his examples and illustrations suggest that he is actually comparing both modern and literary Telugu with English, making English a mediating but silent third term between the two styles of language. In fact, most of Ramamurthy's arguments against classical literary Telugu and in favor of modern Telugu would not make sense without reference to English. Yet because English is never explicitly mentioned as a comparison, it becomes invisible, acting as an apparently external and neutral language in relation to the ostensive conflict between "classical" and "modern" Telugu. Nevertheless, English provides virtually all of the terms through which literary and spoken Telugu are viewed. Although Ramamurthy's use of English gives the appearance of simply translating ideas that already exist in Telugu, he in fact uses many English terms, particularly grammatical terms, that do not exist in Telugu. By doing this he is, in practice, making Telugu and English commensurable in ways never previously known. His numerous examples suggest that he is remaking Telugu into a more suitable medium for the direct and singular translation of English, and more generally European, ideas and concepts. In his Appendix A, he states: "The history of the Telugu language has not yet been studied systematically. No authorities are, therefore, quoted."[65] Rather than refer to the numerous grammatical treatises written on (and in) what he now labels "literary" Telugu, Ramamurthy prefers to use Western grammarians and their models as his authorities.

In describing the differences between modern and literary Telugu he presents the following major sections: Pronunciation, Declension, Conjugation, and Vocabulary and Idiom. In each category he gives examples of "old" Telugu that he argues do not translate into English or that can be translated into English in multiple ways. In contrast, the examples he cites from "modern" Telugu are always given as direct and singular translations, fully commensurable with English—and, most significantly, commensurable in a one-to-one equivalency. For modern Telugu there is one and only one way of saying anything that can be said in English. The following examples illustrate what Ramamurthy repeats throughout his appendix with different grammatical forms:

> ***cheppinan*** (j) The old conditional form *cheppinan* is ambiguous even in the literary language; it means (1) 'when you have said' and (2) 'if you said.' A living language avoids ambiguity. M.T. [modern Telugu] uses *cheppitay* 'if you say,' *cheppinappuḍu* 'when you said,' *cheppinatarvāta* 'after you said,' *cheppinā* 'though you said.'
>
> ***rā(n)ḍu*** (k) O.T. [old Telugu] *rā(n)ḍu*=1. He will not come; 2. He did not come; 3. He does not come. But M.T. has *rāḍu* 'he will not come'; *rālēdu* 'did not come'; *rāvaḍamulēdu* 'he does (did) not come' and thus avoids ambiguity.[66]

These examples show that although he claims to be comparing old Telugu with modern Telugu, he is, in fact, comparing both with English in order to demonstrate that the latter corresponds more closely to categories of thought within English. None of his examples show old Telugu in the context of its use, so we are unable to tell whether ambiguity actually occurs in practice or only in the attempt to translate written Telugu into English and vice versa. He also uses numerous grammatical terms taken directly from English grammar, terms that seemingly correspond exactly with the examples he cites from "modern" Telugu, but not with the examples he provides from "old" Telugu.[67] In this he follows C. P. Brown and other European linguists who have already attempted to describe the language in terms of European grammatical categories.

Another indication of the importance of translation to this entire debate is the fact that the controversy over written Telugu arose in response to the decision in 1910 of the Secondary School Leaving Certificate Board to make mandatory two new examination papers for the school intermediate and final classes. One of these was a paper in translation. Translation and the controversy over the form in which it should occur were indeed fundamental to the emergence of an effort to reform written Telugu. Despite its implicit presence throughout his text though, Ramamurthy never once mentions translation. Not only did English provide a sense of displacement—a new position—from which to view the "Telugu language," but it also provided a reference point against which Telugu—both "Telugus"—could be compared and evaluated. The crucial question for the modern reformers of written Telugu was never "Can one do and say everything with the written language that one needs to do?" Instead, the implicit but unspoken question they were asking was "Can one do and say everything in Telugu the same way one can do and say it in English?"

For the reformers of Telugu, the answer was no, but they were determined to make it yes. By the early decades of the twentieth century, the project of making languages parallel, equivalent, and commensurable with one another had taken over the imaginations of many. A new relationship to language was becoming firmly established.

All of the transitions discussed thus far have led to an acceptance in India today of the naturalness of a single "mother tongue." The need for specific languages to perform specific tasks has been displaced by a belief in the ability to do anything you need to do in your "mother tongue." Not only has this led to the assumption that languages exist in parallel to one another, but this belief in the parallel capacities of language means that today there is no value placed on the unique content available in any one particular language. Once upon a time one would read or recite Valmiki's Ramayana in Sanskrit and study Karnatic music in Telugu. Particular kinds of knowledge had to be learned in or through particular linguistic mediums. Indeed, medium and content were united, with no real distinction made between the one and the other, as is nicely illustrated by the pre-colonial study of music in southern India. Yet with the rise of the belief that everything can be translated, linguistic mediums increasingly became divorced from their content. As long as language was learned in use, content and medium were intimately entwined. As language increasingly came to be studied as an object, it became divorced from its content and began to be learned only as a medium—indeed, devoid of content. When this happened, languages ceased to "contain" anything unique—they began to exist only as mediums through which knowledge can be introduced from other languages via translation. A language viewed only as medium, devoid of content, has little real purpose left but to mark out a domain—and it is here that we can recognize the appearance of the spectre of "culture."

Once content became free-floating, available equally via every language, the only thing left that appeared unique about any particular language was its ability to signify "culture." If all languages can be translated, then there is no longer anything special that can be learned or accomplished in one language as opposed to another. If one can study science, music, geography, or mathematics in one language, then the belief today is that one can learn these subjects equally well in any other language, provided one's competency in that language is adequate and translations have been made available. But once the specific content in a particular language has become available in any language through translation, content and medium are irrevocably separated from one another. The limiting factor is defined by characteristics of the individual rather than by characteristics of the subject to be learned. Again, we see the new attachment of language to person rather than to a task or context. It is precisely such an experience of language that has led to the appearance of a statue of *Telugu Talli,* the personified representation of Mother Telugu, in front of the State Secretariat that no longer requires the use of the Telugu language itself. *Telugu Talli* can today appear in the company of the English language without any reference at all to the actual Telugu language or script and without the slightest appearance of contradiction. Telugu's role as a unique medium is no longer crucial. Its roles as a marker of socio-political identity and foundation for political and cultural authority, however, have never been more important.

CHAPTER 6

Martyrs in the Name of Language? Death and the Making of Linguistic Passion

The Andhra movement didn't become a mass movement until the very end.

—Former Andhra movement leader, Nellore, August 12, 1998

India's new linguistic states, advocated from the 1910s onward and brought into existence in the 1950s, have been widely heralded as more fairly representing the needs and desires of the populace and correcting the historical injustices created by colonial administrative territories. Mohandas Karamchand Gandhi, for example, included the recognition of provincial languages as the eleventh of eighteen guiding points within his 1941 anti-colonial "Constructive Programme" for the achievement of "*Poorna Swaraj* or complete independence by truthful and non-violent means."[1] Gandhi's platform greatly influenced Potti Sriramulu in his decision to undergo his fast-unto-death for a separate Andhra State and to undertake many of his earlier reform activities, and very few of his actions were taken up without first consulting with Gandhi and other political leaders. As early as 1911, a series of articles appeared in the weekly publication *Dēśābhimāni* advocating the formation of a Telugu linguistic state.[2] The historian P. Raghunadha Rao has used these articles to argue that "the Andhras laboured under a double disadvantage." On the one hand, "[t]he British officers who ruled over them had very little knowledge of Telugu." And on the other, "[t]heir subordinates [who were] mostly non-Telugus had very little acquaintance with the Telugu language or the people. As such the grievances of the Telugus were not brought to the notice of the Government."[3]

In the final days before Prime Minister Nehru's declaration of the new state, the widespread gatherings and subsequent violence that occurred in the wake of Potti Sriramulu's death were read by Andhra movement leaders, historians, and journalists alike as evidence of the coming together of the people's passion over the issue of linguistic statehood and of the uniformity of the feelings of Telugu-speakers. In the words of the historian, B. Sreeramulu,

> The news [of Potti Sriramulu's death] shocked the people and the sporadic disturbances that had already begun two or three days prior to his death reached the climax on 16 December, 1952. . . . Wagons were looted. Trains were stopped. . . . Hartals, picketings, processions, condolence meetings, emotional speeches took place throughout the Andhra Province and particularly in the notable towns like Vijayawada, Nellore, Tirupathi and Bellary, unmindful of the police firing, tear gas and *lathi* charges. . . . The great fast unto death undertaken by Potti Sriramulu roused all Andhra into unified activity such as had been unknown for some time past. People all over *Andhra Desa* expressed themselves with one voice to demand the immediate formation of a separate state for themselves.[4]

The outpouring of grief at Potti Sriramulu's death, the processions and strikes in his memory, and the widespread violence and looting have been collapsed within a single narrative leading to the formation of a separate state. It is as though the leaders of the Andhra movement and later historians can conceive of no other possibility than that all those who emerged into public spaces and engaged in any of the activities listed above—looting, processions, meetings, violence, strikes, picketing, and memorials—were all passionately determined to bring about the "immediate formation of a separate state for themselves." As we shall see, however, narratives collected from a wide range of people linked to these 1952 events introduce large and compelling fractures into this seemingly unitary narrative, even while simultaneously illustrating the culmination of the processes discussed in the preceding chapters and the power of language to act as an organizing framework for events, narratives, and human identifications.

How exactly did these events come to be read as evidence of the collective desires and shared anxieties of the majority of speakers of Telugu residing in southern India, and what role did the shifts and transformations discussed in each of the preceding chapters play in this interpretation? Who did discussions of the "masses" actually refer to, and what did it mean in 1952 to say that the Andhra movement had finally become a mass movement? The Andhra movement leader quoted at the beginning of this chapter was not alone in his feeling that it was only at the very end that the Andhra movement achieved mass proportions. As he explained, the movement "originated with the middle-class educated classes, who were in need of jobs. It never really reached a mass movement level until after Potti Sriramulu's death."[5] This was to become a refrain heard again and again as I talked with people about the movement for a separate Telugu-speaking linguistic state. Although most agreed that the nature of the movement changed radically in its last days, not everyone agreed on the extent to which this reflected the desires of the masses. A retired college lecturer and one of the few Andhra movement leaders to come from a non-dominant caste background was more equivocal on the matter, suggesting that it both was and was not a true mass movement. He described the movement by saying: "Before Potti Sriramulu there was no real agitation, only committee meetings. Then there was a one-day hartal. Even I [by that time already a college lecturer] went along with the students."[6] He said that he would call it a mass movement from that point on, "even though poor people didn't participate," justifying his statement with the comment that "for three days after Potti Sriramulu's death all trains were stopped."[7] Elaborating, he explained that "buses were very few in 1952, so stopping trains was a big deal," suggesting that the authenticity of the movement depended upon the level of disturbance of everyday life. Yet despite this, he still characterized the nature of the participation in the Andhra movement as primarily "middle class peasants and students," clarifying that "[t]he actual toilers and laborers weren't involved."[8] On the one hand, he measured the movement's extension to the masses in proportion to the length and effectiveness of efforts to disrupt everyday transportation, communication, and commerce. However, his awareness that participation did not extend to the poor and uneducated—precisely those groups who stood to gain little from a separate state—kept him from wholeheartedly describing it as a mass movement.

His final comments displayed even more ambivalence on this count. An active participant in what he described as the mass struggle of 1942 against the British (during which there was a warrant out for his arrest), he found it difficult to talk of the Andhra movement without comparing it with the earlier anti-colonial Quit India movement. He said with more than a little nostalgia that "in 1952 everyone was reminded of the 1942 struggle.

Nineteen fifty-two was a repetition on a small scale of 1942. Nineteen forty-two was a *real* mass movement."[9] For him, the Andhra movement appeared as a pale imitation of a true mass movement, something that wanted to be what it was not, and that was partly fueled by nostalgia for the excitement and feeling of success of the earlier anti-colonial movement. He described the question of a separate Andhra State as primarily "a superficial problem, one that doesn't go down to the roots," calling it "more of a bureaucratic matter, not something to be emotional about."[10] For this particular leader, then, a true mass movement required two fundamental elements that the Andhra movement lacked. First, it required the participation of poor people, "the actual toilers and laborers," and second, it demanded that the emotions of participants be involved. Without strong passion, in his eyes it could not become a true mass movement.

From a more official perspective, the transition occurred at the moment that violence entered the equation. The deputy inspector-general of police for the Northern Range summarized the view of the special branch of police in a secret inspection report, writing: "The Andhra State agitation, confined till about the middle of December 1952 to conferences, meetings and passing of resolutions culminated in violent activities subsequent to the death of Sri Potti Sreeramulu."[11] Others, too, hold up the widespread violence as evidence of the intensity of passion and emotional engagement. The historian K. V. Narayana Rao tells us that "the disturbances reached the climax on 16 December. Mobs raided the Vijayawada railway station. Wagons were looted. Seven people were killed in police firings in different places. The damage to railway property was estimated by the government at Rs. 50 lakhs [five million rupees]."[12] Others have described the "explosive situation,"[13] the "furious mobs,"[14] and "the resentment and provocation of feelings of the Andhras, some of whom, on hearing of the immolation of Potti Sriramulu became infuriated."[15] The heightened emotional state of "the people" was held up as the cause of the violence experienced throughout the region, but the violence that occurred was also consistently invoked as evidence of the people's passion over the issue of linguistic statehood.

The question of whether those who were killed during the four days of violence were heroes, and whether they should be remembered and honored as such today, forms a second tension within narratives of the culmination of the Andhra movement. Anantha Ramaiah, the octogenarian senior advocate and former president of the Nellore Town Youth League who generously shared with me his extensive personal archive of the event, referred to the four young men who were killed in Nellore—introduced in the introduction—as the *āndhra rāṣṭra mṛta vīrulu* [martyrs of Andhra State], or the *mṛta vīrulu* [lit., "dead heroes"], for short. He also made several concerted efforts to get the government to establish a memorial in front of the Nellore Railway Station for the four young men who were killed by the police so that their contribution to the movement could be publicly recognized and acknowledged—a multi-decade attempt that met with one bureaucratic obstacle after another.[16] At one level such efforts have held these young men up as evidence of the mass nature of the movement and the widespread popular desire for a separate Andhra state. It was precisely the lives that were sacrificed to police bullets, not only in Nellore but also in towns throughout the coastal districts, that were given credit for forcing Nehru's hand, and therefore for bringing the struggle to its ultimate fruition.

Yet at the same time, assertions have also been made that the young men who died as a result of police efforts to subdue unruly crowds were not "real" activists and therefore do not deserve the attention of history. By implication this attitude extended to include many of the others who were present at the railway station that day. When I attempted to elicit memories of the four young Nellore men and the police firings that took their lives from another retired advocate, freedom fighter, and self-proclaimed co-worker of Potti Sriramulu's, he slapped his hand emphatically on the table in front of him and exclaimed that "those four boys were not freedom fighters. Not just *harijans* [untouchables], but also other castes as well, they were not freedom fighters."[17] The vehemence of his comment suggests that he felt that those who were killed in the violence did not, in fact, have a right to claim credit for the ultimate victory of the movement. His repeated use of the term "freedom fighter" invoked an official government of India category for those who participated in the anti-colonial struggle, bringing pensions, special railway counters, and other benefits to those who have been thus officially recognized. He, like others, believed that authentic engagement with the issues at stake could only be manifested through sustained commitment to the movement. Only those who were involved in the long series of meetings, petitions, letter campaigns, and conferences that stretched from 1912 onward were worthy of being recognized as authentic and legitimate freedom fighters. Yet, despite such unwillingness to accept the Johnny-come-latelies who greatly swelled the

FIGURE 6.1. The bodies of Sriramulu, Nageswara Rao, Guruswami, and Ezrah, killed by police at the Nellore Railway Station, December 16, 1952. PHOTO: V. Chinna Rao/ *Courtesy V. Anantha Ramaiah, former president, Nellore Town Youth League* (used by permission).

ranks in the last days as authentic activists, many still read the "huge crowd at Nellore Railway Station on December 16, 1952" as evidence of "a protest against the Congress High Command and prime minister for delaying formation of [a] separate Andhra State."[18]

This claim that "those four boys were not freedom fighters" again demonstrates how much the idioms used for thinking and talking about the Andhra movement were shaped by the earlier nationalist struggle against the British. Five years after independence, no one could have expected that the young men who were killed, who ranged in age from fifteen to nineteen, would have been old enough to have fought in the anti-colonial struggle. Yet, the suggestion remained that their commitment, even to a separate Andhra, was questionable, given the absence of a larger context of participation in meetings, rallies, and other sustained long-term activities to support it. Still others expressed their ambivalence over the contributions made by such individuals in a different way. When asked about the four young men and others who had gone to the railway station that day, a Brahmin who was a retired clerk from the Taluk [sub-district] Office, explained it to me this way. "See," he said, "people want their names to be published in papers, for some reason, good or bad. That's all. And so, some people went to hijack the train, some people went to create some mischief. That is all."[19]

The Participants Imagined

> *We came only after the firings had happened. We came only to stop the violence.*
>
> —Nellore Town Youth League Member, 1952,
> Nellore, October 19, 2002

The power of narratives of the linguistic state movement—both oral and written—to absorb and erase all other narratives concerning the events that occurred in the four days between Potti Sriramulu's death and Nehru's declaration of the new Andhra state is dramatic. The deaths of the four young men at the Nellore Railway Station, along with similar deaths in Anakapalle, Visakhapatnam, Waltair, Guntur, and Srikakulam, are mentioned only to the extent that they support a larger narrative of the swelling passions of the masses and their demand for the immediate formation of a Telugu linguistic state. Except for local newspaper coverage immediately following the events, narratives of these events do not mention the victims by name, but simply use the fact of their deaths as one more example of the extremes of the uncontrollable popular passion that stemmed from impatience with the government's reluctance to act.[20] These narratives treat the specific individuals in question in much the same way that leaders of the Andhra movement treated their bodies—by appropriating them within the larger frame of the achievement of linguistic statehood. There is little interest in the specificities of the individuals' names, backgrounds, stories, concerns, or motives for being at the station that day. Shahid Amin has commented upon the tendency for historians to avoid accounting for events in and of themselves, instead only showing concern for what the events have led to, and the ways in which specific events have supported something larger.[21]

Given the absence of specific details concerning both those who lost their lives and more generally those who participated in the events of December 16, people's impressions of the four young men who died in the police firings provide a window into their ideas of who constitutes "the masses" and reveal a number of intriguing tensions regarding the imagination of "the Andhra people." These tensions place into high relief the power of dominant narratives to erase, absorb, or ignore what does not otherwise easily fit. In many cases thoughts regarding the identities of the four young men were drawn, not from knowledge of the four victims, but from stereotypical ideas of who was thought to have been advocating for a separate Telugu-speaking state. In other cases, it was influenced by tropes pertaining to those elements imagined as most likely to take part in "agitations" regardless of their objective. In all of these examples, the many contradictory statements proffered concerning the identities of the four victims and, more generally, the identities of those who were present at the Nellore Railway Station and in the massive gatherings that occurred in other towns and cities in the wake of Potti Sriramulu's death, tell us more about how people thought about the movement than they do about the identities of those who actually participated.

For some, this meant describing the four victims in what the speaker imagined as the most representative terms possible. The elder brother of one of the four young men killed, for example, described the four victims in representative terms while describing the funeral arrangements: "Three bodies were buried at the burial ground near the Pennar River," he explained. "One Yanadi [a tribal community], one Vaiśya [a "forward" caste community and the community of Potti Sriramulu], one B. C. [member of a Backward Class] . . . Israel's family wanted a Christian burial, so they took his body."[22] One "forward" class, one "backward" class, one Christian, and one tribal—although these don't exhaust all of the representational possibilities, it does reflect a diversity of backgrounds united by their presence at the railway station that day.

A contemporary of Potti Sriramulu (and, like Sriramulu, a Vaiśya), who in 2002 was leading a movement to have the District of Nellore renamed "Potti Sriramulu District," offered a similarly representative impression of the four. He explained that of the four boys who died that day, "one was a Christian, one a Muslim, one a Reddy, and I can't recollect the fourth one." "Was there no Vaiśya among them?" I asked. "No Vaiśya," he replied emphatically. His unequivocal certainty on this last point suggests that since he himself (like Potti Sriramulu) was a Vaiśya, he would have taken special notice of anyone from his own community who had been killed.[23] As Reddys represent one of the most dominant landowning Hindu caste communities in the Telugu-speaking regions of southern India, his characterization of the four young men as Christian, Muslim, and Hindu suggests that he believed the movement to represent not just the interests of a single religious community but larger interests, transcending and shared by all religious communities. Indeed, his comments (in an era of increasing communal tensions) suggest a post-communal ideal in which the population is united by language rather than divided by religion. The fact that he does not imagine any of the victims as members of Scheduled Tribe (ST), Scheduled Caste (SC), or what are today categorized as Other Backward Class (OBC) communities, the three most disadvantaged segments of contemporary society, when, in fact, all four of them belonged to these communities brings into relief the gap between the events and their subsequent conversion to narrative.[24]

His omission contrasts with statements of still others, some with more firsthand knowledge of the events. One former leader, who in his capacity as a member of the Nellore Town Youth League played a central role in the 1952 events, had gone to help quell the violence at the railway station with other members of the League and later helped to raise funds for the victims and their families. He characterized the first victim as a member of a student movement, and a second as the son of a teacher, but did not mention anything about their religious or caste backgrounds or whether they had any specific political associations.[25] Yet another leader described them to me as all members of backward communities (lower, non-dominant castes), "Not scheduled castes, not Dalits, but BCs."[26]

Members of the local Communist Party were also centrally involved in the Andhra movement. Many of the party members with whom I was able to speak wanted me to understand that they had been active in quelling the violence at the railway station but had not been present when it began. Yet others imagined the members of political parties engaging in a very different role. Several imagined those who participated in the commotion, not in religious, caste, or class terms, but in political terms. Once when I was discussing the Andhra movement and Potti Sriramulu's death with a friend in Hyderabad—a well-informed resident of the Telangana region of present-day Andhra Pradesh in his mid-thirties—he told me that "four Communist workers were killed in Nellore" following Potti Sriramulu's death.[27] In this case, caste and religious associations took a back seat to imagined political affiliations. Though both political leaders and immediate family members all stated that none of the four young men had any known connections with either the Communist Party or any other political party, his comment reflects widespread feelings that the agitations were orchestrated by political parties for their own ends, and that the participants were primarily party members. Official secret reports kept by the police likewise suggest a political hand in the events. In describing the violence that occurred subsequent to Potti Sriramulu's death, the deputy inspector general of police wrote:

> The local terrorists took advantage of the unsettled conditions and started vehement campaign against the Congress and Praja Socialists. The agitation on 16–12–52 started with hartals and processions in Nellore town and by the evening the attention of the agitators was diverted to the railway station yard where railway properties were damaged and vehicles burnt. The also tried to over-power the police force that attempted to stop the further damage by the mob.[28]

It is clear from other references within this same report that the term "terrorists" meant members of the Communist Party.

Even within discussions of the involvement of political parties in the events in question, there existed an unusual division of political labor. On the one hand, a number of the former Communist leaders with whom I spoke wanted me to understand how spontaneous the popular reactions to Potti Sriramulu's death had been, and how much they represented the true will of the people—a will that they, too, shared, and that led uncompromisingly toward the formation of a Telugu linguistic state. Yet at the same time I also frequently encountered the suggestion that the actions of these same masses were something from which the educated party organizers preferred to distance themselves. They needed to be able to claim evidence of the "passion" of the "masses," in the form of uncontrollable and "spontaneous" violence and destruction, but at the same time, they also wanted to be able to disassociate themselves from the very acts that provided the evidence they required. The predominantly upper-caste leaders wanted to make clear that they themselves would never participate in any of the rampant and uncontrollable crowd-induced public activities—the burning of rail bogies and police jeeps, the destruction of railway and other government property, the looting and theft of private property, and other acts of violence and crime. These often indirect inferences were generally accompanied by statements that made clear that the speaker would never engage in such acts, but rather was above such associations.

The comments of one Communist leader, for example, suggest that while he may have organized and led pre-planned non-violent actions—meetings, disciplined processions, fundraisers, and other non-destructive events, he would never have participated in something spontaneous that might have become violent or destructive. As a Communist, he told me he had disavowed his Brahmin origins and dropped the brahmanical fixture "Sastri" from the end of his name.[29] Despite this disavowal of caste origins and the attempt to erase explicit differences between himself and others, he was still concerned with distinguishing his contributions to the movement from those of the masses. Somewhat surprisingly, most of the self-proclaimed leaders within the Andhra movement explicitly wanted me to understand that they were not present during the violence—at least not until after the firings occurred. And when they did arrive, they made it clear that they went only "to try and stop the violence. Only to protect others." One Youth League member cited at the beginning of this section was another who claimed to have gone "only to stop the violence," and only after having heard the news of the police firings.

In a lengthy narrative he described to me their role in what happened that day:

> The whole trouble started by some people setting fire. The *bandobast* [security preparation] was there. The Deputy Superintendent of Police then was one Mr. John, a Tamilian [a Tamil-speaker]. Our DSP, supported by MSP—Malabar Special Police—they were there, stationed at the railway station to protect their property.
>
> Then there was a jeep of the police stationed at the north gate of the railway station, near Ranganayalapet. It was set on fire by somebody. Then, the crowd came to the railway station. I was not there. Even Ismail [another prominent leader] was not there. When the mob had swollen, they launched an order. Perhaps some pelted stones. They opened fire on the orders of the DSP, Mr. John. He was transferred the next day. He could not stay here because of that. Then these four boys died. About twenty persons got hurt, including the adopted son of the local college principal, Satyajitanandan Pillai.
>
> When we came to know that the firing was taking place, we ran [to the station]. After *knowing.* First we were not the leaders of that group at the railway station. We might have held some meetings in support of Potti Sriramulu, *in the town.* We didn't participate in that attack on the railway station. That was the job of some others.
>
> So, when nobody went to their rescue, we went in a group

> of about four to five hundred, to help them—to prevent further firing. We reached the station about 6:30–7:00. It was dark. The then Circle Inspector of Nellore Town was one Mr. Venkaiah Naidu. A patriot. And also related to one of the senior advocates, a Mr. G. Sarangapani. Then he saw us, and shouted "Don't shoot." And when we went near him, these are the words he used: "*Arava lanja koḍuku firing order chēsaru.*" That bastard [lit., son of a Tamil whore] ordered the firing.[30] So, then that bastard was hiding to the east of the railway station, under a water tank. Even now, the tank is available.
>
> After we went, people gathered around us. There was no more violence, no firing, no tear gas.[31]

Their role, he emphasized, was in stopping the violence, not in organizing it. This clear distinction between the undisciplined masses and the discipline of leaders was stressed by almost all of the leaders with whom I spoke.

The implicit association between violence and "lumpen elements," as several put it, is something that intersected with both class and caste in consistent ways within most accounts of the events in question. Many of those who repeatedly stressed that they didn't participate in the attack on the railway station also characterized the four young men who were killed as lower caste. "All were B.C.s," stressed one leader. Similar associations between caste and violent or criminal activity pervaded print media accounts of the time, as well. This distinction can be taken a step further, though, as not all print media descriptions of the participants automatically characterized them negatively. Rather, there were clear distinctions made between actions wholeheartedly condoned by political organizers, their fellow journalists, and historians, and actions they condemned but also tacitly accepted as evidence of the "passions" of the "masses" pushed to extremes by the ignorance and neglect of national leaders (such as Nehru, and his hesitancy in acting on the formation of Andhra State). If particular actions were deemed acceptable and worthy of praise, the mob was characterized as "made up primarily of students." If, on the other hand, the actions engaged in were considered more unacceptable by middle-class speakers, the composition of the mob was suddenly changed to "harijans" [Dalits, or those regarded as "untouchable" by orthodox Hindus] and "labourers" or "unruly elements" and "hooligans," often in the same account, sometimes even the same sentence. Benign activities that simply disrupted everyday life but were not violent or destructive, such as the holding of meetings, halting of trains and buses, the closing of businesses and courts, the shouting of slogans, the wearing of armbands, and the boycotting of classes, were represented as activities that students organized and carried out. However, whenever references were made to looting or theft, "harijans" or "labourers" were held responsible. And violence, setting items on fire, or destroying public property were consistently characterized as the work of "unruly elements" or "hooligans." Indeed, there were very few exceptions to these stereotypical descriptions, as the following examples make clear. There was also tremendous agreement between the journalists who reported on the events of December 15 through 19, 1952, as they were happening, and prominent upper-caste Nellore citizens who remember these same events five decades later.[32]

Another of the leaders involved in fundraising efforts displayed this same split in his own representations of demonstrators as both "students" and "unruly elements." On at least one occasion he identified the unruly elements as lower caste and distanced himself from their actions. On another occasion he characterized some of those killed and injured in the police firings as students and explicitly identified with them.[33] In some historical and news accounts the participants were referred to simply as a "mob." In Vijayawada, for example, it was reported that "Vijayawada railway station and surroundings were occupied by a mob, and the railway officials and workers were shoved out of the station precincts at noon to-day."[34] Elsewhere it was reported that "[t]he Southern Railway headquarters have received information that a huge mob raided the Vijayawada railway station, looted the entire building and cut off all communications. Consequently they have cancelled the running of trains of the North-east line between Madras and Waltair."[35] Whenever the mob was characterized as engaging in a criminal act, particularly theft, there was generally a class angle to the description. *The Hindu,* for example, reported that "At Vijayawada Railway Station, a big crowd of labourers, including women, broke open about 300 loaded wagons stabled in the yards with rice, paddy or wheat and carried them away on their heads."[36] Elsewhere, descriptions of similar activities were characterized in terms of the caste identities of the participants, as when *The Hindu* reported the next day that "[t]here was some trouble this morning at Navabpalam, West Godavary district. A crowd of local Harijans started looting rice bags in the railway station. But before the police party arrived, the Harijans left the place throwing away some of the bags on the wayside."[37]

In contrast, there was not a single case of students being described as carrying away rice bags or looting shops. Instead, students were characterized as orderly, disciplined, and engaged in activities disruptive of everyday life, but never violent or destructive. On December 17, *The Hindu* described the Andhras who participated in the demonstrations in Madras during the funeral procession of Potti Sriramulu as "mainly students. . . . Andhra students in various educational institutions abstained from their classes to-day. Batches of college students arrived in procession shouting '*Sriramulu Zindabad*' [Long live Sriramulu!], 'We want Andhra State,' etc. By about 12 o'clock, tram-loads and bus-loads of students from different parts started coming in and they all stood in rows and moved in queues to have a last darshan of Mr. Sriramulu."[38] Not only did "students" not engage in violent and destructive acts, but here they moved only in "rows" and "queues," a remarkable accomplishment for any mob. Elsewhere, students were described as shouting slogans, wearing badges, organizing processions, halting trains and buses, abstaining from classes, and picketing shops—all non-violent, if disruptive, activities, while "unruly elements" and "hooligans" set fire to records and destroyed station premises and signal wires. In Masulipatnam, "several hundred students paraded the thoroughfares on cycles shouting slogans and wearing black badges," as in Guntur, where "students' processions paraded the streets shouting slogans."[39] In Anantapur, "a long procession, mainly of students, went round the streets of the town this morning," and "a big crowd, mostly of college students, held up the No. 68 Down passenger train, running from Guntakal to Bangalore City, at three different points within the railway station limits."[40] Elsewhere, "students went round the streets of the town shouting, 'We demand Andhra State. Sri Ramulu Johar.'"[41] In Vizianagaram, "[a] big procession led by students, proceeded to the Collector's Office, the District Munsif's office and other offices and demanded suspension of work for the day."[42] And the next day, it was reported that "[i]nformation has just been received that over 300 students, marched to Mudanur station this morning near Cuddapah and stood in front of the Bombay Express train bound for Madras."[43]

Clear distinctions, however, were made between the acts of these students and the much less savory actions of the supposedly non-student "unruly elements and hooligans." For example, in Guntur, "On hearing a rumour that some students were detained at the railway station, unruly elements rushed from the public meeting to the railway station and damaged the station premises and burnt some records in the Parcel Office."[44] Here the contrast with students was made explicit. Students were detained, but unruly elements caused damage and burnt records. And in Rajamundry, "[r]eports of hooliganism resulting in damage to railway property including damage to signal wires, traces, etc., are also received from Duggirala, Tenali and Ongole in Guntur district and from several other places in the north-east section of the Southern Railway."[45] It was as though a single mob took its identifying description, not from the individuals who composed it, but rather from the specific actions in which it engaged. If the "mob" burned and destroyed property, it was made up of "hooligans" and "unruly elements." If it stole grain and looted shops, it was made up of "harijans" and "labourers." But if this same "mob" engaged in orderly processions, distribution of armbands, non-violent picketing of shops and halting of trains, then it was made up of "students."

The Relatives' Stories

Having deferred the accounts given by the relatives of the firing victims until now, it is time to turn a careful ear to their stories. I have thus far refrained from writing too much about the four young men who were killed by the police in Nellore in order to re-create the sense of the narratives of these events that predominate in history books, news reports, commemorations of the formation of Andhra State, and popular memory. Small details within a larger narrative of the Andhra movement, even the rare mentions of the names of these young men are inconsistent. *The Hindu* newspaper reported three of the deceased as "Ezra, student, Training School, Nellore; Guruswami, vegetable vendor; Sriramulu, son of a soda vender."[46] By the next day, when the fourth young man, having died after being taken to the hospital, was added to the first three, the names of the dead were no longer relevant. Instead, the "Four Dead in Nellore" simply became an example, as the headline suggests, of the "Situation in Andhra."[47] Only the local Nellore Telugu weekly *Zamin Ryot* took greater interest in the details of the local dead and injured, identifying the dead as "S. Israel, 20 year old Rapur student studying in Higher Grade second year in the Training School; K. Guruswami, vegetable vendor in the shop of Bade Saheb, Chinna Bazaar; Sriramulu, son of Ravilakshmi Ramaiah (alias "soda Ramaiah"), Stonehousepet, 16 years old, a Rebalawari High School third form student; and Potluru Nagesawara Rao, *mashālјī* [lamp-lighter] in the Additional First Class Magistrate Court, 18 years old."[48]

The former president of the Nellore Town Youth League remembered them in the following way:

> The first was N. Israyeel, 19 years old and a Christian. His father was an elementary school teacher, and he himself was in his 2nd year in the Nellore Training School, Higher Grade. After his third year he would have completed his training. The second, K. Guruswamy, was 17 years old. His mother was a vegetable vendor, but his father's name was not available, so he may be difficult to trace. The third was R. Sreeramulu, 15 years old. His father ran a soda shop. And the last was P. Nageswara Rao, 18 years old, a peon—a panka [fan] puller—in the Court of the Additional First Class Magistrate, Nellore.

From the names alone, it is difficult to determine the caste backgrounds of any of the four who were killed in Nellore; however, all belonged to lower castes. The first, Ezrah, was a Christian who had not quite been able to escape the Dalit associations with his identity, despite his father's conversion to Christianity. Ezrah's father was a member of the Mala community —regarded as untouchable by orthodox Hindus—who converted to Christianity under the influence of the American Baptist Church active in his town. The brother of Nageswara Rao, the second firing victim, told me they came from a tribal background and belonged to the Yanadi community. And the remaining two were from what the Indian government refers to as Backward [historically disadvantaged] Class communities. Relatives of the third victim told me they belonged to the *Ediga Balija* community, and the fourth traced his lineage through his mother to a community known as *Bhōgam,* once dancers in the imperial courts. The others who were injured by bullets in the same police firings were likewise predominantly from minority communities. These included several Muslims (mostly railway employees), a handful of laborers of various sorts, one young girl who had been crossing the railway tracks, and several students. There was also at least one merchant from the same community as Potti Sriramulu.[49]

These four deaths may have been reduced to a footnote within the larger narrative of the movement for a separate Telugu linguistic state, but they take on much different meanings within the stories told by their family members. There were three things that struck me as I spoke with surviving relatives of three of the four young men and with others who knew them.[50] The first was the fact that none of the relatives used language that suggested that they viewed the events that led to the death of their family member within a larger narrative of the movement for a separate Telugu linguistic state. One detail that became significant in the accounts that were shared with me was the fact that this was not the first time that Potti Sriramulu had undertaken a fast. Previously, he had begun at least four other public fasts, though never before for the sake of a Telugu linguistic state. And although his final (and fatal) fast had occurred in the city of Madras (now Chennai) some three hours away by train, each of his earlier fasts had been carried out in Nellore town. All four of his earlier fasts had been undertaken for the sake of Dalit, or "untouchable," causes.[51] His first fast, in March of 1946, had been to demand entry for Dalits into the Sri Venugopala Swamy Temple in Nellore and lasted only ten days. The second, in December of the same year, lasted nineteen days and demanded the opening of all temples in Nellore to Dalits. The third and fourth, in 1948 and 1949, both demanded the declaration of a monthly "day of service" to benefit the social uplift of Dalits. Almost everyone I spoke to in Nellore of a certain age also remembered Sriramulu going about the town wearing signboards on his front and back declaring that untouchability was a sin and advocating "*Harijana Dēvālayam Pravēśam*" [Harijan Temple Entry] and "*Sahapankti Bhōjanam*" [Inter-caste Dining].[52]

These earlier fasts and the alliances made by Sriramulu with those of lower-caste backgrounds, particularly Dalits and tribals, are of central importance in understanding the range of motives for why people gathered at the railway station upon hearing the news of Sriramulu's death. Nageswara Rao's elder brother related the story to me in this manner. It seems that his brother generally worked an evening shift at the Additional Magistrate's Court. Of the two brothers, the younger, Nageswara Rao, was the more active and less interested in studies. Once Nageswara Rao had passed his eighth class, his father made the decision to put him into a job and allow his brother to keep studying. I translate: "My father took a right decision," he told me. "My brother told me he would work so that I could keep studying. . . . He had a good personality. People used to think that he was the elder of the two of us."[53] He continued with his memories of the day his brother had died:

> Then, in the evening, after eating rice, around 5:00 or 5:30, in the evening he had to go for duty. So he left from here [the same time he always did]. After that, around 9:00 PM we heard that a big commotion [*pedda galāṭa*] had happened and that four had died. We heard the news that firings had happened and in the firings four had died. Only then did the news come that our boy had also gone there. Why had he gone there, we thought?

Having initially assumed that Nageswara Rao had simply gone to his evening job, as usual, the knowledge that he had gone to the station instead provoked curiosity but did not yet alarm them. By this point in the evening, 9 PM, he and his parents were still not aware that his brother was one of those who had been shot. He went on:

> After that, Radhakrishna, a small boy, came to our house. He had gone there [to the station]. He came around 10:00 PM to our house and said your boy was also one among the four who were killed. He knew very well. Having seen it, he came and told us. Then . . . [he made a gesture expressing a lack of words to say what they felt then].

When asked exactly what had happened at the station, he explained:

> There, he [the one who brought the news] was some *pillakāya* [a child] or the other, wasn't he? He said some big disturbance [*galabha*] had occurred at the station. He also wasn't in that exact spot. Someplace under some tamarind tree, he had heard it happened. It wasn't a direct firing on the part of the police. They fired in the air to scare people. During those firings, a bullet fell down and hit him.

He was quite certain that his brother had no association with any political party and was not an active supporter of the Andhra movement. However, he, his younger brother, and his entire family had great respect [*gauravam*] for Potti Sriramulu. He explained that his brother had certainly gone to the station because of the news of Potti Sriramulu's death, and that, in fact, the news that Potti Sriramulu had been fasting for a separate Andhra State was likely something he had not even known. His explanations referred repeatedly to Potti Sriramulu, who had once lived very close to their own house, and who they used to see frequently roaming around the neighborhood campaigning for various causes and wearing signboards proclaiming his slogans. But that he was fasting this time on behalf of a Telugu linguistic state was news that had not reached their family:

> We had no idea he was fasting for that. Only afterward did we come to know of it. We didn't know anything before that. We knew that Potti Sriramulu would go around for various causes. Only after he died did we come to know that he was fasting for that [for Telugu statehood]. My younger brother also knew nothing about this. He only knew that Potti Sriramulu was a great man. He had great respect for him. That's why he went to the station that day.

Others told me similar stories, but these were all stories that did not fit comfortably within the larger narratives of the event that dominated the press and historical accounts.

The second striking feature of the families' narratives concerned the bodies of the four young men. Each of the family members I spoke with expressed to me their frustration at not being able to reclaim the physical body of their family member. An aunt of the fifteen-year-old who was killed described to me the unwillingness of those she referred to as the "*peddawarlu,*" literally "big people," or "leaders," to hand over the bodies and their inability to convince them otherwise. I translate her Telugu words: "We were told that they wanted to bury all four together, and that we could only come along with them, not take the bodies with us," she said.[54] Their neighborhood was adjacent to the railway station, and Sriramulu was described to me as having come home from school that day, and not finding his mother—who had gone to collect firewood—in the house, he left his school bag and went in search of her. As he passed by the station he must have noticed the big commotion there and climbed up onto a wall to get a better view. It was there, while sitting on the wall, that he fell victim to a bullet. He had not gone along with other friends and had no known connections with any political parties or movements. "He just wanted to find out what was happening," she said. Certainly this account does not exclude the possibility of his being swept up in the mood of the crowd, and likely his story is one that belonged to many others that day who found themselves in the midst of what was going on.

The brother of Nageswara Rao told a similar story about the body of his younger brother. His father, along with some uncles, had gone to the *kōta rūma* [lit. the "cutting room," the post mortem shed] where the four victims had been taken, to collect the body. After spending the whole night and much of the next day there, they came away unsuccessful. He explained:

> The next day, midday, they did the post mortem. After doing the post mortem in the evening around 4:00 PM, they handed them over—the dead bodies. That means, they didn't give them to *us* . . . they didn't hand the dead bodies over to *us*. From the previous night we'd been there, at the post mortem room. But they wouldn't give them to us. They gave them to the party, not to us. After they did the post mortem, they handed them over to the party leaders—the four dead bodies.[55]

When asked why they gave the bodies to the party leaders, when none of the four young men had any relationship with the party, he replied:

> They—the leaders—said that they wanted to go and take them in an *ūrēgimpu* [a procession]. No, he didn't have any relationship with any party. It's in matters like these that the party comes to us, isn't it? Each and every party will come around only when such matters happen. They came only after the deaths, didn't they? Both innocently and accidentally those four boys died, but still all the party people came. They placed them on a wagon and poured flowers all over them. Then they had an enormous procession. They went around the *entire* town. I didn't go along with it. They made a big production [*pedda galāṭa*] out of it. My parents didn't go either. The next day we went ourselves and performed the ceremony of pouring milk on the grave.

With these words, he drew into question the stability not only of histories of the Andhra movement but also of the meanings of the very events in question.

The only family able to reclaim the body of their family member was the Dalit Christian family, and this was only through the intervention of a government official who also happened to be a Dalit Christian from the same community as Ezrah's family. They were successful only at the completion of the procession when they reached the burial grounds where four empty graves had already been dug and lay open and waiting for the bodies. It is perhaps ironic that the name of the government official who intervened to help the family reclaim Ezrah's body, thereby causing the fourth grave to lie empty, was Lazarus. Lazarus narrated to me how he had intervened "to prevent this Christian boy from being buried amongst the Hindus." He, as a government servant with a ranking position in the Labor Office, was able to convince the leaders of the procession of the inappropriateness of burying a Christian boy in that location—successful where Ezrah's own family members, with their much less prestigious social positions, had failed.

Dead Bodies and the "Structure of Visibility"

Descriptions of the actual funeral procession, in which the four bodies were carried to the burial ground, can help us to understand how this event focused people's attention, actions, and even emotions in very particular ways. The event created an effective example of what Naoki Sakai has called a "structure of visibility"—an invitation for people to occupy an already predetermined subject position in relation to a particular object or agenda. He defines the structure of visibility as "a consequence of a certain coordination of technological and discursive arrangements according to which the curiosity and attention of people are solicited, directed, and focused. It consists [of] a series of suggestions which lure viewers into identifying themselves with prearranged subject positions."[56] Sakai has used this term most effectively in the context of the effects of visual and print media upon viewers and readers in nineteenth- and twentieth-century Japan, nicely illustrated by the way the media solicited and directed the nation's attention in relation to the dying body of the emperor Hirohito just before his death in 1989. We can also effectively use it to think critically about the ways in which a publicly orchestrated event—such as the funeral procession and public burial discussed below—interacts with media to shape people's experience and narratives in particular ways. The result is that it becomes increasingly difficult to link alternative narratives or emotions to an event.

Several features of the funeral procession and burial event suggest that it functioned as a way of both soliciting and directing people's attention and emotions. First, the size of the funeral procession was significantly larger than the initial gathering at the railway station in which the firings took place—by most accounts, more than ten times as large. Estimates of the size of the crowd at the railway station in the wake of news of Potti Sriramulu's death averaged between 3,000 and 4,000, whereas most accounts of the funeral procession suggest that at least 40,000 people participated.

Second, the procession and the bodies of the dead effectively drew in and focused the attention of this huge crowd. Anantha Ramaiah provided one perspective on the procession. He narrated how the crowd gathered first at the hospital, moving then, along with the bodies, to the post mortem shed, from where the procession eventually began:

> We stayed all night . . . bringing the injured to the hospital. Some [were taken to] ABM hospital and some to the Government Hospital. The procession started the following evening, because the post mortem on all the four had to be done, certificates had to be prepared, police had to [do other things] . . . Many people, so many people came and saw. Many were taking their relations and all that [from the hospitals] . . .
>
> The next morning (after the firing), we—one Mr. Kantha Rao—the biggest wrestler of Andhra Pradesh at that time. He was known as Nellore Kantha Rao . . . He brought his tire cart. Then we removed the dead in the tire cart, and the police requested us to remove them to the post mortem shed. It is there, beyond Old Hospital, in Santapet. After [the] post mortem, on the 17th, people gathered in thousands at the post mortem shed. According to [the] *Hindu* [newspaper] there were nearly 40,000—estimated by Hindu. We said it was 50,000. Doesn't matter. When someone says 40, it can be 50, it can be 60, nobody counts heads. From there in that cart they were taken in a procession via Chinna Bazaar, and One Town Police Station.
>
> Then all the big shop wallahs, people . . . wherever they could get flowers, they got them, and from their upstairs, they poured them on the victims and came and garlanded. I was not in the photo because I was controlling the crowd attacking the police station. We have to lead, we have to satisfy the police.
>
> Police were not really antagonistic to the demonstration. But if they are attacked, then naturally they will defend themselves. So at One Town Police Station, though the police had not done

> anything, the angry mob, expressing anger at the DSP, John [who had ordered the firings], attacked. So we intervened.
>
> Then, we went around the town. And finally they were taken to Bodigadi Thota, that is the final journey, near Pennar Bridge. Bodigadu was the keeper, so people will understand it even now when you say it is Bodigadi Thota [Bodigadu's Garden]. It is the burial ground, but it will be on the river. But they were buried, I believe, because they are not Brahmins.[57]

The staging of this public procession and the careful movement of the bodies throughout the town on their way to the burial ground took an indirect route through the heart of the city and the most significant business and commercial centers. In this way it drew a great deal of attention to itself. Even more significantly, it also succeeded in framing the position of both the viewers and the participants in the procession in relation to the larger demand for a separate Telugu linguistic state.

Shahid Amin has suggested that most writings on nationalism—and his analysis can be productively extended to writings on regional movements like the Andhra movement—"in their preoccupation with social origins and politics, have tended to bypass the question of nationalist narratives. The ways in which the nation was talked about are considered an aspect of ideology; or alternatively, writing the history of a particular nationalist [or other] struggle itself becomes a part of an ongoing nationalist enterprise. This leaves virtually no space for the *interrogation* of narrative strategies by which a people get constructed into a nation."[58] Extending Amin's interrogation to regional linguistic identification and to the physical strategies that link action and emotion to particular narratives, we can say that emotional attachment to a particular language and linguistic community is neither natural nor inevitable. Rather, it is a relationship that emerges as available and imaginable, even necessary, only at a particular historical moment, under particular historical conditions.

It is certainly not new to suggest that emotional experience is historically shaped through cultural practice. In tracing the appearance of affect in relation to the Telugu language in southern India, my goal has been to understand how people unknown to one another have come to "feel" collectively. In doing so, I have traced the specific mechanisms through which diverse anxieties, concerns, and desires have come to be focused through a single object—in this case, language. The story that the silent bodies of these four young men were made to tell was crucial to the realization of a new linguistic state, yet it was a story that had already been made available for the telling. The relationship to language and linguistic statehood manifested during the funeral procession and burial of these four young men was one that had already been made to appear completely natural in the preceding decades.

Conclusion: Language as a New Foundational Category

The question that remains is whether the violence of 1952 could have been read so easily as evidence of the unified passions of the masses for linguistic statehood had it not been for the many shifts in the representation of and relationship to language that had occurred during the previous century. The argument put forth by this book is that it could not have. Instead, each of the preceding chapters systematically builds the case that without the transformations that had already occurred, the events of the 1950s would undoubtedly have taken a very different direction, and memories of these events would have organized themselves in relationship to different narratives and locally available idioms. These transformations included dramatic changes in patronage practices; the rise of new conventions for representing subjects, especially within narrative; the increasing ease of popular access to the new technologies of printing and lithography; shifts in the relationships between language, place, and person; subtle but important shifts in the representation of the relationships between languages and the meaning of translation; and corresponding shifts in the organization of pedagogical content, historical narratives, and literary canon formation. Especially important was the way that changes in the representation of the relationships between languages led to growing expectations of universal translatability between languages and the assumption that all languages exist more or less in parallel with one another. These new assumptions converged with the reconfiguration of forms of political organization in which new representational mechanisms played a central role, and together they served to force language into a previously unprecedented position as one of the most important foundations for the assertion of socio-cultural and political identity of the twentieth century.

That the bodies of the young men killed by police in Nellore and elsewhere have so easily been assimilated into a story of linguistic statehood is testimony to the dominant availability of language as a compelling and convenient foundation for political organization and identification. By way of conclusion, I would like to trace the rise of language as one of the most dominant and popularly legitimated bases for the organization of knowledge, everyday practice, cultural identification, and political mobilization of the twentieth century, suggesting that although the legitimacy of language as a foundational category grew steadily from the last decades of the nineteenth century and throughout much of the twentieth century, we may be beginning to see its legitimacy wane slightly in the twenty-first century. Such a perspective draws attention not only to the historical rise of language as a foundational category for political and cultural organization, but also to its potential decline. This, in turn, further helps us to see how emotional attachments to language, far from being naturally inherent in speakers' relationships to the words that they use, are historically situated. Even when embodying a choice, language has not always been empowered as a foundation for identification in quite the same ways that it has been over the past century. Indeed, recent evidence suggests that the power of language to form a foundation for ethnic, cultural, or political identification may well be beginning to diminish, at least to a limited extent.

In the year 2000, three new states were added to the Indian union. Chhattisgarh was created out of a portion of southeastern Madhya Pradesh on November 1. Uttaranchal, which changed its name to Uttarakhand in January 2007, was created out of a portion of northern Uttar Pradesh on November 9. And Jharkhand was created out of a portion of southern Bihar on November 15. Although cultural differences played a small role in justifying the movement for separation in each case, the assertion of linguistic difference played a dramatically less significant role than it had in similar demands for new states that had materialized in earlier decades. Indeed, most commentators have remarked that language did not play a primary role at all in any of these three cases. Pradeep Kumar, for example, writing in the period leading up to the formation of the three new states of Chhattisgarh, Uttaranchal, and Jharkhand, commented:

> With the passage of time sentiment for language and culture has given way to the urge for speedier economic development. If in the fifties Samyukta Maharashtra, Visal Andhra or the Maha Gujarat demands aimed at uniting co-linguistic populations from neighbouring states,

> after about three or four decades of lop-sided economic development, it is the issue of unevenness of development that is looming large on the political horizon. The dominant linguistic elite which in the 1950s could subsume the smaller less developed sub-regions into larger linguistic regions, is no more capable of doing so. . . . This perception of non-development, "development of under-development," or retarded development, has transcended the linguistic cohesion which seemed to be such a great cementing force in the initial years of post-colonial political development.[1]

As Kumar so perceptively points out, recent demands for separate political states differ from earlier movements. Even when a contemporary movement appears as a continuation of an earlier political movement—such as the demand that a separate Telangana State be carved out of the existing state of Andhra Pradesh along the lines of the Telugu-speaking regions of the former Nizam's State of Hyderabad—the role of linguistic difference has become increasingly less important. Although advocates of a separate Telangana have been agitating since before the predominantly Telugu-speaking districts of Hyderabad State were joined with Andhra State to form Andhra Pradesh in the All-India Linguistic States Reorganisation of 1956, the terms through which they have articulated their claims have undergone a subtle shift.

Earlier discursive formations of the demand for a separate Telangana State tended to both draw from and reinforce the legitimacy of linguistic difference as an effective foundation for political mobilization. In an interview with me in 1997, the Telangana activist Kaloji Narayana Rao (1914–2002) repeatedly emphasized the linguistic discrimination faced by the children of Telangana. He gave the example of a popular children's radio program on which one would never hear the voices of children from the Telangana region of Andhra Pradesh because their dialect was considered non-standard. Instead, the children who are routinely featured in the call-in section of the program are almost exclusively from the economically prosperous East and West Godavari, Krishna, and Guntur districts of Coastal Andhra, suggesting that only their dialects are acceptable as "standard" Telugu.[2] A poet, writer, and activist who composed in Telugu, Marathi, English, Urdu, and Hindi, reflecting a culture of literacy of an earlier era, Kaloji Narayana Rao's appeal for justice reflected the recognition of language as one of the most legitimate bases for articulating difference, and emphasized the linguistic discrimination experienced by those from other parts of the state. Another woman who grew up in rural Telangana described to me her experience of attending university in Hyderabad. During a botany class, when asked to identify a groundnut plant, she immediately correctly identified it using the term common within her Telangana dialect, only to have her contribution met by peals of laughter from both her classmates and the teacher, for whom the "more standard" Coastal Andhra dialect's term was considered the appropriate answer despite Hyderabad's location in Telangana.[3] Indeed, while conducting the fieldwork for this book, it was not at all uncommon for me to hear Telangana activists in Hyderabad and elsewhere make statements like, "Yes, we speak Telugu, but it's a *different* Telugu, and therefore we should have our own state."[4] Such appeals to the acceptability of linguistic difference as one of the few legitimately recognizable foundations for political mobilization have become increasingly less necessary in twenty-first-century India, as the success of the Chhattisgarh, Uttarakhand, and Jharkhand movements attest.

Paul Brass has argued that in the early decades following independence, the central government followed a set of "four formal and informal rules" that led to the recognition of some demands for separate statehood and the non-recognition of others. These were that the central government would not entertain groups that were making secessionist demands, it would not respond to groups that were making regional assertions based on religious difference, movements had to have demonstrated popular support (not just evidence of widespread use of a particular language), and there had to be strong support from members of more than one interested language group.[5] He uses the last of these reasons to explain why the division of Madras State occurred as early as it did in 1953, given that it had the support of both Tamil- and Telugu-speakers. In contrast, the division of Bombay State took much longer as the movement was initially spearheaded only by Marathi-speakers. Gujarati-speakers were much more reluctant to see the existing state divided, as they feared the loss of Bombay city, and thus it was not until 1960 that the linguistic division of that state was finally successful. What is obvious, however, is that once the idiom of linguistic statehood had demonstrated its success as a method of political mobilization and reformation, others were quick to adopt the model of language as a convenient foundation for political assertion.

A myriad of political concerns was in each case brought into such demands for separate linguistic statehood, most related to specific forms of perceived discrimination—employment, educational opportunities, and resource distribution, in particular. But rather than being made the primary foundation of mid-twentieth-century political demands, these issues took a back seat to the central use of language as the fundamental principle around which political mobilization took place. By tracing the specific processes through which language came to be available for the twentieth-century reorganization of interests, everyday practices, and knowledge production, I have made clearer the historical shifts that were necessary for the making of language as a new foundational category and "mother tongue." The loss of single wealthy patrons powerful enough to support the literary efforts of poets and writers, coupled with the increasing availability of new technologies like printing and lithography, paved the way for appeals to new collectively imagined patrons. These new collective patrons were defined by necessity in relation to their most commonly shared features. Failed attempts to make geographic location this least-common denominator, exemplified in the efforts of Kavali Venkata Ramaswami to make the Deccan region a foundation for the reorganization of literary production, history writing, and identity and therefore a foundation for the construction of a new collective patron, gave way by the end of the nineteenth century to successful efforts to make language stand in as the new foundation. New anthologies of poets, literary production, and history writing, for the first time organized in relationship to language rather that to a dynasty, sect, or lineage, flattered the sensibilities of their desired audiences and created a new canon and historical past with which readers could identify.

New portrayals of language in a personified form used existing devotional idioms to reframe the relationships of speakers to the words they used. Portraying language as a mother worthy of worship, devotion, patronage, or protection created an opportunity for new forms of emotional relationships with language. The demand to be able to sing, pray, conduct business, or simply become literate in a single language now defined as a "mother tongue" displaced a previous understanding of language use as determined by context, geographic location, or purpose rather than by the identity of the speaker. Words from other languages, once an unremarkable part of everyday practice, were reframed as "foreign" and redefined as symbols of oppression and alterity. Efforts to purify language and eliminate "foreign" elements corresponded with the rise of ethnic political assertions that defined some people as more worthy of the benefits the state could provide than others. Pedagogical content, once embodied by teachers who tried to reproduce themselves and their own knowledge in their students, was replaced by externally defined curricula embodied in textbooks that reframed grammatical knowledge as a basic building block for doing things with language. No longer was grammatical knowledge regarded as something only relevant for advanced study and literary composition by already established scholars. As languages began to be regarded as entities parallel to one another rather than complementary, even the meaning of translation was redefined. A belief in universal translatability made languages cease to be imagined as the repository of any particular unique content. By the twentieth century, languages of the land had decisively been converted into languages of the people, making language an increasingly convenient foundation for cultural and political mobilization.

All of these processes have indirectly shaped the ways we are able to read the deaths of the young men killed in Nellore and other towns of Coastal Andhra in 1952. Indeed, the portrayal of emotion as the natural channel linking people with language, defined by the twentieth century as one's "mother tongue," makes it difficult to imagine any other relationships with language or, by extension, with demands for linguistic statehood. That people might have had many other reasons for respecting the efforts of a political activist like Potti Sriramulu, reasons that had nothing at all to do with language or linguistic statehood, found little resonance with the available recognizable meanings and narratives of the 1950s. Sriramulu's earlier fasts on behalf of Dalits, advocating temple entry or non-discrimination against Dalits, have therefore been displaced and erased by narratives of linguistic statehood. That we can now recognize the interests of Dalits, tribals, and members of Other Backward Classes in the stories of the family members of the four young men who were killed in Nellore may have more to do with the recognizable meanings and narratives of the early twenty-first century and their differences from the dominant idioms of the 1950s than it does with any essential elements of the stories themselves.[6] It is only by tracing the multiple historical forces that have helped to produce the dominant available idioms of a particular historico-cultural context—like Coastal Andhra in the first half of the twentieth century—that we can fully understand the process of the making of a mother tongue.

NOTES

Introduction

1. Letter from Potti Sriramulu addressed to B. Lakshminarayana, a Madras lawyer, dated September 15, 1952, reproduced in the English-language periodical *Indian Republic,* December 21, 1952, and cited in B. Sreeramulu, *Socio-Political Ideas and Activities of Potti Sriramulu* (Bombay: Himalaya, 1988), p. 198.

2. K. V. Narayana Rao, *The Emergence of Andhra Pradesh* (Bombay: Popular Prakasan, 1973), p. 32; Sreeramulu, *Socio-Political Ideas,* pp. 200–201; B. Maria John, *Linguistic Reorganisation of Madras Presidency* (Nagercoil: Ajith, 1994).

3. Following Nehru's announcement at the end of 1952, Andhra State was officially brought into existence the following year on October 1, 1953. Although subsequently largely erased from public historical memory, the inclusion of the city of Madras within a new Andhra province was actually the central issue that motivated Sriramulu's decision to undertake his fast. By 1952, and even earlier, there had existed widespread agreement that the districts consisting of an uncontested Telugu-speaking majority should be formed into a new state (Robert D. King, *Nehru and the Language Politics of India,* Delhi: Oxford University Press, 1997, p. 114). It was the controversy over the multilingual city of Madras that was holding up action, and it was to demand a Telugu linguistic state with Madras as its capital that Sriramulu explicitly launched his famous fast. Although Sriramulu's death is today celebrated as the act that launched the agitations that finally brought into being a separate Telugu state, because Nehru's decision to form a new Andhra State explicitly excluded the city of Madras, Sriramulu would most certainly have considered his fast a failure.

4. Sheldon Pollock, "India in the Vernacular Millennium: Literary Culture and Polity, 1000–1500," *Daedalus* 127, no. 3 (1998), p. 64; Velcheru Narayana Rao, "Coconut and Honey: Sanskrit and Telugu in Pre-Modern Andhra," *Social Scientist* 23 (1995), p. 25; Sumathi Ramaswamy, *Passions of the Tongue: Language Devotion in Tamil India, 1891–1970* (Berkeley: University of California Press, 1997), p. 16.

5. Amanul Huq, *International Mother Language Day: Bangla Souvenir,* translated from the original Bangla ed., *Ekusher Tamasuk* by Ahsanul Hoque, Amanul Huq, and A. U. M. Fakhruddin (Dhaka: Shahitya Prakash, 2004).

6. Paul Brass, *Ethnicity and Nationalism: Theory and Comparison* (New Delhi: Sage, 1991), p. 175; Kanwar Jeet Singh, *Master Tara Singh and Punjab Politics: A Study of Political Leadership,* 1978.

7. Ramaswamy, *Passions of the Tongue,* p. 1.

8. Controversy over the establishment of Hindi as the sole national language in the decades immediately following independence, particularly in those regions of India (such as the south) where Hindi is not widely spoken, has ensured that English has continued to be used as an official language.

9. Government of India, "Eighth Schedule," *Constitution of India: Updated up to 94th Amendment Act,* http://lawmin.nic.in/coi.htm, p. 229 (accessed February 20, 2008).

10. The 1961 Census of India—the first census to be conducted following the 1956 All-India Linguistic State Reorganisation—identified 1,652 distinct "mother tongues" in use in India, grouped under 193 language headings and associated with one of four language families: Indo-Aryan (54 languages, including Hindi, Bengali, Marathi, and Gujarati), Dravidian (20 languages, including Telugu, Tamil, Kannada, and Malayalam), Tibeto-Burman (98 languages), and Austric (20 languages), B. Mallikarjun, "Mother Tongues of India according to the 1961 Census," *Language in India* 2, no. 5 (2002), www.languageinindia.com (accessed June 17, 2007).

11. Government of India, Office of the Registrar General and Census Commissioner, India, "General Note," http://www.censusindia.gov.in/Census_Data_2001/Census_Data_Online/Language/gen_note.htm (accessed February 20, 2008).

12. Ibid.

13. Government of India, Office of the Registrar General and Census Commissioner, India, "Scheduled Languages in Descending Order of Speakers' Strength, 2001," http://www.censusindia.gov.in/Census_Data_2001/Census_Data_Online/Language/Statement4.htm (accessed February 20, 2008).

14. Government of India, Ministry of Human Resource Development, Department of Education, "Languages and Media of Instruction," *Fifth All-India Educational Survey,* vol. 1 (New Delhi: Department of Education, 1990), http://www.education.nic.in/cd50years/g/Z/H7/0ZH70E01.htm (accessed June 17, 2007).

15. J. C. Sharma, "Multilingualism in India," *Language in India* 1, no. 8 (December 2001), http://www.languageinindia.com/dec2001/jcsharma2.html (accessed June 17, 2007).

16. Prior to independence, the British colonial administration separated the states of Bihar and Orissa from Bengal on a linguistic basis in 1936. The Andhra movement was the first successful movement to achieve linguistic statehood following Indian independence in 1947.

17. Vennelacunty Soob Row [Vennelakanty Subba Rao], *The Life of Vennelacunty Soob Row (Native of Ongole), Translator and Interpreter of the Late Sudr Court, Madras, From 1815 to 1829, As written by himself* (Madras: C. Foster, 1873), pp. 64–65.

18. Brown, *Miśra Bhāṣā Nighaṇṭu: Brown's Dictionary of Mixed Telugu* (Madras: Christian Knowledge Society Press, 1854), p. iii. (Brown uses the Sanskrit *nighaṇṭu* in his title rather than the Telugu *nighaṇṭuvu* to refer to his dictionary or lexicon.) Brown held official administrative appointments in Cuddapah, Machilipatnam, Rajahmundry, Guntur, and Chittoor in what is today Andhra Pradesh between 1820 and 1834, as well as a one-year appointment in Tiruchirapalli, in the present-day state of Tamil Nadu. After a leave, he served in a range of government appointments in the Presidency capital of Madras (also in present-day Tamil Nadu) from 1838 to 1854 (Peter L. Schmitthenner, *Telugu Resurgence: C. P. Brown and Cultural Consolidation in Nineteenth-Century South India,* Delhi, 2001). It is worth noting that Subba Rao mentions knowing all but two of the nine languages mentioned by Brown—Malayalam and Arabic being the only exceptions.

19. Puduri Sitaramasastri, *Pedda Bāla Śikṣa* (Madras: Vidya Vilasa Mudraksharasala, 1865), pp. iii–iv. This edition opens by introducing the Tamil and English alphabets along with the Telugu alphabet. Chapter 4 provides a more detailed discussion of this primer.

20. Popular legend, for example, has associated eight great poets, the *aṣṭa-dig-*

gajas, with Krishnadevaraya's court. However, it was not until the end of the nineteenth century that these eight poets—and indeed, Krishnadevaraya himself—came to be claimed and celebrated as specifically *Telugu* poets. Velcheru Narayana Rao and David Shulman have suggested that these eight poets may have been assembled within the popular imaginary more than a century later as part of a "retrospective . . . vision of the royal court" reflecting the values of a later era. Velcheru Narayana Rao and David Shulman, eds. and trans., *Classical Telugu Poetry: An Anthology* (Delhi: Oxford University Press, 2002), p. 253. See also P. Chenchiah and M. Bhujanga Rao, *A History of Telugu Literature* (Calcutta: Association Press, 1925), pp. 72, 84; and G. V. Sitapati, *History of Telugu Literature* (Delhi: Sahitya Akademi, 1968).

21. Phillip B. Wagoner, *Tidings of the King: A Translation and Ethnohistorical Analysis of the Rāyavācakamu* (Honolulu: University of Hawaii Press, 1993), p. 93. The quoted passage is from a longer section of the *Rāyavācakamu* taken from the anonymous mid-sixteenth-century *Sabhāpati Vacanamu.* See Wagoner's discussion of this in n. 13, p. 192.

22. Velcheru Narayana Rao, David Shulman, and Sanjay Subrahmanyam, *Symbols of Substance: Court and State in Nayaka Period Tamilnadu* (Delhi: Oxford University Press, 1992), p. 334.

23. Ibid., pp. 203, 334.

24. Indira V. Peterson, "Speaking in Tongues: The Cultural Discourses of Literary Multilingualism in Eighteenth-Century India," unpublished manuscript, 2004. See also her forthcoming book *Imagining the World in Eighteenth-Century India: The Kuravanci Fortune-teller Dramas of Tamil Nadu.*

25. Amanda J. Weidman, "Can the Subaltern Sing? Music, Language, and the Politics of Voice in Early Twentieth-Century South India." *Indian Economic and Social History Review* 42, no. 4 (2005): 485–511.

26. Gurujada Sriramamurti, *Kavi Jīvitamulu* (Chennapattanamu: Empress of India Press, 1893), p. 1. The first edition of *Kavi Jīvitamulu* (Rajahmundry: Vivekavarthani Press, 1878) was subtitled *Modaṭi Bhāgamu: Āndhra bhāṣāvṛttāntamu, Tikkana Sōmayāji Charitrambunu, Bammera Pōtarājukathayunu* [Part 1: Particulars of the Andhra language, biographical narrative of Tikkana Somayaji, and the story of Bammera Potaraju]. A second title page, in English, gives the title as *Biographies of Telugu Poets, with a Series of Discussions Regarding Grammar and Prosody, Part 1.* All translations from Telugu are my own unless otherwise specified.

27. The poet's use of *abhimatā* in the fifth sutra of the Sanskrit *Āndhra Śabda Chintāmaṇi* (attributed to the eleventh-century Nannaya Bhatt, but likely composed much later) may initially appear to some to be a very similar usage. However, it is important to recognize the context in which each author is writing. *Āndhra Śabda Chintāmaṇi* is written in Sanskrit as an effort to justify the respectability of poetry composed in Telugu rather than in Sanskrit, implying that the author is writing for an audience familiar with both languages rather than an audience defined only in relation to Telugu. Conditions of patronage were also quite different in the two contexts. Nannaya Bhatt, *Āndhra Śabda Chintāmaṇi* (Chennapuri: Vavilla Ramaswami Sastrulu and Sons, 1968), p. 4, sutra 5.

28. Charles Philip Brown, *Nighaṇṭuvu Telugu-English: Dictionary Telugu-English,* reprint of 2nd ed. revised by M. Venkata Ratnam, W. H. Campbell, and K. Veeresalingam, 1903 (Madras: Asian Educational Services, 1995), p. 70.

29. Ramaswamy, *Passions of the Tongue,* pp. 5–6.

30. Ibid., p. 5.

31. Ibid., p. 9.

32. See, for example, William Jones, "On the Hindu's [*sic*]," *Asiatick Researches* 1 (1788): 414–432; William Jones, "On the Origin and Families of Nations," *Asiatick Researches* 3 (1792): 479–492; Alexander Duncan Campbell, *Grammar of the Teloogoo language, commonly termed the Gentoo, peculiar to the Hindoos inhabiting the North Eastern provinces of the Indian Peninsula* (Madras: College Press, 1816); and Francis W. Ellis, "Note to the Introduction," in Campbell, *Grammar of the Teloogoo Language*, pp. 1–31.

33. Sheldon Pollock, "Death of Sanskrit," *Comparative Studies in Society and History* 43, no. 2 (2001): 392–426.

34. M. S. S. Pandian, *The Image Trap: M. G. Ramachandran in Film and Politics* (New Delhi: Sage, 1992), p. 18.

35. Ibid., p. 17.

36. Ibid.; Radha Venkatesan, "Politics and Suicides," *The Hindu* [English daily], Sunday, June 2, 2002; Roopa Swaminathan, *M. G. Ramachandran: Jewel of the Masses* (New Delhi: Roopa and Co., 2002), p. 79.

37. Sara Dickey, *Cinema and the Urban Poor in South India* (Cambridge University Press, 1993).

38. Brown, *Nighaṇṭuvu Telugu-English*, p. 70.

39. J. P. L. Gwynn and J. Venkateswara Sastry, *A Telugu-English Dictionary* (Delhi: Oxford University Press, 1991), p. 29.

40. Vaman Shivram Apte, *The Practical Sanskrit-English Dictionary* (Delhi: Motilal Banarsidass, 1965), p. 122.

41. Sigmund Freud, "The Antithetical Meaning of Primal Words," in *Writings on Art and Literature* (Stanford, Calif.: Stanford University Press, 1997), pp. 94–100.

42. The early-fifteenth-century poet Vinukonda Vallabharaya, for example, satirizes earlier descriptions of the relationship between Sanskrit and Telugu:

> They say 'Sanskrit is the mother of all languages,
> but among the languages of the land Telugu is best.' Of course,
> between the aged mother
> and the ravishing young daughter,
> I'll take the daughter any day!

In reading this verse as a parody, Narayana Rao and Shulman are departing from conventional readings of this passage as evidence of ethnic pride and drawing our attention to Vallabharaya's effort to invert the hierarchical relationship between Sanskrit and Telugu. Later citations of Vallabharaya typically omit the context and quote only the phrase "among the languages of the land Telugu is best" [*deśabhāṣālandu telugu lessa*], significantly altering its meaning. Vinukonda Vallabharaya, Krīḍābhirāmamu, trans., in Narayana Rao and Shulman, *Classical Telugu Poetry*, p. 218.

43. Ramaswamy, *Passions of the Tongue*, pp. 79–134.

44. Entry for "mother tongue," *Oxford English Dictionary Online*, draft revision (New York: Oxford University Press, December 2007).

45. **1425** (*a*1400) *Brut* (Corpus Cambr.) 315 Hit was ordeyned . . . that men of lawe . . . fro that tyme forth shold plede in her moder tunge; **1589** *Temporis Filia Veritas* sig.

Aiv[v], God service in the mother tongue, so that now every Carter & Cobler can whistle and sing psalms, *Oxford English Dictionary Online,* draft revision (New York: Oxford University Press, March 2003).

46. **1781** GIBBON *Decline & Fall* III. 15 (*note*) His [*sc.* Shakespeare's] mother-tongue, the language of nature, is the same in Cappadocia and in Britain, *Oxford English Dictionary Online,* draft revision (New York: Oxford University Press, March 2003).

47. Richard Bauman and Charles L. Briggs, *Voices of Modernity: Language Ideologies and the Politics of Inequality* (Cambridge: Cambridge University Press, 2003), p. 9.

48. Ibid., pp. 183–184.

49. Alexander Gode, Introduction to *On the Origin of Language: Two Essays,* trans. with afterword by John H. Moran and Alexander Gode (Chicago: University of Chicago Press, 1966), p. v.

50. Bernard Cohn, *An Anthropologist among the Historians and other Essays* (Delhi: Oxford University Press, 1987); Bernard Cohn, *Colonialism and Its Forms of Knowledge* (Princeton, N.J.: Princeton University Press, 1996).

51. See, for example, Sudipta Kaviraj, "Writing, Speaking, Being: Language and the Historical Formation of Identities in India," in *Nationalstaat und Sprachkonflikte in Süd- und Südostasien,* ed. D. Hellmann-Rajanayagam and D. Rothermund (Stuttgart: Franz Steiner Verlag, 1992); and David Washbrook, "'To Each a Language of His Own': Language, Culture, and Society in Colonial India," in *Language, History, Class,* ed. P. J. Corfield (Oxford: B. Blackwell, 1991).

52. Bernard S. Cohn, "The Command of Language and the Language of Command," in *Subaltern Studies IV: Writings on South Asian History and Society,* ed. Ranajit Guha (Delhi: Oxford University Press, 1985), p. 329.

53. Sreeramulu, *Socio-Political Ideas,* p. 197.

54. Ibid., pp. 206–215. See also the published Medical Report, Kasturi Narayana Murthi, ed., *Sri Potti Sriramulu the Martyr That Fasted for 58 Days to Death from 19–10–1952 to 15–12–1952* (Madras: Antiseptic Press, 1953), cited in Sreeramulu.

55. Interview with former Andhra movement leader, Nellore, October 19, 2002.

56. Fiona Somerset and Nicholas Watson, "Preface: On 'Vernacular,'" in *The Vulgar Tongue: Medieval and Postmedieval Vernacularity,* ed. Somerset and Watson (University Park: Pennsylvania State University Press, 2003), pp. ix–x.

57. Ibid., p. 165.

58. Peter Burke, *Languages and Communities in Early Modern Europe* (Cambridge: Cambridge University Press, 2004), p. 66.

59. E. J. Hobsbawm, *Nations and Nationalism since 1780: Programme, Myth, Reality* (Cambridge: Cambridge University Press, 1990), pp. 52–53.

60. Narayana Rao, *Emergence of Andhra Pradesh,* p. 247; Sreeramulu, *Socio-Political Ideas,* p. 195.

61. Narayana Rao, *Emergence of Andhra Pradesh,* pp. 21–22.

62. Ibid., pp. 22–23.

63. Ibid.

64. Proceedings of the Legislative Council of the Governor, Fort St. George, February 21, 1911, *Fort St. George Gazette,* part 4, March 7, 1911, pp. 133–138, quoted in Narayana Rao, *Emergence of Andhra Pradesh,* p. 27.

65. Ibid.

66. Sreeramulu, *Socio-Political Ideas,* pp. 194–195.

67. Narayana Rao, *Emergence of Andhra Pradesh,* pp. 23, 26.

68. Robert D. King, *Nehru and the Language Politics of India* (Delhi: Oxford University Press, 1997), p. 74; Ramaswamy, *Passions of the Tongue,* p. 170.

69. Narayana Rao, *Emergence of Andhra Pradesh,* p. xiii.

70. Receipts for funds raised for firing victims by the Nellore Town Youth League, private archive of V. Anantha Ramaiah, Nellore.

71. Tape-recorded interviews (male, b. 1932), Nellore, April 16, 2002, October 16, 2002, and October 17, 2002.

72. Interviews with V. Anantha Ramaiah (b. 1922, senior advocate), M. A. Khader (secretary, Nellore District Muslim Welfare Association), Sithalam Krishna Rao (b. 1922, retired wrestling coach), K. V. Ramanaiah (senior journalist), D. C. Veeraswamy Chetty (proprietor, Sri Raghvendra Xerox) and his mother D. Padmavathamma (b. 1917), P. C. Reddy (b. 1916), V. Sundara Rama Dutt, C. C. Subbarayalu (b. 1925), Nellore, June 2000, April 2002, October 2002, and private papers from the personal libraries of V. Anantha Ramaiah and D. C. Veeraswamy Chetty.

73. Gandavaram Sethurami Reddy, *Gandavaram Sēthurāmireḍḍi Jīvitāllō Pradhān Ghaṭṭālu* [Important Events in the Life of Gandavaram Sethurami Reddy] (Nellore: Sethurami Reddy, 2001), pp. 15–16.

74. Narayana Rao, *Emergence of Andhra Pradesh,* pp. 23–25.

75. Government of India, Ministry of Human Resource Development, Department of Education, "Selected Educational Statistics," *Compilation on Fifty Years of Indian Education: 1947–1997,* http://www.education.nic.in/cd50years/g/Z/7H/0Z7H0101.htm (accessed February 20, 2008). These figures are based on Indian census reports and represent an all-India average.

76. I do not intend to suggest that "literate" and "non-literate" form two homogenous and opposed groups, or that these are the primary categories through which individuals thought of themselves and others. The meaning of literacy was itself going through a great transition during the decades leading up to the events discussed in this book. Literacy also does not necessarily correspond with either class or caste identifications. Nonetheless, these statistics and the fact that many who were injured and killed were indeed illiterate raise important questions about the received notions that the Andhra movement was basically a middle-class movement.

77. M. S. S. Pandian, "Towards National-Popular: Notes on Self-Respecters' Tamil," *Economic and Political Weekly* 31, no. 51 (December 21, 1996).

78. Sreeramulu, *Socio-Political Ideas,* p. 225.

79. Interview (male, b. late 1920s), Kavali, August 12, 1998.

80. Tape-recorded interview, Nellore, October 23, 2002.

81. Friedrich A. Kittler, *Discourse Networks 1800/1900* (Stanford, Calif.: Stanford University Press, 1990), p. 369.

82. Ibid., pp. 370–371.

1. From Language of the Land to Language of the People

1. Gurujada Sriramamurti, *Kavi Jīvitamulu,* 3rd ed. (Cennapuri: Vavilla Ramaswami Sastrulu and Sons, 1913), p. 1; Gurujada Sriramamurti, *Kavi Jīvitamulu,* 2nd ed. (Cennapattanam: Empress of India Press, 1893), p. 1.

2. Brown, Charles Philip. *Nighaṇṭuvu Telugu-English: Dictionary Telugu-English,*

reprint of 1903 2nd ed., ed. M. Venkata Ratnam, W. H. Campbell, and K. Veeresalingam (New Delhi: Asian Educational Service, 1995), p. 609.

3. H. S. Brahmananda, *Gidugu Venkata Ramamurti* (New Delhi: Sahitya Akademi, 1990).

4. G. N. Reddy, "Āndhram, Tenugu, Telugu," in *Telugu Bhāṣā Charitra* [History of the Telugu Language], ed. Bh. Krishnamurti (Hyderabad: Potti Sriramulu Telugu University, 2000), p. 1.

5. For example, K. Satyanarayana's two-volume *Study of the History and Culture of the Andhras* begins with the Stone Age (vol. 1, 2nd ed., Hyderabad: Visaalandra, 1999[1979]), while P. Raghunadha Rao's *History and Culture of Andhra Pradesh: From the Earliest Times to the Present Day* (New Delhi: Sterling, 1994) and D. Triveni's *History of Modern Andhra* (Delhi: Surjeet Book Depot, 1986) both begin with the Satavahana Dynasty, close to a millennium before the first appearance of Telugu.

6. Andhra Province Standing Committee, *For and Against the Andhra Province* (Masulipatam: M. Krishna Rao, 1913); N. Subbarau, *The Second Andhra Conference 1914, Held at Bezvada: The Address of the President Mr. N. Subbarau Pantulu* (Bezvada: Vani Press, 1914); K. S. Narain Rao, ed., *Report of the Third Andhra Conference held at Vizagapatam on 12th and 13th May, 1915* (Vizag: Observatory Press, 1915); Andhra Provincial Congress Committee Correspondence in the All India Congress Committee Manuscripts Collection, NMML; *Reorganization of Indian Provinces: Being a Note Presented to the Indian National Congress* (Bezwada: Vani Press, 1916).

7. See, for example, Kasinathuni Nageswara Rao, *Āndhra Vāŋmaya Sūchika* [Andhra Literary Index] (Hyderabad: Prāchī, 1929), which attempts to catalogue every Telugu work written or published.

8. The decision for Telangana to join with the other two regions was not unanimous, with a major Telangana faction opposed to the union and three out of the ten District Congress Committees in Telangana voting in favor of a separate Telangana State. These factions ultimately lost to the proponents of the Viśālāndhra (Greater Andhra) movement. See Raghunadha Rao, *History and Culture of Andhra Pradesh,* p. 303; Triveni, *History of Modern Andhra,* pp. 215–218. Dissatisfaction with the union has largely centered on economic disparities and underdevelopment and has continued to the present. S. Simhadri and P. L. Vishweshwar Rao, eds., *Telangana: Dimensions of Underdevelopment* (Hyderabad: Centre for Telangana Studies, 1997).

9. See, for example, Raghunadha Rao, *History and Culture of Andhra Pradesh,* p. 114–120; and Suryanath U. Kamath, *A Concise History of Karnataka* (Bangalore: Archana Prakashana, 1980), pp. 176–178.

10. Kunduri Iswara Dutt, *Prāchīnāndhra Chāritraka Bhūgōlamu* [Ancient Historical Geography of Andhra Pradesh: An Identification and Demarcation of the Ancient Geographical and Administrative Divisions of Andhra Pradesh] (Hyderabad: Andhra Pradesh Sahitya Akademi, 1979 [1963]), pp. 63, 207, 283, 299, and 306; P. Appa Row, *The Historical Geography of Madras Presidency* (Tenali: Kalavani, 1928); Goparaja Ramanna, ed., *Koṇḍavīṭi Sīmā Daṇḍakavile Nakalu: Ancient Record Containing Geography and Chronological History of Telugu Country* (Madras: Markandeya Sarma, 1921).

11. Cynthia Talbot, *Precolonial India in Practice: Society, Region, and Identity in Medieval Andhra* (New Delhi: Oxford University Press, 2001), p. 36.

12. Velcheru Narayana Rao and David Shulman, introduction to *Classical Telugu Poetry: An Anthology,* ed. and trans. Narayana Rao and Shulman (Delhi: Oxford University Press, 2002), p. 6.

13. Ibid., pp. 6–7.

14. Xiang Biao, *Global "Body Shopping": An Indian Labor System in the Information Technology Industry* (Princeton, N.J.: Princeton University Press, 2007), pp. 30–31.

15. P. Chenchiah and M. Bhujanga Rao, *A History of Telugu Literature* (Calcutta: Association Press, 1925), p. 14.

16. Ibid.

17. Raghunadha Rao, *History and Culture of Andhra Pradesh,* p. viii. In the author's preface he writes that the book is "intended for the students of the B.A. and M.A. classes of the Universities of Andhra Pradesh, who have offered history and culture of Andhra Pradesh as one of their subjects of study," but he goes on to suggest that it "would be useful to the general reader" and "also the candidates of the various civil services examinations of Andhra Pradesh" (p. v).

18. Other texts with a similar objective include K. Gopalachari, *Early History of the Andhra Country,* K. A. Nilakanta Sastri, ed., Madras University Historical Series (Madras: University of Madras, 1941); Nagolu Krishna Reddy, *Social History of Andhra Pradesh (Seventh to Thirteenth Century: Based on Inscriptions and Literature)* (Delhi: Agam Kala Prakashan, 1991).

19. Talbot, *Precolonial India in Practice.*

20. Ibid., p. 10.

21. Ibid., p. 36.

22. Narayana Rao and Shulman, *Classical Telugu Poetry,* pp. 254–256.

23. Talbot, *Precolonial India in Practice,* p. 172, cited in Sanjay Subrahmanyam, "Whispers and Shouts: Some Recent Writings on Medieval South India," *Indian Economic and Social History Review* 38, no. 4 (2001): 462.

24. Talbot, *Precolonial India in Practice,* p. 10. We must consider her statements that "other allegiances were circumscribed by the linguistic region" and that "we can point to language as the most important cultural affiliation in the medieval South" (ibid.) in light of arguments she makes elsewhere that "the rising popularity of the religious patronage of gods and brahmans is testimony to the spread of a pan-Indic culture that valued the expression of piety in such forms" (p. 18). Although it is clear from her discussion that the *use* of Telugu in inscriptions is increasing rapidly from the eleventh through the thirteenth centuries (the period on which she focuses), the idea that this also implies "the increasing salience of a Telugu cultural identity" (p. 16) is not supported. The spread of shared religious practices (including the practice of making endowments) across multiple linguistic mediums, including Kannada, Tamil, Marathi, and even Sanskrit, demonstrates the importance of distinguishing between shared usage of a language and the explicit marking of language as a representation of identity.

25. G. V. Sitapati, *History of Telugu Literature* (New Delhi: Sahitya Akademi, 1968), p. vii.

26. Ibid., p. viii.

27. Sheldon Pollock, "Literary History, Indian History, World History," *Social Scientist* 23, no. 10–12 (1995): 112–142; "The Sanskrit Cosmopolis, 300–1300: Transculturation, Vernacularization, and the Question of Ideology," in *Ideology and Status of Sanskrit: Contributions to the History of the Sanskrit Language,* ed. Jan E. M. Houben (Leiden: E. J. Brill, 1996), pp. 197–247; "The Cosmopolitan Vernacular," *Journal of Asian Studies* 57, no. 1 (1998): 6–37; "India in the Vernacular Millennium: Literary Culture and Polity, 1000–1500," *Daedalus* 127, no. 3 (1998): 41–74; "The Death of Sanskrit," *Comparative Studies in Society and History* 43, no. 2 (2001): 392–426.

28. Velcheru Narayana Rao, David Shulman, and Sanjay Subrahmanyam, *Symbols*

of Substance: Court and State in Nayaka Period Tamilnadu (Delhi: Oxford University Press, 1992); Velcheru Narayana Rao and David Shulman, *A Poem at the Right Moment: Remembered Verses from Premodern South India* (Berkeley: University of California Press, 1998); Velcheru Narayana Rao, David Shulman, and Sanjay Subrahmanyam, *Textures of Time: Writing History in South India, 1600–1800* (Delhi: Permanent Black, 2001).

29. Pollock, "India in the Vernacular Millennium," p. 46.

30. Ibid., p. 64.

31. See Velcheru Narayana Rao's critique of Nannaya's canonical status in his essay "Multiple Literary Cultures in Telugu: Court, Temple, and Public," in *Literary Cultures in History: Reconstructions from South Asia,* ed. Sheldon Pollock (New Delhi: Oxford University Press, 2004), pp. 383–436, especially pp. 390–391.

32. S. Nagaraju, "Emergence of Regional Identity and Beginnings of Vernacular Literature: A Case Study of Telugu," *Social Scientist* 23, nos. 10–12 (1995): 13–14, 16.

33. Ibid., p. 14.

34. Ibid., p. 11.

35. Ibid., p. 14.

36. Ibid., pp. 14–15.

37. Ibid., p. 19.

38. Mallikarjuna Panditaradhya, *Śivatattvasāramu,* verses 263 and 264, quoted in Nagaraju, "Emergence of Regional Identity and Beginnings of Vernacular Literature," p. 18.

39. Ibid., verse 275.

40. Enugula Veeraswamy, *Kāśiyātra Charitramu* (Hyderabad: Telugu University, 1992). Another Telugu edition was published from New Delhi: Asian Educational Services, 3rd ed., 1991. An English translation has also been published: P. Sitapati and V. Purushottam, ed. and trans., *Enugula Veeraswamy's Journal* (Hyderabad: Andhra Pradesh Government Oriental Manuscripts Library and Research Institute, 1973). All translations from Telugu are my own unless otherwise specified, and therefore all page numbers refer to the Telugu-language edition published by Telugu University. The title of this work, *Kāśiyātra Charitramu,* was added later. In a letter written in English and addressed to C. P. Brown, author Enugula Veeraswamy refers to his writing as a "journal," though the work was composed in Telugu in the form of letters addressed to Veeraswamy's friend in Madras, Komaleswarapuram Srinivasa Pillai. Although written by Veeraswamy in Telugu, the collection of letters was first published in Tamil, and only later appeared in Telugu (Vadlamudi Gopalakrishnaiah, preface to the English edition of *Enugula Veeraswamy's Journal,* P. Sitapati and V. Purushottam, ed. and trans., pp. ix–x).

41. I have provided the original Telugu for those who would like to consider my translation: *"Kaḍapa vadilinadi modaluga aravabhāṣa telisi māṭlāḍa taginavāru sakrittugā nunnāru. Tenugu māṭalu sarvasādhāraṇamugā rāgasariḷigā ceppucunnāru. . . . Hindūstāni turakamāṭalu tarucugā dēśalayinanduna ā māṭalu tenugubhāṣalō kalipi māṭlāḍucunnāru. Ī dēśamulō īgelu bahu bādhapeṭṭucunnavi"* (Veeraswamy, *Kāśiyātra Charitramu,* pp. 53–54).

42. The original passage reads, *"Kāyarā anē yūru modalu tenugubhāṣa sakrittugā nunnadi. Brāhmaṇulu modalayina jātulanni mahārāṣṭra bhāṣatō māṭlāḍucunnāru. Hindūsthāni, turaka bhāṣa sarvajana sādhāraṇamugā nunnadi"* (ibid., p. 61).

43. Translated by Sitapati and Purushottam, *Enugula Veeraswamy's Journal,* p. 40.

44. Velcheru Narayana Rao, "Coconut and Honey: Sanskrit and Telugu in Medieval Andhra," *Social Scientist* 23 (1995): 25. See also note 42 in the introduction.

45. Ibid.

46. Lewis McIver, "The Report," vol. I, *Imperial Census of 1881: Operations and Results in the Presidency of Madras* (Madras: Government Press, 1883), p. 2. The 1871 census was the first all-India census attempted under British rule; however, due to its incompleteness and general inconsistency in categories used in each presidency, its results were not widely trusted. Bernard Cohn writes: "A full census of India was to have been attempted in 1861 but because of the dislocations caused by the suppression of the rebellion of 1857–9 and of the sensitivity which the British had developed to what, at least in North India, might be constructed as undue interference in the life of the people, the census was postponed until 1871–2. A census of most of the provinces and princely states was carried out in 1871 and 1872, but such imperfections, both in administration and in conception, developed that not much reliance was put in the census at the time." Bernard Cohn, "The Census, Social Structure and Objectification in South Asia," in *An Anthropologist among the Historians,* Delhi (Oxford University Press, 1987), p. 238.

47. W. R. Cornish, *Report on the Census of the Madras Presidency, 1871* (Madras: Government Gazette Press, 1874), p. 67. The last of the six total figures given includes "Ooriya and Hill languages."

48. Ibid., p. viii.

49. Ibid.

50. In the twentieth century, also, questions of property ownership were raised in debates over how the boundaries of the new linguistic states should be determined. See, for example, the article "Border Talks," in *The Indian Express,* September 9, 1955, in which the issue is raised. "Another very important question to be considered," writes the correspondent, "is whether the numerical strength for the time-being including persons without any property who can migrate at any time should alone be taken into consideration, or whether great importance should be attached to the permanent residence of the people and their property and other permanent interests in the village."

51. Cornish, *Report on the Census of the Madras Presidency,* p. 23.

52. Ibid., p. 24.

53. Ibid.

54. "Specimen Form of Schedule," in ibid., p. 26.

55. Lewis McIver, *Imperial Census of 1881: Operations and Results in the Presidency of Madras,* vol. I (Madras: Government Press, 1883), p. 9.

56. Ibid.

57. Ibid., p. 11.

58. Ibid., p. 123.

59. Ibid., p. 124.

60. Ibid., pp. 125–126.

61. Cavelly Venkata Ramaswamie [Kavali Venkata Ramaswami], *Biographical Sketches of Dekkan Poets* (Calcutta: 1829).

62. C. V. Ramaswamy [Kavali Venkata Ramaswami], *A New Map of the Ancient Division of the Deckan Illustrative of the History of the Hindu Dynasties with Discriptions [sic] of the Principle Places* (Calcutta: Asiatic Lithographic Press, 1827); Cavelly Venkata Ramaswami [Kavali Venkata Ramaswami], *Descriptive and Historical Sketches of Cities and Places in the Dekkan; to which is prefixed, An Introduction, containing a brief description of The Southern Peninsula, and A succinct History of its ancient Rulers: The Whole Being to Serve as a Book of Reference to A Map of Ancient Dekkan* (Calcutta: 1828).

63. Ramaswami was a member of a literate multilingual world that Narayana Rao, Shulman, and Subrahmanyam have labeled "*karaṇam*" culture. "The *karaṇam,*" they

write, "tends to know more than one language, can read in different scripts, and in particular has access to trans-local, universalist ('imperial') languages such as Persian and Sanskrit." For further discussion of this multilingual world, see Narayana Rao et al., *Textures of Time,* pp. 19–20, and Narayana Rao and Shulman, *Poem at the Right Moment,* p. 186.

64. Lisa Mitchell, "Literary Production at the Edge of Empire: The Crisis of Patronage in Southern India under Colonial Rule," in *Fringes of Empire,* ed. Elizabeth Kolsky and Sameetah Agha (Delhi: Oxford University Press, 2009).

65. Mackenzie himself helped to create this negative impression of Ramaswami when he praised the faithfulness of Ramaswami's elder brother Lakshmaiah, extolling his good qualities, and then wrote, "As to Ramaswami, his brother, I look upon him in a different light" (quoted in W. C. Mackenzie, *Colonel Colin Mackenzie: First Surveyor-General of India* [Edinburgh: W. and R. Chambers, 1952], p. 185). Mackenzie also initially included Ramaswami by name in his will, later revising it to write him out. Colin Mackenzie's Will, dated August 3, 1811, with later revisions dated February 18, 1815, and January 21, 1816 (IOIC, BL, IOR/L/AG/34/29/33), pp. 249–253. C. V. Ramachandra Rao has provided other evidence that Ramaswami may have been the most independent and innovative of the Kavali brothers when he mentions that "C. P. Brown, the Telugu scholar, in one of his Telugu memos mentions that Ramaswami, brother of Lakshmaiah knew Bengali well and that he was headstrong and refractory (*pogarumōtu*—Telugu)." C. V. Ramachandra Rao, *The Kavali Brothers, Col. Colin Mackenzie and the Reconstruction of South Indian History and Cultural Resurgence in South India* (Nellore: Manasa, 2003), p. 15. See also the Telugu literary historian Arudra's discussion of Ramaswami in comparison with the other Kavali brothers: Arudra, *Samagra Āndhra Sāhityam,* vol. 9: *Kumpiṇī Yugam* (Vijayawada: Praja Shakti Book House, 1990), pp. 115–128.

66. The fact that scholars have largely accepted Mackenzie's colonial assessment of Ramaswami has blinded subsequent readers to Ramaswami's uniquely creative and innovative responses to the changing conditions of nineteenth-century India. See Mitchell, "Literary Production at the Edge of Empire," and Lisa Mitchell, "Knowing the Deccan: Enquiries, Points, and Poets in the Construction of Knowledge and Power in Early Nineteenth-Century Southern India," in *The Madras School of Orientalism,* ed. Thomas R. Trautmann (Delhi: Oxford University Press, forthcoming).

67. Ramaswami's father was descended from a line of hereditary ministers and ambassadors to the Vijayanagaram sovereigns, which suggests that part of Ramaswami's motivation may have stemmed from a general anxiety within a community traditionally supported through their attachment to a royal court. Ramaswami includes his elder brother Borraiah as one of the poets in his *Biographical Sketches of the Dekkan Poets.* In his biography, Ramaswami writes that Borraiah was "of a respectable tribe of Brahmins, being one of the sons of Cavelly Venkata Soobeah, who was lineally descended from a branch of the Areveti Niyogi Brahmins, who was hereditary minister and ambassador of the Vejayanagaram sovereigns" (Ramaswami, *Biographical Sketches,* ed. C. V. Ramachandra Rao, 1975, p. 91).

68. See Narayana Rao and Shulman, introduction to *Classical Telugu Poetry,* especially pp. 62–66, and their "After-Essay," in *Poem at the Right Moment,* especially pp. 148–159.

69. A. D. Campbell, "On the State of Education of the Natives in Southern India," *Journal of the Madras Literary Society* I (1833–34): 354.

70. Thomas R. Trautmann, *Languages and Nations: The Dravidian Proof in Colonial Madras* (Berkeley: University of California Press, 2006), pp. 146–150.

71. Madras Public Consultations, September 28, 1813, letter of May 2, 1813, quoted in Trautmann, *Languages and Nations,* p. 147.

72. Ibid., Mamadi Venkaya to Collector, July 1, 1813, quoted in Trautmann, *Languages and Nations,* p. 148.

73. Trautmann, *Languages and Nations,* p. 148.

74. Andrew S. Cook, "The Beginning of Lithographic Map Printing in Calcutta," in *India: A Pageant of Prints,* ed. Pauline Rohatgi and Pheroza Godrej (Bombay: Marg, 1989). The first lithographic press was introduced to India in 1822, and experiments in reproducing maps began in March 1823. Local climatic conditions meant that it took some time for adjustments to the European process, and initially only the government made use of the press. Ramaswami's map in 1827 was likely one of the very earliest applications of lithographic technology issuing from a non-governmental source in India. See Mitchell, "Knowing the Deccan," for additional discussion of Ramaswami's lithographic mapmaking, use of subscriptions, and other creative efforts.

75. Mitchell, "Knowing the Deccan."

76. I am grateful to Phillip Wagoner for pointing out to me the fact that entries in Ramaswami's *Descriptive and Historical Sketches of Cities and Places in the Dekkan* are taken, often verbatim, from texts collected as part of the Mackenzie manuscripts, making it clear that Ramaswami was one of the only individuals ever to publish from Mackenzie's massive project. Wagoner is currently completing a book on Mackenzie's assistants that will make a much-needed contribution to our understanding of low local knowledge experts responded to the conditions of colonial rule.

77. Mitchell, "Knowing the Deccan."

78. See Ramachandra Rao, *Kavali Brothers,* for details regarding his specific publications.

79. Ibid. See also Rama Mantena's and Phillip Wagoner's forthcoming work.

2. Making a Subject of Language

1. Rama Sundari Mantena, "Vernacular Futures: Colonial Philology and the Idea of History in Nineteenth-Century South India," *Indian Economic and Social History Review* 42, no. 4 (2005): 513–534. See also her forthcoming book on the subject, *Estranged Pasts: Archive and Historical Time in Colonial India* (in progress).

2. The song with which this chapter opens, *Mā Telugu Tallikī Mallepū Daṇḍa* [A Garland of Jasmine Flowers for Our Mother Telugu], was composed in Telugu by Shankarambadi Sunderachari around 1942 (my translation). It is today used as a state anthem and learned by schoolchildren throughout Andhra Pradesh, appearing in textbooks and primers such as Buddiga Subbarayan's *Surabhi Pedda Bāla Śikṣa* (Hyderabad: Educational Products of India, 1998), pp. 340–341.

3. Some of these associations may have been historically accurate, though others were apocryphal or served the purpose of creating an imagined shared past for a later community that identified with them. Velcheru Narayana Rao and David Shulman have suggested that these eight poets—despite widespread popular belief that places them all together in Krishnadevaraya's court—may have been assembled within the popular imaginary more than a century later as part of a "retrospective . . . vision of the royal

court" reflecting the values of a later era. Velcheru Narayana Rao and David Shulman, ed. and trans., *Classical Telugu Poetry: An Anthology,* Delhi: Oxford University Press, 2002), p. 253. See also P. Chenchiah and M. Bhujanga Rao, *A History of Telugu Literature* (Calcutta: Association Press, 1925), pp. 72, 84; and G. V. Sitapati, *History of Telugu Literature* (Delhi: Sahitya Akademi, 1968).

4. Velcheru Narayana Rao, David Shulman, and Sanjay Subrahmanyam, *Symbols of Substance: Court and State in Nayaka Period Tamilnadu (*Delhi: Oxford University Press, 1992), p. 334. They also describe the ways in which courtly dramas mixed Telugu with colloquial Tamil, recorded in Telugu script.

5. Velcheru Narayana Rao and David Shulman, *A Poem at the Right Moment: Remembered Verses from Premodern South India* (Berkeley: University of California Press, 1998), p. 23.

6. Ibid., pp. 186–187.

7. For example, even in written anthologies of *cāṭus,* such as Madiki Singanna's fifteenth-century collection *Sakala-nīti-sammatamu,* Telugu is the medium in which these poems are collected and written, rather than the marker of what unites them. Ibid., p. 6.

8. Gurujada Sriramamurti, *Kavi Jīvitamulu* (Rajahmundry: Vivekavarthani Press, 1878). In the preface to his second edition in 1893, he claims to have begun work on this in 1876.

9. Sriramamurti, *Kavi Jīvitamulu,* 2nd ed., p. 1.

10. Charles Philip Brown, *Essay on the Language and Literature of the Telugus* (New Delhi: Asian Educational Services, 1991), pp. 13; 9 (reprint of original 1840 ed.). See also Brown's manuscript "Analysis of Telugu Prosody" (Tel. D. 1260), Government Oriental Manuscripts Library, Chennai.

11. Colin Mackenzie's manuscript collection contains a "List of the most Celebrated Caveeswars [poets] in the Andra or Tellinga language," compiled in 1801 by Ramaswami's elder brother, Kavali Venkata Boraiah (Mack Gen/21). Rama Mantena, panel on Language, Genre, and Identity in Colonial South India, Association for Asian Studies Annual Meeting, New York, March 28, 2003. The existence of such a list points to the impact of Mackenzie's information-gathering practices in shaping the ways his assistants collected and organized data. Although lists of poets and titles of works appear in the Mackenzie manuscripts in ways that could be interpreted as being organized by both language and geographic territory, Ramaswami is the first to compile narratives of poets' *lives* specifically, and Gurujada Sriramamurti to explicitly use language as the organizational foundation.

12. Kandukuri Viresalingam, *Rājaśēkhara Charitramu* [The Life Story of Rajasekhara] (Hyderabad: Visalaandhra, 1991). Although many biographers and contemporaries of Viresalingam have agreed with Viresalingam's claim that this was the first Telugu novel, more recent literary historians have suggested several literary works published prior to *Rājaśēkhara Charitramu* that may lay claim to the honor of being the first Telugu novel, including Narahari Gopalakrishna Chetty's *Śrī Ranga Rāja Charitramu* [The Story of Sri Ranga Raja] published in 1872 (see John Greenfield Leonard, *Kandukuri Viresalingam (1848–1919): A Biography of an Indian Social Reformer* [Hyderabad: Telugu University, 1991, reprint of his Ph.D. dissertation in comparative tropical history submitted to the University of Wisconsin in 1970], pp. 84–85) and Kokkonda Venkataratnam's *Mahāsweta* (see D. Anjaneyulu, *Kandukuri Viresalingam* [Delhi: Publications Division, Ministry of Information and Broadcasting, Government

of India, 1976], p. 88). The fact that this is now a contested matter points to the constructed nature of literary categories and the difficulty of defining genres of writing. Viresalingam's novel was the first to attempt to appeal to a general audience, as seen in his use of simpler, more accessible language. It was also the first novel to be concerned with social issues. Evidence that it was viewed as the first Telugu novel at the time it was published includes a reference to it in *The Hindu,* where it was described as marking "an era in the annals of Telugu literature. It is the first Telugu novel that has yet appeared, and as an attempt in a new direction, we must consider it a success" (quoted in Leonard, *Kandukuri Viresalingam,* p. 84).

13. Sitapati, *History of Telugu Literature,* pp. 246–247.

14. Gwynn and Sastry, *Telugu-English Dictionary,* p. 180.

15. Charles Philip Brown, *Nighaṇṭuvu Telugu-English,* p. 406.

16. Velcheru Narayana Rao, David Shulman, and Sanjay Subrahmanyam, *Textures of Time: Writing History in South India, 1600–1800* (Delhi: Permanent Black, 2001).

17. See, for example, M. M. Bakhtin's famous essay "Epic and Novel," in *The Dialogic Imagination,* ed. Michael Holquist (Austin: University of Texas Press, 1981), pp. 3–40.

18. Anjaneyulu, *Kandukuri Viresalingam,* p. 89.

19. Ibid., p. 90.

20. English translation taken from K. Viresalingam, *Fortune's Wheel: A Tale of Hindu Domestic Life,* trans. J. Robert Hutchinson (London: Elliot Stock, 1887), pp. 198–199.

21. The earliest known Telugu *Dēśa Charitramu* [History of the Country] is D. Venkataranga Setti's, published in 1890, followed by another published in 1916 by Gidugu Venkata Sitapati. In the preface to his 1893 edition of *Kavi Jīvitamulu,* Gurujada Sriramamurti also claims to have been working on a *Dēśa Charitramu* [History of the Country], his work on this preventing him from completing the second edition of his *Lives of Poets* earlier than 1893, but there is no evidence that he ever published such a text. Sriramamurti offers this as an explanation for why Kandukuri Viresalingam was able to publish the first volume of his *Āndhra Kavula Charitramu* in 1887, six years prior to the completion of his own full edition (Sriramamurti, *Kavi Jivitamulu,* 1893).

22. P. Gopala Rao Naidu, *Āndhra Bhāṣā Charitra Sangrahamu* [Summary of the History of the Andhra Language] (Rajahmundry: Vivekavarthani Press, 1896). This was followed by Mangu Venkataramanuja Rao, *Āndhra Bhāṣā Charitra Sangrahamu* [Summary of the History of the Andhra Language] (Elluru [Eluru], 1899), and much later by Chilukuri Narayana Rao, *Āndhra Bhāṣā Charitramu* [History of the Andhra Language] (Madras: Anand Mudranalayam, 1937).

23. Chilukuri Veerabhadra Rao, *Āndhrula Charitramu, Prathama Bhāgamu: Purva Yugamu* [History of the Andhras, vol. 1: Ancient Period] (Cennapuri [Madras]: Ananda Mudrayantrashalaya, 1910), and *Āndhrula Charitramu, Dvitiya Bhāgamu: Madhya Yugamu* [History of the Andhras, vol. 2: Medieval Period] (Cennapuri [Madras]: Jyotishmati Mudrayantrashalaya, 1912).

24. Sriramamurti, *Kavi Jīvitamulu* (1893), p. 1.

25. William P. Trent, "Biographical Sketch of Macaulay," in *Johnson and Goldsmith: Essays by Thomas Babington Macaulay, with Additional Material for Study,* ed. William P. Trent (Boston: Houghton Mifflin, 1906), pp. xvi–xvii. Although published slightly later than the period under question, such a framework for the teaching of biographical essays appears to have been a part of the lessons to which students in English educational institutions in India would also have been exposed. Late-nineteenth-century syllabi in

Madras University included items such as J. T. Fowler, *Johnson's life of Addison, from the Lives of the Poets, for the Use of University Students* (Madras: J. T. Fowler, 1867) and J. T. Margoschis, *Life of Addison by Samuel Johnson, LL.D., reprinted from his 'Lives of the most Eminent English Poets,' with notes* (Madras: Messrs. C. Foster, 1875). See also Oxford graduate, *First Part of the Adelphi Press, First Arts Text Book for 1870* (Madras: Messrs. Grantz Brothers, 1870); Government of India, *The Idolatrous and Immoral Teaching of Some Government and University Text Books in Madras, India* (Madras, 1872); Madras University Calendars, 1873–1880, OIOC; Government of India, *Report of the Committee for the Revision of English, Telugu, and Tamil School Books in the Madras University*, vol. 44 (Madras: Selections of the Madras Government, 1875); John Murdoch, *Education in India: Letter to His Excellency the Most Honourable Marquis of Ripon, Viceroy and Governor-General of India* (Madras: S.C.K.S. Press, Vepery, 1881); Government of India, Indian Education Commission, *Report of the Madras Provincial Committee* (Calcutta, 1884); and Government of India, *Papers Relating to Discipline and Moral Training in Schools and Colleges in India* (Madras, 1890).

26. Jayanti Ramayya, *An Essay on Telugu Language and Literature* (Vizagapatam: S. S. M. Press, 1896).

27. Ibid., p. 18.

28. Ibid., p. 19.

29. Sitapati, *History of Telugu Literature*, p. 254.

30. Arudra, *Samagra Āndhra Sāhityam*, vol. 12: *Zamīndāri Navya Sāhitya Yugālu* (Vijayawada: Praja Shakti Book House, 1991), p. 76.

31. Kandukuri Viresalingam, *The Complete Works of Rao Bahadur K. Veeresalingam Pantulu*, vol. 10: *Telugu Poets*, part 1, 2nd ed. (Rajahmundry: Sree Rama Press, 1937 [1917]), pp. 1–84.

32. A text that initially appears to be an exception to this argument is the mid-eighteenth-century *Tañjāvūri Āndhra Rājula Charitra* [History of the Tanjavur Telugu Kings], written by an unknown author and published by Veturi Prabhakara Sastri in 1914. Yet it appears likely that the title of this published edition was added by Prabhakara Sastri only in 1914. "The title may have been given by the learned editor, Veṭuri Prabhakara Sastri, who published it, from a single surviving manuscript, in 1914," write Narayana Rao, Shulman, and Subrahmanyam in their book *Textures of Time: Writing History in South India, 1600–1800* (Delhi: Permanent Black, 2001), p. 129. This suggests that the apparent emphasis on the collective history of *Telugu* kings of Tanjavur, as suggested by the title, rather than the genealogy of the last king discussed, may, in fact, more accurately reflect the categories and ways of structuring knowledge of the early twentieth century rather than those of the eighteenth century.

33. Benedict Anderson, *Imagined Communities: Reflections on the Origins and Spread of Nationalism*, rev. ed. (London: Verso, 1991).

34. C. Gopinatha Rao, *Library Movement in Andhra Pradesh* (Hyderabad: Dept. of Public Libraries, Government of Andhra Pradesh, 1981).

35. Velcheru Narayana Rao and David Shulman dismiss this debate with the comment that "[m]uch ink has been wasted in an attempt to show that this beloved figure was identical with the *kāvya* poet called Tenāli Rāmakr̥ṣṇa, again of the sixteenth century. There is, however, no reason whatsoever to believe that the jester Tenāli Rāmalingaḍu was a historical person, let alone that the great *kāvya* poet attracted this role to himself. Jesters existed at Hampi and elsewhere; but Tenāli Rāmalingaḍu belongs, by right, to the moment when the Telugu *cāṭu* system crystallized in a retrospective

frame. The system needed just such an outrageous figure; his appearance in the stories is one sure sign that we are dealing not with memory but with a critical imagination working on materials suited to the middle-level elite of late-medieval Andhra." See *A Poem at the Right Moment,* p. 185. They also suggest that this quick-witted jester-clown "in some sense epitomizes the *cāṭu* vision—innovative, subversive, trenchant in judgment, spontaneous, and heavily weighted toward the oral as opposed to the scholarly-literate" (ibid.).

Narayana Rao and Shulman refer to the sixteenth-century *kāvya* poet as Tenali Ramakrishna and the figure of the court-jester as Tenali Ramalingadu, despite the fact that as many popular collections of stories about the court-jester published between 1860 and 1920 use the name Tenali Ramakrishna as use Ramalingadu. Sriramamurti uses Ramakrishna but mentions that he also went by Ramalingadu and occasionally uses that name as well in his *Kavi Jīvitamulu.* To further add to the confusion, the *kāvya* poet Tenali Ramakrishna also is known to have composed some works under the name Tenali Ramalinga. Narayana Rao and Shulman, in a brief history of the *kāvya* poet, write that "Tenāli Rāmakṝṣṇa was the son of a Śaiva priest, Gārlapāṭi Rāmayya, who served in the temple of Rāmalingeśvarasvāmi in Tenāli. The son was named after this deity. His earliest work was probably the *Udbhaṭārādhya-charitramu,* where he calls himself Tenāli Rāmalinga" (*Classical Telugu Poetry,* p. 291). They speculate that his later name change may have reflected "a conversion from Śaivism to Vaiṣṇavism, as is also suggested by the shift from a Śaiva to Vaiṣṇava cultic focus in the poet's works" (ibid.).

36. Nelaturu Venkatasubba Sastri, *Tenāli Rāmakṛṣṇa Kathalu* (Saraswati Vilasa Press, 1860). There appears to be some discrepancy over the actual date of Gurujada Sriramamurti's writing on *Tenali Ramakrishna.* A copy of his *Tenāli Rāmakṛṣṇa-kavi Jīvitamu* from 1915 survives in the British Library's collection in London, but as his title suggests, he thinks of it as a *jīvitamu* (life) rather than a collection of *kathalu* (stories), a significant distinction and one illustrated by the arrangement of his table of contents. Kasinathuni Nageswara Rao, in his 1929 *Āndhra Vāŋmaya Sūchika* [Index of Andhra Literature], lists the date of publication of Sriramamurti's *Tenali Ramakrishna* as 1860, followed by subsequent editions of Tenali Rama stories published by a wide variety of different authors in 1882, 1907 (works by two different authors), 1908, 1911, 1912, and 1917. Arudra, in his thirteen-volume *Samagra Āndhra Sāhityam* [Complete Andhra Literature], appears to take his dates directly from Kasinathuni Nageswara Rao's *Index,* as the number of authors, titles, and dates he cites are exactly the same (vol. 12, p. 74). He, too, claims that Sriramamurti was the first to publish a written collection of the popular oral Tenali Ramakrishna stories and gives 1860 as the date of publication. But given the general consensus that Sriramamurti was born in 1851, this is improbable. N. Sivanarayya, M. Pramila Reddy, and N. Jangaiah in *Telugu Sāhitya Kosamu: Ādhunika Sāhityam (1851–1950)* (Hyderabad: Telugu Akademi, 1986), p. 1131, give the date of 1880 with a question mark, which is a much more likely publication date for the first collection of Sriramamurti's. For the purpose of my argument, however, the exact date of publication and the original author/editor are not as important as the fact that a written version of oral tales *about* a poet was printed and became popular long before the actual literary compositions *by* a poet (previously available only on palm-leaf manuscripts) were printed and made popularly available.

37. Nageswara Rao, *Āndhra Vāŋmaya Sūchika,* p. 109.

38. Arudra, *Samagra Āndhra Sāhityam,* vol. 12, p. 74 (my translation).

39. Of the twenty-four poets included in Sriramamurti's 1893 six-part edition of

Kavi Jīvitamulu, it appears that the works of most were not published until the early decades of the twentieth century—some not until the middle of the century. The only notable exceptions are Telugu versions of the *(Maha-)Bharatamu, Ramayanamu,* and *Bhagavathamu* composed by these authors. As chapter 4 explores in more detail, these were three of the most popularly used manuscript-texts studied in schools at the beginning of the nineteenth century (prior to the availability of printed schoolbooks), and many school children devoted large sections of these to memory. By 1867, for example, four editions of *Bhaskara Ramayanam* (attributed to Bhaskara, one of the poets included by Sriramamurti) had been printed by the Viveka Vithia Nilayam Press, in Peddu Naick's Petta, Madras. The *Quarterly List of Publications* published from Madras described the work in 1868 as follows: "Parts of this work are selected annually, as they well deserve to be, for the Matriculation Examination of the Madras University in the Telugu language" (1868, vol. 2, p. 14, OIOC). This text was also the most commonly mentioned manuscript used in schools in the 1820s (see Venelakanty Subba Rao, A. D. Campbell, and Raz Ram's descriptions of school curriculum in chapter 4.) A printed version of the *Āndhrabhāgavatamu* [Telugu Bhagavata] of Bammera Potana was published in 1875, the year before Sriramamurti says he began working on assembling his *Lives of Poets,* with sections of Pōtana's Bhagavatam appearing even earlier (Kasinathuni Nageswara Rao, *Āndhra Vāŋmaya Sūchika,* p. 14). Of this work, Velcheru Narayana Rao and David Shulman write that this text "remains the most widely copied and the most frequently read and performed text in Telugu, its verses learned by heart by many" (*Classical Telugu Poetry,* p. 202). A section of Tikkana's *Mahabharata* was prescribed for the F.A. Examination at Madras University in 1901, and an edition was published by Madras University the preceding year (OIOC 14174.k.45.3). It is likely that earlier versions may also have been printed. Aside from these few exceptions, the works of the other poets Sriramamurti discusses were not published until well after his *Lives of Poets* came out. Regardless of when these and other works appeared, the fact remains that we have evidence that in the last decades of the nineteenth century there was as great a fascination with stories and narratives of the lives of well-known poets as with their works. Indeed, interest in stories about their lives seems to have actually been more popular than their works themselves.

40. K. V. R. Krishna Rao, *Āndhra Bhāṣābhivṛddhi* [The Progress of Telugu Language] (Rajahmundry: Viveka Varthani Press, 1896).

41. *Abhivṛddhi* comes into the Telugu language from Sanskrit. This definition is taken from Gwynn and Sastry, *Telugu-English Dictionary,* p. 29. An earlier definition, "increase, improvement, progress, augmentation," is taken from Brown, *Nighaṇṭuvu Telugu-English,* p. 71.

42. From "Farbas Vilāsa" (recounting a literary gathering organized by Alexander Kinlok-Forbes in 1852), published in *Buddhiprakāś* (1857), cited in Sheldon Pollock, "The Death of Sanskrit," *Comparative Studies in Society and History* 43, no. 2 (2001): 394.

43. V. S. Srinivasa Sastri, "The Improvement of Vernaculars," *Indian Review* 1 (December 1900): 560.

44. Informal conversation, August 11, 1998.

45. Ibid.

46. Interview, Madras, July 28, 1998.

47. Interview, Nellore, August 12, 1998.

48. *Vaartha* (Hyderabad ed.), November 1, 2002, p. 1 (my translation).

49. Ibid. The inscription was subsequently changed to Telugu. See Figure 2.4.

50. Sumathi Ramaswamy has discussed this phenomenon in the context of Tamil. See her article "En/gendering Language: The Poetics of Tamil Identity," *Comparative Studies in Society and History* 35, no. 4 (1993): 683–725. See also Sumathi Ramaswamy, "Maps and Mother Goddesses in Modern India," *Imago Mundi* 53 (2001): 97–114.

51. Interview, July 13, 2000.

52. Tape-recorded interview, August 7, 2000.

53. Informal conversation, July 13, 2000.

54. Velcheru Narayana Rao, "Coconut and Honey: Sanskrit and Telugu in Premodern Andhra," *Social Scientist* 23 (1995): 24–40.

55. Narayana Rao and Shulman, *Classical Telugu Poetry,* p. 256.

3. Making the Local Foreign

1. Naoki Sakai, *Translation and Subjectivity: On "Japan" and Cultural Nationalism* (Minneapolis: University of Minnesota Press, 1997), p. 20; and Discussant Comments, American Anthropological Association, panel entitled "Adventures in Heteroglossia," December 2, 2001.

2. Kathryn Woolard and Bambi B. Schieffelin, "Language Ideology," *Annual Review of Anthropology* 23 (1994): 55.

3. Ibid., p. 56.

4. Joseph Errington, "Colonial Linguistics," *Annual Review of Anthropology* 30 (2001): 19–39.

5. Robert Hardgrave, *The Dravidian Movement* (Bombay: Popular Prakashan, 1956); Eugene F. Irschick, *Politics and Social Conflict in South India: The Non-Brahman Movement and Tamil Separatism, 1916–1929* (Berkeley: University of California Press, 1969); Jyotirindra Dasgupta, *Language Conflict and National Development: Group Politics and National Language Policy in India* (Berkeley: University of California Press, 1970); Karat Prakash, *Language and Nationality Politics in India* (Bombay: Orient Longman, 1973); Paul R. Brass, *Language, Religion and Politics in India* (Cambridge: Cambridge University Press, 1974); R. Suntharalingam, *Politics and Nationalist Awakening in South India, 1852–1891* (Tuscon: University of Arizona Press, 1974); Marguerite Barnett, *The Politics of Cultural Nationalism in South India* (Princeton, N.J.: Princeton University Press, 1976); K. Nambi Arooran, *Tamil Renaissance and Dravidian Nationalism, 1905–1944* (Madras: Koodal, 1980); Eugene Irschick, *Tamil Revivalism in the 1930s* (Madras: Cre-A, 1986); David Washbrook, *The Emergence of Provincial Politics: The Madras Presidency, 1870–1920* (Cambridge: Cambridge University Press, 1976); David Washbrook, "Caste, Class, and Dominance in Modern Tamil Nadu: Non-Brahmanism, Dravidianism, and Tamil Nationalism," in *Dominance and State Power in Modern India: Decline of a Social Order,* ed. Francine R. Frankel and M. S. A. Rao (Delhi: Oxford University Press, 1989), pp. 204–265; Paul Brass, *Ethnicity and Nationalism: Theory and Comparison* (New Delhi: Sage, 1991); Sudipta Kaviraj, "Writing, Speaking, Being: Language and the Historical Formation of Identities in India," in *Nationalstaat und Sprachkonflikte in Süd- und Südostasien,* ed. Dagmar Hellmann-Rajanayagam and Dietmar Rothermund (Stuttgart: Franz Steiner Verlag, 1992), pp. 25–68; and V. Geetha and S. V. Rajadurai, *Towards a Non-Brahmin Millennium: From Iyothee Thass to Periyar* (Calcutta: Samya, 1999).

6. V. Ravindiran, "The Unanticipated Legacy of Robert Caldwell and the Dravidian Movement," *South Indian Studies* 1 (1996): 83–110; Thomas R. Trautmann, "Hullabaloo about Telugu," *South Asia Research* 19, no. 1 (1999): 53–70; Trautmann,

"Inventing the History of South India," in *Invoking the Past: The Uses of History in South Asia,* ed. Daud Ali (New Delhi: Oxford University Press), pp. 36–54; Trautmann, "Dr Johnson and the Pandits: Imagining the Perfect Dictionary in Colonial Madras," *Indian Economic and Social History Review* 38, no. 4 (2001): 375–397.

7. Nannaya Bhatt, *Āndhra Śabda Chintāmaṇi* (Chennapuri: Vavilla Ramaswamisastrulu, 1968), chapter 1, verse 6. See also C. P. Brown's notes on a manuscript version of this text, GOML, Tel. D. 1237.

8. Boddupalli Purushottam, *The Theories of Telugu Grammar* (Thiruvananthapuram: International School of Dravidian Linguistics, 1996), p. 3.

9. Mulaghatika Ketana, *Āndhra Bhāṣā Bhūṣaṇamu* (Tenali: Ajanta Art Press, 1953), p. 23, verse 19. Unlike *Āndhra Śabda Chintāmaṇi,* Ketana's grammar has not encouraged the production of commentaries, causing Boddupalli Purushottam to place it in its own separate grammatical school (*Theories of Telugu Grammar,* pp. 11–12).

10. Kakunuri Appakavi, *Appakavīyamu* (Chennapuri: Vavilla Ramaswamisastrulu and Sons, 1951), p. 38, verse 101.

11. Although I have included the most well-known and influential Telugu grammars, these are but a small portion of preserved grammars. For a more comprehensive overview of Telugu grammars and the influences of Sanskrit and Prakrit grammars, see (in Telugu) Tumati Donappa, *Bhāṣa Charitraka Vyāsāvali* [Collection of Essays on the History of Language] (Hyderabad: Andhra Sarasvata Parishat, 1972); Tumati Donappa, *Vaikṛta Pada Svarūpa Nirūpaṇamu: Old and Middle Indo-Aryan Loan Words in Literary Telugu* (Hyderabad: Felicitation Committee of the Sixtieth Birthday Celebrations, 1987); Boddupalli Purushottam, *Tenugu Vyākaraṇa Vikāsamu: The Origins and Development of Telugu Grammar* (Guntur: Girija Prachuranalu, 1968); G. Lalitha, *Telugu Vyākaraṇamula Charitra* [History of Telugu Grammars] (Madras: Velagapudi Foundation, 1996); Rajeswara Sarma, *Āndhra Vyākaraṇa Vikāsamu,* 2 vols. (Kamareddi: Praca Vidya Parishat, 1973); Nayani Krishna Kumari, *Telugu Bhāṣa Charitra: Tulanatmaka Pari Silana* [The History of Telugu Language: A Comparative Study] (Hyderabad: Telugu Akademi, 1984); Bhagavatamu Rama Rao, "Telugu nighaṇṭuvulalō dēśyapadamula pai chinna chūpu," *Bharati* (1968), pp. 39–45; Amareesham Rajeswara Sarma, *Āndhra Vyākaraṇa Vikāsamu* (Kamareddi: Prācya Vidyā Parishat, part 1, 1973, and part 2, 1977); and (in English) Purushottam, *Theories of Telugu Grammar;* Purushottam, "Classification of Telugu Vocabulary," *Proceedings of the First All India Conference of Dravidian Linguists, 1971,* ed. V. I. Subramoniam (Trivandrum: St. George's Press, 1972), pp. 202–205; Korada Mahadeva Sastri, *Historical Grammar of Telugu with Special Reference to Old Telugu c. 200 BC–1000 AD* (Anantapur: Sri Venkateswara University, 1969); and G. J. Somayaji, "The Influence of Sanskrit Grammar on Telugu Grammar," *Journal of Andhra History and Culture* I, no. 3 (1943): 129–135. See also S. Kuppuswami Sastri, *A Descriptive Catalogue of the Telugu Manuscripts in the Government Oriental Manuscripts Library, Madras,* vol. 5, *Grammar, Prosody and Lexicography* (Madras: Superintendent, Government Press, 1935).

12. Vedam Pattabhirama Sastri, *Āndhra Vyākaraṇamu: Padya Kāvyamu* (Chennapuri: Vavilla Ramaswamisastrulu, 1951 [1825]); Ravipati Gurumurti Sastri, *Telugu Vyākaraṇamu* (Chennapattanam: Mission Press, 1836; reprinted Chennapuri: Vavilla Ramaswamisastrulu, 1951); and Paravastu Chinnaya Suri, *Bāla Vyākaraṇamu* (Chennapuri: Vavilla Ramaswamisastrulu, 1967 [1858]).

13. Eivind Kahrs, "What Is a *Tadbhava* Word," *Indo-Iranian Journal* 35, nos. 2–3 (1992): 232–233.

14. I am not suggesting here that the literary languages of southern India were not

recognized as distinct languages prior to the colonial period, but rather that pre-colonial grammarians show little preoccupation with formally documenting the distinctions between one regional language and another, or with identifying "pure" and "foreign" linguistic forms of one group of people vis-à-vis other regional groups, in the ways that colonial and post-colonial scholars have tended to do. Instead, the categories used by pre-colonial grammarians document a spectrum of available language use by categorizing all known words in relation to their usefulness and prestige rather than in relation to the ethnic identities of those who use them, with prestige measured according to the intelligibility of words by educated multilinguals in other regions. Ashok Aklujkar makes a similar argument regarding the characterization of language as a continuum by early Indian grammarians. "The Early History of Sanskrit as a Supreme Language," in *Ideology and the Status of Sanskrit: Contributions to the History of the Sanskrit Language,* ed. J. Houben (Leiden: E. J. Brill, 1996), p. 74.

15. Kahrs, "What Is a *Tadbhava* Word," p. 233.

16. Ibid., p. 226.

17. Ibid., p. 245.

18. Ibid., pp. 226, 236.

19. Purushottam, *Theories of Telugu Grammar,* p. 103.

20. A. D. Campbell, *A Grammar of the Teloogoo Language,* 2nd ed. (Madras: College Press, 1820 [1816]), p. xviii.

21. Ibid., pp. xiv–xv.

22. Thomas R. Trautmann, "Hullabaloo," pp. 53–70; Trautmann, "Inventing the History," pp. 36–54; Trautmann, "Dr Johnson and the Pandits," pp. 375–397.

23. Trautmann, "Hullabaloo," pp. 44–45; "Inventing the History," p. 60.

24. Campbell, *Grammar of the Teloogoo Language,* p. xvii.

25. Ibid., pp. xvii–xviii.

26. Appakavi, *Appakavīyamu,* p. 39, verse 105; Pattabhirama Sastri, *Āndhra Vyākaraṇamu,* p. 23; Gurumurti Sastri, *Telugu Vyākaraṇamu,* p. 27, verse 82.

27. Campbell, *Grammar of the Teloogoo Language,* p. 37.

28. Ibid., p. xviii.

29. Francis W. Ellis, "Note to the Introduction," in A. D. Campbell, *Grammar of the Teloogoo Language,* p. 21.

30. Ibid.

31. Mamadi Vencaya [Venkaya], *The Andhra Deepica, a Dictionary of the Telugu Language,* Tel. D. 1332 and Tel. D. 1333, Oriental Manuscripts Library, Chennai. The best of several surviving handwritten copies of this dictionary housed in Chennai's Oriental Manuscripts Library is labeled "published at Masulipatam AD 1806 but never printed" (Vencaya, Tel. D. 1333, p. 4), prefaced by a note from C. P. Brown dated Masalipatam, August 12, 1824, which states, "This copy was prepared under my directions, and is very accurate. It was transcribed from the original copy in the author's handwriting" (p. 1).

32. Ellis, "Note to the Introduction," p. 15.

33. Ibid., p. 17, emphasis added.

34. Charles Philip Brown, *Essay on the Language and Literature of the Telugus* (Madras: J. B. Pharoah, 1840), p. 12; Charles Philip Brown, *A Grammar of the Telugu Language,* 2nd ed. (Madras: Christian Knowledge Society, 1857), p. 357.

35. Brown, *Essay on the Language and Literature of the Telugus,* p. 12. See also Brown's notations on a manuscript copy of Appakavi's grammar, the *Appakavīyamu,* GOML, Tel. D. 1261.

36. Ibid., emphasis added.
37. Ibid.
38. Brown, *Grammar of the Telugu Language,* p. 355.
39. Ibid., emphasis added.
40. Ibid., p. 357, emphasis added.
41. Appakavi, *Appakavīyamu,* p. 39, verse 105.
42. Ibid., verse 106.
43. Ibid., verse 108.
44. Ellis, "Note to the Introduction," p. 16.
45. Purushottam, *Theories of Telugu Grammar,* p. 101.
46. Ellis, "Note to the Introduction," p. 17.
47. Ibid., p. 4; Campbell, *Grammar of the Teloogoo Language,* p. xxi. A manuscript version of an earlier work by Pattabhiramma Sastri, *Paṭṭābhirāmapaṇḍitīyamu, Written after the manner of Āndhraśabdhacintāmaṇi by a Pandit of Presidency College* is preserved in the GOML, Tel. D. 1246.
48. Pattabhirama Sastri, *Āndhra Vyākaraṇamu,* pp. 23–24.
49. Ellis, "Note to the Introduction," p. 21.
50. Campbell, *Grammar of the Teloogoo Language,* p. 37.
51. Trautmann, "Hullabaloo," pp. 60–61; "Imagining the Perfect Dictionary," p. 379.
52. Aklujkar, "Early History of Sanskrit," p. 74.
53. Daud Ali, *Courtly Culture and Political Life in Early Medieval India* (Cambridge: Cambridge University Press, 2004), p. 171.
54. Ibid., emphasis added.
55. Sheldon Pollock, "The Cosmopolitan Vernacular," *Journal of Asian Studies* 57, no. 1 (1998): 11.
56. J. P. L. Gwynn and J. Venkateswara Sastry, *A Telugu-English Dictionary* (Oxford: Oxford University Press, 1991); P. Sankaranarayana, *Telugu-English Dictionary* (New Delhi: Asian Educational Services, 1998). For an example of an early-twentieth-century effort to compose a dictionary of *accha telugu,* see Koti Venkanna, *Āndhrabhāṣarnavamu: Accha Tenugu Nighaṇṭuvu* (Chennapuri: Vavilla Ramaswamy Sastrulu and Sons, 1931).
57. Ketana, *Āndhra Bhāṣā Bhūṣaṇamu,* p. 23, verse 19.
58. Purushottam, *Theories of Telugu Grammar,* p. 105.
59. Ketana, *Āndhra Bhāṣā Bhūṣaṇamu,* p. 27, verse 22.
60. G. V. Sitapati, *History of Telugu Literature* (New Delhi: Sahitya Akademi, 1968), p. 49.
61. Ibid.
62. Appakavi, *Appakavīyamu,* p. 39, verse 110.
63. Gurumurti Sastri, *Telugu Vyākaraṇamu,* p. 27, verse 82.
64. Ibid., prefatory page; Brown, *Essay on the Language and Literature,* pp. 16–17.
65. Brown, *Grammar of the Telugu Language,* p. 357.
66. Charles Philip Brown, *Brānya Telugu Nighaṇṭu* [Brown's Telugu Dictionary] (Madras: Christian Knowledge Society, 1852).
67. Charles Philip Brown, *Nighaṇṭuvu Telugu-English,* p. 27.
68. Brown, *Brānya Telugu Nighaṇṭu,* p. 449.
69. Brown, *Nighanṭuvu Telugu-English,* p. 609, emphasis added.
70. Charles Philip Brown, *Miśrā Bhāṣā Nighaṇṭu: Brown's Dictionary of Mixed Telugu* (Madras: Christian Knowledge Society Press, 1854), p. i. A copy of a manuscript effort by

Brown to produce a glossary of mixed Telugu, entitled *Ābhāṣāndhranighaṇṭuvu, Glossary of mixed Telugu explaining origin, local, foreign or corrupt. Based on Board of Revenue vocabulary with Telugu and Sanskrit omitted,* is housed in the GOML, Tel. D. 1372.

71. Ibid., p. iv.

72. Ibid., p. iii.

73. Brown, *Nighaṇṭuvu Telugu-English,* pp. v–vi.

4. From Pandit to Primer

1. Appendix to *The First Report of the Madras School Book Society for the Year 1823* (1823: 43-C), reprinted in Vennelakanty Subba Rao [Vennelacunty Soob Row], *The Life of Vennelacunty Soob Row (Native of Ongole), Translator and Interpreter of the Late Sudr Court, Madras, From 1815 to 1829, As written by himself, Published for the Information of his Relations and Friends by the Son Vennalacunty Venkata Gopal Row, District Munsiff-Trivellore* (Madras: C. Foster, 1873), p. 65.

2. Ibid., pp. 72–73, emphasis added.

3. Eric Stokes, *The English Utilitarians and India* (Delhi: Oxford University Press, 1982), pp. 45–47; Gauri Viswanathan, *Masks of Conquest: Literary Study and British Rule in India* (New York: Columbia University Press, 1989), pp. 34–45.

4. Subba Rao [Soob Row], *Life of Vennelacunty Soob Row,* p. 68.

5. Velcheru Narayana Rao, David Shulman, and Sanjay Subrahmanyam, *Textures of Time: Writing History in South India, 1600–1800* (Delhi: Permanent Black, 2001), p. 20. See also fn. 63 in chapter 1.

6. In an earlier book on court and state in the Nayaka period (sixteenth to eighteenth centuries) Velcheru Narayana Rao, David Shulman, and Sanjay Subrahmanyam have written, "The Nayaka courts produced a large literature in Telugu, Sanskrit, and Tamil, aimed at an educated multi-lingual audience of courtiers, courtesans, pandits and officials," and they describe the ways in which courtly dramas mixed Telugu with colloquial Tamil, recorded in Telugu script. Narayana Rao, Shulman, and Subrahmanyam, *Symbols of Substance: Court and State in Nayaka Period Tamilnadu* (Delhi: Oxford University Press, 1992), p. 334. Elsewhere Narayana Rao and Shulman have discussed the multilingual context in which the literary genre of *cāṭu* verses were generated and circulated, describing "language boundaries as porous [such that] *cāṭu* verses moved easily from one language to another." Narayana Rao and Shulman, *A Poem at the Right Moment: Remembered Verses from Premodern South India* (Berkeley: University of California Press, 1998), pp. 186–187.

7. Srinatha, *Śrī Bhīmēsvara-purāṇamu,* quoted in Narayana Rao et al., *Textures of Time,* p. 20.

8. The quoted passage is originally from the anonymous mid-sixteenth-century *Sabhāpati Vacanamu.* Phillip B. Wagoner, *Tidings of the King: A Translation and Ethnohistorical Analysis of the Rāyavācakamu* (Honolulu: University of Hawaii Press, 1993), p. 93; fn. 13, p. 192). Many of these languages were used within dramatic presentations to represent specific types of characters. For example, Paishachi was generally used to represent demonic characters.

9. T. P. Santhanakrishnan, *The Regional Language in the Secondary School* (Madras: South India Saiva Siddhanta Works Publishing Society, 1950), p. 57.

10. Ibid., emphasis added.

11. Ibid.

12. Ibid.

13. Subba Rao [Soob Row], *Life of Vennelacunty Soob Row.*

14. Ibid., p. 64.

15. Ibid., p. 73.

16. Ibid, pp. 67–68, emphasis added.

17. Ibid, p. 73.

18. A. D. Campbell, "On the State of Education of the Natives in Southern India," *Journal of the Madras Literary Society* 1 (1833–34): 354.

19. Ibid., p. 355.

20. Ibid., pp. 353–354, emphasis added.

21. Subba Rao [Soob Row], *Life of Vennelacunty Soob Row,* p. 67.

22. Campbell, "On the State of Education," p. 354. Lest the reader get the impression from this statement that there is nothing left for Campbell to praise after this critique of local schools, let me set the record straight by relating the sentence just prior to this. Campbell writes, "The economy with which children are taught to write in the native schools, and the system by which the more advanced scholars are caused to teach the less advanced, and at the same time to confirm their own knowledge, is certainly admirable, and well deserved the invitation it has received in England" (p. 354). The Madras chaplain Dr. A. Bell introduced this method of having senior pupils tutor younger ones in England "as a cheap and efficient method of educating the poor." Suresh Chandra Ghosh, *The History of Education in Modern India, 1757–1998* (New Delhi: Orient Longman, 2000), p. 9. It became popular in England as the Monitorial or Madras System, writes Ghosh.

23. Campbell, "On the State of Education," p. 353.

24. Subba Rao [Soob Row], *Life of Vennelacunty Soob Row,* pp. 72–73.

25. Campbell, "On the State of Education," p. 354.

26. Great Britian, *Parliamentary Debates, 1813,* 26: 562, quoted in Gauri Viswanathan, *Masks of Conquest,* p. 24.

27. "Public Letter from the Madras Government dated 31st December 1813," *Parliamentary Papers on East India Affairs* (London, August 16, 1832), pp. 684–685, cited in J. Mangamma, *Book Printing in India, with Special Reference to the Contributions of European Scholars to Telugu (1746–1857)* (Nellore: Bangorey Books, 1975), p. 101.

28. See Mangamma, *Book Printing in India,* pp. 38–42. Mangamma speculates that the East India Company must have had earlier access to a printing press in Madras, despite official accounts that refer to the press captured from the French in 1761 as the first press to be established in Madras. She also provides a good discussion of earlier presses in southern India, including the press established at Tranquebar in 1711 by the Society for the Promotion of Christian Knowledge, used almost entirely for missionary work.

29. Ibid.

30. B. S. Kesavan, *History of Printing and Publishing in India: A Story of Cultural Re-awakening,* vol. 1 (New Delhi: National Book Trust, 1985), p. 62. Kesavan tells us that the French, who had brought the press to Pondicherry in 1758, used it primarily for printing notes of credit.

31. Ibid.

32. Kesavan, *History of Printing and Publishing in India,* vol. 2 (New Delhi: National Book Trust, 1988), p. 414.

33. Katharine Smith Diehl, "Early Madras-Printed Books," http://www.intamm.com/l-science/smith.htm, accessed July 29, 2003.

34. Several accounts suggest that this did not occur until 1831, and that the government obtained a press then solely for the purpose of publishing the *Fort St. George Gazette,* a periodical first issued in 1832. The government press apparently printed "general military orders, Queen's orders and job-work on a very limited scale." Mangamma, *Book Printing in India,* p. 112. The government press did not begin to print books until company rule had ended in 1858. Thereafter, government involvement in book printing rapidly expanded, with a press in every district by 1859 (p. 108).

35. Ibid., p. 101. There is no evidence of anything being printed by this press until 1815–16, as books were initially obtained from the College of Fort William in Calcutta.

36. Thomas Munro, *Minute on Native Education,* March 10, 1826, in *The Life of Major-General Thomas Munro, Bart. and K.C.B., Late Governor of Madras, with extracts from his correspondence and private papers,* ed. G. R. Gleig, vol. 2 (1830; reprint, London: Colburn and Bentley, 1930), p. 410. This was in response to a proposal made by the Madras School Book Society in 1824.

37. Ibid., p. 409.

38. Viswanathan, *Masks of Conquest,* p. 34.

39. Subba Rao [Soob Row], *Life of Vennelacunty Soob Row,* 68.

40. There is some controversy over the date of the initial printing of the first *Bāla Śikṣa* reader. Kasinathuni Nageswara Rao's 1929 *Āndhra Vāŋmaya Sūchika* [Andhra Literary Index] gives a publication date of 1868 for Sitaramasastri's *Bāla Śikṣa* and 1885 for Sitaramasastri's *Pedda Bāla Śikṣa* (Hyderabad: Prāchī, 1929, pp. 127 and 115). In his thirteen-volume *Samagra Āndhra Sāhityam* [Complete Andhra Literature], the Telugu literary historian Arudra has most likely used Nageswara Rao as his source, for he also dates the first publication of Chadaluvada Sitaramasastri's *Pedda Bāla Śikṣa* in 1885 and does not mention the publication of the earlier basic primer, *Bāla Śikṣa,* vol. 12, *Zamīndārī Navyasāhitya Yugelu II* (Vijayawada: Prajā Śakti Buk Haws, 1991), p. 103. Both of these dates are clearly wrong. In a forward to the 1998 edition of the new *Surabhi Pedda Bāla Śikṣa,* Arudra offers a more detailed history of the publication with new (and perhaps more accurate) publication dates, though he unfortunately fails to mention his sources. He writes: "In 1832, an Englishman, Mister Clulow caused the book *Bāla Śikṣa* to be written by the hand of his protégé Pudūru Chadalavāda Sītārāmaśāstri. . . . In the *Bāla Śikṣa* that was released in 1856, 24 years after the first publication, there were 78 pages, demi-octavo size. In the printing in 1865, nearly ten years later, there were 90 pages. That means it grew by 12 pages. Literary subjects, metrical rules, Sanskrit slokas, and geographic topics, which didn't exist in the old edition, were added. That was produced as *Bāla Vivēka Kalpa Taruvu.* Thereafter the new name *Pedda Bāla Śikṣa* was given to the book that had been accepted up until then as *Bāla Śikṣa.* We can't say how many printings the original went into. . . . From 1865 it achieved fame as *Pedda Bāla Śikṣa,* even though the author called it *Bāla Vivēka Kalpa Taruvu.*" Arudra, "Ānanda Vākyālu" [Comments of Delight], in Buddiga Subbarāyan, *Surabhi Pedda Bāla Śikṣa,* 2nd ed. (Hyderabad: Educational Products of India, 1998), n.p. Arudra also mentions that after obtaining the patronage of the Englishman Clulow, "in 1830 Chadalawada Sītārāmaśāstri wrote an Andhra grammar for adults called *Praśnōttara Ratnamāla.* Two years later, in 1832 he formulated *Bāla Śikṣa*" (ibid.).

The Oriental and India Office Collection of the British Library has a copy of Puduri Sitaramasastri's *Bāla Śikṣa* identified as an 1856 publication. This copy contains

78 pages, corresponding with Arudra's description. Their collection also contains a copy of *Pedda Bāla Śikṣa* dated July 30, 1865 (Madras: Vidyā Vilāsa Mudrāksharaśāla). Although Puduri Sitaramasastri's name is not printed on the title page of this edition, he is acknowledged in the preface [*Pīṭhika*] and identified in the catalogue. This edition has iv + 90 pages, which also agrees with Arudra's description. However, the 1865 copy of *Bāla Vivēka Kalpa Taruvu* available in the British Library has only 50 pages, not 90 as mentioned by Ārudra. It is therefore not clear what the relationship between *Bāla Vivēka Kalpa Taruvu* and *Pedda Bāla Śikṣa* may have been. According to J. Mangamma, an advertisement for *Bāla Śikṣa* appeared in 1842 in an issue of the Telugu periodical *Vārtamanatarangini,* but neither this nor any copy earlier than 1842 has been attested. The earlier 1832 date may refer to the first printing of the book, to a manuscript copy, or to the date when Sitaramasastri began to formulate the project.

41. What she seemed to remember most vividly in association with *Pedda Bāla Śikṣa* were the names of the sixty years within the cycle of Telugu years, a way of identifying years little used today except in contexts where "culture" is explicitly invoked.

42. Campbell, "On the State of Education," p. 353.

43. David Shulman, personal communication, August 31, 2000.

44. Ram Raz, "A Short Sketch of the State of Education among the Natives at Bangalore," Appendix no. 6, January 6, 1824, published in *The Second Report of the Madras School-Book Society* (Madras, 1827), pp. 28–29.

45. Mangamma, *Book Printing in India,* p. 127. She continues: "Colebrooke consulted the Sanskrit dictionaries, vocabularies and a few grammatical works before he wrote his own commentary and English meaning to *Amara Cosha.* The work is of 393 pages and the correction and additions are 29 pages followed by an alphabetical index of 219 pages" (ibid.).

46. Charles Philip Brown, "Some Account of the Literary Life of Charles Philip Brown, Written by Himself," in C. P. Brown, *English-Telugu Dictionary,* 1866, 2nd ed., Madras, 1895: xv, quoted in Bernard Cohn, "The Command of Language and the Language of Command," in *Subaltern Studies IV,* ed. Ranajit Guha (New Delhi: Oxford University Press, 1985), p. 328.

47. Kandukuri Viresalingam, *Svīya Charitramu* [Autobiography], trans. V. Ramakrishna Rao and T. Rama Rao (Rajahmundry: Addepally, 1970). In his introduction Viresalingam writes, "This forms the very first attempt at an autobiography [*svīya charitramu*] in the Telugu language" (p. ix).

48. Ibid., p. 77.

49. J. P. L. Gwynn and J. Venkateswara Sastry, *A Telugu-English Dictionary* (Delhi: Oxford University Press, 1991), p. 37.

50. Viresalingam, *Svīya Charitramu,* pp. 77–78.

51. Ibid., p. 79.

52. U. V. Swaminatha Iyer, *En Charittiram, The Story of My Life,* part 2, translated from the Tamil original by Kamil V. Zvelebil (Madras: Institute of Asian Studies, 1994), p. 333. Here he is referring to a date sometime between 1878 and 1880.

53. John Greenfield Leonard, *Kandukuri Viresalingam* (Hyderabad: Telugu University, 1991), p. 58. Elsewhere Leonard has traced Viresalingam's partners and has demonstrated that three of them were extremely powerful within local politics. See John Greenfield Leonard, "Local Politics in a Traditional Indian Religious Centre: Rajahmundry," unpublished paper presented at the American Historical Association meetings, Washington, D.C., 1969.

54. Leonard, *Kandukuri Viresalingam,* p. 59.
55. Narayana Rao and Shulman, *Poem at the Right Moment,* p. 190.
56. Ibid., pp. 196–197.
57. Ibid., p. 197.
58. Ibid., p. 195.
59. Ibid.
60. Ibid., p. 197.
61. Ibid., pp. 190–191.
62. Ibid., p. 191.
63. The Avadhana Saraswathi Peetham USA, with head office located in Hyderabad, Andhra Pradesh, and branch office in Durham, North Carolina, for example, an organization of one of the most well-known *avadhānam* performers, offers opportunities to sponsor "a great scholar as a prichhoka (questioner)" for various periods of time. According to the "Appeal for Sponsorship" flyer distributed by the Avadhana Saraswathi Peetham, for $1,116.00 one can "sponsor a great scholar as a prichhoka for 125 days." In exchange, the "Sponsor's name will be announced in the Avadhana Sabha. A 5 hr VCD of Avadhanam will be given free. ¼ page advertisement and colour photo of the donor will be published in the souvenir and a copy of it will be sent to the sponsor."
64. The Telugu entertainment website, teluguone.com, charges a membership fee in order to have on-line access to video recordings of *avadhānam* performances and other cultural entertainment.
65. Narayana Rao and Shulman, *Poem at the Right Moment,* p. 196.
66. Ibid., p. 197, footnote 36.
67. Telusa, March 10, 1999, "Re: From TANA Conference Literary Committee," http://groups.yahoo.com/group/telusa/message/2043 (accessed July 30, 2003).
68. Telusa, March 11, 1999, "Re: From TANA Conference Literary Committee," http://groups.yahoo.com/group/telusa/message/2046 (accessed July 30, 2003).
69. Subbarayan, *Surabhi Pedda Bāla Śikṣa,* back cover (emphasis in original).
70. Subbarayan, "Nā Māṭa" [My Word/Preface], *Surabhi Pedda Bāla Śiksha,* n. p. (my translation, emphasis added).

5. From the Art of Memory to the Practice of Translation

1. In making a distinction between "language" and "languages," I am differentiating between the use of this term as a mass noun and as a count noun. In the former instance I am referring to linguistic acts collectively in whatever linguistic medium or mediums they may occur. In the latter case, I am referring to bodies of linguistic acts that have come to be associated with particular linguistic mediums, recognizable as "languages" today. These latter languages can be listed, counted, inventoried, and so on.
2. Vennelakanty Subba Rao [Vennelacunty Soob Row], *The Life of Vennelacunty Soob Row (Native of Ongole), Translator and Interpreter of the Late Sudr Court, Madras, From 1815 to 1829, As written by himself, Published for the Information of his Relations and Friends by the Son Vennalacunty Venkata Gopal Row, District Munsiff-Trivellore* (Madras: C. Foster, 1873), pp. 67–68; and A. D. Campbell, "On the State of Education of the Natives in Southern India," *Journal of the Madras Literary Society* 1 (1833–34): 353–354.
3. Naoki Sakai, *Translation and Subjectivity: On "Japan" and Cultural Nationalism* (Minneapolis: University of Minnesota Press, 1997), p. 20.

4. Ibid.

5. Benedict Anderson, *Imagined Communities: Reflections on the Origin and Spread of Nationalism,* rev. ed. (New York: Verso, 1991), p. 35.

6. Ibid., p. 38.

7. H. M. J. Maier, "From Heteroglossia to Polyglossia: The Creation of Malay and Dutch in the Indies," *Indonesia* 56 (October 1993): 37–65.

8. Ibid., pp. 47–48.

9. Puduru Sitaramasastri, *Pedda Bāla Śikṣa* (Madras: Vidya Vilasa Mudraksharasala, 1865), pp. iii–iv. In comparing the contents of Sitaramasastri's 1865 text with Buddiga Subbarayan's 1998 *Surabhi Pedda Bāla Śikṣa* (Hyderabad: Educational Products of India), we must be cautious not to make the 1865 edition of *Pedda Bāla Śikṣa* represent some sort of "traditional" past that existed prior to that moment. Indeed, such a reading would ignore how revolutionary the idea of a single printed book containing the sum total of basic knowledge required by a beginning student in southern India would have been in the middle of the nineteenth century. As such, it was one of many new printed books being produced in the middle decades of the nineteenth century. Textbooks for use in schools represented one of the first significant markets for print literature in southern India.

10. Subba Rao [Soob Row], *Life of Vennelacunty Soob Row,* pp. 66–67.

11. Although in reading this quotation outside the context of Subba Rao's larger narrative one might assume that the primacy given to Tamil in this passage stems from the location of the presidency's capital at Fort St. George in Madras, it is clear from the rest of his account that this is not the case. Most of his own education takes place in regions that are now identified as predominantly Telugu-speaking, and his years of employment take him to Kannada-, Telugu-, and Tamil-speaking regions, finally culminating in his employment in the Sudr [High] Court in the linguistically cosmopolitan city of Madras. In fact, if anything, his journal entries privilege the nature of educational practices within Telugu schools, making his comment that boys generally learn the Tamil script first because of its fewer letters even more startling to our contemporary linguistic sensibilities. His own education begins in "a Telugu school at Ongole," and in the letter to the Madras School Book Society introduced above, he mentions in passing that "Masters of Telugu Schools at Madras are Brahmins and generally invited from the northward, for the Telugu language of the Northern Provinces is much preferred to that of the Southern or Western county."

12. Subba Rao and others writing about education in the early decades of the nineteenth century claim that there was little variation in basic education according to caste, occupation, gender, or even what we might today characterize as "mother tongue." Subba Rao writes: "The study of the school-boys is not consistent with the profession of their families respectively, and the general mode of education is universally the same for boys of all castes indiscriminately. In the native schools in this Country, boys of all castes are taught as I have already observed; and the only persons of the female sex educated in public schools are the dancing girls, for whom it is indispensably necessary to learn to write and read to enable them to get by heart the songs which they sing out in concerts." Subba Rao [Soob Row], *Life of Vennelacunty Soob Row,* pp. 68–69. Ram Raz also concurs with this view, writing that in all of the schools of Bangalore, "these scholars are composed of all sects indiscriminately." The only exception to this is that "[t]he poorer class of people being frequently obliged to take their children from it and put them to some labour or employment before they have learned the first principles of education."

Ram Raz, "Short Sketch of the State of Education," p. 25. Campbell, too, writes that the curriculum and routine of the different schools in Bellary District differ very little: "The internal routine of duty for each day will be found, with very few exceptions and little variation, the same in all the schools," Campbell, "On the State of Education of the Natives," p. 351. Yet Ram Raz also states:

> The richer class of Merchants, Artificers and Shopkeepers usually possess some knowledge in the rudiments of learning, by means of which, they are capable of keeping their own account and transacting their own business, while the poorer class remain totally unacquainted with letters. Among the Brahmans, the Laucicás or the laity, who fill almost the whole of the civil offices in this country, are well versed in reading letters on business, and in the mode of keeping accounts in one, and frequently, in two of the vernacular languages; and most of the Vaydicás or the clergy, unite to a knowledge of reading and writing the ability of reciting a part of their Védás, a qualification which is considered indispensably necessary to maintain their sacerdotal dignity; but their learning seldom extends so far as to enable them to understand the import of their scriptures, for it is but one in fifty that possesses a competent knowledge of the Sanscrit language. "Short Sketch of the State of Education," p. 25.

This suggests that, in fact, there actually was some variation in education according to caste and economic status.

13. The appearance of languages in different scripts was quite common in medieval India. This is particularly true in the case of Sanskrit texts in southern India, but there are also examples of other languages, such as Tamil, appearing in Telugu script.

14. Campbell, "On the State of Education of the Natives," p. 352.

15. Subba Rao [Soob Row], *Life of Vennelacunty Soob Row,* p. 12.

16. Ibid., passim. In a letter cited in Subba Rao's account, dated March 14, 1815, T. Fraser praises Subba Rao's knowledge of English, Persian, and Hindoostanee (p. 32). Subba Rao was appointed translator and interpreter of the Madras Sudr Court "in the Tamil, Telugoo and Canarese languages" on April 6, 1815 (pp. 33–34). In 1819 he was appointed "Canarese and Mahratta Interpreter" to the Supreme Court, in addition to his position in the Sudr Court (p. 44). In addition to these seven languages he also mentions several Sanskrit books typically read in primary schools, suggesting an intimate familiarity with Sanskrit also. He reports attending a Telugu school for a few years in his childhood, from 1790 to 1794 (p. 2), living with an uncle who taught him Telugu for a few months in 1794 (p. 2), learning to write letters and accounts from another relative (p. 3), studying English in a small school sporadically for a period of one year during 1798 (p. 4), and gaining "further acquirement in the English language under the benevolent protection of Navaloor Pareatomby Pillah, the Accountant in the Military Paymaster's Office" in Innacondah in 1799 (p. 4). Other than this, the only explicit reference he makes to "learning a language" is a passing comment made to his study of Tamil over the course of several days in 1815: "On the 1st of April 1815, I left Nellore and arrived at Madras on the evening of the 4th. During my travel I employed a Tamil Moonshee and had, through his assistance, recourse to my old Tamil study" (pp. 32–33). He makes no mention of how he acquires Canarese (Kannada), Mahratta (Marathi), Persian, or Hindustani, suggesting that he was either taught these scripts along with others in school, or that he has picked them up in the specific contexts where he needed to use them.

17. Ibid., pp. 2–3.
18. Ibid., pp. 4–5.
19. Ibid., p. 68.
20. Ibid., pp. 65–66.
21. Ibid., p. 67.
22. Ibid., p. 66.
23. Ibid.
24. Campbell, "On the State of Education of the Natives," p. 352.
25. Charles Philip Brown, *Miśra Bhāṣā Nighaṇṭu: Brown's Dictionary of Mixed Telugu* (Madras: Christian Knowledge Society's Press, 1854), p. 1.
26. Ibid.
27. Thomas R. Trautmann, "Dr. Johnson and the Pandits: Imagining the Perfect Dictionary in Colonial Madras," *Indian Economic and Social History Review* 38, no. 4 (2001): 393.
28. Ibid.
29. M. Sankara Reddy argues that there must have been some sort of oral lexicon passed on from the days of Nannaya's *Mahabharatha* onward. Reddy, *Reference Sources in Telugu* (New Delhi: B. R., 1996), p. 23. However, the earliest Telugu lexicon that appears to have been recorded in writing, *Āndhra Nāma Sangrahamu,* is attributed to the seventeenth-century Paidipati Lakshmana Kavi (Vijayawada: Maithili, 1993).
30. Charles Philip Brown, *Essay on the Language and Literature of the Telugus* (New Delhi: Asian Educational Services, 1991), p. 5. Additional evidence that language was not the primary locus of community or identity before the (late) nineteenth century is apparent in Brown's other comments concerning this lexicon: "There are also several vocabularies, imitated from the Amara Cosha, as has been already noticed; being the Siva Andhram; and its rival the Vishnu Andhram, the Andhra Ratnacaram, the Andhra Bhash Arnavam (now about to be printed), and many more" (p. 13).
31. *Vēnkaṭēśuḍu* is the name of another deity popular in southern India, worshipped (among other places) at the temple in the Tirumala hills above Tirupati.
32. Charles Philip Brown, *Karkambāḍi Nighaṇṭu,* GOML, Tel. MSS. D. 1373. His notes on the Telugu verse rendering of the Sanskrit Amara Kośa lexicon, *Āndhrabhāṣārṇavaśabdasūci,* are also preserved at the GOML, Tel. MSS. D. 1370. See also Peter L. Schmitthenner's discussion of Brown's lexicographical efforts in his book *Telugu Resurgence: C. P. Brown and Cultural Consolidation in Nineteenth-Century South India* (New Delhi: Manohar, 2001), pp. 137–150; L. S. Ramaiah, *Bibliography of Dravidian Languages and Lingusitics,* vol. 3: *Telugu Language and Linguistics* (Chennai: T. R., 1998); and Sankara Reddy, *Reference Sources in Telugu,* p. 26.
33. Gidugu Venkata Ramamurthy, *A Memorandum on Modern Telugu* (Madras: Guardian Press, 1913), p. 40.
34. Brown, *Essay on the Language and Literature,* pp. 17–18.
35. For further evidence of the presence of words today considered to be of other languages, see L. Chakradhararao, "Urdu and Marathi Loan Words in Literary and Inscriptional Telugu (Up to 1800 AD)," (Ph.D. diss., Andhra University, Waltair, 1965); Boddupalli Purushottam, "Classification of Telugu Vocabulary," in *Proceedings of the First All India Conference of Dravidian Linguists, 1971,* ed. V. I. Subramoniam (Trivandrum: St. George's Press, 1972), pp. 202–205; Tumati Donappa, "Śrīnātha Sāhithilō Anya Dēśeya Padālu" [Foreign Words in the Literature of Srinatha], *Akāśa Bhārati* (Hyderabad: Sudhara, 1988), pp. 77–86; Saiyyad Jamaluddin, *Linguistic Study of Arabic and Persian*

Loan Words in Telugu (Agra: Kendreeya Hindi Samgtha, 1964); and G. V. S. R. Krishnamurthy, "A Study of Loan Words in Telugu from Cognate Languages" (Ph.D. diss., Andhra University, Waltair, 1977). L. S. Ramaiah's *Bibliography of Dravidian Languages and Lingusitics,* vol. 3, also has an excellent list of additional studies on loan words, borrowing, dictionaries, and lexicography.

36. Cited in J. Mangamma, *Book Printing in India: With Special Reference to the Contribution of European Scholars to Telugu, 1746–1857* (Nellore: Bangorey Books, 1975), p. 125.

37. H. T. Colebrooke, *Amaracosha* (Serampore, 1808).

38. T. M. Kistnasawmy Pillay, *A Polyglot Vocabulary in the English, Teloogoo and Tamil Languages* (Madras: Hindu Press, 1851).

39. Thomas Antoni Pillai, *The English, Tamil, Telugu and Hindustani Sonmalai, or An easy way of learning to speak four languages* (Madras, 1880); Raja Gopalu Shetti, *Telugu, Canarees, Tamil, English and Hindustani Paṇchabhāṣīya* [Five Language] *Vocabulary* (Bellary, 1887).

40. Imani Venkataramaya Sitaramaswami, *Trībhāṣa-manjari (Se-zubani): A Vocabulary in Telugu, Hindi, and Persian* (Masulipatam, 1890).

41. V. Madhura-Muttu Mudaliyar, *Ṣaṭ-bhāṣā Śabdārtha Chandrika: A Vocabulary Containing Six Languages, viz. Telugu, Kannada, Tamil, English, Hindustani, and Marathi* (Madras, 1896); P. S. Rangasvami Rau, *The Linguist's Self-instructor (in Telugu, Kannada, Malayalam, Marathi, Tamil, and English)* (Madras, 1900).

42. Copies of these and other multilingual lexicons from this period are available in the Oriental and India Office Collection of the British Library in London. In addition to these lexicons, texts such as Franz Bopp's *A Comparative Grammar of the Sanskrit, Zend, Greek, Latin, Lithuanian, Gothic, German, and Slavonic Languages* (London: Madden and Malcolm, 1845–53) and the Rev. G. U. Pope's *Our Blessed Lord's Sermon on the Mount, in English, Tamil, Malayalam, Kanarese and Telugu, in the Anglo-Indian character with a vocabulary, minute grammatical praxis and inflexional tables* (Madras, 1860) suggest both the widespread support of such efforts among linguists, missionary groups, and others, as well as one of the objectives which such lexicons would have supported—the project of translation of texts thought to be of use to local residents unable to read or understand English.

43. Sivashankara Pandyaji, *Āndhra Hūna Bhāṣantarikarna Chintāmaṇi* [Telugu-English Translation Guide] (n.p., 1886), OIOC, British Library.

44. In the Telugu context, Gurujada Apparao's famous play *Kanyāśulkam,* first published in 1897, was the first literary composition to be composed in a language more closely resembling educated Telugu speech. Apparao, *Kanyāśulkam* (Madras: M. Seshachalam, 1968). See also the recent translation by Velcheru Narayana Rao of Apparao's *Girls for Sale: Kanyasulkam: A Play from Colonial India* (Bloomington: Indiana University Press, 2007). This play is widely regarded as having launched the Spoken Telugu Movement (also known as the Modern Telugu Movement), a movement to make written Telugu more closely resemble educated speech, discussed in more detail below. See Gurujada Apparao, *The Minute of Dissent to the Report of the Telugu Composition Sub-Committee* (Madras, 1914).

45. Amanda J. Weidman, "Can the Subaltern Sing? Music, Language and the Politics of Voice in Early Twentieth Century South India," *Indian Economic and Social History Review* 42, no. 4 (2005): 485–511; and Weidman, *Singing the Classical, Voicing*

the Modern: The Postcolonial Politics of Music in South India (Durham, N.C.: Duke University Press, 2006), pp. 150–191.

46. Sumathi Ramaswamy, *Passions of the Tongue: Language Devotion in Tamil India, 1891–1970* (Berkeley: University of California Press, 1997), pp. 137–144.

47. Sakai, *Translation and Subjectivity*, p. 2.

48. Ibid.

49. Charles Philip Brown, *Essay on the Language and Literature of the Telugus,* p. 8. First published in the *Madras Journal of Literature and Science* (1839).

50. One of the six chapters of Gurujada Sriramamurti's *Kavi Jīvitamulu* [Lives of Poets], is devoted entirely to "Āndhra Dvyarthi Kāvya Kavulu" [Poets Who Composed Double-Meaning Verse Compositions], suggesting the prominence of this important genre within Telugu literature and its role in helping to establish a poet's name and reputation.

51. S. Nagaraju, following other Telugu scholars, suggests that it is likely "that *kāvya* literature in Telugu may have started five or six centuries earlier than Nannaya." Nagaraju, "Emergence of Regional Identity and Beginnings of Vernacular Literature: A Case Study of Telugu," *Social Scientist* 23, no. 10–12 (1995): 10. He identifies at least two literary texts which he says most scholars agree date to the pre-Nannaya period: Padmakavi's *Jinēndra Purāṇa* and Sarvadeva's *Ādipurāṇa,* both authored by Jains (p. 16). The evidence he provides suggests that Nannaya's desire to compose the Mahabharata in Telugu may have been influenced not by any sense of linguistic patriotism or desire to see such a work in Telugu, but rather by a desire to counter the religious ideas that were being spread in Telugu with more brahmanical ideals. In celebrating Nannaya as the "first" poet of Telugu, later literary historians seem to likewise have been composing a particularly brahmanical history of the Telugu language and literature, ignoring earlier non-brahmanical literature.

52. P. Chenchiah and M. Bhujanga Rao Bahadur, *A History of Telugu Literature* (Delhi: Asian Educational Services, 1988 [1925]), p. 19.

53. G. V. Sitapati, *History of Telugu Literature* (New Delhi: Sahitya Akademi, 1968), p. 7.

54. Paravastu Cinnaya Suri, *Nītichandrika* [Moral Tales] (Vijayawada: Sri Sailaja, 1999); Cinnaya Suri and Kandukuri Viresalingam, *Sampūrṇa Nītichandrika* [Complete Collection of Moral Tales], ed. Jannalagadda Mrutyunjaya Rao, 3rd ed. (Rajahmundry: Rohini, 2000).

55. Jayanti Ramayya, in commenting on these compositions, writes: "These three authors derived the subject-matter of their books from the same source—the Sanskrit *Panchatantram* and elaborated it. Their styles of composition exhibit characteristic differences, though all professed to follow the same model. It must be remembered that these books were written for school boys by schoolmasters." Ramayya, *A Defense of Literary Telugu* (Madras: Addison, 1913), pp. 2–3.

56. Vaman Shivram Apte, *The Practical Sanskrit-English Dictionary* (Delhi: Motilal Banarsidass, 1965), p. 74.

57. See note 12 in chapter 2.

58. Jayanti Ramayya, one of the key participants in the debate over the reform and modernization of the Telugu language, likewise uses both the terms "translation" and "adaptation" in his *Defense of Literary Telugu* (p. 3), suggesting that he, too, finds it important to distinguish between the two.

59. Gidugu Venkata Ramamurthy, *A Memorandum on Modern Telugu* (Madras: Guardian Press, 1913).

60. Although the emergence of this movement is difficult to date exactly, the publication of Gurujada Apparao's social drama *Kanyāśulkam* [Bride Price] in 1897 is generally regarded as the first example of literature in modern Telugu. In his preface, Apparao explicitly takes up the issue of language reform: "If it is intended to make the Telugu literary dialect a great civilizing medium, it must be divested of its superfluous, obsolete and Sanskrit elements, and brought closer to the spoken dialect from which it must be thoroughly replenished." Apparao, quoted in Bh. Krishnamurti, "Classical or Modern—A Controversy of Styles in Education in Telugu," in *Language Movements in India,* ed. E. Annamalai (Mysore: Central Institute of Indian Languages, 1979), p. 7. However, this effort of Apparao's confined itself primarily to the use of spoken Telugu in dialogues and continued to use literary Telugu for the narration. Apparao published a second edition of *Kanyāśulkam* in 1909 which displayed a much more radical break with earlier literary Telugu. In 1906 J. A. Yates was posted as inspector of schools for the districts of Godavari, Visakhapatnam, and Ganjam. Discussions occurred between Ramamurthy, Apparao (who was working as epigraphist to the maharaja of Vizianagaram), P. T. Sreenivasa Iyengar (principal of the Mrs. A. V. N. College in Visakhapatnam), and Yates. A literary association called the Andhra Sahitya Sanghamu (Andhra Literary Organization) was formed in 1907 in Vizianagaram with K. Ramanujacharyulu (principal of the maharajah's college) as president and Ramamurthy as vice-president. This organization held conferences in Kovvuru and Yelamanchili in support of the spoken language (ibid., pp. 8–11). See also Gurujada Apparao, *The Minute of Dissent to the Report of the Telugu Composition Sub-Committee* (Madras, 1914); Undavalli Nagabhusanamu, *Vyāvahārika Bhāṣā Sampradāya Vimarśaṇamu* [Critique of the Colloquial Language Movement] (Kakinada: Sri Saraswati Press, 1914); Andhra University, *Report of the Vernacularisation Committee Together with Minutes of Dissent, Questionnaire and Replies Thereto* (Bezwada: Vani Press, 1928); Gidugu Venkata Ramamurthy, *Vyāsāvaḷi: Vartamānāndhra Bhāṣa Caritrakūpanyāsamulu* [Collection of Essays: Discourses on the History of Contemporary Andhra Language] (Guntur: Telikicherla Venkataratnam, 1933); Tekumalla Kamesvara Rao, *Vāḍukabhāṣa: Racanaki Konni Niyamālu* [Colloquial Language: Some Rules for Writing]. (Guntur: Navya Sahitya Parishattu, 1938); Budaraju Radhakrishna, *Vyāvahārika Bhāṣā Vikāsam* [Development of Colloquial Language] (Hyderabad: Visalaandhra, 1999 [1972]); the Telugu Language Committee on the Use of Modern Standard Telugu (Siṣṭavyāvahārika) for Teaching and Examination for All University Courses, *A Report to the Andhra University* (Waltair: Andhra University, 1973); Akkiraju Ramapati Rao, *Grānthika Vyāvahārika Vāda Sūcika* [Bibliography of Classical and Colloquial Telugu Controversy], ed. B. Radha Krishna (Hyderabad: Telugu Akademi, 1980); and K. Brahmayya, *Kanyāśulkastha Grāmya Bhāṣāvāda Vimarśanamu* [Review of the Argument over the Common Language used in Kanyasulkam] (Kakinada: Srisaraswati Mudraksharashaala, n.d.).

61. Quotation marks are Ramamurthy's.

62. Peri Suryanarayana, *A Short Biography of the Late Mr. Gurujada Venkata Appa Rao* (Vijayawada: Saibaba Press, 1968), p. 63. Suryanarayana uses the terms "classical" and "modern" when he discusses the options given to students regarding the language in which these examinations are to be written. Suryanarayana also refers to the debate in terms of literary Telugu and spoken Telugu.

63. See, for example, Krishnamurti, "Classical or Modern," who uses the terms "classicists" and "modernists."

64. Ibid., p. 18.

65. Ramamurthy, *Memorandum,* p. 35.

66. Ibid., pp. 46–47.

67. Occasionally he does mention Telugu grammatical terms, though usually only to illustrate how confusing or unnecessary they are. In a section on conjugation in old Telugu, he writes, "What is called present tense in one grammar is called future in another and both are equally authoritative! The term *Taddharma* as a tense form is most misleading. The past tense is now formed quite differently to the ancient usage." Ramamurthy, *Memorandum,* p. 43. *Taddharma* is the indefinite aorist tense (an indefinite past tense), which exists in Sanskrit, literary Telugu, and also in Greek, but not in English. One cannot help but wonder whether the real problem he has with it is simply that it doesn't have an English equivalent and therefore cannot be translated directly into an existing English category.

6. Martyrs in the Name of Language?

1. M. K. Gandhi, *The Collected Works of Gandhiji* (Delhi: Publication Division, Ministry of Information and Broadcasting, Government of India, vol. 75), p. 146, quoted in B. Sreeramulu, *Socio-Political Ideas and Activities of Potti Sriramulu* (Bombay: Himalaya, 1988), p. 143.

2. P. Raghunadha Rao, *History of Modern Andhra,* rev. and enlarged ed. (New Delhi: Sterling, 1997), p. 89.

3. Ibid.

4. Sreeramulu, *Socio-Political Ideas,* p. 225.

5. Interview, Nellore, August 12, 1998.

6. Interview, Kavali, August 12, 1998.

7. Ibid.

8. Ibid. In India, the term "peasant" does not necessarily indicate the class background of individuals, but rather describes their relationship to land and cultivation. In this sense, it is often used to refer to those who make their living primarily from agriculture, including large and very powerful landowners, as well as poorer tenants and small holders. In this example, the term "peasant" is used in opposition to the "actual toilers and labourers," suggesting that he is referring to landlords and landowners who earn their income from the land rather than those who physically cultivate the land.

9. Ibid.

10. Ibid.

11. "Inspection Notes of the District Special Branch, Nellore (Secret)," A. N. Rai, I. P., deputy inspector-general of police, Northern Range, Waltair, April 16, 1953 (District Special Branch [Police] Records Room, Nellore).

12. K. V. Narayana Rao, *The Emergence of Andhra Pradesh* (Bombay: Popular Prakashan, 1973), p. 249. A lakh is equivalent to one hundred thousand (100,000).

13. Raghunadha Rao, *History of Modern Andhra Pradesh,* p. 155.

14. D. Triveni, *History of Modern Andhra* (Delhi: Surjeet Book Depot, 1986), p. 240.

15. Sreeramulu, *Socio-Political Ideas,* p. 225

16. The private archive of V. Anantha Ramaiah contains correspondence with various government officials, as well as sketches of the planned memorial. At one stage, the district collector had expressed his interest in going ahead with the plans, but before funding was approved that district collector was transferred, and the new collector was not sympathetic to the project. Anantha Ramaiah's archive also included, among other items, detailed account books from fundraising events showing the sources of funds raised and league expenses, programs from events held, lists of members and donations, and money order receipts and other hand written receipts for funds disbursed to victims. In addition, it was Anantha Ramaiah who first told me about those who died in the wake of the news of Potti Sriramulu's death—individuals not only in Nellore but also in other towns. And it was the addresses from these money order receipts—each conveying Rs. 75 to the families of those who were killed and Rs. 25 to those who were hospitalized—that eventually enabled me to locate surviving family members of the victims. It was also through him that I was introduced to numerous other Youth League members, Andhra movement leaders, and other activists.

17. *Harijan* is a term popularized by Gandhi to refer to communities considered "untouchable" by orthodox Hindus. Tape-recorded interview, Nellore, October 17, 2002.

18. P. C. Reddy, *A Guide to Writings, Libraries, Books, Manuscripts of Prof. P. C. Reddy* (Nellore: P. C. Reddy Trust, n.d.: no page number).

19. Tape-recorded interview, Nellore, October 23, 2002.

20. The December 19, 1952, issue of the local Nellore weekly Telugu newspaper, the *Zamin Ryot*—the longest continuously running Telugu newspaper—offers details of the four who were killed and twelve who were injured in the firings, including the locations of bullet wounds, in which of the several rounds of firing they were caught, and some limited personal details, if known, such as occupation, father's name, and place of residence.

21. Shahid Amin, *Event, Metaphor, Memory: Chauri Chaura, 1922–1992* (Delhi: Oxford University Press, 1995). Amin's influences on my techniques of listening to and reading the narratives used in this chapter should be evident.

22. Tape-recorded interview, April 16, 2002.

23. Tape-recorded interview, Nellore, October 23, 2002.

24. "Scheduled Caste" (SC) and "Dalit" are both terms that are used today to refer to those regarded as "untouchable" by orthodox Hindus. "Scheduled Castes" and "Scheduled Tribes" (STs) are Government of India designations, referring to the inclusion within an official constitutional schedule or list of extremely marginalized communities that are targeted for special government support. This support has largely taken the form of an affirmative action–style program known as "reservations." Government offices and educational institutions maintain quotas for hiring and admission of members of SC and ST communities. "Dalit" is a term that has been embraced by members of SCs as a term of self-identification, especially in the context of political mobilization. More recently the reservation system has been expanded to include groups that the Indian government classifies as "Other Backward Classes" (OBCs), also defined as historically disadvantaged.

25. Interview, Nellore, August 12, 1998.

26. Interview, Nellore, June 18, 2000.

27. Personal conversation, Hyderabad, March 17, 2000.

28. "Inspection Notes of the District Special Branch, Nellore (Secret)," A. N. Rai, I. P., Deputy Inspector-General of Police, Northern Range, Waltair, April 16, 1953 (District Special Branch [Police] Records Room, Nellore).

29. Interview, Nellore, August, 1988.

30. *Arava* is a Telugu word that was used in the nineteenth and early twentieth centuries (and likely even earlier) to refer to "Tamil." It appears to be little used today. The term may be related to *aravandam* (n.) "state of confusion, state of mystification, blankness, inability to understand," which would suggest it is used to refer to the Tamil language only by those who do not understand Tamil.

31. Tape-recorded interview, Nellore, October 19, 2002. My interview brought together two former movement leaders who had not met in thirty years. Both had been active in the Nellore Town Youth League and had raised funds for the victims' families. One had organized the sale of photographs of the four deceased young men signed by cinema stars (see Figure 6.1), and the other had organized a drama, the admission proceeds of which went to benefit the injured and the families of the victims.

32. The comment earlier that the circle inspector was related to one of the senior advocates, a Mr. G. Sarangapani (his own colleague), exemplifies the social links between government officials, public figures, political leaders, and also journalists and historians.

33. Interviews, August 1998 and June 2000.

34. *The Hindu* [English daily], December 17, 1952, p. 4, col. 5.

35. Ibid.

36. *The Hindu,* December 17, 1952, p. 9, col. 2. This is also the only mention of women's presence or participation in any of the events that occurred following Sriramulu's death.

37. *The Hindu,* December 18, 1952, p. 8, col. 2.

38. *The Hindu,* December 17, 1952, p. 4, col. 3.

39. Ibid., p. 9, col. 3.

40. Ibid., p. 9, col. 2.

41. Ibid.

42. Ibid., p. 9, col. 2–3.

43. Ibid., December 18, 1952, p. 8, col. 4.

44. Ibid., p. 8, col. 5.

45. Ibid., p. 8, col. 4.

46. *The Hindu,* December 17, 1952, p. 6, col. 3.

47. *The Hindu,* December 18, 1952, p. 8, col. 2. The full headline is "Situation in Andhra: Police Firings in Three Centres," with a smaller subheading announcing "Four Dead in Nellore." No specific names are given in this day's reports.

48. *Zamin Ryot,* December 19, 1952 (my translation from the Telugu).

49. Private archive of V. Anantha Ramaiah.

50. I have been unable thus far to locate any relatives of the fourth young man, Gurunadham. After I left Nellore, A. Subrahmanyam, a friend and fellow academic scholar who has taken great interest in this project, was able to locate the son of Gurunadham's employer, Bada Saheb. The son said that Gurunadham very intentionally went to join the agitation at the railway station that day. It appears he was to go to Venkatagiri on work but postponed the journey in order to join the gathering at the railway station. Why he went is not clear. Personal communication with A. Subramanyam, December 30, 2002.

51. Potti Sriramulu used the term *harijan,* popularized by Gandhi, whenever he referred to those treated as untouchables by orthodox Hinduism.

52. Interviews, August 1998, June 2000, April 2002, and October 2002.

53. Tape-recorded interview, Nellore, April 15, 2002. All translations from the Telugu narratives collected from the families are my own. None of the family members spoke with me in English.

54. Tape-recorded interview, Nellore, April 18, 2002.
55. Tape-recorded interview, Nellore, October 16, 2002.
56. Naoki Sakai, *Translation and Subjectivity*, p. 73.
57. Tape-recorded interview with Anantha Ramaiah, October 19, 2002.
58. Shahid Amin, *Event, Metaphor, Memory*, p. 2.

Conclusion

1. Pradeep Kumar, "Demand for New States: Cultural Identity Loses Ground to Urge for Development," *Economic and Political Weekly*, 35–36 (August 26–September 2, 2000): 3078–3079.

2. Kaloji Narayana Rao, tape-recorded interview, Warangal, April 22–23, 1997. See also his autobiography, *Idī Nā Goḍava* [This Is My Struggle] (Vijayawada: Padmanabha Printing Works, 1995).

3. Interview, June 21, 1997.

4. Interview, April 28, 1997.

5. Paul Brass, *The Politics of India since Independence* (Cambridge: Cambridge University Press, 1990), pp. 149–152.

6. I am grateful to Partha Chatterjee for his insightful questions on these matters.

BIBLIOGRAPHY

Unpublished Records

Government Oriental Manuscripts Library, Chennai

Āndhrabhāṣārṇavaśabdasūchi (verse rendering of Amara Kōśa), with notes by C. P. Brown, Tel. D. 1370.

Āndhraśabdhchintāmaṇi, with notes by C. P. Brown, Tel. D. 1237.

Analysis of Telugu Prosody, in English, notes by C. P. Brown, Tel. D. 1260.

Appakavīyamu (3rd Āśvāsa), with explanation on Telugu text in English by C. P. Brown, Tel. D. 1261.

Brown, C. P. *Āndhra Vyākaraṇamu,* Tel. D. 1235.

Brown, C. P. *Ābhāsāndhranighaṇṭuvu,* Glossary of mixed Telugu explaining origin, local, foreign, or corrupt. Based on Board of Revenue vocabulary with Telugu and Sanskrit omitted, Tel. D. 1372.

Brown, C. P. *Karkambāḍi Nighaṇṭuvu,* Tel. D. 1373.

Paṭṭābhirāmapaṇḍitīyamu, written after the manner of *Āndhraśabdhchintāmaṇi* by a Pandit of Presidency College, Tel. D. 1246.

Vencaya [Venkaya], Mamadi. *The Andhra Deepica, a Dictionary of the Telugu Language* (Telugu and Sanskrit words arranged in alphabetical order with their meanings), Tel. D. 1332.

———. *The Andhra Deepica, a Dictionary of the Telugu Language,* copy prepared under direction of C. P. Brown with his notes, Tel. D. 1333.

Nehru Memorial Museum and Library, Delhi

All India Congress Committee Manuscripts Collection (Boundary Disputes; Andhra Provincial Congress Committee Correspondence; Constructive Programme Department Correspondence; Resolutions)

Oriental and India Office Collection, British Library, London

Mackenzie General Collection.

Memoirs Illustrative of the Geography of South India (Mack Gen/60).

Mackenzie Miscellaneous Collection.

Mackenzie Translations.

Correspondence of the Committee of Public Instruction (Eur MSS J821).

Colin Mackenzie's Will (IOR/L/AG/34/29/33).

Madras Educational Proceedings, 1874–1915.

Madras University Calendars, 1873–1880.

Quarterly List of Publications, Madras.

Ramaswamy, C. V. [Kavali Venkata Ramaswami], A New Map of the Ancient Divisions of the Deckan Illustrative of the History of the Hindu Dynasties with Discriptions [*sic*] of the Principle Places (Calcutta: Asiatic Lithographic Press: 1827).

Royal Asiatic Society, London

Pamphlets (bound volumes)
Second Report of the Madras Schoolbook Society, 1827, vol. 39.

District Special Branch Records, Inspector of Police, Nellore

Inspection Notes of the District Police Special Branch (Secret).

Records Room, Office of the District Collector, Nellore

Disposal Lists (LD, D, R).
General Series.
Magisterial Series.

Private Papers

V. Anantha Ramaiah, President, Town Youth League, Nellore (1950s).
P. C. Reddy, Nellore.
D. C. Veeraswamy Chetty, Nellore (Correspondence with Potti Sriramulu).

Periodicals

Newspapers

Eenadu (Telugu)
The Hindu (English)
The Indian Express (English)
Vaartha (Telugu)
Zamin Ryot (Telugu)

Published Sources

Telugu and Sanskrit Sources

Appakavi, Kakunuri. *Appakavīyamu.* Ed. Gidugu Ramamurthy, Utpala Venkatanarasimhacharyulu and Ravuri Dorasami Sharma. Chennapuri: Vavilla Ramaswami Sastrulu and Sons, 1951.
Apparao, Gurujada. *Kanyāśulkam* [Bride Price]. Madras: M. Seshachalam, 1968.

Appa Row, P. *Chennarājadhāni Bhūgōlamu: The Historical Geography of Madras Presidency.* Tenali: Kalavani, 1928.
Arudra. "Ānanda Vākyālu" [Preface, lit. "Phrases of Delight"]. In *Surabhi Pedda Bāla Śikṣa,* ed. Buddiga Subbarayan. Hyderabad: Educational Products of India, 1998.
———. *Samagra Āndhra Sāhityam* [Complete Andhra Literature]. Vol. 9: Kumpiṇī Yugam [Company Era]. Vijayawada: Praja Shakti Book House, 1990. Vol. 12: *Zamīndāri Navya Sāhitya Yugālu* [Zamindar and New Literature Eras]. Vijayawada: Praja Shakti Book House, 1991.
Brahmananda, H. S. *Gidugu Venkata Ramamurti.* New Delhi: Sahitya Akademi, 1990.
Brahmayya, K. *Kanyāśulkastha Grāmya Bhāṣāvāda Vimarśanamu* [Review of the Argument over the Common Language used in Kanyāśulkam]. Kakinada: Srisaraswati Mudraksharashaala, n.d.
Chinnaya Suri, Paravastu. *Bāla Vyākaraṇamu* [Basic Grammar, lit. "A Child's Grammar"]. Ed. Bulusu Venkataramanayya. Chennapuri: Vavilla Ramaswamy Sastrulu and Sons, 1967 [1858].
———. *Nīti Chandrika* [Moral Tales, lit. "Light of Morals".' Vijayawada: Sri Sailaja, 1999.
Chinnaya Suri, Paravastu, and Kandukuri Viresalingam. *Sampūurna Nītichandrika* [Complete Collection of Moral Tales, lit. "Complete Light of Morals"]. Ed. Jonnalagadda Mrutyunjaya Rao. 3rd ed. Rajamandry: Rohini, 2000.
Donappa, Tumati. "Śrīnātha Sāhithilo Anya Dēśeya Padālu" [Foreign Words in the Literature of Srinatha]. In *Akāśa Bhārati.* Hyderabad: Sudhara, 1988.
———. *Bhāṣā Chāritraka Vyāsāvali* [Essays on the History of Language]. Hyderabad: Andhra Sarasvata Parishat, 1972.
———. "Telugulō Buḍatakīcu Nudulu" [Portugese Words in Telugu]. In *Bhāṣā Chāritraka Vyāsāvali,* 214–301. Hyderabad: Andhra Sarasvata Parishettu, 1972.
———. *Vaikṛta Pada Svarūpa Nirūpaṇamu* [Old and Middle Indo-Aryan Loan Words in Literary Telugu]. Hyderabad: Felicitation Committee of the Sixtieth Birthday Celebrations, 1987.
Ekamranatha. *Pratāparudra Charitramu* [Biographical Narrative of Prataparudra]. Ed. C. V. Ramachandra Rao. Hyderabad: Andhra Pradesh Sahitya Akademi, 1984.
Gopala Rao Naidu, P. *Āndhra Bhāṣa Charitra Sangrahamu* [Summary of the History of the Andhra Language]. Rajahmundry: Vivekavarthani Press, 1896.
Gurumurti Sastri, Ravipati. *Telugu Vyākaraṇamu* [Telugu Grammar]. Chennapuri: Vavilla Ramaswami Sastrulu and Sons, 1951 [1836].
———. *Telugu Vyākaraṇamu* [Telugu Grammar]. Chennapattanam: Mission Press, 1836.
Iswara Dutt, Kunduri. *Prācīnāndhra Chāritraka Bhūgōlamu* [Ancient Historical Geography of Andhra Pradesh]*: An Identification and Demarcation of the Ancient Geographical and Administrative Divisions of Andhra Pradesh.* Hyderabad: Andhra Pradesh Sahitya Akademi, 1979 [1963].
Kamesvara Rao, Tekumalla. *Vāḍukabhāṣa: Rachanaki Konni Niyamālu* [Colloquial Language: Some Rules for Writing]. Guntur: Navya Sahitya Parishattu, 1938.
Ketana, Mulaghatika. *Āndhra Bhāṣā Bhūṣaṇamu* [lit., "Ornament of the Andhra Language"]. Chennapuri: Vavilla Ramaswami Sastrulu and Sons, 1932.
Krishna Kumari, Nayani. *Telugu Bhāṣa Charitra: Tulanātmaka Pari Sīlana* [The History of Telugu Language: A Comparative Study]. Hyderabad: Telugu Akademi, 1984.
Krishna Rao, K. R. V. *Āndhra Bhāṣa Abhivṛddhi* [The Progress of Telugu Literature]. Rajahmundry: Vivekavarthani Press, 1896.

Krishnamurti, Bhadriraju. *Telugu Bhāṣa Charitra.* Hyderabad: Potti Sriramulu Telugu University, 2000.

Lakshmana Kavi, Paidipati. *Āndhra Nāma Sangrahamu.* Vijayawada: Maithili, 1993.

Lalitha, G. *Telugu Vyākaraṇamula Charitra* [History of Telugu Grammars]. Madras: Velagapudi Foundation, 1996.

Mudaliyar, V. Madhura-Muttu. *Ṣaṭ bhāṣā Śabdārtha Chandrika: A Vocabulary Containing Six Languages, viz. Telugu, Kannada, Tamil, English, Hindustani, and Marathi.* Madras, 1896.

Nagabhusanamu, Undavalli. *Vyāvahārika Bhāṣā Sampradāya Vimarśaṇamu* [Critique of the Colloquial Language Movement]. Kakinada: Sri Saraswati Press, 1914.

Nageswara Rao, Kasinathuni. *Āndhra Vāŋmaya Sūchika* [Catalogue of Telugu Literature]. Hyderabad: Prācī, 1929.

Nannaya Bhatt. *Āndhra Śabda Chintāmaṇi* [lit., "Andhra Word Guide"]. Chennapuri: Vavilla Ramaswami Sastrulu and Sons, 1968.

Narayana Rao, Chilukuri. *Āndhra Bhāṣā Charitramu* [History of the Andhra Language]. Madras: Anand Mudranalayam, 1937.

Narayana Rao, Kaloji. *Idī Nā Goḍava* [This Is My Struggle/Headache]. Vijayawada: Padmanabha Printing Works, 1995.

Pandyaji, Sivashankara. *Āndhra Hūṇa Bhāṣāntarīkarṇa Chintāmaṇi* [Telugu-English Translation Guide], 1886.

Pattabhirama Sastri, Vedam. *Āndhra Vyākaraṇamu* [Andhra Grammar]. Chennapuri: Vavilla Ramaswami Sastrulu, 1951 [1825].

Purushottam, Boddupalli. *Tenugu Vyākaraṇa Vikāsamu: The Origin and Development of Telugu Grammar.* Guntur: Girija Prachuranalu, 1968.

Radhakrishna, Budaraju. *Vyāvahārika Bhāṣā Vikāsam* [Development of Colloquial Language]. Hyderabad: Vishaalaandhra, 1999 [1972].

Rajeswara Sarma, Amareesham. *Āndhra Vyākaraṇa Vikāsamu.* Part 1. Kamareddi: Prācya Vidyā Parishat, 1973.

———. *Āndhra Vyākaraṇa Vikāsamu.* Part 2. Kamareddi: Prācya Vidyā Parishat, 1977.

Rama Rao, Bhagavatamu. "Telugu Nighaṇṭuvulalō Dēśyapadamula Pai Chinna Chūpu" [A Small Look at the Dēsya Words in Telugu Lexicons]. *Bharati* (1968): 39–45.

Ramamurthy, Gidugu Venkata. *Vyāsāvaḷi: Vartamānāndhra Bhāṣa Caritrakūpanyāsamulu* [Collection of Essays: Discourses on the History of Contemporary Andhra Language]. Guntur: Telikicherla Venkataratnam, 1933.

Ramanna, Goparaju, ed. *Koṇḍavīṭi Sīmā Daṇḍakavile Nakalu: Ancient Record Containing Geography and Chronological History of Telugu Country.* Madras: Markandeya Sarma, 1921.

Ramapati Rao, Akkiraju, R. Tirumala Rao, and Budaraju Radhakrishna. *Grānthika Vyāvahārika Vāda Sūchika* [Index to the Literary-Colloquial Debate]. Ed. Budaraju Radhakrishna. Hyderabad: Telugu Akademi, 1980.

Ranganayakulu Shresti, Chunduru. *Āndhra Dīpika* [Telugu Lexicon, lit., "Andhra Lamp"]. 3rd ed. Madras: Viveka Kalanidhi, 1882.

Reddy, G. N. "Āndhram, Tenugu, Telugu." In *Telugu Bhāṣa Charitra,* ed. Bhadriraju Krishnamurti. Hyderabad: Potti Sriramulu Telugu University, 2000.

Schultze, Benjamin. *Grammatica Telugica* [Telugu Grammar]. Halle: Martin Luther University, 1984 [1728].

Sethurami Reddy, Gandavaram. *Gandavaram Sēthurāmireḍḍi Jīvitāllō Pradhān Ghaṭṭālu*

[Important Events in the Life of Gandavaram Sethurami Reddy]. Nellore: Sethurami Reddy, 2001.
Shetti, Raja-Gopalu. *Telugu, Canarees, Tamil, English and Hindustani Pānchabhāṣiya* [Five Language] *Vocabulary.* Bellary, 1887.
Sitaramasastri, Puduri. *Bāla Śikṣa* [A Child's Primer]. 1856.
———. *Pedda Bāla Śikṣa* [Expanded Child's Primer]. Madras: Vidya Vilasa Mudraksharasala, 1865.
Sriramamurti, Gurujada. *Kavi Jīvitamulu: Biographies of Telugu Poets, with a Series of Discussions Regarding Grammar and Prosody.* Part 1. Rajahmundry: Vivekavarthani Press, 1878.
———. *Kavi Jīvitamulu.* 2nd ed. Vol. 1, Telugu Vizianagaram Historical Series. Chennapattanam: Empress of India Press, 1893.
———. *Kavi Jīvitamulu.* 3rd ed. Vizianagara Caritra Grantha Samudāyamu. Chennapuri: Vavilla Ramaswami Sastrulu and Sons, 1913.
———. *Tenāli Rāmakṛṣṇa Kavi Jīvitamu. Hāsya Kathalu* [Life of the Poet Tenali Ramakrishna: Humorous Stories]. Chennapuri: Vavilla Ramaswami Sastrulu and Sons, 1915.
Subbarayan, Buddiga. *Surabhi Pedda Bāla Śikṣa.* Hyderabad: Educational Products of India, 1998.
Tañjāvūri Āndhra Rājula Charitra [History of the Tanjavur Telugu Kings]. Ed. Veturi Prabhakara Sastri. Hyderabad: Manimanjari Pracurana, 1984 [1914].
Veerabhadra Rao, Chilukuri. *Āndhrula Charitramu, Dvitiya Bhāgamu: Madhya Yugamu* [History of the Andhras; vol. 2: Medieval Period]. Chennapuri [Chennai]: Jyotishmati Mudrayantrashalaya, 1912.
———. *Āndhrula Charitramu, Prathama Bhāgamu: Purva Yugamu* [History of the Andhras; vol. 1: Ancient Period]. Chennapuri [Chennai]: Ananda Mudrayantrashalaya, 1910.
Veeraswamy, Enugula. *Kāśiyātra Charitramu* [Narrative of a Pilgrimage to Varanasi]. 3rd ed. New Delhi: Asian Educational Services, 1991.
———. *Kāśiyātra Charitramu.* Hyderabad: Telugu University, 1992.
Venkanna, Koti. *Āndhrabhāṣarṇavamu: Accha Tenugu Nighaṇṭuvu* [Ocean of the Andhra Language: A Lexicon of "Pure" Telugu]. Chennapuri: Vavilla Ramaswamy Sastrulu and Sons, 1931.
Venkataramanuja Rao, Mangu. *Āndhra Bhāṣa Charitra Sangrahamu* [Summary of the History of the Andhra Language]. Elluru [Eluru], 1899.
Venkataramaya Sitaramaswami, Imani. *Trībhāṣa-manjari (Se-zubani): A Vocabulary in Telugu, Hindi, and Persian.* Masulipatam, 1890.
Venkataranga Setti, D. *Dēśa Charitramu* [History of the (Telugu) Country], 1890.
Venkatasubbasastri, Nelaturu. *Tenāla Rāmakṛṣṇuni Kathalu* {Stories of Tenali Ramakrishna]. Saraswati Vilasa Press, 1860.
Viresalingam, Kandukuri. *Āndhra Kavula Charitramu, Dvitīya Bhāgamu: Madhya Kālapu Kavulu* [Biographical Narrative of Andhra Poets, Part 2: Poets of the Medieval Period]. Rajahmundry: Avanti Press, 1949.
———. *Āndhra Kavula Charitramu, Prathama Bhāgamu: Telugu Poets.* Part 1. In *The Complete Works of Rao Bahadur K. Veeresalingam Pantulu,* vol.10, 2nd ed. Rajahmundray: Sree Rama Press, 1937 [1917].
———. *Āndhra Kavula Charitramu, Tṛtīya Bhāgamu: Ādhunika Kavulu* [Biographical

Narrative of Andhra Poets, Part 3: Modern Poets]. Rajahmundry: Avanti Press, 1959.
———. *Rājasēkhara Charitramu* [The Story of Rajasekhara]. Hyderabad: Visalaandhra, 1991 [1880].
———. *Sangraha Vyākaraṇamu, Concise Grammar, for Use in Schools.* 11th ed. Chennapuri: Śri Cintāmaṇi Mudrākṣaraśāla, 1900.
———. *Swīya Charitramu* [Autobiography]. Vijayawada: Visalaandhra, 1982 [1910].

English Sources

Aklujkar, Ashok. "The Early History of Sanskrit as a Supreme Language." In *Ideology and the Status of Sanskrit: Contributions to the History of the Sanskrit Language,* ed. J. Houben. Leiden: E. J. Brill, 1996.
Ali, Daud. *Courtly Culture and Political Life in Early Medieval India.* Cambridge: Cambridge University Press, 2004.
Amin, Shahid. *Event, Metaphor, Memory: Chauri Chaura, 1922–1992.* Delhi: Oxford University Press, 1995.
Anderson, Benedict. *Imagined Communities: Reflections on the Origin and Spread of Nationalism.* Rev. ed. London: Verso, 1991.
Andhra Province Standing Committee. *For and Against the Andhra Province.* Masulipatam: M. Krishna Rao, 1913.
Andhra University. *Report of the Vernacularisation Committee Together with Minutes of Dissent, Questionnaire and Replies Thereto.* Bezwada: Vani Press, 1928.
Anjaneyulu, D. *Kandukuri Viresalingam.* Delhi: Government of India, Publications Department, Ministry of Information and Broadcasting, 1976.
Apparao, Gurujada. *The Minute of Dissent to the Report of the Telugu Composition Sub-Committee.* Madras, 1914.
———. *Girls for Sale: Kanyasulkam, A Play from Colonial India.* Trans. Velcheru Narayana Rao. Bloomington: Indiana University Press, 2007.
Apte, Vaman Shivram. *The Practical Sanskrit-English Dictionary.* Delhi: Motilal Banarsidass, 1965.
Bakhtin, M. M. "Epic and Novel." In *The Dialogic Imagination,* ed. Michael Holquist, 3–40. Austin: University of Texas Press, 1981.
Barnett, L. D. *A Catalogue of the Telugu Books in the Library of the British Museum.* London: British Museum, 1912.
Barnett, Marguerite. *The Politics of Cultural Nationalism in South India.* Princeton, N.J.: Princeton University Press, 1976.
Bauman, Richard, and Charles L. Briggs. *Voices of Modernity: Language Ideologies and the Politics of Inequality.* Cambridge: Cambridge University Press, 2003.
Benjamin, Walter. "Theses on the Philosophy of History." In *Illuminations,* ed. Hannah Arendt, 253–264. New York: Schocken, 1969.
———. "The Work of Art in the Age of Mechanical Reproduction." In *Illuminations,* ed. Hannah Arendt, 217–251. New York: Schocken, 1969.
Bopp, Franz. *A Comparative Grammar of the Sanskrit, Zend, Greek, Latin, Lithuanian, Gothic, German, and Slavonic Languages.* Trans. Lieut. Eastwick. Ed. H. H. Wilson. London: Madden and Malcolm, 1845–53.
Brass, Paul R. *Ethnicity and Nationalism: Theory and Comparison.* New Delhi: Sage, 1991.

———. *Language, Religion and Politics in India.* Cambridge: Cambridge University Press, 1974.
———. *The Politics of India since Independence.* Cambridge: Cambridge University Press, 1990.
Brown, Charles Philip. *Brānya Telugu Nighaṇṭu* [Brown's Telugu Dictionary]. Madras: Christian Knowledge Society, 1852.
———. *Essay on the Language and Literature of the Telugus.* New Delhi: Asian Educational Services, 1991. [Reprint of original ed., Madras: J.B. Pharoah, 1840].
———. *A Grammar of the Telugu Language.* 2nd ed. Madras: Christian Knowledge Society, 1857.
———. *Miśra Bhāṣā Nighaṇṭu: Brown's Dictionary of Mixed Telugu.* Madras: Christian Knowledge Society Press, 1854.
———. *Nighaṇṭuvu Telugu-English: Dictionary Telugu-English.* Reprint of 2nd ed., rev. and ed. M. Venkata Ratnam, W. H. Campbell and K. Veeresalingam. New Delhi: Asian Educational Service, 1995 [1903].
Burke, Peter. *Languages and Communities in Early Modern Europe.* Cambridge: Cambridge University Press, 2004.
Campbell, Alexander Duncan. *Grammar of the Teloogoo language, commonly termed the Gentoo, peculiar to the Hindoos inhabiting the North Eastern provinces of the Indian Peninsula.* Madras: College Press, 1816.
———, ed. *A Grammar of the Teloogoo Language.* 2nd ed. Madras: College Press, 1820.
———. "On the State of Education of the Natives in Southern India [on Bellary]." *Journal of the Madras Literary Society* 1 (October 1834): 350–359.
Carey, William. *A grammar of the Telingana language.* Serampore: Mission Press, 1814.
Chakradhararao, L. "Urdu and Marathi Loan Words in Literary and Inscriptional Telugu (Up to 1800 A.D.)." Ph.D. diss., Andhra University, Waltair, 1965.
Chenchiah, P., and M. Bhujanga Rao Bahadur. *A History of Telugu Literature.* Delhi: Asian Educational Services, 1988 [1925].
Cohn, Bernard. *An Anthropologist among the Historians and Other Essays.* Delhi: Oxford University Press, 1987.
———. *Colonialism and Its Forms of Knowledge.* Princeton, N.J.: Princeton University Press, 1996.
———. "The Command of Language and the Language of Command." In *Subaltern Studies IV,* ed. Ranajit Guha, 276–329. New Delhi: Oxford University Press, 1985.
Colebrooke, H. T. *Amaracosha.* Serampore, 1808.
Cook, Andrew S. "The Beginning of Lithographic Map Printing in Calcutta." In *India: A Pageant of Prints,* ed. Pauline Rohatgi and Pheroza Godrej. Bombay: Marg, 1989.
Cornish, W. R. *Report on the Census of the Madras Presidency, 1871.* Madras: Government Gazette Press, 1874.
Dasgupta, Jyotirindra. *Language Conflict and National Development: Group Politics and National Language Policy in India.* Berkeley: University of California Press, 1970.
Deshpande, Madhav M. *Sanskrit and Prakrit: Sociolinguistic Issues.* Delhi: Motilal Banarsidass, 1993.
Dickey, Sara. *Cinema and the Urban Poor in South India.* Cambridge: Cambridge University Press, 1993.
Diehl, Katharine Smith. *Early Madras-Printed Books.* http://www.intamm.com/l-science/smith.htm, 2003 (accessed July 29, 2003).

Ellis, Francis W. "Note to the Introduction." In *A Grammar of the Teloogoo Language*, ed. A. D. Campbell, 1–31. Madras: College Press, 1816.

Fowler, J. T. *Johnson's life of Addison, from the Lives of the Poets, for the use of University Students.* Madras: J. T. Fowler, 1867.

Freud, Sigmund. "The Antithetical Meaning of Primal Words." In *Writings on Art and Literature*, 94–100. Stanford, Calif.: Stanford University Press, 1997.

Geetha, V., and S. V. Rajadurai. *Towards a Non-Brahmin Millennium: From Iyothee Thass to Periyar.* Calcutta: Samya, 1999.

Ghosh, Suresh Chandra. *The History of Education in Modern India, 1757–1998.* New Delhi: Orient Longman, 2000.

Gode, Alexander. Introduction to *On the Origin of Language: Two Essays.* Trans. with afterword by John H. Moran and Alexander Gode. Chicago: University of Chicago Press, 1966.

Gopalachari, K. *Early History of the Andhra Country.* Ed. K. A. Nilakanta Sastri. Madras University Historical Series. Madras: University of Madras, 1941.

Gopinatha Rao, C. *Library Movement in Andhra Pradesh.* Hyderabad: Dept. of Public Libraries, Government of Andhra Pradesh, 1981.

Government of India. Eighth Schedule, Constitution of India Constitution: Updated up to 94th Amendment Act. http://lawmin.nic.in/coi.htm, p. 229 (accessed February 20, 2008).

———. Indian Education Commission. *Report of the Madras Provincial Committee.* Calcutta, 1884.

———. Ministry of Human Resource Development, Department of Education. "Languages and Media of Instruction," *Fifth All-India Educational Survey,* vol. 1. New Delhi: Government of India, 1990. http://www.education.nic.in/cd50years/g/Z/H7/0ZH70E01.htm (accessed June 17, 2007).

———. Ministry of Human Resource Development, Department of Education. "Selected Educational Statistics," *Compilation on Fifty Years of Indian Education: 1947–1997.* http://www.education.nic.in/cd50years/g/Z/7H/0Z7H0101.htm (accessed February 20, 2008).

———. Office of the Registrar General and Census Commissioner, India. "General Note." http://www.censusindia.gov.in/Census_Data_2001/Census_Data_Online/Language/gen_note.htm (accessed February 20, 2008).

———. *Report of the Committee for the Revision of English, Telugu, and Tamil School Books in the Madras University.* Vol. 44. Madras: Selections of the Madras Government, 1875.

———. "Scheduled Languages in Descending Order of Speakers' Strength, 2001." http://www.censusindia.gov.in/Census_Data_2001/Census_Data_Online/Language/Statement4.htm (accessed February 20, 2008).

Gwynn, J. P. L., and J. Venkateswara Sastry. *A Telugu-English Dictionary.* Delhi: Oxford University Press, 1991.

Hardgrave, Robert. *The Dravidian Movement.* Bombay: Popular Prakashan, 1956.

Heidegger, Martin. *Nietzsche,* vol. 1, trans. David Farrell Krell. San Francisco: Harper and Row, 1991.

Hobsbawm, E. J. *Nations and Nationalism since 1780: Programme, Myth, Reality.* Cambridge: Cambridge University Press, 1990.

Huq, Amanul. *International Mother Language Day: Bangla Souvenir,* trans. from the original Bangla ed., *Ekusher Tamasuk* by Ahsanul Hoque, Amanul Huq, and A. U. M. Fakhruddin. Dhaka: Shahitya Prakash, 2004.

Irschick, Eugene F. *Politics and Social Conflict in South India: The Non-Brahman Movement and Tamil Separatism, 1916–1929.* Berkeley: University of California Press, 1969.

———. *Tamil Revivalism in the 1930s.* Madras: Cre-A, 1986.

Jamaluddin, Saiyyad. *Linguistic Study of Arabic and Persian Loan Words in Telugu.* Agra: Kendreeya Hindi Samgtha, 1964.

Jones, Sir William. "On the Hindu's [*sic*]." *Asiatick Researches* 1 (1788): 414–432.

———. "On the Origin and Families of Nations." *Asiatick Researches* 3 (1792): 479–492.

Kahrs, Eivind. "What Is a *Tadbhava* Word?" *Indo-Iranian Journal* 35, no. 2–3 (1992): 232–233.

Kamath, Suryanath U. *A Concise History of Karnataka.* Bangalore: Archana Prakashana, 1980.

Karat Prakash. *Language and Nationality Politics in India.* Bombay: Orient Longman, 1973.

Kaviraj, Sudipta. "Writing, Speaking, Being: Language and the Historical Formation of Identities in India." In *Nationalstaat und Sprachkonflikte in Süd- und Südostasien,* ed. Dagmar Hellmann-Rajanayagam and Dietmar Rothermund, 25–68. Stuttgart: Franz Steiner Verlag, 1992.

Kesavan, B. S. *History of Printing and Publishing in India: A Story of Cultural Re-awakening.* Vols. 1 and 2. New Delhi: National Book Trust, 1985.

King, Robert D. *Nehru and the Language Politics of India.* Delhi: Oxford University Press, 1997.

Kistnasawmy Pillay, T. M. *A Polyglot Vocabulary in the English, Teloogoo and Tamil Languages.* Madras: Hindu Press, 1851.

Kittler, Friedrich. *Discourse Networks 1800/1900.* Trans. Michael Metteer. Stanford, Calif.: Stanford University Press, 1990.

Krishna Reddy, Nagolu. *Social History of Andhra Pradesh (Seventh to Thirteenth Century: Based on Inscriptions and Literature).* Delhi: Agam Kala Prakashan, 1991.

Krishnamurti, Bh. "Classical or Modern—A Controversy of Styles in Education in Telugu." In *Language Movements in India,* ed. E. Annamalai. Mysore: Central Institute of Indian Languages, 1979.

Krishnamurthy, G. V. S. R. "A Study of Loan Words in Telugu from Cognate Languages." Ph.D. diss., Andhra University, Waltair, 1977.

Kumar, Pradeep. "Demand for New States: Cultural Identity Loses Ground to Urge for Development." *Economic and Political Weekly* 35–36 (2000): 3078–3082.

Kuppuswami Sastri, S. *A Descriptive Catalogue of the Telugu Manuscripts in the Government Oriental Manuscripts Library, Madras.* Vol. 5: *Grammar, Prosody and Lexicography.* Madras: Superintendent, Government Press, 1935.

Leonard, John Greenfield. *Kandukuri Viresalingam (1848–1919): A Biography of an Indian Social Reformer.* Hyderabad: Telugu University, 1991.

———. "Local Politics in a Traditional Indian Religious Centre: Rajahmundry." Paper presented at the American Historical Association meeting, Washington, D.C., 1969.

Mackenzie, W. C. *Colonel Colin Mackenzie: First Surveyor-General of India.* Edinburgh: W. and R. Chambers, 1952.

Mahadeva Sastri, Korada. *Historical Grammar of Telugu with Special Reference to Old Telugu c. 200 BC–1000 AD* Anantapur: Sri Venkateswara University, 1969.

Maier, H. M. J. "From Heteroglossia to Polyglossia: The Creation of Malay and Dutch in the Indies." *Indonesia* 56 (1993): 37–65.

Mallikarjun, B. "Mother Tongues of India according to the 1961 Census." *Language in India* 2, no. 5 (2002). www.languageinindia.com (accessed July 17, 2007).

Mangamma, J. *Book Printing in India, with Special Reference to the Contributions of European Scholars to Telugu (1746–1857).* Nellore: Bangorey Books, 1975.

Manibhai Jasbhai, Dewan Bahadur. *A Memorandum on Our Vernaculars, as Media of Elementary Instruction; and the Development of Vernacular Literature, with Special Reference to Technical Education.* Bombay: Bombay Gazette Steam Printing Works, Fort, 1899.

Mantena, Rama Sundari. "Vernacular Futures: Colonial Philology and the Idea of History in Nineteenth-Century South India." *Indian Economic and Social History Review* 42, no. 4 (2005): 513–534.

Margoschis, J. T. "Life of Addison by Samuel Johnson, LL.D., Reprinted from his 'Lives of the Most Eminent English Poets,' with Notes." Madras: Messrs. C. Foster, 1875.

Maria John, B. *Linguistic Reorganisation of Madras Presidency.* Nagercoil: Ajith, 1994.

McIver, Lewis. "The Report." In *Imperial Census of 1881: Operations and Results in the Presidency of Madras.* Vol. 1. Madras: Government Press, 1883.

Mitchell, Lisa. "Knowing the Deccan: Enquiries, Points, and Poets in the Construction of Knowledge and Power in Early Nineteenth-Century Southern India." In *The Madras School of Orientalism,* ed. Thomas R. Trautmann. Delhi: Oxford University Press, forthcoming.

———. "Literary Production at the Edge of Empire: The Crisis of Patronage in Southern India under Colonial Rule." In *Fringes of Empire,* ed. Elizabeth Kolsky and Sameetah Agha. Delhi: Oxford University Press, 2009.

Morris, Henry. *Simplified Grammar of the Telugu Language.* London: Kegan Paul, Trench, Trubner, 1890.

Morris, J. C. *Teloogoo Selections, with Translations and Grammatical Analysis; to which is added, A Glossary of Revenue Terms Used in the Northern Circars.* Madras: College Press, 1823.

Muller, Friedrich Max. *Lectures on the Science of Language, Delivered at the Royal Institution of Great Britain in April, May, and June 1861.* New York: Scribners, 1862.

Munro, Thomas. "Minute on Native Education," March 10, 1826. In G. R. Gleig, *The Life of Major-General Thomas Munro, Bart. and K. C. B., Late Governor of Madras, with Extracts from His Correspondence and Private Papers.* Vol. 2. London: Colburn and Bentley, 1930.

Nagaraju, S. "Beginnings of Telugu Literature: A Socio-historical Approach." Paper presented at the Andhra Pradesh History Congress, 11th annual session, Nagaram, S.V.R.M. College, January 5, 1987.

———. "Emergence of Regional Identity and Beginnings of Vernacular Literature: A Case Study of Telugu." *Social Scientist* 23, no. 10–12 (1995): 8–23.

Nambi Arooran, K. *Tamil Renaissance and Dravidian Nationalism, 1905–1944.* Madras: Koodal, 1980.

Narain Rao, K. S., ed. *Report of the Third Andhra Conference Held at Vizagapatam on 12th and 13th May, 1915.* Vizag: Observatory Press, 1915.

Narayana Rao, K. V. *The Emergence of Andhra Pradesh.* 1st ed. Bombay: Popular Prakashan, 1973.

Narayana Rao, Velcheru. "Coconut and Honey: Sanskrit and Telugu in Pre-modern Andhra." *Social Scientist* 23 (1995): 24–40.

———. "Multiple Literary Cultures." In *Literary Cultures in History: Reconstructions from South Asia,* ed. Sheldon Pollock. Berkeley: University of California Press, 2003.

———. "Texture and Authority: Telugu Riddles and Enigmas." In *Untying the Knot: On Riddles and Other Enigmatic Modes,* ed. Galit Hasan-Rokem and David Shulman. New York: Oxford University Press, 1996.

Narayana Rao, Velcheru, and David Shulman, eds. *Classical Telugu Poetry: An Anthology.* Delhi: Oxford University Press, 2002.

———. *A Poem at the Right Moment: Remembered Verses from Premodern South India.* Berkeley: University of California Press, 1998.

Narayana Rao, Velcheru, David Shulman, and Sanjay Subrahmanyam. *Symbols of Substance: Court and State in Nayaka Period Tamilnadu.* Delhi: Oxford University Press, 1992.

———. *Textures of Time: Writing History in South India, 1600–1800.* Delhi: Permanent Black, 2001.

Narullah, Syed, and J. P. Naik. *A History of Education in India during the British Period.* 2nd rev. ed. Bombay: Macmillan, 1951.

Natarajan, J. *History of Indian Journalism.* Delhi: Government of India, Publications Division, Ministry of Information and Broadcasting, 1955.

Nayar, Baldev R. *National Communication and Language Policy in India.* New York: F. A. Praeger, 1969.

Oxford graduate, An. *First Part of the Adelphi Press, First Arts Text Book for 1870.* Madras: Messrs. Grantz Brothers, 1870.

———. *First Part of the Adelphi Press, First Arts Text Book for 1871.* Madras: Messrs. Grantz Brothers, 1871.

Pandian, M. S. S. *The Image Trap: M. G. Ramachandran in Film and Politics.* New Delhi: Sage, 1992.

———. "Towards National-Popular: Notes on Self-Respecter's Tamil." *Economic and Political Weekly* 31, no. 51 (1996): 3323–3329.

Pillai, Thomas Antoni. *The English, Tamil, Telugu and Hindustani Sonmalai; or, An Easy Way of Learning to Speak Four Languages.* Madras, 1880.

Pollock, Sheldon. "The Cosmopolitan Vernacular." *Journal of Asian Studies* 57, no. 1 (1998): 6–37.

———. "The Death of Sanskrit." *Comparative Studies in Society and History* 43, no. 2 (2001): 392–426.

———. "India in the Vernacular Millennium: Literary Culture and Polity, 1000–1500." *Daedalus* 127, no. 3 (1998): 41–74.

———, ed. *Literary Cultures in History: Reconstructions from South Asia.* Berkeley: University of California Press, 2003.

———. "Literary History, Indian History, World History." *Social Scientist* 23, no. 10–12 (1995): 112–142.

———. "The Sanskrit Cosmopolis, 300–1300: Transculturation, Vernacularization, and the Question of Ideology." In *Ideology and the Status of Sanskrit: Contributions to the History of the Sanskrit Language,* ed. Jan E. M. Houben, 197–247. Leiden: E. J. Brill, 1996.

Pope, George U. *Our Blessed Lord's Sermon on the Mount, in English, Tamil, Malayalam, Kanarese and Telugu, in the Anglo-Indian character with a vocabulary, minute grammatical praxis and inflexional tables.* Madras, 1860.

Purushottam, Boddupalli. "Classifiction of Telugu Vocabulary." In *Proceedings of the First All India Conference of Dravidian Linguists, 1971,* ed. V. I. Subramoniam, 202–205. Trivandrum: St. George's Press, 1972.

———. *The Theories of Telugu Grammar.* Thiruvananthapuram: International School of Dravidian Linguistics, 1996.

Raghunadha Rao, P. *History and Culture of Andhra Pradesh: From the Earliest Times to the Present Day.* Delhi: Sterling, 1994.

———. *Modern History of Andhra Pradesh.* Rev. and enlarged ed. Delhi: Sterling, 1997.

Ragunatha Sarma, S. "The Treatment of Tatsama Forms in Nannaya." In *Proceedings of the First All India Conference of Dravidian Linguists, 1971,* ed. V. I. Subramoniam, 389–391. Trivandrum: St. George's Press, 1972.

Rajagopala Rao, T. *A Historical Sketch of Telugu Literature.* New Delhi: Asian Educational Services, 1984 [1933].

Ramachandra Rao, C. V. *The Kavali Brothers, Col. Colin Mackenzie and the Reconstruction of South Indian History and Cultural Resurgence in South India.* Nellore: Manasa, 2003.

———. "Politico-Geographic Identity of Andhra Desa." Unpublished manuscript, n.d.

Ramaiah, L. S. *Telugu Language and Linguistics.* Chennai: T. R., 1998.

Ramamurthy, Gidugu Venkata. *A Memorandum on Modern Telugu.* Madras: Guardian Press, 1913.

Ramapati Rao, Akkiraju. "List of Telugu Swiiya Caritralu." In *Telugu Swiiya Caritralu,* 59–60. Secunderabad: Yuvabharati, 1984.

Ramaswami, Kavali Venkata [Ramaswamie, Cavelly Venkata]. *Biographical Sketches of Dekkan Poets.* Calcutta, 1829.

———. *Biographical Sketches of the Dekkan Poets.* Ed. C. V. Ramachandra Rao. Nellore: Nellore Progressive Union, 1975 [1829].

———. [Ramaswami, Cavelly Venkata]. *Descriptive and Historical Sketches of Cities and Places in the Dekkan, to Which is Prefixed and Introduction, containing a brief description of the Southern Peninsula, and a succinct History of the Ancient Rulers, the whole being intended to serve as a book of reference to A Map of Ancient Dekkan.* Calcutta: W. Thacker, St. Andrew's Library, 1828.

——— [Ramaswamy, C. V.]. "A New Map of the Ancient Division of the Deckan Illustrative of the History of the Hindu Dynasties with Discriptions [*sic*] of the Principle Places." Calcutta: Asiatic Lithographic Press, 1827.

Ramaswamy, Sumathi. "En/Gendering Language: The Poetics of Tamil Identity." *Comparative Studies in Society and History* 35, no. 4 (1993): 683–725.

———. "Feminizing Language: Tamil as Goddess, Mother, Maiden." In *Passions of the Tongue: Language Devotion in Tamil India, 1891–1970,* 79–134. Berkeley: University of California Press, 1997.

———. "Maps and Mother Goddesses in Modern India." *Imago Mundi* 53 (2001): 97–114.

———. *Passions of the Tongue: Language Devotion in Tamil India, 1891–1970.* Berkeley: University of California Press, 1997.

Ramayya, Jayanti. *A Defense of Literary Telugu.* Madras, 1913.

———. *An Essay on Telugu Language and Literature.* Vizagapatam: S. S. M. Press, 1896.

Ram Raz. "A Short Sketch of the State of Education among the Natives at Bangalore." Appendix no. 6, January 6, 1824. In *The Second Report of the Madras School-Book Society.* Madras, 1827.

Rangasvami Rau, P. S. *The Linguist's Self-instructor (in Telugu, Kannada, Malayalam, Marathi, Tamil, and English).* Madras, 1900.
Ravindiran, V. "The Unanticipated Legacy of Robert Caldwell and the Dravidian Movement." *South Indian Studies* 1 (1996): 83–110.
Reddy, P. C. *Forgotten Martyr Potti Sriramulu: Architect of the Linguistic States of India.* 3rd. ed. Nellore: Acharya P. C. Reddy Trust, 1998.
———. *A Guide to Writings, Libraries, Books, Manuscripts of Prof. P. C. Reddy.* Nellore: P. C. Reddy Trust, n.d.
Reorganization of Indian Provinces: Being a Note Presented to the Indian National Congress. Bezwada: Vani Press, 1916.
Rousseau, Jean-Jacques, and Johann Gottfried Herder. *On the Origin of Language.* Trans. John H. Moran and Alexander Gode. Chicago: University of Chicago Press, 1966.
Sakai, Naoki. "Adventures in Heteroglossia: Navigating Terrains of Linguistic Difference in Local and Colonial Regimes of Knowledge." Discussant comments presented at the American Anthropological Association, Washington, D.C., 2001.
———. *Translation and Subjectivity: On "Japan" and Cultural Nationalism.* Minneapolis: University of Minnesota Press, 1997.
Sankara Reddy, M. *Reference Sources in Telugu: A Comprehensive Guide.* Delhi: B. R., 1996.
Sankaranarayana, P. *Telugu-English Dictionary.* New Delhi: Asian Educational Services, 1998.
Santhanakrishnan, T. P. *The Regional Language in the Secondary School.* Madras: South India Saiva Siddhanta Works Publishing Society, 1950.
Satyanarayana, K. *A Study of the History and Culture of the Andhras: Consolidation of Feudalism.* Vol. 2, 1st ed. New Delhi: People's, 1982.
———. *A Study of the History and Culture of the Andhras: From Stone Age to Feudalism.* Vol. 1, 2nd ed. Hyderabad: Visalaandhra, 1999 [1975].
Schmid, Bernhard. "Observations on Original and Derived Languages." *Journal of Madras Literary Society* 4 (July 1836): 121–127.
Schmitthenner, Peter L. *Telugu Resurgence: C. P. Brown and Cultural Consolidation in Nineteenth-Century South India.* Delhi: Manohar, 2001.
Selections in English Prose, for the use of Schools in the Madras Presidency. Part 1. Madras: Madras Educational Department, 1867.
Sharma, J. C. "Multilingualism in India," *Language in India* 1, no. 8 (December 2001), http://www.languageinindia.com/dec2001/jcsharma2.html (accessed June 17, 2007).
Simhadri, S., and P. L. Vishweshwar Rao, eds. *Telangana: Dimensions of Underdevelopment.* Hyderabad: Centre for Telangana Studies, 1997.
Singh, Kanwar Jeet. *Master Tara Singh and Punjab Politics: A Study of Political Leadership.* 1978.
Sitapati, G. V. *History of Telugu Literature.* New Delhi: Sahitya Akademi, 1968.
———. *Mahakavi Guruzada Apparao.* Hyderabad: Sagar Publications, 1978.
Somayaji, G. J. "The Influence of Sanskrit Grammar on Telugu Grammar." *Journal of Andhra History and Culture* 1, no. 3 (1943): 129–135.
Somerset, Fiona, and Nicholas Watson, eds. *The Vulgar Tongue: Medieval and Postmedieval Vernacularity.* University Park: Pennsylvania State University Press, 2003.
Soob Row, Vennelacunty [Vennelakanty Subba Rao]. *The Life of Veenelacunty Soob Row*

(Native of Ongole), Translator and Interpreter of the Late Sudr Court, Madras, From 1815 to 1829, As written by himself. Madras: C. Foster, 1873.

Sooryanarayana Sastrulu, D., and C. Sundara Rama Sastulu. *Notes of the Lives of Telugu Poets and Sateemani.* Madras: Madras Central Book Depot, 1901.

Sreeramulu, B. *Socio-Political Ideas and Activities of Potti Sriramulu.* Bombay: Himalaya, 1988.

Srinivasa Aiyangar, P. T. *Death or Life,—A Plea for the Vernaculars,* 1911.

Srinivasa Sastri, V. S. "The Improvement of Vernaculars." *Indian Review* I (1900): 560.

Stokes, Eric. *The English Utilitarians and India.* Delhi: Oxford University Press, 1982.

Subba Rao, G. V., ed. *History of Andhra Movement (Andhra Region).* 2 vols. Hyderabad: Committee of History of Andhra Movement, 1982.

Subbarau, N. *The Second Andhra Conference 1914, Held at Bezvada: The Address of the President Mr. N. Subbarau Pantulu.* Bezvada: Vani Press, 1914.

Subbarayan, P. "Minute of Dissent." In *Report of the Official Language Commission,* 315–30. New Delhi: Government of India, 1956.

Subrahmanyam, Sanjay. "Whispers and Shouts: Some Recent Writings on Medieval South India." *Indian Economic and Social History Review* 38, no. 4 (2001).

Suntharalingam, R. *Politics and Nationalist Awakening in South India, 1852–1891.* Tuscon: University of Arizona Press, 1974.

Suryanarayana, Peri. *A Short Biography of the Late Mr. Gurujada Venkata Appa Rao.* Vijayawada: Saibaba Press, 1968.

Swaminatha Iyer, U. V. *The Story of My Life [En Carittiram].* Trans. Kamil V. Zvelebil. Ed. M. Shanmugam Pillai and A. Thasarathan. Madras: Institute of Asian Studies, 1990.

Swaminathan, Roopa. *M. G. Ramachandran: Jewel of the Masses.* New Delhi: Roopa, 2002.

Talbot, Cynthia. *Precolonial India in Practice: Society, Region, and Identity in Medieval Andhra.* New Delhi: Oxford University Press, 2001.

Telugu Language Committee on the Use of Modern Standard Telugu (Śiṣṭavyāvahārika) for Teaching and Examination for All University Courses. *A Report to the Andhra University.* Waltair: Andhra University, 1973.

Thongchai, Winichakul. *Siam Mapped.* Honolulu: University of Hawaii Press, 1994.

Trautmann, Thomas R. "Dr Johnson and the Pandits: Imagining the Perfect Dictionary in Colonial Madras." *Indian Economic and Social History Review* 38, no. 4 (2001): 375–397.

———. "Hullabaloo about Telugu." *South Asia Research* 19, no. 1 (1999): 53–70.

———. "Inventing the History of South India." In *Invoking the Past: The Uses of History in South Asia,* ed. Daud Ali, 36–54. New Delhi: Oxford University Press, 1999.

———. *Languages and Nations: The Dravidian Proof in Colonial Madras.* Berkeley: University of California Press, 2006.

Trent, William P. "Biographical Sketch of Macaulay." In *Johnson and Goldsmith: Essays by Thomas Babington Macaulay, with Additional Material for Study,* ed. William P. Trent, xvi–xvii. Boston: Houghton Mifflin, 1906.

Triveni, D. *History of Modern Andhra.* Delhi: Surjeet Book Depot, 1986.

Vaikuntham, Y. *Education and Social Change in South India: Andhra, 1880–1920.* Madras: New Era, 1982.

Veeraswamy, Enugula. *Enugula Veeraswamy's Journal* [*Kasiyatra Charitra*—English translation]. Trans. P. Sitapati and V. Purushottam. Ed. Komaleswarapuram

Srinivasa Pillai (compiled Telugu original). Afzalgunj, Hyderabad: Andhra Pradesh Government Oriental Manuscripts Library and Research Institute (State Archives), 1973.

Venkata Rao, N. "Pioneers of English Writing in India: The Cavally Telugu Family," 1–33.

Venkatarangaiya, M. "A History of Andhra." *Journal of Andhra History and Culture* 1, no. 1 (1943): 24–25.

Venkatesan, Radha. "Politics and Suicides." *The Hindu,* Sunday, June 2, 2002.

Venkayya, T. *Telugu Grammar for the Use of Schools [Andhra Vyaakaranamu].* Madras: C. Coomaraswamy Naidu and Sons, 1911.

Viresalingam, Kandukuri. *Autobiography of Kandukuri Veeresalingam Pantulu.* Part 1. Trans. V. Ramakrishna Rao and T. Rama Rao. Rajahmundry, India: Addepally, 1970.

———. *Autobiography of Kandukuri Veeresalingam Pantulu.* Part 2. Trans. Tharakam and C. Sitharamamurthi. Rajahmundry, India: Addepally, 1972.

———. *Fortune's Wheel: A Tale of Hindu Domestic Life.* Trans. J. Robert Hutchinson. London: Elliot Stock, 1887.

Viswanathan, Gauri. *Masks of Conquest: Literary Study and British Rule in India.* New York: Columbia University Press, 1989.

Vittal Rao, Y. *Education and Learning in Andhra under the East India Company.* Reprint of 1968 Ph. D. thesis, Karnatak University. Secunderabad: N. Vidyaranya Swamy, 1979 [1968].

Wagoner, Phillip B. "Precolonial Intellectuals and the Production of Colonial Knowledge." *Comparative Studies in Society and History* 41, no. 3 (2003): 783–814.

———. *Tidings of the King: A Translation and Ethnohistorical Analysis of the Rayavacakamu.* Honolulu: University of Hawaii Press, 1993.

Washbrook, David. "Caste, Class, and Dominance in Modern Tamil Nadu: Non-Brahmanism, Dravidianism, and Tamil Nationalism." In *Dominance and State Power in Modern India: Decline of a Social Order,* ed. Francine R. Frankel and M. S. A. Rao, 204–265. Delhi: Oxford University Press, 1989.

———. *The Emergence of Provincial Politics: The Madras Presidency, 1870–1920.* Cambridge: Cambridge University Press, 1976.

———. "'To Each a Language of His Own': Language, Culture, and Society in Colonial India." In *Language, History, Class,* ed. Penelope J. Corfield, 179–203. Oxford: B. Blackwell, 1991.

Weidman, Amanda J. "Can the Subaltern Sing? Music, Language and the Politics of Voice in Early Twentieth Century South India." *Indian Economic and Social History Review* 42, no. 4 (2005): 485–511.

———. *Singing the Classical, Voicing the Modern: The Postcolonial Politics of Music in South India.* Durham, N.C.: Duke University Press, 2006.

Wilson, H. H. *The Mackenzie collection: A descriptive catalogue of the oriental and other articles illustrative of the literature, history, statistics and antiquities of the south of India.* Madras: Higganbotham, 1882 [1828].

Woolard, Kathryn, and Bambi B. Schieffelin. "Language Ideology." *Annual Review of Anthropology* 23 (1994).

Xiang Biao. *Global "Body Shopping": An Indian Labor System in the Information Technology Industry.* Princeton, N.J.: Princeton University Press, 2007.

INDEX

Page numbers in italics refer to illustrations.

CONTEMPORARY INDIAN STUDIES

Published in association with the American Institute of Indian Studies

The Edward Cameron Dimock, Jr. Prize in the Indian Humanities

Temple to Love: Architecture and Devotion
in Seventeenth-Century Bengal
PIKA GHOSH

Art of the Court of Bijapur
DEBORAH HUTTON

India's Immortal Comic Books: Gods, Kings, and Other Heroes
KARLINE MCLAIN

Language, Emotion, and Politics in South India:
The Making of a Mother Tongue
LISA MITCHELL

The Joseph W. Elder Prize in the Indian Social Sciences

The Regional Roots of Developmental Politics in India:
A Divided Leviathan
ASEEMA SINHA

Wandering with Sadhus: Ascetics in the Hindu Himalayas
SONDRA L. HAUSNER

Wives, Widows, and Concubines:
The Conjugal Family Ideal in Colonial India
MYTHELI SREENIVAS

LISA MITCHELL is Assistant Professor of Anthropology and History in the Department of South Asia Studies at the University of Pennsylvania.